INSIDE CONGRESS

SECOND EDITION

Timely Reports to Keep
Journalists, Scholars and the Public
Abreast of Developing Issues, Events and Trends

October 1979

CONGRESSIONAL QUARTERLY
1414 22ND STREET, N.W., WASHINGTON, D.C. 20037

Congressional Quarterly Inc.

Congressional Quarterly Inc., an editorial research service and publishing company, serves clients in the fields of news, education, business and government. It combines specific coverage of Congress, government and politics by Congressional Quarterly with the more general subject range of an affiliated service, Editorial Research Reports.

Congressional Quarterly was founded in 1945 by Henrietta and Nelson Poynter. Its basic periodical publication was and still is the CQ *Weekly Report,* mailed to clients every Saturday. A cumulative index is published quarterly.

The CQ *Almanac,* a compendium of legislation for one session of Congress, is published every spring. *Congress and the Nation* is published every four years as a record of government for one presidential term.

Congressional Quarterly also publishes books on public affairs. These include the twice-yearly *Guide to Current American Government* and such recent titles as *Energy Policy* and *The Middle East: U.S. Policy, Israel, Oil and the Arabs, Fourth Edition.*

CQ Direct Research is a consulting service which performs contract research and maintains a reference library and query desk for the convenience of clients.

Editorial Research Reports covers subjects beyond the specialized scope of Congressional Quarterly. It publishes reference material on foreign affairs, business, education, cultural affairs, national security, science and other topics of news interest. Service to clients includes a 6,000-word report four times a month bound and indexed semiannually. Editorial Research Reports publishes paperback books in its fields of coverage. Founded in 1923, the service merged with Congressional Quarterly in 1956.

Major Contributors: Mary M. Neumann, Margaret C. Thompson.
Contributors: Irwin B. Arieff, Christopher R. Conte, Ann Cooper, Linda Cumbo, Alan Ehrenhalt, John Felton, Mark Gruenberg, Sari Horwitz, Lynda McNeil, David R. Tarr, Andrea J. Yank.
Art Director: Richard A. Pottern. **Staff Artist:** Gwendolyn Hammond.
Production Manager: I. D. Fuller. **Assistant Production Manager:** Maceo Mayo.
Book Department Editor: Patricia Ann O'Connor.

Library of Congress Cataloging in Publication Data

Congressional Quarterly, inc.
  Inside Congress.

  Bibliography: p.
  Includes index.
  1. United States. Congress — Reform. I. Title.

JK1041.C65 1979   328.73   79-20000
ISBN 0-87187-177-7

Table of Contents

Editor's Note

Inside Congress, second edition, contains new and updated information on the procedures, leadership, membership and committee structure of Congress. The first edition of this book, published in January 1976, covered fundamental changes that had taken place during the early 1970s in the way Congress was organized and operated. This second edition includes those changes and takes a look at additional reforms instituted or studied since then.

Topics discussed include:

● Reforms in congressional procedures in the 1970s, including restrictions on the Senate filibuster and the growth in the use of suspension of the rules in the House.

● The new congressional budget process approved in 1974 and how it has fared.

● Congressional perquisites and publicity, with chapters on legislative branch funds, members' benefits, congressional travel, televising sessions of the House and the increased use of computers on Capitol Hill.

● Characteristics of the membership as well as the functions of the Democratic Caucus, Democratic whips and the Republican Steering Committee.

● Revisions of the committee system, growth of subcommittees and proposed reforms.

● Techniques of congressional oversight: the Senate confirmation process, controversy surrounding use of the legislative veto and proposals to enact sunset legislation.

● Congressional ethics, with chapters on the 1977 ethics codes, recent investigations into alleged ethical misconduct on the part of some members and congressional financial disclosures.

There is also a selected bibliography and index.

Introduction

When the 96th Congress convened in January 1979, inflation, the budget and energy — issues that had dominated previous Congresses in the 1970s — were again at the head of the agenda for debate. But Congress itself had undergone both subtle and far-reaching transformations. For one thing, although the average age of members in the House and Senate was 49.5 years — the lowest such figure in more than 30 years — political observers expected the 96th Congress to be more conservative than its most recent predecessors. One sign of that was the increase in Republican membership. Three more were elected to the Senate in November 1978, and 12 were added to the House, making the lineup 276 Democrats and 159 Republicans in the House and 59 Democrats and 41 Republicans in the Senate.

Beyond the facts and figures, however, were more intangible factors that had contributed to a Congress that in 1979 was far different from its predecessors of the 1960s. Beginning in the late 1960s and early 1970s, membership in the House and Senate changed dramatically, with the election of new younger members who were bent on reforming the institution and revising its procedures. Between 1970 and 1975, Congress substantially rewrote the rules governing the way it conducted its business. The House in particular revised its committee and floor procedures. As a result of actions instigated by the House Democratic Caucus, the powers of committee chairmen were weakened, the seniority system of selecting them was challenged and the powers and numbers of subcommittees were upgraded, allowing newer members access to influential positions. In the Senate, similar reforms that assured better committee seats for more junior members were implemented, and in 1975, the chamber restricted the filibuster as a major method to obstruct legislation by lowering the number of votes needed for cloture (cutting off debate) to a "constitutional majority" of three-fifths of the full Senate — or 60 votes if there were no vacancies. A limit on post-cloture debate was adopted in 1979.

Both chambers in the early 1970s took steps to make themselves more accountable to the public by opening up committee meetings, including markup and conference sessions, to outside scrutiny. The House went a step further in 1979 by allowing television cameras (albeit strictly controlled) to record its floor procedures.

Problems of 'Democracy'

Although these and other changes resulted in a Congress that was more democratic and open, they created problems as well — problems that made it difficult for President Carter to get many of his legislative programs through Congress, even though a substantial majority of its members was from his own party. In the House, the growth of subcommittees had diffused power, making the legislative process more time consuming; and in both chambers, many of the newer, younger members were less willing to toe the party line than were their more senior colleagues. The impact of this new assertiveness was reflected in the Senate by an increase in obstructionism, where a few members were able to hold up action on a number of major bills.

In addition, although committee "sunshine" rules and the increase in the number of roll calls in the House made members more accountable to their constituents, it also made them subject to pressures by lobbyists and special interest groups which, as a result, had proliferated in the 1970s.

While these reforms may have had their drawbacks, few observers or members advocated a return to the previous, more autocratic and secret method of operation. And, too, during the 1970s, Congress enacted several measures that were designed to streamline the legislative process. One of the major changes came in 1974, with enactment of a new congressional budget control system intended to bring order out of the prevailing chaos of the legislative appropriations process. And in 1977, the Senate revised its committee structure in an effort to reduce the conflicts and contradictions in committee jurisdictions that were based on a scheme drawn up in 1946 when many 1970s problems, such as energy use and environmental protection, were unknown. The House began to follow suit in 1979, by creating a committee to study similar reforms.

Recognizing the need to enhance their ability to oversee federal programs, members of both chambers introduced "sunset" legislation that would call for periodic review — and possible termination — of federal programs and agencies. One vehicle for oversight pushed by many members in the House — but opposed by most in the

Senate — would attach a "legislative veto" proviso to bills. In recognition of the fact that effective oversight also involved the officials administering federal programs, the Senate began to look into tightening its investigatory procedures during the confirmation process.

Ethics Issues

Besides procedural problems, a series of embarrassing accusations of criminal or unethical behavior involving members plagued both the House and Senate in the years 1976-79. In 1976, Rep. Wayne L. Hays, D-Ohio, was forced to resign as chairman of the House Administration Committee because of allegations by 33-year-old Elizabeth Ray that he had given her a job on the committee in exchange for her sexual favors. (Hays later resigned from Congress.)

Also that year, the House voted to reprimand Robert L. F. Sikes, D-Fla., for financial misconduct. The Hays case prompted the House to set up a special committee to study reforms in the congressional payroll system and to change its perquisites rules, while the Sikes case created pressures for stricter financial disclosure. Shortly after the 95th Congress convened in 1977, special committees in both the House and the Senate began drawing up comprehensive new codes of ethics which were adopted by both chambers in March. The new rules were codified in law in 1978 and extended to top officials in the executive and judicial branches. The legislation placed strict limits on the amount of outside income members could earn. But while the

House in 1978 refused by a large margin to repeal the limit, the Senate in 1979 voted to postpone the ceiling.

During 1978, three House members were indicted on felony charges, and one of them later was convicted. Four members were charged with ethical violations by the House Committee on Standards of Official Conduct, and the Senate Ethics Committee investigated two senators for alleged unethical behavior.

The full Senate was not called upon in 1978 to act in either the ethics cases investigated by its committee or in a separate probe of South Korean influence-peddling. But the House conducted a bitter, divisive debate after its ethics panel recommended punishment for three members charged with wrongdoing in the South Korean scandal.

The committee recommended that the House reprimand California Democrats Charles H. Wilson and John J. McFall and censure Edward R. Roybal, D-Calif. However, after a debate featuring criticism of the committee's procedures and its differing recommendations for punishment, the House rejected a resolution to censure Roybal and instead voted reprimands — the lightest possible punishment — for all three Californians.

For the first time in more than 50 years, the House voted July 31, 1979, to censure one of its members, Rep. Charles C. Diggs, Jr., D-Mich., who had been convicted in 1978 on charges of mail fraud.

Congressional Procedures

CQ

Congress and Procedural Reform in the 1970s

Beginning in 1970, with passage of the Legislative Reorganization Act, Congress enacted a number of procedural reforms that made it in 1979 a far different institution than it had been a decade earlier.

The changes were made in the rules and procedures of the Senate and House under the unremitting pressure of middle- and low-ranking members. The result of their efforts, which reached a peak in 1974-75, produced a basic upheaval in the manner that power was held and exercised in Congress.

Four years later, however, some observers — and members of Congress themselves — were questioning whether some of the reforms had impeded Congress' efficiency.

The 95th Congress that ended a few weeks before the 1978 elections was not an especially unwieldy Congress, but there were new indications of institutional developments that would make both the Senate and House more difficult chambers in which to pass legislation.

In both houses, leaders experienced obstacles to operations that — if not entirely new — at least showed signs of becoming major elements in the legislative process.

Both House and Senate faced delays during the session, and were accused — both by members and outside observers — of becoming unmanageable institutions. The final legislative record didn't prove that Congress was beyond the control of the leadership, but there was little doubt that many new forces were making it a more unwieldy place than it used to be.

A considerable amount of the most difficult legislative work that Congress had to do was left for the last six weeks of the session.

Although it is not unusual for delays to appear toward the end of a session, there appeared to be more to the problem in 1978 than the traditional year-end logjam that held up many bills in both chambers. Interviews with more than two dozen members showed that many believed poor legislative relations by President Carter and his White House aides were a factor; but most members thought that Congress itself was an even bigger problem.

Many reasons were cited. Among those mentioned most often were:

House Reforms. The substantial reforms in House procedures made during the preceding 10 years, said by many members to have made the chamber more democratic but also more difficult to manage. Power was scattered and new power centers were created.

Senate Rules. Increased obstructionism in the Senate, where rules make it relatively easy for a handful of members to stall or kill bills. The principal development was new use of the old filibuster technique to keep legislation from coming to a vote.

Assertiveness. Increased congressional assertiveness, which began in the early 1970s when large Democratic majorities in both houses found their plans frequently frustrated by Republican administrations.

Having learned to flex its muscles more, the Democratic Congress was no longer inclined to automatically embrace administration proposals just because they came from a Democratic president.

More Lobbyists. The proliferation of lobbyists — representing everyone from the Chamber of Commerce to the National Electric Sign Association — who had developed sophisticated tactics to fight bills. In addition, the growth of single-issue lobbying organizations put a new type of pressure on members; these groups cared little for a member's overall record, but only whether he or she supported or opposed the organizations' positions.

Lobbying played a prime role in defeat of labor law reform, no-fault auto insurance, hospital cost control and consumer protection agency bills in 1978. It also killed a bill that would have required lobbyists to reveal more about their activities to the public.

Public Mood. A public mood that seldom showed a consensus on major issues because of narrow self-interests. This was a consideration that could change in another Congress, but it reinforced the many other factors that made the 95th Congress a slow-moving one with little apparent overall philosophy guiding it.

House Reforms

In the House, many members said a series of reforms approved over the previous decade had produced delays and made many chamber operations more difficult.

By breaking the autocratic grip of committee chairmen, the reforms dispersed power and created a more democratic House where junior members had unprecedented opportunities to speak up.

But the House also found that democracy takes up more time. More members demanded consideration of more bills and amendments, sometimes tying up floor action so long that the House began to resemble the Senate during a filibuster.

In addition, democracy enabled many young Democrats to refuse to go along with the party line with far less reprisal from their elders, making it more difficult for party leaders to muster votes.

There were certain efficiencies in the "old system" that governed the House until recent years, said Thomas S. Foley, D-Wash. "But they're not efficiencies I would like to go back to," he hastened to add.

The "old system" was one that concentrated power in the hands of House committee chairmen and party leaders who were always the most senior members. It was "efficient" in the sense that if an administration or anyone else with a bill could persuade a handful of leaders to support it, the legislation usually would pass.

Now, however, "you have to deal with and negotiate with a lot of congressmen," said House Budget Committee Chairman Robert N. Giaimo, D-Conn. For instance, instead of just going to the chairman of the Ways and Means Committee to get a tax bill passed, it was necessary to lobby all 37 members of the committee, Giaimo said.

Moreover, on the major 1978 tax bill, another half dozen factions with amendments or substitutes had to be negotiated with, he said.

The old autocratic system was broken up gradually, beginning in the late 1960s when the Democratic Caucus was reactivated by reform-minded members. Although seniority was still the key to power, committee chairmen lost much of the control they used to have over colleagues and over the flow of legislation.

One reason was that subcommittees proliferated in the mid-1970s, giving dozens of additional members the chance to head a panel and push out legislation on their own. Moreover, new rules gave subcommittees protection from the whims of full committee chairmen.

Accompanying the shift in power was the move to open more House activities to public scrutiny.

In 1973, the House required that all committee and subcommittee bill-drafting sessions and other business meetings be open to the public unless a majority of the committee in open session voted to close the doors to the public. Bill-drafting sessions traditionally had not been open to the public.

In 1970, the House ended non-recorded teller votes by which many key issues were decided. In 1973, the House began use of an electronic voting system that simplified roll-call voting. The change was dramatic. In 1969, the House took 177 roll-call votes; in 1972, 329; in 1973, 541; in 1978, 834.

This opening of committee work sessions and the increase in roll calls enabled constituents and lobbyists to know exactly how each member stood on key issues. But it also created pressure to abandon party loyalty and vote solely on the basis of benefits to a member's district or to special interest groups that support him or her. That made it more difficult for leaders to round up votes, which in turn forced delays in floor action on controversial bills.

The results of those changes were "subtle things" that added up to a considerable impact on the work flow, said House Majority Whip John Brademas, D-Ind. Taken together, the changes increased the obstacles to passage of all bills.

"The bottom line is that reforms have worked to inform the public but also to slow down legislation," said Rep. John W. Jenrette Jr., D-S.C., a member of the class of 1974 that was instrumental in reform changes. But neither Jenrette nor any other House member interviewed suggested that the reforms should be undone in the interest of efficiency.

Senate Filibuster

By 1978, a new mood of militancy had turned the clubby, custom-bound Senate into a battleground where minorities — often just one or two senators — were increasingly willing to manipulate the rules in order to kill or delay legislation.

Unlike the House, which limits legislative debates, Senate rules allowed a minority of members to conduct a filibuster (unlimited debate) on any bill unless three-fifths of the full Senate voted to invoke cloture (end debate).

The only thing restricting the number of filibusters was Senate custom, which in recent decades had limited senators to only occasional use of the disruptive tactic.

But in a Senate much less inclined to play by the unwritten rules of the past, the filibuster threat was becoming one of the most popular ways to fight legislation. The more militant members who found themselves in a minor-

ity — some liberal Democrats as well as the conservative Republicans — made it clear that cloture alone would not stop their filibusters.

Noting the proliferation of filibuster threats in the Senate in 1978, Majority Leader Robert C. Byrd, D-W.Va., said: "It used to be that it was resorted to only infrequently and on the great national issues, mostly civil rights. But anymore, it's just resorted to promiscuously, I think."

Conservative Republican Jesse Helms, N.C., a supporter of some filibuster threats in 1978, dismissed Byrd's protest. "If the shoe were on the other foot, he would be doing exactly what [some] of us have been doing and will probably do to a greater extent in the future," Helms said. "Senator Byrd never fails to use the rules to his advantage, so why the outcry when the minority uses them?"

Actually, there was only one real filibuster in 1978. Because the Senate refused to cut off the six-week talkathon against the labor law reform bill (HR 8410), it never moved into the more controversial post-cloture phase that the bill's opponents were prepared for.

But the long fight over labor law, coupled with lengthy debate on the Panama Canal treaties, took a three-month chunk from the Senate schedule and created a time crunch that made the mere mention of a filibuster as effective as carrying one out.

"One or two members can, when time is running out, resort to obstructionist tactics and endanger any bill that they're opposed to," said Byrd. "And while they're doing that they're also endangering passage of other measures which will be caught in the backlog."

The Senate took a step to rectify the situation in February 1979, when it passed a resolution limiting post-cloture debate.

Following is a discussion of the major changes in the rules governing both chambers during the years 1970-79.

Background: 1970-75

Congress in the first half of the 1970s approved numerous and fundamental changes in its procedures that ended the nearly absolute authority enjoyed by senior members and redistributed power among junior and even freshmen members.

The reform action began in the 1970 Legislative Reorganization Act and reached a height in late 1974 and in 1975.

In the House, Democrats transferred the authority to make committee assignments to its Steering and Policy Committee, a unit representative of all the party members and of the leadership. This power, which was taken from Democrats on the Ways and Means Committee, led to the defeat of three sitting chairmen — an action that completely undermined the already eroded seniority system.

The House also further strengthened subcommittees by approving additional staff for them, made Appropriations subcommittee chairmen subject to election, and decided to open conference committee sessions to the public. *(Subcommittee power, p. 63; conference committee changes, p. 67)*

In the Senate, the filibuster rule was modified to make cloture easier to invoke, committee chairmen were made subject to caucus election, and open committee meetings, including conference sessions, were approved.

The impact of the revisions was on the way Congress conducts its business. The changes made the two chambers — and the House in particular — more pluralistic by spreading power among many members. The changes did not divest senior members of control, but they made them subject to influence by junior members — a situation that was almost unheard of in the past. And the changes also made Congress a more open institution by exposing most committee work sessions to the public and the press.

House

A number of the changes involved the Democratic Party in the House and were accomplished through the party's caucus. These revisions in effect influenced how the House was run because Democrats were in the majority. In addition, changes were made in the House's rules that applied to all members.

Committee Chairmen. Democrats in 1975 decided to make all nominees for committee chairmanships subject to automatic, secret-ballot election by the caucus. This change began modestly in 1971 with a requirement that 10 or more caucus members could demand a separate vote on any chairman nominee. It was known as the kamikaze rule because the challengers had to stand up publicly in the caucus to demand the vote. The 1973 expansion of the requirement made all chairmen accountable to their Democratic colleagues without the possibility of retribution by chairmen. In 1975, the automatic election requirement was extended to the chairmen of Appropriations subcommittees.

In 1975, Democrats slightly refined their method of selecting chairmen by allowing competitive nominations for the posts to be made on the caucus floor if the original selection, made by the Democratic Steering and Policy Committee, was voted down. Existing rules provided for a vote on the next Steering Committee choice.

In 1971, the Democrats had decided that no member could be chairman of more than one legislative subcommittee. That broke the hold of senior Democrats on key subcommittees. When adopted, it gave 16 Democrats elected since 1958 their first subcommittee chairmanships. This was expanded in 1975 to prevent a chairman of a legislative committee from chairing any other committees including special, select or joint ones.

Steering Committee. Democrats in 1973 created a Steering and Policy Committee to assist the leadership in developing party and legislative priorities.

Committee Assignments. Democrats in 1973 adopted a party rule guaranteeing each Democrat a major committee assignment. In December 1974, at an organizing session for the next Congress, the caucus gave the power to assign Democrats to House committees to the party's Steering and Policy Committee, composed of party leaders and their nominees and regionally elected members. The action took the appointive power away from Ways and Means Committee Democrats, who had held it since 1911.

In an effort to assure that all Democrats had a chance at good subcommittee slots, the caucus in December 1974 specified that beginning in 1975 no member could become a member of a second subcommittee on any full committee until every member of the full committee had chosen one subcommittee position. A grandfather clause allowed existing subcommittee members to protect two slots. The change was aimed at the Appropriations subcommittees where senior Democrats dominated the important units handling defense, agriculture, health, education and welfare funding.

Committee Rules. Committees are required to have written rules. This rule, adopted in the 1970 Legislative Reorganization Act, opened the way to checking the arbitrary use of power by committee chairmen.

Subcommittees. Subcommittee members were protected by a "bill of rights" adopted by the Democratic Caucus in 1973. The new rules established a Democratic caucus on each committee and forced committee chairmen to start sharing authority with other Democratic members. Each committee caucus was granted the authority to select subcommittee chairmen, establish subcommittee jurisdictions, set party ratios on subcommittees to reflect the ratio in the full House, provide adequate subcommittee budgets and guarantee all members a major subcommittee slot where vacancies make that possible. In 1974, the caucus gave the subcommittee members the power to determine the number of subcommittees their committee would have.

Under the "bill of rights," committee chairmen no longer could kill legislation by quietly pocketing it. They were required to refer bills to subcommittees within two weeks.

All committees with more than 20 members must establish at least four subcommittees. This requirement was made in 1974 and modified slightly in 1975. It was aimed at the Ways and Means Committee, which had not had subcommittees since 1961, but it also institutionalized subcommittees for the first time.

Subcommittee Staffing. In 1975, House rules were changed to allow subcommittee chairmen and ranking minority members to hire one staff person each to work directly with them on their subcommittees. The new staffing power strengthened subcommittees.

Proxy Voting. The House restricted the use of proxy voting in committee. The practice was banned in 1974, but partially restored by Democrats in 1975 by allowing committees to decide if proxies could be used. If they were, they could be used only on a specific amendment or on procedural matters and they had to be in writing and given to a specific person. The proxy vote also had to be dated and could not be used to make a quorum. General proxies, often given between Democrats for use as the recipient saw fit, no longer were possible. Republicans had long complained that Democrats abused proxy votes by using them to control committee activity even though few Democrats were present.

Open Meetings. The House in 1973 required that all committee and subcommittee bill-drafting sessions and other business meetings be open to the public unless a majority of the committee in open session voted to close the doors to the public. Hearings had been open, but markup sessions to draft legislation usually were closed. The change allowed interested citizens and — more importantly — reporters to watch bill-drafting work to see how committee members were performing and how they were voting on amendments and other changes in legislation.

The House in 1975 went a step further and voted to require that conference committee sessions be open to the public. The Senate went along later in the year.

Closed Rule. Democrats in 1973 modified the closed rule which had been used almost exclusively by the Ways and Means Committee to protect its bills from change on the House floor. Under the revision, 50 or more Democrats could bring a proposed amendment to the caucus. If a majority of the caucus approved the recommendation of the 50, the Democratic members of the Rules Committee would be instructed to write a rule allowing that specific amendment to reach the House floor for a vote when the bill to which it pertained came up.

Rules Committee Members. The Democrats in 1974 took a step to strengthen the party's leadership by allowing the Speaker to nominate all Democratic members of the Rules Committee, subject to caucus ratification.

Organization. In 1974, the House decided that beginning that year it would return between Dec. 1 and 20 in election years to organize the next Congress in advance. The purpose was to speed action on substantive matters at the beginning of new Congresses.

Teller Votes. The House took an important step to make members' actions more visible by requiring that teller votes on the floor be recorded. In the past, these votes were tabulated only in total; no record was made of each member's position even though the procedure was used to decide some of the most controversial issues that came before the House. The change was adopted in the 1970 Legislative Reorganization Act and put the House on a par with the Senate, where all important floor votes can be — and usually are — recorded.

Minority Rights. The 1970 Legislative Reorganization Act extended certain safeguards to minority members of Congress. For example, the minority was assured the right to call witnesses, House minority party conferees on a bill were given control over one-half of the debate time when the conference report came to the floor and minority members of a committee were given a specific length of time to get their views in a committee report.

Proceedings. The 1970 Legislative Reorganization Act made many changes in Senate and House procedures designed to expedite congressional activity and make more information available to members. For example, House committees were allowed to sit during a House session, House quorum calls were shortened, committee reports in both chambers had to be available at least three days before the bill was taken up on the floor and a minimum 10 minutes' debate was provided for any amendment on the House floor if the proposal had been printed previously in the *Congressional Record* so that members had an opportunity to study it.

Senate

There were fewer changes approved by the Senate during this period, but the Senate was a more open body and power was more evenly distributed than in the House. This was because Senate debate was unrestricted and floor amendments could be offered under most circumstances, and because the relatively small size of the Senate allowed most members to have good committee seats and at least one committee or subcommittee chairmanship and often more than one. Nevertheless, a number of fundamental changes were made.

Filibuster. Rule 22, which prescribed the way to terminate filibusters, was modified in 1975 after years of battle. The existing rule required two-thirds of senators present and voting to invoke cloture and bring a proposal to a vote. The 1975 change set the number of votes required at three-fifths of the full Senate, or 60 if there were no vacancies. Advocates believed the change would ease the task of ending filibusters.

Open Meetings. The Senate in 1975 voted to require each standing, select or special committee or subcommittee to open all its meetings, including bill-drafting sessions, to the public and press. Sessions could be closed by a majority vote of the members taken in open session, but only for one of about half a dozen reasons written into the new rule. In this regard, the open-meetings requirement was more strict than the similar House rule which set no standards for voting to close a meeting.

The Senate in 1975 also agreed — like the House — to open conference committee sessions.

Committee Chairmen. Senate Democrats in 1975 decided in their caucus to select committee chairmen by secret ballot whenever one-fifth of the caucus requests it. The procedure to carry out the change provides that a list of chairmen nominees by the Democratic Steering Committee will be distributed to all Democrats. The Democrats will check off the names of the nominees they wish to subject to a secret ballot and will submit the list without signing it. If at least 20 percent of the caucus members wants a secret vote on a nominee it will be held automatically two days later.

Staff Assistance. Junior senators in 1975 obtained committee staff assistance to aid them on legislative matters. The change allowed them to hire up to three staffers who would work on a senator's committees. In the past, committee staffs were tightly controlled by senior senators; junior senators rarely had access to the staffers.

1976 Developments

The year 1976 was not a particularly good year for Congress as an institution.

This branch of government was troubled and embarrassed by sex and payroll scandals, by abuses of House travel allowances benefits by a few members, by allegations of campaign finance law violations, by conflict of interest charges and by inaction on various proposals to halt these problems.

Some of the bad press Congress received was due to normal election year pressures, some to the lack of strong leadership in both chambers and some simply to the expected foibles of a body composed of diverse personalities and interests.

However, the year was not without some redeeming events for Congress. Both chambers completed the first full year under stringent open meeting requirements for committee work sessions. In the Senate, two special committees began to examine the procedural and management problems of the chamber as well as the all-important committee structure. In the House, special committees studied the chamber's housekeeping and administrative practices and other rules to see whether additional changes beyond those made in recent years were called for.

Nevertheless, the image Congress projected to the public was not favorable. The principal element in this picture was the revelation in the spring that powerful Rep. Wayne L. Hays, D-Ohio, maintained a woman on his office payroll to serve as his mistress. The woman, Elizabeth Ray, said she did no congressional work for the pay and possessed no office skills.

The revelations, which were first made by Ray to newspaper reporters, led initially to Hays' resignation as chairman of the House Administration Committee and the Democratic Congressional Campaign Committee, which hands out campaign money to Democratic candidates, and eventually, on Sept. 1, from his seat in Congress.

More significant than his departure, however, were House reforms that followed the publicity about the sex-payroll controversy. Over the years, Hays had built his Administration Committee into a power base by getting the

House to grant it authority to provide allowances and other perquisites (such as office space, mechanical equipment and so on) that make life more comfortable for members.

A few months after the Hays-Ray scandal broke, the House took back from the committee many of these powers and vested final decisions on them in the full House. The legislators also made other changes in internal procedures designed to prevent similar abuses of power and to make the House look better in the public's eye. The changes were engineered by Democrats and criticized by Republicans who charged that they were a whitewash of the scandal and were inadequate as reforms.

Although the ethics controversies dominated the news about Congress, there were a number of other important matters in 1976 that concerned the way in which Congress functioned.

Rule 22 Change. The Senate April 6 amended its cloture rule (Rule 22), under which filibusters can be stopped, to allow the introduction of amendments to pending legislation until the announcement of the outcome of a cloture vote. No amendment can be considered after cloture is invoked unless it was formally read or considered read before the cloture vote was taken. In practice, the Senate routinely granted unanimous consent to consider read all amendments at the Senate desk at the time of the cloture vote. Supporters said the change merely formalized the existing informal practice, but opponents said it could allow bill foes to introduce many more amendments that could delay action on a measure even after cloture was invoked.

House Two-Hour Rule. In an effort to improve its operations, the House Feb. 26 changed its rules to prevent consideration of a legislative proposal unless copies of the legislation had been available to members at least two hours before it was taken up on the floor. The change, adopted 258-107, applied to bills, resolutions and conference committee reports.

Under existing rules, legislation had to be available in printed form for members to study at least three days before the House could consider it. H Res 868 did not eliminate the three-day layover rule, but gave the House the alternative of taking up legislation two hours after copies of it became available. However, the Rules Committee and the House would have to sanction use of the two-hour period by voting to waive the three-day rule. (Existing rules allowed waiver of the three-day requirement by majority vote of the House.)

H Res 868 also allowed the Rules Committee and the full House by majority vote to suspend the two-hour rule entirely. If this were done, the legislation under consideration would not have to be delayed at all and conceivably could be considered before printed copies were available. Such situations might occur in hectic final days of congressional sessions as both houses attempted to pass many bills.

H Res 868 was sponsored by Rep. John L. Burton, D-Calif., who said he wanted to protect members against legislating blindly without a bill to study.

The change was strongly opposed by Rep. John B. Anderson, R-Ill., Republican Conference chairman. Anderson's basic concern was that committees might be encouraged to utilize the new two-hour rule in lieu of the three-day requirement. He said that committees could slip in controversial items that members might not notice if they had only two hours to examine the bill or conference report before a House vote.

1977 Action

The 95th Congress, younger but less iconoclastic than its immediate predecessor, convened on Jan. 4, selected new leaders and began to organize itself to deal with a government that, for the first time in eight years, was united under the same political party.

The House installed Thomas P. O'Neill Jr., D-Mass., as Speaker, formally ratifying a decision that had in reality been made more than a month earlier at the Democrats' organizational meeting and had been a foregone conclusion since the previous Speaker, Carl Albert, D-Okla., announced his retirement on June 5, 1976.

Senate Democrats also did the expected, picking Robert C. Byrd, W.Va., as their floor leader to replace the retiring Mike Mansfield, Mont. But Senate Republicans produced a surprise as Howard H. Baker Jr., Tenn., won a close election over Robert P. Griffin, Mich., for minority leader. *(Leadership, box, p. 8)*

The House quickly adopted a package of rules changes agreed on by the Democrats in December 1976, and then settled down to decide committee assignments and chairmen for the coming two years. The House committee chairmen were chosen in succeeding weeks, with fewer challenges to the seniority system than in recent years.

In the Senate, the issue of how to realign committees became the first order of business as the Rules Committee opened hearings on a resolution (S Res 4) proposing the first major overhaul of the Senate committee system since 1947. Action on the reorganization was completed Feb. 4.

House Rules Changes

After the Speaker was officially elected Jan. 4, the House turned to another matter that had also been largely played out in December Democratic Caucus meetings — changes in the House rules. The package of changes (H Res 5) was adopted over the vocal objections of Republicans.

Less dramatic than the changes made at the start of the 94th Congress, the new rules aimed largely at streamlining House committee and floor procedures, the Democratic leadership said during the one hour of debate permitted on the rules changes.

Republicans, incensed at what they called a "gag rule" procedure that in effect prohibited them from offering amendments to the caucus' proposals, warned that adoption of the new rules would permit a legislative stampede. Republicans lost their bid to open the proposed House rules to amendment when the Democrats won a key procedural test on a straight party-line vote of 261-140.

H Res 5 then was adopted on a 256-142 vote, with all but two voting Democrats supporting the changes.

The new House rules made changes in four areas:

● The powers of the Speaker were enhanced.

● Committee privileges and powers were broadened; a quorum for conducting business — including mark-up sessions — was set at one-third of a committee's membership, and committee subpoena power was substantially broadened.

● House floor procedures were modified in a number of ways, including restrictions on quorum calls and a doubling of the number of days each month the House could deal with bills under a suspension of the rules procedure, barring floor amendments.

● The House Committee on Standards of Official Conduct and the Joint Committee on Atomic Energy were stripped of their legislative jurisdictions.

95th Congress Leadership

SENATE

President Pro Tempore — James O. Eastland, D-Miss.

Deputy President Pro Tempore — Hubert H. Humphrey, D-Minn.*

Majority Leader — Robert C. Byrd, D-W.Va.

Majority Whip — Alan Cranston, D-Calif.

Democratic Conference Secretary — Daniel K. Inouye, D-Hawaii

Minority Leader — Howard H. Baker Jr., R-Tenn.

Minority Whip — Ted Stevens, R-Alaska

Republican Policy Committee Chairman — John G. Tower, R-Texas

Republican Conference Chairman — Carl T. Curtis, R-Neb.

Republican Conference Secretary — Clifford P. Hansen, R-Wyo.

HOUSE

Speaker — Thomas P. O'Neill Jr., D-Mass.

Majority Leader — Jim Wright, D-Texas

Majority Whip — John Brademas, D-Ind.

Minority Leader — John J. Rhodes, R-Ariz.

Minority Whip — Robert H. Michel, R-Ill.

Republican Conference Chairman — John B. Anderson, R-Ill.

Republican Policy Committee Chairman — Del Clawson, R-Calif.

* Position specially created for Humphrey and not continued after Humphrey's death in January 1978.

Republican Criticism. Launching the Republican attack on the proposed rules changes, Minority Leader John J. Rhodes, R-Ill., objected that the resolution was "brought to the floor under a situation in which the minority has only one-half hour to debate and no ability at all to offer amendments." In all but one of the four previous Congresses, House rules had been adopted on the first day of the first session. In the 92nd Congress, adoption came on the second day.

In response to this complaint, Majority Leader Jim Wright, D-Texas, declared that the majority party "from time immemorial" had had "the responsibility of organizing Congress and therefore has the obligation of establishing the rules under which that Congress can operate."

Moving to substantive questions, Republican Conference Chairman John B. Anderson, Ill., said the changes offered "not greater efficiency," but rather a "license for absenteeism in the House," adding that the net result would be "legislation without representation."

Republicans found most noxious the reduced size of legislative committee quorums — particularly for mark-up sessions — extension of the subpoena power to subcommittees as well as committees, and the augmented use of suspension of the rules. They also objected to provisions limiting quorum calls during House debate and making it more difficult to prevent committee meetings when the House is in session.

W. Henson Moore, R-La., voiced a common complaint of Republicans when he cited the potential for abuse in giving committee and subcommittee chairmen "a free hand at issuing subpoenas, regardless of the issue, witness, or time." He also offered a gloomy forecast of "legislative steamrolling of substantive legislation" by the Democrats under more frequent suspensions of the rules.

Reviewing the prospect of fewer quorum calls and more committee meetings while the House is in session, Bill Frenzel, R-Minn., sarcastically noted that the rules conferred "a great new obligation to be absent from the floor for committee work." He added that the quorum limitation would not "allow very many silly interruptions like making sure one-half the members of the House are alive."

Debate ranged beyond the text of the resolution to perennial Republican complaints about minority party staffing of committees and other matters. Twice in six years (1970 and 1974) the Democratic majority had agreed to allot one-third of each committee's staff funds to the Republicans, only to rescind the agreement later. Minority staffing on committees during the 94th Congress was estimated at 20 percent, according to Robert McClory, R-Ill., who argued that Republican members were thus unfairly denied "legislative tools available to Democrats" because of their political affiliation.

House Committee Changes. Once the leadership was elected and new rules changes adopted, the House had one major housekeeping item left to attend to: the naming of House committee and subcommittee chairmen. Decisions were made in Democratic Caucus meetings Jan. 11, 18 and 26. On Jan. 19 and 27 the House by voice votes then adopted resolutions (H Res 117, 118 and 198) ratifying party choices for committee assignments in the 95th Congress.

Unlike 1975, when three powerful committee chairmen were toppled in a major revolt against the seniority system, House Democrats in 1977 accepted the elevation of senior members to the top posts on most committees.

More dramatic than the votes on committee chairmen was a 189-93 Jan. 26 caucus vote to oust Robert L. F. Sikes, D-Fla., as chairman of the House Military Construction Appropriations Subcommittee. In 1976 Sikes had been reprimanded by the full House for conflict of interest and for failure to disclose ownership of stocks as required by House rules. The action had grown out of an investigation of Sikes' financial holdings by Common Cause.

Congressional Ethics

Both the House and Senate moved swiftly in 1977 to enact new codes of ethics. The groundwork — and the impetus — for the action was laid in the 94th Congress and in earlier years as a result of scandals that had tarnished Congress' public image.

The 1977 codes were adopted as part of Senate and House rules, and violations of their provisions were punishable through traditional congressional procedures such as censure, reprimand, expulsion or loss of seniority. Both chambers planned to merge their codes and write the resulting product into statutory law that would carry legally enforceable penalties. But little progress toward this goal had been made by the end of 1977.

In the House, the ethics code was adopted on March 2. It was the work of the Commission on Administrative Review, headed by Rep. David R. Obey, D-Wis., that had been set up in July 1976 after the Hays scandal.

Democratic Caucus Votes on 1977 Reforms

All of the rules changes adopted on the House floor at the beginning of the 95th Congress had been considered during marathon sessions of the Democratic Caucus Dec. 6-9, 1976. Other proposed reforms were rejected by the caucus. Following were the votes on major proposals.

Ways and Means Subcommittees

One of the central goals of the House liberals was to make the Ways and Means Committee's subcommittee chairmen subject to an election by the caucus, in the same manner as full committee chairmen and subcommittee chairmen on the Appropriations Committee. Reformers argued that because Ways and Means, like Appropriations, was an exclusive committee with broad powers, its subcommittee chairmen also should be elected by the caucus.

"There is no single reform that is any more important than the matter pending," said Phillip Burton, Calif., in arguing for the change. "We should extend the democratic process to those who chair the most critical subcommittees in the House."

But Richard Bolling, Mo., opposed the move, charging that it would "fractionalize the legislative process" and force the caucus to "deal too much in detail."

Ways and Means Committee members — from Martha Keys, Kan., to Joe D. Waggonner Jr., La., to Charles B. Rangel, N.Y. — lined up against the proposal. When Richard L. Ottinger, N.Y., moved to adopt the change, the motion lost on a standing vote of 22-98.

Joint Atomic Energy Committee

A major victory for reform advocates came when the caucus voted to strip the Joint Atomic Energy Committee of its legislative powers and to distribute its jurisdiction among four standing committees.

Opponents of the committee had argued that it was too close to the nuclear industry to provide a balanced approach to energy matters, that it had outlived its time and that it violated the principle of the bicameral legislature.

Backers of the committee said that to divide up the jurisdiction over atomic energy would upset the nuclear program.

"This would splinter the jurisdiction and cause hopeless confusion," said Mike McCormack, Wash., in opposing the change.

The caucus agreed to back the change on a voice vote after defeating, 133-97, a motion by John Young, Texas, to refer the issue to the Steering and Policy Committee for further study.

Ethics Committee

The Committee on Standards of Official Conduct was the only committee in the House with equal numbers of Democrats and Republicans. For this reason, and because of widespread dissatisfaction in the House with the panel's failure to act on a number of accusations about improper conduct, the Democrats voted to strip the panel of its power over legislation — primarily lobby reform and financial disclosure laws.

The amendment, sponsored by Andrew Maguire, N.J., passed by voice vote.

Also by voice vote the Democrats endorsed a resolution sponsored by Berkley Bedell, Iowa, calling on the ethics committee to launch an immediate investigation into allegations of influence peddling on Capitol Hill by agents of the government of South Korea.

Open Conference Meetings

In a major extension of the movement toward open meetings, the Democrats endorsed a change in the House rules that would open all House-Senate conference committee meetings to the public except when the House specifically voted to close such a session.

Bob Carr, Mich., who sponsored the amendment, said it would expose the working of the Congress to the "maximum sunlight" and prevent "powerful conference committees from bargaining and making deals in secret."

Bob Eckhardt, Texas, said that the mechanism of a House vote to close committee meetings was "absolutely unworkable." Members of the Armed Services Committee opposed the change on the grounds that it might endanger national security.

But in a surprisingly strong vote the caucus adopted the Carr amendment by a recorded vote of 129-92. It then adopted, by voice vote, an amendment sponsored by Thomas J. Downey, N.Y., to allow all members access to all meetings of full committees and subcommittees unless the House voted to close the meetings.

Budget Committee

The Democrats voted to make several changes in the new Budget Committee.

The caucus first voted, 75-44, to strip the chairmen of the Ways and Means and Appropriations Committees of their power to nominate members of the Budget Committee and to vest that power in the Steering and Policy Committee.

Such a change, said outgoing Budget Committee Chairman Brock Adams, Wash., would enable the Budget Committee to begin operations sooner, without having to wait until late January after the Ways and Means and Appropriations Committees had been organized and chairmen elected.

Waggonner, a member of Ways and Means, argued against the proposal, charging that it would give the Steering and Policy Committee the "potential for philosophical stacking of the committee."

The caucus also voted to scrap the existing system of rotating membership on the Budget Committee and instead voted to empower the Steering and Policy Committee each session to nominate eight sitting members and eight new members to the panel. The change set the stage for a fight among several contenders for chairman of the committee.

Roll-Call Votes: A Waste of Time?

According to Rep. George E. Danielson's calculations, members of the House spent 172 hours during the first six months of 1978 "doing nothing but putting a card in a slot and punching a button."

That's the process the California Democrat and his colleagues must perform to record their votes on bills and amendments.

It's the same process they often have to go through in order to record their position on the minutes of the previous session, to answer frequent quorum calls and to vote on measures that Danielson thinks are . . . well, less than earthshaking.

The Senate, which has rules allowing unlimited debate, has always been more vulnerable to time-wasting tactics than the House. But Danielson put together in 1978 statistics that he said showed certain members were squandering House time by demanding quorum calls and recorded votes on non-controversial matters.

Obviously, there are some different opinions about the importance of the votes. But Danielson's figures did show that roll calls and quorum calls have escalated considerably in the previous eight years. There were 449 taken in all of 1970; in the first six months of 1978 the House was well beyond that with 517. (By the end of the year, the total had risen to 834.)

Danielson calculated those 517 roll calls took up 172 hours — or 33.4 percent of the 515 hours the House was in session from January through June. Five hours were spent just approving the previous day's journal and 59 hours were spent voting on measures that passed with the support of at least 90 percent of the House.

Danielson's figures are inflated, but he argued that was necessary to compute the actual time spent on roll calls. Officially, votes last for 15 minutes. Danielson calculated them at 20 minutes each, which would cover time taken up making the request for a vote, making vote switches and announcing the outcome, he said.

The increased demand for roll calls and quorum calls has made the House a less efficient institution, said Danielson. It is also one of the factors that could contribute to the death of some major bills, he contended.

Because they eat up time the House needs to get through its overburdened schedule, many roll calls amount to harassment, said Danielson. Although he did not single out any alleged harassers, Danielson did have a document listing all roll calls and quorum calls and who requested them.

Members Forcing Most Roll Calls

The most frequent requester was Rep. Robert E. Bauman, R-Md. (51 requests), followed by Reps. John M. Ashbrook, R-Ohio (41), John H. Rousselot, R-Calif. (24), Ronald M. Mottl, D-Ohio (20) and Steven D. Symms, R-Idaho (17). Together, those five members accounted for almost one-fourth of the roll calls and quorum calls requested in the first six months of 1978.

Self-restraint is the only cure Danielson offered for the rash of roll calls and quorum calls. But to make up for time lost, he suggested the House might make these procedural changes:

● Decrease the time alloted to debate the rule governing floor debate of a bill.

● Limit members to one speech per amendment.

● Encourage the Rules Committee to grant some rules limiting debate time on amendments.

● Encourage the Rules Committee to screen out bills "which do not deserve the priority of congressional attention."

The latter suggestion appeared unlikely to gain much favor because every member would argue that his or her bill is important. However, said Danielson, "We spend an unacceptable amount of time on a lot of things which don't deserve it."

A second factor was a $12,900 pay raise that members received effective Feb. 20, 1977. House Speaker Thomas P. O'Neill Jr. (D Mass.) had promised early in the year that the House would adopt the toughest ethics code of any legislative body in the country. His promise resulted partly from public resentment over the size of the pay raise.

But to deliver on that promise, O'Neill had to whip into line almost all his party troops, many of whom had been on the verge of rebellion against one or more of the new code's provisions.

The resolution (H Res 287) establishing the House code brought important changes to the way of life in the House. One of the most basic came from a provision that limited to 15 percent of his or her official salary the amount of money a member may earn from a job outside Congress.

In addition, the time-honored practice of members earning income by making public speeches was limited. The new code also put an end to unofficial office accounts—the last remaining device by which members could accept unreported contributions from organizations or individuals and use the funds for virtually any purpose.

Finally, the idea that a congressman's personal financial activities are nobody's business but his own—long a key argument against financial disclosure

legislation—disappeared. One section of the new code required extensive public disclosure of the amount and sources of a member's income.

In the Senate, the story was much the same. That chamber drew on the work of the Obey Commission, but moved quickly in the spring to draft and pass a code. Final approval came June 1 after two weeks of debate and much opposition to some parts of the code—particularly those limiting outside income (S Res 110).

The financial aspects of the Senate code were quite similar to those of the House. But the Senate code also included enforcement provisions, a section guaranteeing that senators would not discriminate against employees because of race, sex, national origin or age and other areas not covered by the House code.

Obey Commission Proposals. Having swallowed strong medicine on ethics reform and allowance changes, the House in October refused to consider a package of administrative changes, committee reform and anti-discrimination efforts. The decision came when the House by a 160-252 vote rejected the rule for floor consideration of a package of proposals drafted by the Commission on Administrative Review, the group that proposed the ethics codes adopted earlier in the year. Although on a parliamentary issue, the vote was a clear statement that the House didn't want to consider any more reforms in 1977. Democratic leaders agreed they lost by pushing a package (H Res 766) that had enough controversial proposals to alienate much of the House.

Senate Committee Reforms

The Senate approved the most sweeping overhaul of its committee system in 30 years. The changes made under the resolution (S Res 4) touched nearly all aspects of Senate work — although some of the changes would not occur for several years. The reorganization effort began in 1976 when the Senate created a temporary select committee to study the problem. As approved by the Senate in February, S Res 4 limited each senator to service on a limited number of committees and subcommittees, limited the number of chairmanships a senator could hold, reduced the number of Senate committees and revised jurisdictions to provide more logical legislative responsibilities including concentration of nearly all energy legislation in one committee.

The 96th Congress

The 96th Congress began its life Jan. 15, 1979, in a deceptively harmonious atmosphere. As the House and Senate performed their routine opening-day business, there were few hints of the fiscal fights, inflation debates and foreign and defense policy battles that were expected to dominate the session.

During the short House and Senate meetings Jan. 15, newly-elected members were sworn in, top party leaders in both houses were returned to their posts and House Democrats easily pushed through a package of procedural rules changes they had approved at party caucuses in December.

The new House rules were aimed at reducing the number of floor votes in the House and eliminating or limiting several parliamentary procedures that Democratic leaders said had been used as dilatory tactics by Republicans.

In the Senate, debate began Jan. 15 on the controversial issue of limiting filibuster tactics. A package of proposed filibuster changes had been introduced by Majority Leader Robert C. Byrd, D-W.Va. Most of Byrd's proposals (S Res 9) were aimed at limiting dilatory tactics used to delay a final vote on a bill even after three-fifths of the Senate had voted to invoke cloture (cut off debate). However, S Res 9 also included pre-cloture debate limits.

After six weeks of sporadic and often desultory debate, the Senate Feb. 22 approved the part of the package that set a 100-hour limit on post-cloture action. Byrd's six other proposals appeared unlikely to be approved in 1979.

House Rules Changes

House Democrats, meeting to organize for the 96th Congress, elected leaders and voted on dozens of changes in caucus and House rules.

During the caucuses Dec. 4 through 7, 1978, Democrats re-elected Thomas P. O'Neill Jr., D-Mass., as Speaker of the House, Jim Wright, D-Texas, as majority leader, and Thomas S. Foley, D-Wash., as chairman of the Democratic Caucus. John Brademas, D-Ind., was reappointed to his post as Democratic whip. All four leaders first held those posts in the 95th Congress. (*Leadership, box, this page*)

Democrat also voted to adopt a proposal by David R. Obey, D-Wis., to increase from two to three the number of

---

96th Congress Leadership
SENATE

President Pro Tempore — Warren G. Magnuson, D-Wash.
Majority Leader — Robert C. Byrd, D-W.Va.
Majority Whip — Alan Cranston, D-Calif.
Democratic Conference Secretary — Daniel K. Inouye, D-Hawaii

Minority Leader — Howard H. Baker Jr., R-Tenn.
Minority Whip — Ted Stevens, R-Alaska
Republican Policy Committee Chairman — John Tower, R-Texas
Republican Conference Chairman — Bob Packwood, R-Ore.
Republican Conference Secretary — Jake Garn, R-Utah

HOUSE

Speaker — Thomas P. O'Neill Jr., D-Mass.
Majority Leader — Jim Wright, D-Texas
Majority Whip — John Brademas, D-Ind.

Minority Leader — John J. Rhodes, R-Ariz.
Minority Whip — Robert H. Michel, R-Ill.
Republican Conference Chairman — John B. Anderson, R-Ill.
Republican Policy Committee Chairman — Bud Shuster, R-Pa.

---

terms members can serve on the House Budget Committee. In addition, they made changes that would:

● Help junior members get better subcommittee assignments.

● Prohibit Democrats from serving on more than five subcommittees.

● Reduce time spent taking roll-call votes in the House.

● Maintain at least a two-to-one ratio of Democrats to Republicans on most House committees.

The caucus approved two changes affecting Democratic membership on subcommittees.

The first, requiring committees to let each member choose one subcommittee assignment before any member could pick a second one, should open up more choice assignments to junior members. Democrats elected in the last two congresses pushed for the change.

The second change limits each Democrat to five subcommittee assignments on standing committees of the House. It was adopted as a substitute to an amendment offered by John F. Seiberling, D-Ohio, which would have limited members to four assignments.

Seiberling's proposal — which affected 102 Democrats who had more than four assignments — had the backing of members first elected to the 94th and 95th Congresses. Phillip Burton, D-Calif., offered the substitute that eventually was approved by the caucus.

Burton said Democrats should be cautious about limiting assignments, since no one knew what effect the limit might have in abolishing some subcommittees. Once members had given up assignments in order to meet the limit, some subcommittees might be left with no members, he said.

Burton's amendment was adopted, 82-30.

Other caucus rules changes approved during the organizational meetings included:

●**Budget Committee Terms.** The Obey proposal extending the number of terms which members can serve on the Budget Committee from two to three. The change also would permit an incumbent Budget Committee chairman to serve four terms if he or she was not elected chairman until the third term served on the committee. Giaimo could not serve a fourth term because he was elected Budget chairman during his second term on the panel.

●**Naming Subcommittee Chairmen.** An amendment offered by Berkley Bedell, D-Iowa, and supported by the 94th caucus, locking in place current practices for selecting subcommittee chairmen. The new rule provides that all committees — except Appropriations — must continue to allow bidding for subcommittee chairmanships by seniority on the full committee. It would permit the Appropriations Committee to continue its practice of bidding for chairmanships by seniority on the subcommittee. Bedell's amendment was approved by voice vote.

●**Getting Subcommittee Seats.** A proposal by Thomas J. Downey, D-N.Y., requiring continuous bidding for subcommittee seats. Currently, senior members can retain two subcommittee assignments before freshmen can make their first choice. Downey's amendment required committees to allow each of their members to choose one subcommittee assignment before any member could choose a second one. The Appropriations Committee was exempted from the change. The amendment, sponsored by the 94th and 95th caucuses, was approved by voice vote.

●The Burton amendment limiting each member to five subcommittee assignments was approved, 82-30.

●**Bills Under Suspension.** An amendment by Allen E. Ertel, D-Pa., formalizing guidelines for bills considered under suspension of the rules. The guidelines prohibit any bill with an estimated cost of over $100 million in a single fiscal year from being put on the suspension calendar unless the Democratic Steering and Policy Committee granted a request from the Speaker to waive the rule. If an exception was made by the committee, members would have to be notified at least four days in advance that the bill was coming up under suspension.

The guidelines also required at least three legislative days advance notice of all other bills brought up under suspension. The guidelines would not apply in some emergency situations or in the last few days of a congressional session, when the House normally waives some of its procedural rules.

Ertel's amendment, which provided several exceptions not contained in earlier versions he had proposed, was a compromise worked out with Speaker O'Neill. It was approved by voice vote.

Several changes were offered by the Democratic leadership in order to cut down on what Majority Leader Jim Wright, D-Texas, called "dilatory tactics sometimes employed by the other party." Most of the leadership proposals made minor procedural changes that would reduce House time consumed by roll-call votes.

Leadership Proposals. The leadership proposals — all approved by voice vote — made these changes:

●Only one vote on approving the previous day's journal would be allowed.

●Members could not demand reading of a conference report if the report had been available for three days prior to floor consideration.

●If a recorded quorum call were demanded just prior to a vote on an amendment to a bill, a recorded vote on the amendment could be limited to five minutes (instead of the 15 minutes currently required). The same change was approved for a vote on final passage of a bill if that vote came immediately after a roll call on a motion to recommit the bill to committee. The shortened vote would have to be announced prior to the quorum call or recommital vote.

●The Speaker would be authorized to name the House's three non-voting delegates and the resident commissioner from Puerto Rico to select committees and House-Senate conference committees.

●The Speaker could defer and "cluster" roll-call votes on final passage of bills and on adoption of rules reported from the Rules Committee. Existing rules allow "clustering" — delaying votes on several bills until the end of business — on legislation brought up under suspension of the rules. The change approved by the caucus would require the clustered votes to be deferred until the following legislative day, when the first vote would last for 15 minutes and all others would last five minutes.

●A requirement for a second on a motion to suspend the rules and pass a bill would be eliminated unless the bill had not been made available to members at least one day prior to the vote.

Other Changes. Other rules changes approved by the caucus that were adopted by the House in January included:

●Printed copies of reports on bills would have to be available to members at least two days — instead of just two hours, as existing rules require — before the legislation could be brought up on the House floor.

●As part of the House ethics code, members would be prohibited from letting any outside group use the words "Congress of the United States," "House of Representatives," or "official business" on a letterhead or envelope.

●The number of members required to stand in support of a request for a recorded vote on an amendment considered in the committee of the whole would be increased from 20 to 25.

●A proposal increasing the limit on the amount a member can accept as a speaking fee from $750 to $1,000 was approved.

Republican Changes. Republicans made one important change in party rules during the organizational meetings. They approved an amendment forbidding any Republican from being the ranking minority member on more than one standing, select or ad hoc committee. Previously, the limit applied only to the ranking position on standing committees.

The new rule would require at least two Republicans to give up their ranking positions on committees. ∎

Senate Limits Post-cloture Filibusters

The Senate in 1979 tightened its rules to prevent future use of the post-cloture filibuster tactic by a minority of members who want to kill a bill.

By a 78-16 vote Feb. 22, the Senate approved a resolution (S Res 61) guaranteeing that when three-fifths of the Senate has voted to invoke cloture (cut off debate) on a bill, a final vote on it must be taken after no more than 100 hours of debate. All time spent on quorum calls, roll-call votes and other parliamentary procedures would be counted in computing the 100-hour limit.

The vote came almost six weeks after Senate Majority Leader Robert C. Byrd, D-W.Va., first brought a more ambitious proposal (S Res 9) to the Senate floor. He had introduced his package of proposed filibuster changes on the opening day of the 96th Congress after routine business and formalities were completed.

The 100-hour limit — the first major proposal approved by the Senate in 1979 — will curtail a tactic used by both conservatives and liberals to delay or threaten several major bills in recent years.

But despite its potentially far-reaching effect on controversial legislation, the often desultory debate on post-cloture limits drew few senators and little public attention during the weeks it occupied the Senate.

Much of the discussion of filibuster changes took place behind the scenes, with just a handful of Republicans and Democrats working on the issue.

Republicans drafted a substitute approach, which would have put new restrictions on post-cloture debate without setting an overall time limit. The substitute was defeated on a straight party-line vote Feb. 22.

After that loss, most Republicans supported Byrd's plan. Among those who voted against the final resolution were several conservative Republicans who threatened to conduct post-cloture filibusters in the 95th Congress.

Cap Was Key Reform

The 100-hour cap on post-cloture debate was the most important change Byrd sought in the filibuster rules.

The Senate rejected a provision to permit as little as 30 hours. That limit would have been significant primarily at the end of a session when time for debate runs short.

But despite the amendment, supporters said the final resolution still would prevent the emotional, divisive kind of filibuster conducted against a natural gas pricing bill in 1977 and threatened on other bills since then.

"This takes away a chunk of the psychology of obstructionism," said Fred Wertheimer, vice president of Common Cause, whose group lobbied for the post-cloture limit.

The 100-hour limit was only one of seven changes in Byrd's original proposal. However, as soon as S Res 9 was unveiled Jan. 15, Republicans indicated that post-cloture debate limits were likely to be the only part of the proposal they were willing to discuss.

Byrd agreed Feb. 7 to split off the post-cloture time limit from his other proposals, but he indicated he would pursue the rest of S Res 9 later. However, Byrd told Republicans that if they allowed action on the scaled-down proposal, S Res 61, he would not try to push through his other rules changes by majority vote.

That promise was important to Republicans, who wanted to avoid a confrontation on the issue of whether Byrd could cut off a filibuster against rules changes by majority vote at the beginning of a Congress. Byrd had threatened to use majority cloture to pass S Res 9 when it was first introduced.

James A. McClure, R-Idaho, one of 15 Republicans who voted against S Res 61, said opponents of the change did not try to block it by filibuster partly because of Byrd's promise not to seek other changes by majority vote. Once S Res 61 was approved, Byrd adjourned the Senate, a parliamentary move which means that any filibuster on other proposed rules changes during the 96th Congress could be stopped only by a two-thirds cloture vote.

McClure also said it was "obvious" Byrd had "maintain[ed] strict party discipline" in voting on the issue.

New Filibuster Technique

Senate Rule 22, governing filibusters, already permitted each member just one hour to talk on a bill after cloture. For years, that limit was enough to restrain debate because the minority conducting a filibuster acknowledged defeat once cloture was invoked.

But the hour-per-senator limit was nullified in 1976 when the late James B. Allen, D-Ala. (1969-78) began using parliamentary tactics to eat up far more time than his one-hour allotment.

Allen, often dubbed a parliamentary wizard by his contemporaries, managed to win compromises by continuing to filibuster after cloture with such parliamentary maneuvers as demanding quorum calls and roll-call votes on dozens of amendments. The time consumed in calling the roll did not count against Allen's one-hour limit.

Byrd first sought to cut off those tactics in early 1977, but wasn't successful.

A few months later, filibuster history entered a new era when Howard M. Metzenbaum, D-Ohio, and former Sen. James Abourezk, D-S.D. (1971-1978) used Allen's techniques to block a vote on a natural gas pricing bill.

Although the Senate voted 77-17 to invoke cloture, the two Democrats managed to tie up debate for nine more days. Byrd's maneuvering to cut them off provoked an emotional fight on the floor.

Many members, recalling the fiasco of the natural gas debate, became worried by the increasing number of threatened filibusters against bills in 1978.

Many of the threats came from conservative Republicans, who found they could block or delay bills and win compromises by introducing hundreds of amendments and implying each would be called up even if cloture were invoked.

The new mood of militant obstructionism helped Byrd win support for post-cloture limits.

Senate Cloture Votes, 1919-1978 . . .

Between 1917, when Senate Rule 22 was adopted, and the end of 1978, 140 cloture votes were taken; 41 (in **dark type**) were successful.

Cloture efforts through March 7, 1975, required a two-thirds majority for success. (Figures in the right-hand column through that date are hypothetical: the vote majorities that would have been needed to invoke cloture had Rule 22 required only a three-fifths majority of senators present and voting, as reform advocates wanted. Italic lines show votes that would have succeeded under that standard.) In 1975, Rule 22 was changed so that three-fifths of the full Senate, or 60 votes, was required for cloture after March 7. (There had been no cloture votes taken in the 96th Congress as of August 1979.)

Issue	Date	Vote	Yeas Needed 2/3 Majority	Yeas Needed 3/5 Majority
Versailles Treaty	Nov. 15, 1919	78-16	63	57
Emergency tariff	Feb. 2, 1921	36-35	48	43
Tariff bill	July 7, 1922	45-35	54	48
World Court	Jan. 25, 1926	68-26	63	57
Migratory birds	June 1, 1926	46-33	53	47
Branch banking	Feb. 15, 1927	65-18	56	50
Disabled officers	Feb. 26, 1927	51-36	58	52
Colorado River	Feb. 26, 1927	32-59	61	55
D.C. buildings	Feb. 28, 1927	52-31	56	50
Prohibition Bureau	Feb. 28, 1927	55-27	55	49
Banking Act	Jan. 19, 1933	58-30	59	53
Anti-lynching	Jan. 27, 1938	37-51	59	53
Anti-lynching	Feb. 16, 1938	42-46	59	53
Anti-poll tax	Nov. 23, 1942	37-41	52	47
Anti-poll tax	May 15, 1944	36-44	54	48
Fair Employment Practices Commission	Feb. 9, 1946	48-36	56	50
British loan	May 7, 1946	41-41	55	49
Labor disputes	May 25, 1946	3-77	54	48
Anti-poll tax	July 31, 1946	39-33	48	43
Fair Employment	May 19, 1950	52-32	64*	58*
Fair Employment	July 12, 1950	55-33	64*	58*
Atomic Energy Act	July 26, 1954	44-42	64*	58*
Civil Rights Act	March 10, 1960	42-53	64	57
Amend Rule 22	Sept. 19, 1961	37-43	54	48
Literacy tests	May 9, 1962	43-53	64	58
Literacy tests	May 14, 1962	42-52	63	57
Comsat Act	Aug. 14, 1962	63-27	60	54
Amend Rule 22	Feb. 7, 1963	54-42	64	58
Civil Rights Act	June 10, 1964	71-29	67	60
Legislative reapportionment	Sept. 10, 1964	30-63	62	56
Voting Rights Act	May 25, 1965	70-30	67	60
Right-to-work repeal	Oct. 11, 1965	45-47	62	55
Right-to-work repeal	Feb. 8, 1966	51-48	66	59
Right-to-work repeal	Feb. 10, 1966	50-49	66	59
Civil Rights Act	Sept. 14, 1966	54-42	64	58
Civil Rights Act	Sept. 19, 1966	52-41	62	56
D.C. Home Rule	Oct. 10, 1966	41-37	52	47
Amend Rule 22	Jan. 24, 1967	53-46	66	59
Open Housing	Feb. 20, 1968	55-37	62	55
Open Housihg	Feb. 26, 1968	56-36	62	55
Open Housing	March 1, 1968	59-35	63	57
Open Housing	March 4, 1968	65-32	65	58
Fortas Nomination	Oct. 1, 1968	45-43	59	53
Amend Rule 22	Jan. 16, 1969	51-47	66	59
Amend Rule 22	Jan. 28, 1969	50-42	62	55
Electoral College	Sept. 17, 1970	54-36	60	54
Electoral College	Sept. 29, 1970	53-34	58	53
Supersonic transport	Dec. 19, 1970	43-48	61	55
Supersonic transport	Dec. 22, 1970	42-44	58	52
Amend Rule 22	Feb. 18, 1971	48-37	57	51
Amend Rule 22	Feb. 23, 1971	50-36	58	52
Amend Rule 22	March 2, 1971	48-36	56	50
Amend Rule 22	March 9, 1971	55-39	63	57
Military Draft	June 23, 1971	65-27	62	55
Lockheed Loan	July 26, 1971	42-47	60	54
Lockheed Loan	July 28, 1971	59-39	66	59
Lockheed Loan	July 30, 1971	53-37	60	54
Military Draft	Sept. 21, 1971	61-30	61	55
Rehnquist nomination	Dec. 10, 1971	52-42	63	57
Equal Job Opportunity	Feb. 1, 1972	48-37	57	51
Equal Job Opportunity	Feb. 3, 1972	53-35	59	53
Equal Job Opportunity	Feb. 22, 1972	71-23	63	57
U.S.-Soviet Arms Pact	Sept. 14, 1972	76-15	61	55
Consumer Agency	Sept. 29, 1972	47-29	51	46
Consumer Agency	Oct. 3, 1972	55-32	58	53

The Debate

Although Byrd kept the Senate meeting most days on his proposed filibuster changes, debate did not begin in earnest until he agreed to bring up the post-cloture change by itself.

But after Feb. 9, the Senate was interrupted for a week and a half by a Washington's birthday recess and a crippling snowstorm that kept many senators from getting back to the capital.

When debate resumed Feb. 21, Ted Stevens, R-Alaska, offered the Republican substitute.

Under that proposal, every member would have been entitled to one hour of debate after cloture but any time taken up by quorum calls or roll-call votes requested by a member would be charged to his or her time. The substitute allowed a senator to yield an hour to another senator, but no member could get more than 10 hours for debate.

Stevens' proposal didn't contain an overall cap on post-cloture debate, although he argued it effectively would limit debate to 100 hours. But Byrd charged that without an absolute limit, senators would find ways to string out debate after cloture.

Byrd's proposal did not charge individual members for time spent on roll calls or quorum calls, but it did count that time in computing the 100-hour limit.

Republicans objected to that approach, saying it would permit one member — employing the techniques developed by Allen — to use up the entire 100-hour period. They argued that each member should be guaranteed the opportunity to debate and offer amendments.

"We are looking to protect individual senators' rights while at the same time agreeing to a 100-hour cap," Stevens said. Byrd said S Res 61 did guarantee each member an opportunity to debate after cloture.

The proposal required that before any one senator could offer more than two amendments, all other senators must be given an opportunity to offer amendments. "I cannot envision there ever coming a time when senators are going to use up all the cap and a senator is going to be denied the opportunity to obtain recognition in order to call up an amendment," said Byrd.

...41 Successful Cloture Efforts

Issue	Date	Vote	Yeas Needed 2/3 Majority	Yeas Needed 3/5 Majority	Issue	Date	Vote	Yeas Needed 2/3 Majority	Yeas Needed 3/5 Majority
Consumer Agency	Oct. 5, 1972	52-30	55	49	Tax Reduction	March 20, 1975	59-38		60
School Busing	Oct. 10, 1972	45-37	55	49	**Tax Reduction**	March 21, 1975	83-13		60
School Busing	Oct. 11, 1972	49-39	59	53	**Agency for Consumer Advocacy**	May 13, 1975	71-27		60
School Busing	Oct. 12, 1972	49-38	58	53	**Senate Staffing**	June 11, 1975	77-19	64**	
Voter Registration	April 30, 1973	56-31	58	53	New Hampshire Senate Seat	June 24, 1975	57-39		60
Voter Registration	May 3, 1973	60-34	63	57	New Hampshire Senate Seat	June 25, 1975	56-41		60
Voter Registration	May 9, 1973	67-32	66	59	New Hampshire Senate Seat	June 26, 1975	54-40		60
Public Campaign Financing	Dec. 2, 1973	47-33	54	48	New Hampshire Senate Seat	July 8, 1975	57-38		60
Public Campaign Financing	Dec. 3, 1973	49-39	59	53	New Hampshire Senate Seat	July 9, 1975	57-38		60
Rhodesian Chrome Ore	Dec. 11, 1973	59-35	63	57	New Hampshire Senate Seat	July 10, 1975	54-38		60
Rhodesian Chrome Ore	Dec. 13, 1973	62-33	64	57	**Voting Rights Act**	July 21, 1975	72-19		60
Legal Services Program	Dec. 13, 1973	60-36	64	58	**Voting Rights Act**	July 23, 1975	76-20		60
Legal Services Program	Dec. 14, 1973	56-29	57	51	Oil Price Decontrol	July 30, 1975	54-38		60
Rhodesian Chrome Ore	Dec. 18, 1973	63-26	60	54	Labor-HEW Appropriations	Sept. 23, 1975	46-48		60
Legal Services Program	Jan. 30, 1974	68-29	65	58	**Labor-HEW Appropriations**	Sept. 24, 1975	64-33		60
Genocide Treaty	Feb. 5, 1974	55-36	61	55	**Common-Site Picketing**	Nov. 11, 1975	66-30		60
Genocide Treaty	Feb. 6, 1974	55-38	62	56	Common-Site Picketing	Nov. 14, 1975	58-31		60
Government Pay Raise	March 6, 1974	67-31	66	59	**Common-Site Picketing**	Nov. 18, 1975	62-37		60
Public Campaign Financing	April 4, 1974	60-36	64	58	Rail Reorganization	Dec. 4, 1975	61-27		60
Public Campaign Financing	April 9, 1974	64-30	63	57	**New York City Aid**	Dec. 5, 1975	70-27		60
Public Debt Ceiling	June 19, 1974	50-43	62	56	**Rice Production Act**	Feb. 3, 1976	70-19		60
Public Debt Ceiling	June 19, 1974	45-48	62	56	**Antitrust Amendments**	June 3, 1976	67-22		60
Public Debt Ceiling	June 26, 1974	48-50	66	59	**Antitrust Amendments**	Aug. 31, 1976	63-27		60
Consumer Agency	July 30, 1974	56-42	66	59	**Civil Rights Attorneys' Fees**	Sept. 23, 1976	63-26		60
Consumer Agency	Aug. 1, 1974	59-39	66	59	Draft Resisters Pardons	Jan. 24, 1977	53-43		60
Consumer Agency	Aug. 20, 1974	59-35	63	57	Campaign Financing	July 29, 1977	49-45		60
Consumer Agency	Sept. 19, 1974	64-34	66	59	Campaign Financing	Aug. 1, 1977	47-46		60
Export-Import Bank	Dec. 3, 1974	51-39	60	54	Campaign Financing	Aug. 2, 1977	52-46		60
Export-Import Bank	Dec. 4, 1974	48-44	62	55	**Natural Gas Pricing**	Sept. 26, 1977	77-17		60
Trade Reform	Dec. 13, 1974	71-19	60	54	Labor Law Revision	June 7, 1978	42-47		60
Fiscal 1975 Supplemental Funds	Dec. 14, 1974	56-27	56	50	Labor Law Revision	June 8, 1978	49-41		60
Export-Import Bank	Dec. 14, 1974	49-35	56	50	Labor Law Revision	June 13, 1978	54-43		60
Export-Import Bank	Dec. 16, 1974	54-34	59	53	Labor Law Revision	June 14, 1978	58-41		60
Social Services Programs	Dec. 17, 1974	70-23	62	56	Labor Law Revision	June 15, 1978	58-39		60
Tax Law Changes	Dec. 17, 1974	67-25	62	55	Labor Law Revision	June 22, 1978	53-45		60
Rail Reorganization Act	Feb. 26, 1975	86-8	63	57	**Revenue Act of 1978**	Oct. 9, 1978	62-28		60
Amend Rule 22	March 5, 1975	73-21	63	57	**Energy Taxes**	Oct. 14, 1978	71-13		60
Amend Rule 22	March 7, 1975	73-21	63	57					

* Between 1949 and 1959, the cloture rule required a two-thirds majority of the Senate membership, rather than two-thirds of senators who voted.

** In 1975, Rule 22 was changed to require a three-fifths majority of the Senate membership for cloture except for changes in Senate rules, in which a two-thirds majority of senators voting still would be required.

Even after the 100 hours, a senator who had not spoken on the bill was guaranteed 10 minutes to talk, Byrd pointed out. But Republicans said that wasn't enough, because a senator couldn't offer an amendment during the 10 minutes.

The vote on the substitute was postponed until Feb. 22, when a Byrd motion to table Stevens' proposal was approved 51-38. Both Democrats and Republicans held ranks in the voting, although Robert Morgan, D-N.C., originally voted on Stevens' side until Byrd had an earnest discussion with him on the Senate floor. When asked later why he switched his vote to Byrd's side, Morgan said he did not want to talk about the vote.

Another Stevens amendment, to delete a provision allowing 60 senators to vote a reduction of the debate cap to 30 hours, was approved 92-2 after Byrd said he would support the change. The resolution still permitted 60 senators to vote to increase the 100-hour cap.

Other amendments tabled by the Senate were:

● A Stevens proposal to allow senators to transfer their post-cloture debate time to any member, which would allow some members up to three hours of debate time. Tabled, 51-43.

● A proposal by Jesse Helms, R-N.C., to limit post-cloture Senate sessions to no more than eight hours each calendar day. Tabled, 52-39.

Provisions

As approved by the Senate Feb. 22, S Res 61:

● Required that after the Senate voted to invoke cloture on a measure, a final vote must occur after no more than 100 hours of post-cloture debate.

● Provided that if the 100-hour limit ran out, senators who had not used at least 10 minutes of their time were each guaranteed 10 minutes to speak on the issue.

● Permitted the Senate by a three-fifths majority vote to increase post-cloture debate time beyond 100 hours. Specified that any extended time agreed on would be divided equally between the majority and minority. Specified that a motion to extend the time was not debatable.

● Provided that if a bill were reprinted after cloture was invoked, amendments that were in order to the original version would continue to be in order.

● Prohibited any senator from calling up more than two amendments until every senator had a chance to call up an amendment.

● Permitted a senator to yield all or part of his or her hour of debate to the majority or minority floor managers of the bill or to the majority or minority leaders.

● Prohibited floor managers or party leaders from having over two hours of time yielded to each of them.

● Permitted waiver of the reading of any amendment after cloture if it were available to members in printed form 24 hours in advance.

● Required that, in order to be eligible for consideration after cloture, all amendments in the first degree must be submitted by 1 p.m. the day after filing of a cloture petition, and amendments in the second degree must be submitted at least one hour prior to the start of the vote on cloture.

House Use of Suspensions Grows Drastically

One House Democrat paused on the way to cast his fourth in a rapid-fire series of votes in the last days of the 95th Congress.

"I don't know a goddamn thing about the Amateur Sports Act of 1978," he said, referring to a bill he was about to vote on. "So I'll just have to ask someone on the floor. And frankly I couldn't care less."

Another young Democrat dashed onto the House floor to record his vote on one bill in the series, then emerged a minute later and admitted, "I can't tell you what the next vote is." Scanning his Democratic Study Group summary of bills, he added ruefully, "Normally I do better than I'm doing today."

Other members expressed similar confusion while the House was taking votes — one every five minutes — on some of the 11 bills it had debated under suspension of the rules Sept. 26, 1978. Few had attended the brief debate on each bill, and members were relying on party fact sheets, staff advice or their friends to tell them how to vote on what most considered minor bills.

The day before, Sept. 25, the House had considered 24 bills under suspension. And the week before, 22 bills had

---

Passing legislation under suspension of the rules is widely seen as a useful way to deal with minor bills. But many members of both parties object to increased use of the suspension calendar for bills they believe deserve full debate and amendment.

---

been considered under suspension in a two-day period. The 57 bills taken up in those four days rivaled the 70 suspensions the House considered in all of 1972.

Congressional Research Service figures show the recent spate of suspensions is part of a steady growth in use of the procedure since the 90th Congress, when 167 bills were considered under suspension. The 95th Congress considered 449 bills under suspension. (The procedure is used almost exclusively in the House. In the Senate motions to suspend the rules are rarely made and are subject to filibusters.)

At the end of the 95th Congress, the suspension calendar was particularly crowded as House leaders tried to clear a backlog of bills before the Oct. 15 House adjournment. By early September, the suspension calendar was clogged with 80 bills that committee chairmen realized had no chance for regular floor action in 1978. Most of those bills were passed under suspension by the end of the month, and another 23 were scheduled for suspension Oct. 3.

"It's too many," said Abner J. Mikva, D-Ill. "On the other hand, at the close of the session what would the alternative be?"

Many members are not at all bashful about admitting they can't keep up with the pace when faced with a dozen or more suspension bills in a single day. Attendance during debates of suspension bills in September 1978 usually averaged less than two dozen members, and most members didn't go to the floor at all until roll-call votes began after all suspensions had been debated.

"This is the ultimate test of the committee system," said Edward W. Pattison, D-N.Y. "You have to rely on the fact that [suspension bills] are not controversial and that the Republicans and Democrats on the committee are reasonably expert in these things."

But relying so heavily on committees can be dangerous, said Leon E. Panetta, D-Calif. "I frankly had no idea what the impact would be," he said of several tax bills being considered. "Too much of this is done by the seat of our pants."

However, most members still said the process was a valuable parliamentary tool for dealing quickly with relatively minor bills.

What some members — both Democrats and Republicans — do object to is increased use of the suspension calendar for bills that they feel should come up under regular House rules for full debate and consideration of amendments.

"We're not following the [informal] guidelines" dictating use of the suspension calendar only for non-controversial bills, said Christopher J. Dodd, D-Conn.

"It used to be the suspension calendar was used only for non-controversial items. Now it's for anything they think they can get by," said Robert E. Bauman, R-Md.

James M. Collins, R-Texas, who protested when several large health program authorization bills were brought up under suspension in September 1978, complained that suspension bills are "greased pigs. You turn 'em loose and you can't get hold of them."

The Process

The suspension process is supposed to be a time-saving procedure for passing non-controversial House legislation.

Under the procedure, regular House rules for debate are suspended, only 40 minutes of debate are allowed and no amendments can be offered unless they are included in

---

"It's too many. On the other hand, at the close of the session what would the alternative be?"

—Rep. Abner J. Mikva, D-Ill.

---

the floor manager's motion to suspend the rules.

Two-thirds of the members voting are required to pass a bill under suspension.

There are no formal restrictions on what bills a committee chairman can ask the Speaker to put on the suspension calendar. The unwritten rule is that suspensions are not supposed to be controversial, but it is left up to committee chairmen to define which of their bills are non-controversial.

"The committee wouldn't recommend it for suspension if it thought it would fail," contended an aide to the Democratic leadership.

But increasingly, suspensions are failing.

Thirty-one bills were defeated under suspension of the rules in the 95th Congress, compared to 25 in the 94th Congress and only one in the 93rd Congress.

Members say defeat of suspensions, which often surprise even those opposing the bills, has increased because of occasional abuse of the system by leaders anxious to ram through bills that otherwise might be subject to sharp debate or amendment.

Also contributing to the number of defeats is a growing unhappiness with the large number of bills considered under suspension.

Growth of the suspension process has paralleled a growth in legislation that is being pushed through Congress. In the House, a proliferation of subcommittees has given dozens of newer members the chance to push out more bills, and most have taken advantage of their new-found power.

To accommodate all the bills, suspensions — once taken up only every other Monday — were allowed on both Mondays and Tuesdays in 1973. That year, suspensions jumped to 173, more than double the number considered in 1972. In the 95th Congress, suspensions were allowed on Mondays and Tuesdays of every week.

The expanded days for considering suspensions has proved a legislative Parkinson's Law, according to William A. Steiger, R-Wis. "All it did was give committees another excuse to report out another bill," he said.

Defeats

Probably the most embarrassing suspension vote for Democratic leaders in 1978 came in March, when the leadership tried to undercut supporters of tuition tax credit legislation by scheduling an education grant bill (HR 11274) on the suspension calendar.

The grant bill had been offered by President Carter as an alternative to tuition tax credits, which the president opposed. Fearful that the tax credit supporters might succeed in attaching their bill as an amendment if the grant bill was brought up under regular procedures, Democratic leaders put Carter's bill on the suspension calendar so no amendments could be offered.

Angered by the maneuver, the House didn't even give the grant bill a majority vote. It was soundly defeated, 156-218.

After the March 1978 vote, grumbling about the procedure usually focused on large authorization bills brought up under suspension. But the complaints were often inconsistent.

For instance, several members told Congressional Quarterly they voted against a $1.49 billion health planning bill (HR 11488) Sept. 18, 1978, because it involved too much money to be on the suspension calendar. But some of the same members also voted for a $1.9 billion health centers reauthorization bill (HR 12460) under suspension the next day.

Explained Don Young, R-Alaska; "My friend John Rousselot spoke to me about the planning bill, but nobody approached me on the health centers bill." Rousselot, R-Calif., had argued that the planning bill was too big to be on the suspension calendar, Young said.

Controversial Procedure

In the last weeks of the 95th Congress, the suspension procedure was almost as much a focus of debate as the merits of the bills brought up under the procedure. A variety of House members — from liberal Democrats to conservative Republicans — seized the suspension procedure as an argument for voting against bills they opposed.

The argument often works, said Collins, because some members who hear even a hint of controversy about a suspension bill will vote against it. Once the tide starts rolling against a bill during a roll-call vote, other members will come in, see the scoreboard, and vote no just because it's controversial, he said.

Agreed Pattison: "Those kinds of things happen in waves around here the minute someone hears something controversial about it."

As arguments against bills under suspension have focused more on the procedure itself, several members have found it relatively easy to drum up the one-third of the votes needed to defeat a suspension bill.

Armed with a stack of one-page, double-spaced letters, Bob Carr, D-Mich., worked the floor for about four hours Sept. 26, 1978, in a successful solo effort to defeat a hydroelectric power plant authorization bill (HR 9333).

Carr said that although members had been notified the week before that the bill was scheduled for Sept. 26, he was not aware it would come up until 11 a.m. the day of

---

"It used to be the suspension calendar was used only for non-controversial items. Now it's for anything they think they can get by."

—Rep. Robert E. Bauman, R-Md.

---

the vote. He spent the afternoon buttonholing Democrats and Republicans who wandered on the House floor, interrupting some who were reading newspapers to deliver an explanation of his "Dear Colleague" letter opposing the bill.

Carr said some members pledged to vote against the bill solely because it was brought up under suspension against his wishes. The bill was defeated, 263-143.

Another defeat involved a bill (HR 5265) to temporarily suspend import duties on fluorspar, a mineral mined in the districts of Paul Simon, D-Ill., and a handful of other House members.

Since the effect of the bill would be to increase U.S. imports of fluorspar, Simon's mining constituents could have been hurt economically. But instead of arguing about protecting the nation's 1,000 fluorspar miners, Simon focused on a related issue that seemed certain to have more emotional appeal.

South Africa is the major source of fluorspar imports into the U.S., and a temporary duty suspension would benefit companies in that country. Simon's staff mounted a plan of attack based on the theory that "if people voted for economic sanctions for Rhodesia they're probably going to feel the same way about South Africa," said an aide.

Using a recent vote on the foreign military assistance bill (HR 12154) to remove U.S. economic sanctions against Rhodesia in 1979, Simon's staff targeted 80 members who had voted against lifting sanctions. Phone calls to those 80 offices and a "Dear Colleague" letter to all members arguing against giving South Africa an economic break generated the votes Simon needed to defeat the fluorspar bill Sept. 12. "We might have been lucky in having South Africa as the major supplier of fluorspar," acknowledged a Simon aide.

Self-Policing

Some members said those and other defeats are evidence that the suspension system is a self-policing one that rejects bills that are too controversial. "I think if there are hookers in there, it's discovered and made known," said Charles W. Whalen Jr., R-Ohio.

But others complained that the sheer number of suspensions makes it difficult to know where the "hookers" might be.

One Democrat said he was sure some suspension votes "will come back to haunt me."

"Yesterday was really bad news," he said, referring to the 24 suspension bills considered Sept. 25, 1978. "Fortunately a couple didn't get [roll-call] votes. We were smart enough not to take votes on ones we didn't know about."

Many members tried to keep up with the votes by regularly checking party fact sheets that briefly summarized each bill. "Most of us follow some poop sheet or other," said Mikva, whose Democratic Study Group puts out one of the most respected summaries used by members.

Others had staff-prepared memos. Don Wolfensberger, an aide to John B. Anderson, R-Ill., had typed a two-page summary sheet of the 25 bills scheduled for Sept. 18, starring any that involved more than $100 million in spending or any kind of controversy.

However, brief summaries don't keep members adequately informed, most admitted. Collins said few members felt they could oppose several recent health bills taken up under suspension, but he argued that more might have

voted against them if they had time to see what was in them. "If you name a bill right, you're on the side of the gods before you start," he said.

Most members said they often relied on the scoreboard and their friends to tell them whether a suspension bill was controversial.

"You could crucify people if you stand on the floor and ask them what they're voting on," said one Democrat.

Some members would like to change that by curtailing use of the suspension calendar.

One proposal (H Res 1332) was introduced by Allen E. Ertel, D-Pa., in September 1978. Under Ertel's plan, any bill that authorized or appropriated over $100 million in a single fiscal year would not be allowed on the suspension calendar.

If that restriction had been in effect during 1978, 21 bills considered under suspension would not have been allowed on the calendar.

Although Ertel acknowledged his $100 million cutoff was "arbitrary," he said, "anytime we start talking about programs that cost $100 million or more, we should be able to amend the legislation."

Meeting in December 1978, the House Democratic Caucus by voice vote approved Ertel's amendment formalizing guidelines for bills considered under suspension of the rules. The guidelines prohibited any bill with an estimated cost of over $100 million in a single fiscal year from being put on the suspension calendar unless the Democratic Steering and Policy Committee granted a request from the Speaker to waive the rule. If an exception was made by the committee, members would have to be notified at least four days in advance that the bill was coming up under suspension.

The guidelines also required at least three legislative days advance notice of all other bills brought up under suspension. The guidelines would not apply in some emergency situations or in the last few days of a congressional session, when the House normally waives some of its procedural rules.

Ertel's amendment, which provided several exceptions not contained in earlier versions he had proposed, was a compromise worked out with Speaker Thomas P. O'Neill Jr., D-Mass. It was formally approved by the House in January 1979. ∎

Membership and Party Groups

CQ

96th Congress: Younger, Fewer Lawyers

Critics of Congress often picture the institution as a collection of aging mossbacks waiting patiently for the seniority system to reward them with power. But whatever truth that stereotype might once have contained, the fact is that Congress has been getting younger every year.

When the House and Senate convened in January 1979 for the 96th time, the average age in the two chambers was 49.5 years, the lowest such figure in more than 30 years. This was the first Congress since World War II in which the average age dropped below 50.

Of the 433 sitting members of the House of Representatives at the opening session, 220 had served four years or less. Of 100 senators, 55 had served six years or less.

For the second Congress in a row, there were no House members 80 years old or more. Before 1977, there was an octogenarian in every House since 1939.

As usual, the House was younger than the Senate. A larger-than-normal influx of 77 new House members reduced the average age of that chamber to 48.8. (Two additional members won seats in the spring.) The Senate remained above 50, with an average of 52.7, but even that figure was the lowest recorded for the Senate in the postwar period.

Republicans were younger than Democrats, although not by very much. In the two chambers together, Republicans averaged 49.1 years, Democrats 49.8.

A Consistent Trend

The most striking thing about this shift to youth in Congress was its consistency over the past decade. The average age of the House has declined every two years since 1969, when it stood at 52.2, the highest in the past 20 years. The Senate has been getting steadily younger since 1965, when the average member was 57.7 years old.

For Congresses before World War II, precise age figures are not easily available. But a spot check of the 71st Congress, which met in 1929, indicated an age breakdown similar to the ones of the late 1960s. The Senate averaged 57.7 years, the House 53.1. The only significant difference was that Republicans were older than Democrats.

Until the 20th century, Congresses tended to be younger than they are now. Membership in the House or Senate was a part-time job, physically demanding but not especially prestigious at home. Politicians tended to pass it around. At one time in the mid-19th century, the senior member of the House had served only 14 years.

After 1900, though, the development of the seniority system and the political security of Democrats in the South and Republicans in the Midwest led members to think of Congress as a permanent job. "Few die, and none retire," critics said of House members just a decade ago, with some justification.

Only in the past ten years has this careerism begun to reverse itself. Congress these days is not only a full-time job but a year-round one, something even politically secure members sometimes tire of after 10 or 15 years. The switch from party-based to individually-based campaigning has made almost any complacent incumbent potentially vulnerable to an ambitious, well-financed newcomer. This requires members to perform feats of constituent service many of them find unpleasant as they grow older.

As a result of these things, the number of congressional retirements has been increasing and the average retirement age has been decreasing. In 1968, there were only 11 House members who retired voluntarily to private life. In 1978 there were 31. In 1968, the retirement age averaged 64.3, down from a figure of 67.3 in 1958. The average was down to 60.2 in 1978.

At the same time, the average age of the newcomers has been going down. Ten years ago the average House first-termer was 44 years old. In 1979, he was 40. The decline of party service as a political credential in many areas makes it possible for younger people with the energy and resources to win a seat in Congress without paying many dues.

Fewer Lawyers

Lawyers may dominate American politics, but their numbers in Congress have been slowly declining. The 96th Congress had fewer lawyers in it than any Congress during the 30 years in which Congressional Quarterly has been keeping occupational statistics. Some 270 senators and representatives had law degrees, just over 50 percent of the membership.

The number of lawyers in the Senate has remained relatively constant, although the 1979 figure of 65 represents a slight decline from two years ago. But the House figures have changed dramatically. In the 96th Congress,

Changing Age Structure Of Congress

(Average ages at start of first session)

	House	Senate	Congress
1949	51.0	58.5	53.8
1951	52.0	56.6	53.0
1953	52.0	56.6	53.0
1955	51.4	57.2	52.2
1957	52.9	57.9	53.8
1959	51.7	57.1	52.7
1961	52.2	57.0	53.2
1963	51.7	56.8	52.7
1965	50.5	57.7	51.9
1967	50.8	57.7	52.1
1969	52.2	56.6	53.0
1971	51.9	56.4	52.7
1973	51.1	55.3	52.0
1975	49.8	55.5	50.9
1977	49.3	54.7	50.3
1979	48.8	52.7	49.5

for the first time in at least 30 years, lawyers made up less than a majority of the House. The 205 sitting members with law degrees were outnumbered by the 228 members who did not have them. The drop in the number of lawyers from 220 in 1977 to 205 in 1979 marked the steepest decline recorded in any two-year period.

Whatever the reason, the legal profession was not represented among incoming House members the way it once was. Only 28 of the first-term representatives in 1979 had law degrees. No such trend was evident, however, among senators. Fourteen of the 20 people elected to the Senate for the first time in 1978 were lawyers, a higher percentage than in the chamber as a whole.

Religious Affiliation, Changes

Members of Congress are much more likely than most people to claim a religious affiliation. During the past decade, as church affiliation in the country as a whole has hovered near the 60 percent mark, the number of members of Congress identifying with one denomination or another has remained above 90 percent.

In the 96th Congress, 505 of the 533 sitting members cited a specific religious affiliation, according to a survey by Congressional Quarterly. Twenty-three others said they were "Christian" or "Protestant" but specified no denomination. Only five cited no religious connection at all.

It is not so clear whether members of Congress actually go to church more often than other people, or whether they are simply reluctant to say that they don't.

But while the number of members of Congress identifying with one denomination or another has remained constant over the past two decades, the denominational breakdown has changed considerably. Since the early 1960s, the Protestant groups which traditionally dominated congressional delegations have been losing strength, and Jewish and Roman Catholic representation has increased significantly.

This has been most noticeable in the House. In 1961, the first year Congressional Quarterly kept track of these

Members' Occupations

(As of January 1979)

	House			Senate			Congress
Occupation	D	R	Total	D	R	Total	Total
Agriculture	10	9	19	2	4	6	25
Business or Banking	71	56	127	15	14	29	156
Education	44	13	57	4	3	7	64
Engineering	0	2	2	0	0	0	2
Journalism	6	5	11	2	0	2	13
Labor leaders	3	1	4	0	0	0	4
Law	135	70	205	43	22	65	270
Law enforcement	4	1	5	0	0	0	5
Medicine	1	5	6	1	0	1	7
Public service/Politics	22	19	41	7	5	12	53
Clergymen	4	2	6	0	1	1	7
Scientists	2	0	2	1	1	2	4

statistics, some 31 percent of the House members were either Methodist or Presbyterian, then the two most common Protestant affiliations in the House. In 1979 the figure for the two denominations was 25 percent. Catholics, who comprised 20 percent of the House in 1961, in 1979 made up 27 percent — an increase in absolute numbers from 88 to 116. In 1961 there were 11 Jewish members of the House of Representatives. In 1979 there were 23. The number of Jewish senators has risen from one to seven.

Perhaps most interesting, many of the new Catholic and Jewish members of the 96th Congress came from overwhelmingly Protestant areas, something that was not common in the past. In the 96th Congress, Nevada, South Dakota, Arizona and Vermont were all represented by Catholic senators. There were Jewish House members from Dallas, Wichita, and Kalamazoo. In 1961, eight of the 11 Jewish House members came from the New York City area, with one each from Chicago, Philadelphia and Baltimore. ∎

GOP Freshmen Seek Power Broker Role

Freshman House Republicans have developed a cohesiveness and militancy that could have an important effect on the chamber's balance of power in the 96th and later Congresses.

Already by mid-1979, it was clear that the GOP freshmen were working hard to shift the focus of attention in the House from its liberal-to-moderate majority and award both the limelight and the power of winning votes to a newly strengthened conservative coalition.

It seemed unlikely they could accomplish this while they were still freshmen, but their zest for the task — combined with a fortuitous conservative trend in the House — suggested the goal was not as unrealistic as their small number — only 37 in a 435-member chamber — might suggest.

Key Elements

Much depended on whether the younger House Republicans could continue to stick together on issues and to push their brand of partisanship, and whether like-minded GOP members were elected to replace both Democrats and more senior Republicans. Replacing more moderate senior GOP members was particularly significant because many such Republicans in office in 1979 often voted with the Democrats on key issues. This happened enough in 1979 to cause the younger party members to gnash their teeth and complain — both publicly and privately — about sellouts of party principles.

The 1980 elections could become a central event in this play. House Republicans in 1979 numbered 159 — a slightly shrunken minority from their typical number over the last 35 years. (Since 1945, Republicans have averaged 183 members in each Congress; the number has been 176 in the 15 Congresses since then in which they were the minority party. They were the majority in two Congresses.)

It seemed possible, as of mid-1979, that the GOP could pick up 10 to 20 House seats if energy, inflation and possibly a recession plague the nation as much in November 1980 as many political observers expect. If this occurs — and any sizable number of the new Republicans are ideologically similar to the 1979 freshmen — House conservatives should be in a position to exert much greater pressure on legislative events than in recent years.

Reshaping the Party

The GOP freshmen's immediate goal has been to provide a distinct alternative approach to important national issues and a more unified opposition to the House liberal-moderate majority by solidifying the Republican position on major legislation.

The freshmen have set out to reshape their party into a vocal, independent and more effective opposition party. Under their strategy, the party actions would be aimed at selling the party line to the public and winning elections, rather than seeking a consensus with the majority on important issues or merely opposing the Democratic posi-

tion. Their goal was to win a Republican majority in the House in 1980. Almost no one, except perhaps some of the freshmen themselves, believed this was possible. But in the meantime, the freshmen's selling job might have produced dividends beyond those they originally sought.

Closing the Vote Gap

Instead of merely improving their image, the freshman Republicans and their allies have brought their group to within striking distance of winning some important floor fights when Republicans vote in large numbers with Democratic conservatives. Republicans were outnumbered in the House 276 to 159 in 1979. They had no hope of winning battles on the floor unless some conservative Democrats joined them, and few of their own numbers deserted to the Democratic side. Both of these conditions have been present on a number of important votes in 1979, but not quite enough to produce victories for the GOP and their conservative Democratic allies.

An analysis of 33 important House votes suggests that a handful of GOP members — numbering about two dozen — cast their votes with Democrats frequently enough to give victory to the Democratic leaders. For the most part, these defections have come from senior Republicans who have been in Congress for a number of years. The group also included a number of sophomores. It included almost no freshman Republicans.

It was this trend that could cause Democratic leaders more grief in coming years if the Republican Party developed even more cohesion than it had in 1979. (Democratic leaders might offset this development to some extent by leaning harder on party colleagues who have supported Republicans in floor fights to stick with the Democratic Party position. This assumes, however, greater Democratic unity than has been evidenced in recent years in the House, particularly among the younger members.) Even without actual victories, however, the emerging conservative bloc has pumped new life into conservative issues that had fared poorly in earlier years.

More Aggressive Stance

To get their party to vote more often as a bloc, the freshmen have been needling their GOP leaders to take a more aggressive stance on national issues before the House and to push party unity. "The freshman Republicans have been raising hell with the leadership because our leaders have been absent from the floor at times they could have been creating cohesiveness," commented Gerald B. Solomon, R-N.Y.

The Republican freshmen also held regular meetings in 1979 — independent of the regular party leaders — to develop policy positions on key issues before Congress. They pushed the benefits of party unity by encouraging the regular leaders to adopt their positions and lobby for them with the more senior House Republicans. As the freshman class of Republican House members in the 96th Congress

Vote Analysis Shows Freshman Unity

To analyze voting patterns of House Republicans, Congressional Quarterly studied 33 recorded votes taken during the first six months of the 96th Congress. The votes were chosen on the basis of how Republicans divided on the votes, as well as on the importance of the particular issue to conservatives.

The votes were grouped into four categories and concerned legislation on foreign aid, Panama Canal treaties implementation, U.S. relations with Taiwan, and budget and spending priorities — all controversial issues in the 96th Congress and of special significance to conservative lawmakers.

Among the factors considered in including a vote in the study were the following:

● Whether a vote involved an important controversy of particular significance to conservatives;

● Whether a vote was basically along party lines, in that it showed a clear split between the predominant Republican position and the predominant Democratic position;

● Whether the total Republican vote was split between the predominant Republican and predominant Democratic position;

● Whether the final tally showed Republican unity actually resulting in victory for the conservative position, or — had the Republicans voted more as a bloc — having the potential for, or coming close to resulting in, a victory for the conservative position.

The voting percentages shown in the box on p. 27 were calculated on the basis of the number of votes actually cast by the member; the name of members absent for more than half of the votes studied in any one category is marked with an asterisk in the table.

Freshman Unity

The study pointed to some trends that affected the outcome of a number of important votes in 1979:

1. Among Republicans, the freshman class that began service in January 1979 has shown more unity than either sophomores or more senior GOP members in opposing the Democratic majority on key votes.

2. There were enough Republicans above the freshman level, including a number in the sophomore class, who voted with the Democrats to assure a victory for the Democrats on some close roll-call votes.

3. There was a handful of Republicans, primarily in the more senior ranks, who voted repeatedly (a few even 100 percent of the time) with the Democrats on key issues.

The table below shows the number of House Republicans who voted at least 40 percent of the time with Democratic colleagues in (Col. 1) two of the four categories, (Col. 2) three of the four categories and (Col. 3) four of the four categories. The figures on the left are the number of Republicans in the three classifications: freshmen, sophomores, all other senior members.

	(Col. 1) 2 of 4 categories	(Col. 2) 3 of 4 categories	(Col. 3) 4 of 4 categories
Senior members (102)	26	15	8
Sophomores (20)	5	4	2
Freshmen (37)	1	0	0

Who They Are

Specifically, of the GOP freshmen, only Rep. Charles F. Dougherty, Pa., voted with the Democrats more than 40 percent of the time on votes in more than one of the four categories of votes studied.

Dougherty voted with the majority of Democrats six times and with the Republicans three times on the nine foreign aid votes used in the study. On the seven votes setting budget priorities, he voted with the majority of Democrats four times, and with the majority of Republicans two times; he was absent for a seventh vote.

Only four other freshman Republicans — Reps. Douglas K. Bereuter, Neb., Tom Tauke, Iowa, Ron Paul, Texas, and Arlen Erdahl, Minn., voted with the majority of Democrats more than 40 percent of the time in even one category.

By contrast, in the more senior GOP ranks, members voting with the Democratic position more than 40 percent of the time in all four categories were Reps. John Buchanan, Ala., Silvio O. Conte, Mass., Millicent Fenwick, N.J., Paul Findley, Ill., Frank Horton, N.Y., James P. Johnson, Colo., Paul N. McCloskey Jr., Calif., and Joel Pritchard, Wash.

Republican sophomores voting with the Democratic position more than 40 percent of the time in all four categories were Reps. S. William Green, N.Y., and Marc L. Marks, Pa.

Minority Leader Rhodes voted with the Democratic position over 60 percent of the time in two categories of votes: Panama Canal and foreign aid. On budget priority issues, he voted with the Democrats 14 percent of the time; on Taiwan relations, he voted with the Democrats 36 percent of the time.

Votes Selected

The Congressional Quarterly analysis included 11 votes taken during March 1979 House consideration of the Taiwan relations legislation (HR 2479); nine votes taken during April 1979 consideration of foreign economic aid (HR 3324) and State Department authorizing (HR 3363) legislation; six votes taken during June 1979 debate on legislation to implement the Panama Canal treaties (HR 111), and seven votes taken during May 1979 House floor consideration of the fiscal 1980 budget targets (H Con Res 107).

viewed the matter, their party under existing leaders often had been a willing servant of the Democrats and had put legislative compromise above partisan gain. Too often in the past, freshman Republicans noted in a series of interviews, their party had been content to play the role of the "reasonable opposition." On other occasions, the freshmen said, instead of setting out party goals, they had merely opposed whatever it was the Democrats wanted.

These postures had made it easier for the majority to set national goals and priorities, freshmen argued, and had

Where the Democrats Got Their Help

This table lists House Republicans who voted frequently with Democrats on 33 significant votes in the first six months of 1979. The percentages indicate how often the member sided with the Democrats in each category of votes.

Entered Congress	Taiwan	Foreign Aid	Panama Canal	Budget Issues
83rd (1953)		*Rhodes 67%	Rhodes 83%	
		Wilson 80%		
85th (1957)	Broomfield 91%	Broomfield 56%		
86th (1959)	Conte 45%	Conte 100%	Conte 67%	Conte 71%
		Derwinski 50%	Derwinski 100%	
87th (1961)		Anderson 100%		*Anderson 100%
	Findley 91%	Findley 67%	Findley 100%	Findley 43%
88th (1963)	Horton 75%	Horton 67%	Horton 50%	Horton 43%
		*McClory 50%	McClory 67%	
	McDade 50%	McDade 56%		McDade 43%
89th (1965)	Buchanan 64%	Buchanan 89%	Buchanan 100%	Buchanan 43%
		Conable 50%	Conable 50%	
	Edwards (Ala.) 88%			
	Erlenborn 82%	Erlenborn 50%	Erlenborn 100%	
		Stanton 44%	Stanton 50%	
90th (1967)	Heckler 64%	Heckler 71%		
	*McCloskey 100%	McCloskey 100%	McCloskey 100%	McCloskey 86%
				Miller 43%
		Railsback 67%	Railsback 100%	
		Winn 56%		
91st (1969)		Coughlin 40%	Coughlin 50%	
		Fish 91%	Fish 100%	Fish 60%
	Forsythe 64%			Forsythe 50%
				Goldwater 50%
	Whitehurst 91%	*Sebelius 67%		
92nd (1971)			Butler 100%	
	Frenzel 50%	Frenzel 44%	Frenzel 50%	
		McKinney 100%	McKinney 100%	McKinney 100%
				Spence 43%
93rd (1973)				Daniel (Va.) 43%
	Johnson (Colo.) 82%	Johnson 100%	Johnson 100%	Johnson 40%
		Gilman 89%		Gilman 43%
	Madigan 71%	Madigan 67%	Madigan 50%	
		*O'Brien 100%		
	Pritchard 91%	Pritchard 67%	Pritchard 100%	Pritchard 43%
				Rinaldo 57%
			Treen 60%	
94th (1975)		*Hyde 100%		
	Fenwick 100%	Fenwick 100%	Fenwick 100%	Fenwick 57%
	*Jeffords 50%	Jeffords 56%		Jeffords 43%
95th (1977)		Dornan 80%		
		Evans (Del.) 56%		Evans 43%
	Green 82%	Green 100%	Green 100%	Green 57%
		Hollenbeck 100%	Hollenbeck 67%	Hollenbeck 71%
		Leach (Iowa) 67%		
			Livingston 50%	
	Marks 90%	Marks 100%	Marks 100%	Marks 57%
		Pursell 83%	Pursell 50%	Pursell 83%
			Sawyer 100%	
				Stockman 43%
96th (1979)		Bereuter 44%		
		Dougherty 67%		Dougherty 67%
		Erdahl 50%		
				Paul 43%
		Tauke 43%		

Absences excluded in computing percentages in each category. Any person absent for at least half the votes is marked with an asterisk.

done nothing to strengthen the minority party's voice or to win elections. "The classic majority coalition in the House this year [1979] has been about 195 votes from the majority party and about 25 votes from the minority party," observed freshman Republican Newt Gingrich, R-Ga. "For a great part of its minority life, the Republican Party has allowed itself to become co-opted as an arm of government. Too often it has allowed itself to be cajoled into providing the necessary votes for the majority party to win."

A unified House GOP, the freshmen reasoned, might not have the strength in numbers to win on every vote, but it would give the party a stronger national image and would make it a more significant force to reckon with in the House power structure — particularly when GOP and conservative Democratic votes could make a majority.

Freshmen *vs.* the Leaders

The dissatisfaction of freshman Republicans and some of their most conservative senior colleagues with party leaders has been rooted in what the former saw as the leadership's failure to take a sufficiently aggressive stance on important national issues. The dissatisfaction highlighted the differences between low-key Republican leader John J. Rhodes, Ariz., on the one hand, and the freshmen and more militant senior conservatives, such as Robert E. Bauman, Md., John H. Rousselot, Calif., and John M. Ashbrook, Ohio, on the other. These freshmen, when working with their more senior conservative GOP allies and Democratic conservatives, have become the House minority leaders on a number of occasions. "On many days, Rousselot and Bauman are the effective minority party leaders," Gingrich said.

"The Republican leaders, many of them 10- and 15-term veterans, are of a decidedly different generation than the younger Republicans," commented Dave Stockman, R-Mich., a sophomore. "Their view is going to be different [from] that [of] the younger Republicans in their first or second term and still eager to take on the world."

"You have a very uneasy kind of dissatisfaction at the present time," Stockman said. "People are going to have to start talking to each other."

Rather than lead the party, Gingrich commented, the leadership has "had a tendency to be the nurse that says, 'I know this tastes bad, but hold your nose and swallow it.' " This should not be the case, Gingrich claimed. Instead, the Republicans should provide a meaningful opposition to the Democrats. "If the majority party is content to run the House like a plantation, they can do so," he said. "But they can't make me dress up and serve mint juleps with a smile."

But Gingrich and many of his freshman colleagues frequently have given back with one hand what they have taken away from the official GOP leaders with the other. For example, Gingrich admitted differences in style with the Republican leaders but insisted they have understood the freshmen, shared their philosophy, and have allowed them complete freedom to pursue their interests. Referring to references in the press to the clashes between the younger members and the leaders, he commented: "You don't see the 200 things on which we work together. Instead you see the two things on which we don't." The leaders "are saying, 'we will back you, we will support you,' " Gingrich said.

Leadership Response

The freshmen even said the leadership has taken some steps to respond to their concerns, and has encouraged them to act independently to pursue their goals.

Nonetheless, there was friction in the relationship. The younger members' desire to reshape the regular House leadership was illustrated in mid-1979 by an attempt to push their own candidate for the chairmanship of the House Republican Conference. That effort was defeated by middle-of-the-road Republicans June 20 when Henry J. Hyde, Ill., a two-term conservative who was the freshmen's candidate, lost his race for the chairmanship by three votes to 11-term representative Samuel L. Devine, Ohio.

The freshmen had asked Hyde to seek the office after interviewing Devine and the other candidates and declining to back them. Although the freshmen lost on this occasion, they voted as a bloc and proved themselves a force to be reckoned with.

"Sure, they lost, but they put up a good fight," commented one veteran Democrat. "Now, anybody who runs for a Republican leadership post knows they're going to have to deal with those guys." ∎

House Democratic Whips: Massing Support

Freshman Rep. Leon E. Panetta, D-Calif., was having a tough time finishing his phone call in the House cloakroom.

First, Majority Leader Jim Wright, D-Texas, interrupted. Wright was followed by several other Democrats, who took turns breaking in. Then a page brought Panetta a note saying Speaker Thomas P. O'Neill Jr., D-Mass., wanted to see him. Panetta found no escape on the House floor. As he left the cloakroom and strode down an aisle into the crowded chamber, Jim Mooney, chief aide to Majority Whip John Brademas, D-Ind., spotted him. Mooney grabbed Norman Y. Mineta, D-Calif., and steered him toward Panetta.

"Can you give us a vote on this?" asked Mineta. Panetta said no, resisting his friend's plea to change the vote he had just cast in favor of an amendment by Joseph L. Fisher, D-Va., to cut about $7 billion from the first fiscal 1979 budget resolution (H Con Res 559).

Undaunted by the rejection, Mineta turned to court other Democrats who had voted for the amendment — and against the wishes of the Democratic leadership.

Meanwhile, Wright wove his way through a crowd of younger members in the well of the chamber, urging them to switch their votes by signing little red cards stacked on a nearby table. O'Neill and Brademas stalked up the aisle, looking like hunters in search of prey. They, too, sought vote switchers. By the time the leaders stopped stalking — 10 minutes after the House scoreboard showed time had elapsed on the roll-call vote — 16 Democrats had trooped down to the well to change their votes. The amendment, which had been a sure winner when time ran out, instead was defeated, 195-203. The last-minute victory was credited to the arm-twisting of the Democratic leadership — O'Neill, Wright and Brademas. But backing up that highly visible trio were Mineta and other members of the leadership's intelligence-gathering network — the Democratic whips.

While the praise or blame for the Democratic record in the House ultimately rests with the party's leaders, many of the leadership's decisions are based on information the whips gather in their monitoring of members. It is the whips' advice that helps determine whether — and when — bills should be taken to the House floor. It is also the whips — representing the leadership — who can provide some of the muscle needed to get those bills passed.

Vote Hunters

Party whips originated in the British House of Commons, where they were named after the "whipper-in" — the rider who keeps the hounds together during a fox hunt. The first Democratic whip in the U.S. House was appointed in 1900 — three years after the Republicans named a party whip.

Unlike the British system, where political parties are well disciplined and a whip's major concern is good party attendance, whips in the United States House cajole as well as count noses.

In the 95th Congress, where Democrats held a nearly 2-1 edge over Republicans and enjoyed administration support on most major bills, it might have seemed unusual for the Democratic whips to be called on for more than an occasional nose count. But by May 1978 Brademas had had his troops out counting — and coaxing — votes on 63 bills or amendments since he became majority whip in 1977.

Expanding Empire

And when Brademas expanded his empire by adding seven new whips in 1978, he was not featherbedding, said several experienced whips. The additional people were needed to combat changes in the House that have made the whip's job of gathering votes for the leadership "a hell of a lot more difficult than it used to be," explained George E. Danielson, D-Calif., who was serving his eighth year as a whip.

Changes in the House make gathering votes "a hell of a lot more difficult than it used to be."

—Whip George E. Danielson, D-Calif.

The major change cited by several whips has been the increasing independence of members elected in recent years, which makes a party loyalty appeal for votes much more difficult.

"At one time you'd blow a whistle and say this is what the party wants and the members would line up and say, 'Yes sir, yes sir, yes sir,'" said Joe Moakley, D-Mass., an at-large whip in Brademas' operation and once the sole Democratic whip in the Massachusetts House.

However, younger members no longer are kept meekly disciplined by the House seniority system. "Today they get elected on Monday and they are giving a [floor] speech on Tuesday," said Moakley.

A glimpse of the new independence can be seen in the reactions of some younger members who switched their votes on the Fisher budget amendment. The leadership and its whips worked feverishly to get members to change their votes on the amendment, but some younger members who switched seemed to resent any suggestion that a leadership appeal might have swayed them.

Emotional Appeals

Panetta, who said he did not switch because he had made public statements in his district in favor of Fisher-type cuts, described the numerous last-minute approaches made to him as "strong emotional appeals."

"It can get very heavy," he said. "It's a point at which it's really no longer the issue as much as the fact that it could have an impact on the overall legislation, that the welfare of the Congress needs this, or the Speaker wants this."

One who did switch after hearing from Brademas, O'Neill and others was Toby Moffett, D-Conn. But Moffett said he changed his vote for other reasons, insisting that a leadership appeal "wouldn't have done it by itself, I'll tell you."

Peter H. Kostmayer, D-Pa., who lingered in the well of the House for several minutes before changing his "yea" vote to a "no" on the Fisher amendment, also portrayed his decision to switch as one immune from party appeals. Kostmayer said he switched after realizing that the amendment — which called for cuts in a wide variety of federal programs — would reduce some programs especially helpful to the Northeast.

Danielson was one whip who was particularly disturbed by the trend among younger members of ignoring party positions. "Party loyalty has really withered away," he lamented. "It shouldn't be that way. They didn't get elected on their own. A lot of these guys wouldn't have been elected if they didn't have Democrat behind their name."

How It Works

The whip organization has grown in size gradually since the early 1900s. Under Brademas, it consisted of a chief deputy whip, three deputy whips, 10 at-large whips and 22 zone whips.

The House Appropriations Committee voted to give Brademas $416,800 to run the majority whip's office in the Capitol during fiscal 1979 — more than the majority leader was allotted. The figure, much of which pays salaries of the majority whip's aides, was about 330 percent larger than the amount provided the majority whip in 1970.

Among the more mundane tasks Brademas is responsible for is the preparation of whip notices, which summarize the major issues involved in each bill that comes to the House floor. Among his more lively duties is the organization of a whip meeting every Thursday morning at 9:15. Surrounded by Brademas' office art collection, all of the Democratic whips spend 45 minutes with their party leaders in what one whip described as "a no holds barred exchange." Policy, scheduling and gripes are regular agenda items.

The zone whips, who are elected by the Democrats from the areas they cover, usually function primarily as tally keepers. The rest of the whips, appointed by the party's three leaders, are vote seekers as well as tally keepers. The decision to make a whip check is made by the Speaker, by the Steering and Policy Committee (a Speaker-dominated organization) or by the three House leaders. A check is usually begun several days before a bill reaches the floor.

Much of the nuts and bolts work is done by Brademas aide Mooney, who assembles material for the whips, compiles the information they send back to him and consults with them about strategy in gathering votes.

Questions for the whips to ask are selected with the help of the committee chairman managing a bill. The chairman is expected to give advice on matters that will be controversial so the whips know whether to count noses on adoption of the rule, controversial amendments, final passage or other issues. No more than three questions are asked on a whip check because most members "don't like to be probed that much," Mooney said. When it comes to actually wording the questions, advice of the committee chairmen is often ignored. "They want me to ask, 'Will you vote against the ill-advised, ill-conceived Joe Doakes amendment?' " said Mooney.

Unloaded Questions

To get an accurate count, it is important to avoid such loaded questions, according to Mooney. At the same time, "A whip check is a declaration of party policy. These are not Gallup polls," he said. The party position is implicit in the typical opening phrase of a whip question: "Will you vote for. . . ?" Said Mooney: "The question is always phrased so the right answer is yes." In one exception, the whips were instructed to ask, "Do you intend to vote for. . . ?" in order to signal members that the leadership was neutral.

The questions and a packet of background material on the bill to be checked are given to each zone whip. Although zone whips are supposed to make the initial check in person, several members said that in reality much of the checking is done by staff. The zone whips report their findings to Brademas' office, categorizing each member as for or against the bill, leaning for, leaning against or undecided. Members are also asked whether they will be present the day the bill is to be considered. A couple of members never respond to whip inquiries, while a handful of others so routinely give unreliable answers that they are not counted when a vote is close, according to Mooney.

Past Democratic whips have had problems getting complete information from their assistants. For instance, in 1966 a large bloc of western Democrats stopped reporting to their whip how individual members would vote. They complained that the whip polls had been shown to the administration and outside lobbyists, resulting in pressure on those members who did not support the party position.

Secrecy and Accuracy

Brademas' policy of keeping confidential the whip poll information on individual members was designed to help the whips get accurate information. Whip counts are "a very close-knit matter of trust," said at-large whip John W. Jenrette Jr., D-S.C. If individual names were given to lobbyists, "It would start a stampede" of lobbying pressure on members, he said. "Once it breaks down we would not ever be trusted again."

As the information from zone whips is reported to the majority whip's office, Mooney compiles lists of their data. A couple of times, these initial checks have shown such overwhelming support for a bill that no further action by the whips was needed. But if there is any question about passage, the at-large and deputy whips are called in for a briefing with the three leaders and the committee chairman. The list of undecided and "leaning" members is divided up, with the whips taking names of members they feel they could influence to vote with the leadership. Zone whips might help with this second stage if they support the leadership position on the bill.

'If You Need Me. . . .'

When the Democratic zone whips fan out to check how their party colleagues will vote on a bill, they put them in categories such as "undecided" or "leaning yes."

Subsequent visits by other whips are aimed at getting a firm "yes" from those who were uncommitted on the first check.

But sometimes a member falls back on a qualified commitment. In this case, the member would rather vote against the party position. But he or she promises a whip to go along with the leadership "if you need me."

Slipperiest Category

" 'If you need me' is the slipperiest category," said Jim Mooney, assistant to Majority Whip John Brademas.

Since the House chamber is crowded and noisy during roll-call votes, a member who had made an "if you need me" pledge could walk in during the middle of a vote, see that the leadership position was winning, vote the other way, and leave without consulting a whip. Later, the member could claim that it didn't look like his or her vote was needed — even though the leadership might go on to lose the final tally.

To avoid that, the whips keep close tabs on the "if you need mes" during a vote.

A vote in May 1978 that drew a number of "if you need me" commitments was the leadership's attempt to defeat an amendment by John M. Ashbrook, R-Ohio, reducing the Health, Education and Welfare budget by $3.15 billion.

Ashbrook won an initial 198-189 victory May 9, catching the Democratic leadership by surprise. Mooney said the whips had not been called in to work against Ashbrook's proposal because the leadership had assumed it would be defeated.

After Ashbrook's victory, the leadership went to work trying to change votes to repeal the amendment the next day. They picked up enough sure switches to reverse the vote on Ashbrook — if all other factors remained the same. They also picked up some "if you need me" commitments, providing a bit of insurance in case of unexpected absentees or other vote switches.

Before the second vote on Ashbrook's amendment May 10, Norman Y. Mineta, D-Calif., one of 10 at-large Democratic whips, was given a list of seven members who had voted for Ashbrook the first time but gave "if you need me" commitments for the second vote.

As soon as the vote began, Mineta spotted one of his sophomore colleagues who was on the list of seven. "I'm monitoring your vote," he told the friend before going in search of others on his list. Mineta said the "if you need me" commitments have to be carefully watched to "make sure they follow through on their promises."

When it became apparent in the closing seconds that the leadership had a comfortable victory, Mineta told his colleague his vote wasn't needed. Just before time elapsed on the vote, the member punched his card into the electronic voting system, casting his vote for the Ashbrook amendment. Ashbrook was defeated, 192-205.

The Real Vote

Mooney, who carries the "if you need me" commitments in his head along with a staggering amount of other data on whip counts, talks of votes in terms of the public tally and the "real" vote that would have occurred if the whips had called in all of their commitments.

There were six of those commitments on a leadership-backed bill to set up a consumer protection agency. That bill was defeated earlier in 1978 by a margin too large for the "if you need mes" to have made a difference.

Mooney pointed out that while it appeared the bill would have passed the House if 20 members had switched their votes. "We really lost by 14."

Although there are no hard and fast rules for dividing up the names, geography, committee assignments and friendship are factors. "I tend to get people from Tennessee and Missouri quite a bit," said deputy whip Bill Alexander, from the neighboring state of Arkansas. At-large whip Jenrette said he usually took the names of southerners.

Armed with their lists of names, the whips then pay a visit to each member to "lay it on him, so to speak," Jenrette said. This time, the whips stress the party position, ask members what troubles them about the bill and what might make them change their minds to vote for it. "It's always a question of, 'Can you help us?' " said Alexander. Again, Mooney and Brademas get reports from the whips including tips on what might turn a member around — such as an amendment or a call from the Speaker or the president. Depending on how soon the bill is scheduled for floor action, those who are still undecided could get more visits from other whips. "We don't send the same whip back to keep badgering the same guy," said Mooney. Repeat visits create more pressure — and more commitments. "Taking a whip count is like fishing. The more you do, the more you catch," said Mooney.

As the list of commitments is firmed up, the leadership studies the whip information to make a final determination on whether to bring a bill to the floor or postpone it. After one whip check in spring 1978, the leadership decided to postpone floor action on a financial disclosure bill (HR 1). The whip check showed a large number of members who were refusing to make a commitment for or against an amendment the leadership considered damaging. The Democratic leaders decided not to take a chance that the undecideds would vote their way, and the bill was pulled from the calendar.

Ephemeral Data

While the leadership decision on scheduling a bill is largely based on the intelligence gathered in a whip poll, the whips' data can prove ephemeral. For instance, some members who indicated they would vote for final passage of the fiscal 1979 budget resolution couldn't be counted on after the House began changing it substantially with amendments. "A commitment is like a piece of hamburger. It only keeps for so long," said Mooney. Wright and O'Neill are usually saved for last-minute vote-getting, to apply "the heavy party loyalty shtick. Then it's more personalities than issues. There are some members who can only be gotten by the Speaker or the Majority Leader," said Mooney.

"In a close case, the prestige of the Speaker is very great [in winning votes]," said at-large whip Tom Bevill, D-Ala. On a few particularly controversial or complex bills, O'Neill has begun the practice of appointing a task force to supplement the whip operation. Task forces — formed on the budget resolution, energy and Social Security bills, and others — are made up of members who support the leadership positions on the bill. They function like whips, asking members for vote commitments.

Once a bill reaches the floor, some whips "work the doors," lining up for one last shot at members as they enter the chamber to vote. Brademas said he tries to vote early so anyone looking at his name on the electronic scoreboard can see what the leadership position is. During the vote a machine on the floor will give the whips a computer printout of Democrats who have voted yea or nay. If a vote is close, the whips use that list as a guide to seek possible vote switches.

Horsetrading

The whips say their primary tools of persuasion are making appeals to party loyalty and arguing the merits of the bills supported by the leadership. Ten whips interviewed by Congressional Quarterly said the whip operation does not have any authority to offer members favors in exchange for votes. Nor is it in a position to arrange vote exchanges, such as certain voting blocs might agree to within the House. For instance, many members from urban districts vote in favor of farm bills in exchange for the support of farm state members on mass transit or other urban interest legislation.

Several of the whips said only the three Democratic leaders have the authority to grant or withhold favors in exchange for party support. "There is a little horsetrading [by the leadership] every once in awhile," said one House source who did not want to be identified. "But it's the exception because there isn't that much to trade." This source and others said that committee chairmen and party leaders in recent years have lost much of their once powerful authority to grant favors, such as assuring a member of a public works project for his or her district or passage of a pet bill. Favors now are confined to such plums as paving the way for a choice committee assignment or promising help in moving a bill, they said.

Some whips said that while they had no authority to engage in horsetrading to win a vote, more subtle political forces often help them influence members to vote with the leadership. "One of the things you do without anybody telling you around here is you can't be crossing people all the time because you'll want their vote one day," said Danielson.

Track Record

Although the Democratic leadership took a beating on several bills in 1978, most of its defeats came on measures that were not worked by its whip network. According to Mooney's figures as of May 1978, whip advice to the leadership in the 95th Congress was very accurate — even on leadership losses.

Mooney said that 60 of the 63 bills or amendments checked by the whips eventually went to the floor for a vote. The leadership position prevailed on 55 of the 60 votes, he said. Of the five leadership losses, only one came as a surprise. The other four bills were brought up — in spite of very close tallies in the whip checks — for other reasons, according to House leaders.

The first big defeat for the leadership and the whips in the 95th Congress came in March 1977, on labor's common-situs picketing bill. Based on the count done by Brademas' whips, the leadership considered pulling the bill from the calendar. But organized labor insisted it had the votes, and the leadership agreed to schedule it. "I have to give the whips credit that, frankly, they were very accurate," said AFL-CIO lobbyist Victor Kamber. "We were hearing intelligence from our local people that didn't turn out to be correct."

Whip counts also indicated trouble for the labor-backed oil cargo preference bill before it was taken up in October 1977. But the leadership brought it up at the insistence of Merchant Marine and Fisheries Committee Chairman John M. Murphy, D-N.Y., and it was defeated.

A third defeat in 1977 — the one surprise — came on a package of administrative reforms proposed by the House Commission on Administrative Review. Prior to the vote, whips had counted noses for votes on the previous question, one amendment and final passage. They had not counted votes on adoption of the rule, which was rejected — thus killing the bill. Mooney said that, based on rumors picked up by the whips, the opposition had been expected to try to defeat the bill on the previous question. He added: "We misgauged the sentiment of the House."

Several whips said that the count they did in early 1978 on a bill to set up a consumer protection agency was extremely accurate. None was surprised when the legislation was defeated. In that instance, White House insistence — not the whip check — prompted scheduling of the bill, House leaders said. The bill had been pulled from the calendar in late 1977 because a whip check then showed it probably wouldn't pass.

Public Financing Dispute

A controversial bill to revise federal campaign finance law, which the leadership had hoped to use as a vehicle for considering public financing of congressional elections, was defeated in March 1978. Brademas played two roles in the bill — one as a member of the House Administration Committee that wrote the legislation and one as a whip trying to round up votes for it. Prior to floor action on the campaign bill, Republicans and Democrats became embroiled in a partisan squabble over Democratic-backed committee amendments to the bill that Republicans viewed as an attempt to throttle GOP fund-raising. As a result, backers of public financing — including Common Cause — bitterly attacked Brademas and others who had put together the bill for angering Republicans and jeopardizing the chance to pass public financing. House Republicans voted unanimously to kill the measure, although some had previously said they supported public financing of congressional elections.

Brademas insisted that public financing — not the partisan fight — had been the real issue in the vote. While others urged the leadership to delay action on the bill, the recommendation from the whip's office was to go ahead with it. Mooney said that, based on the whip check, the recommendation was a gamble. However, Brademas did not believe the prospects for public financing would be improved by waiting. In unusually bitter public criticism,

Common Cause officials disagreed with Brademas. Common Cause President David Cohen called the recommendation to bring the campaign finance bill to the floor "an unnecessary roll of the dice. The partisan atmosphere would have cooled down some. I think time would have been a plus [for gaining votes in favor of public financing] because the atmosphere was just so thick in terms of partisanship."

Outside Assessments

Lobbyists asked to assess the Democratic whip organization under Brademas usually tied their judgment to the outcome of major bills they supported.

For instance, while Cohen was highly critical of Brademas' role in the campaign finance bill, he expressed satisfaction with the whip's role in the decision to delay the financial disclosure bill. "I think where they did not show prudence on public financing, they did show prudence on financial disclosure," Cohen said.

Mark Green, director of Ralph Nader's Congress Watch, was critical of the leadership decision — based on a whip count — to postpone the consumer protection agency bill in fall 1977. Green said his own lobbying checks showed at least a dozen members who voted against the bill in February 1978 would have supported it in the previous fall. Nader had urged action then — as well as in February, when it was defeated.

Mooney, however, insisted that the Democratic whip counts are the most accurate ones in town because members answer other members more honestly than they answer lobbyists. "Members of Congress are very skilled at telling people what they like to hear but without really saying, 'Yeah, I'll vote for it.' That's why our counts are invariably the best. Members don't bull-shit each other."

List Kept Secret

However, several lobbyists said it would be impossible to judge the accuracy of the Democratic whips because their lists are kept confidential. Outside groups pushing a leadership-backed bill readily share their vote counts with the whips. But the only information that lobbyists — including the administration — get in return are the total number of yes votes or general guidance such as, "Your figures are way off in Indiana."

"They very jealously guard individual reports," said AFL-CIO lobbyist Ken Young. He contended that a whip's statement that their count was within one or two votes of the actual outcome could be misleading. "It's always easy to come close on a number and be wrong on individual members," said Young.

Printed whip counts carry a stern warning at the top that they are to be kept confidential. Only the whips, the leadership, the committee chairman working with the whips on a bill and a few aides are supposed to see the counts. Mooney said he knew of only one instance in the 95th Congress where the policy was breached, when a committee aide gave copies of a whip count to lobbyists.

Not all Democratic whips have kept such tight wraps on whip counts, and several lobbyists said Brademas' policy was "frustrating" to them. However, all agreed that the confidentiality probably increases the accuracy of whip counts. White House lobbyist Bill Cable said, "The best lobbying effort is a member to member effort. It's a whole lot more difficult to be cute with a fellow member." ∎

Party Caucus Role on Legislative Issues

More than ten years after House Democrats revitalized their long-dormant caucus, they continued to bicker about what the caucus should do on legislative issues.

The caucus has been used in that period to make significant reforms in House procedures. But there has been much disagreement about the rare attempts to use the body to influence legislation.

One example of such an attempt began in March 1978, when Democrats anxious for an election-year rollback of planned Social Security tax increases appeared headed for an impasse with the House power structure.

The Democrats needed a prod to get some action from a stubborn Ways and Means Committee, which would have to send a rollback bill to the floor. But they could not rely on the House leadership to help them get a floor vote because Speaker Thomas P. O'Neill Jr., D-Mass., agreed with the Carter administration's opposition to a change in Social Security financing.

As their election-year jitters grew, the Democrats turned to the caucus — the organization of all House party members. In April, a resolution urging Ways and Means to act on rollback legislation breezed through the caucus on a 150-57 vote.

Although the vote had no binding effect, the power of the caucus is potentially so strong that committees take heed when it speaks. Most observers believed that, in the wake of the caucus vote, Ways and Means would approve some sort of tax rollback.

In May the House Ways and Means Committee agreed by a one-vote margin to roll back Social Security taxes. However, the next week, it rejected the tax cut proposal by a 16-21 vote. The dramatic reversal was seen by some committee Democrats who had favored the rollback as a direct rebuke to the House Democratic Caucus.

The Social Security vote marked the first legislative stand the caucus had taken in more than three years.

Source of Power

The key to caucus power in setting legislative policy lies in its authority to select committee chairmen, who for decades held power only by virtue of their longevity in the House. The theory is that when the caucus "urges" a committee to take an action, the committee chairman heeds or faces the consequences. Another lever is the caucus' ultimate control over Democratic committee assignments.

However, the caucus in recent years has primarily confined itself to in-House actions such as making committee assignments, electing party leaders, and recommending changes in House rules and procedures at the beginning of each Congress. (Role in procedural reforms, box, p. 37)

There is little dispute about its authority to act on such procedural questions. But when the caucus tries to move into legislative policy-making, such as the Social Security vote, members part ways on the question of how far the caucus should extend itself into the bill-writing responsibilities of the legislative committees.

The most powerful House policy-makers — including committee chairmen and Speaker O'Neill — have resisted the notion of having the caucus tell them what to do. Older members, who remember when the caucus was moribund, have said they felt some major issues such as Social Security were worthy of caucus attention — but only in rare instances. And some younger members felt the caucus was a slumbering giant that ought to be awakened as a new voice for the party, setting broad policy and legislative priorities and endorsing occasional specific bills.

Caucus Revival

After decades of dormancy, the caucus was given new life in the early 1970's by Democratic liberals and moderates who wanted to tip the balance of House power away from some conservative, autocratic committee chairman. (Story, p. 3)

The revival led to a long series of procedural changes to reform committee operations and make chairmen more responsive to the Democratic majority. But the caucus still proceeded with extreme caution when it came to legislative policy.

Then, in 1975, caucus votes on legislative positions screeched to a halt when older members became alarmed at a series of caucus votes pushed by freshman members.

The End-the-War Push

The last straw for many came in February 1975 when Bob Carr, D-Mich., persuaded the caucus to pass a resolution opposing military aid to Cambodia and South Vietnam.

Already that year, the caucus had deposed three committee chairmen and ordered the Rules Committee to let the House vote on repealing the oil depletion allowance.

Even though only two of the actions involved legislation, "that was about as much as some of the old fogeys could digest," said Fortney H. (Pete) Stark, D-Calif.

Republicans began shouting an old epithet, "King Caucus," warning of a return to days when the Democratic Caucus had an iron grip on its members. And some Democrats fumed that if the caucus was going to vote on policy before hearing from committees, the committee system might as well be abolished and witnesses on bills could just come directly to the caucus.

Continued Discontent

Carr's anti-war resolution became the last legislative position the caucus took until the 1978 Social Security vote.

Although they had not tried another assault, Carr and some of his colleagues in the junior ranks of the House said in interviews in 1978 that they were not happy that the caucus had been neglected as a party policy-making arm.

"The caucus has fallen down miserably," said Stark, one of the principal sponsors of the earlier Social Security resolution.

Rep. Toby Moffett, D-Conn., who called a special caucus meeting in the spring of 1978 to discuss the troubled energy bill, described the caucus as "almost inoperative." Although Moffett withdrew a request for a caucus vote on the energy bill, he said such votes are a proper function of the party. In addition, he said the caucus should meet more frequently to discuss major issues such as arms sales and national health insurance.

Carr said the caucus should increase its initiatives in adopting legislative priorities, now set almost entirely by committee chairmen. Stark was more cautious, noting that too many orders to committees could become meaningless. "It's conceivable the committee wouldn't do it. Then what do you do?" he said.

Besides taking votes on policy, the caucus could fill an information gap by informing members about upcoming legislation, said Norman Y. Mineta, D-Calif. "The only information mechanism we have now is the whip advisory, but that's just on the bills that are [on the floor] next week." Mineta said.

He recommended meetings twice a month (the caucus now meets monthly) just to talk about major issues and hear reports from chairmen about the bills their committees are considering. "Otherwise, how does a member who's not on the committee get their two cents in?" Mineta said.

But Mineta acknowledged that such meetings would still meet leadership resistance, because "the leadership gets uptight" about the possibility of policy votes when the caucus meets. He offered no solution for breaking down the adversary relationship between the caucus and House leaders.

Although these newer members did not blame caucus inactivity directly on its chairman, Thomas S. Foley, D-Wash., they regarded him as a far less activist leader than his predecessor, Phillip Burton, D-Calif., was. Foley is "a very establishment guy" who is not inclined to buck the leadership's traditional dislike of the caucus, said Stark.

Foley countered such criticisms by describing his own role as "the servant of the caucus" and maintaining that, "The members can determine how active the caucus is."

Under caucus rules, any member who can find 50 supporters to sign a petition can ask for a special caucus meeting. Thus, complaining that the caucus doesn't do enough is like saying "there's no litigation in the court and blaming the judge for the lack of litigation," Foley said.

It is not his role, Foley contended, to actively seek issues for the caucus to deal with. And the younger members' criticism was contradicted by the fact that he received relatively few formal requests for caucus action, Foley said.

If younger members did organize an effort for more caucus action on legislative policy, Foley said he thought they would be rebuffed by the party. "I have no reason to believe that the majority wants to jump in" to a larger policy-setting role, he said.

Other Democrats concurred with Foley's opinion that members would rather keep the caucus as "a kind of gun behind the door."

"I think they'd have an awful time if they tried [to set party policy in the caucus]," Richard Bolling, D-Mo., told Congressional Quarterly. "It's better left to the committee system."

Abner J. Mikva, D-Ill., another backer of the 1978 Social Security resolution, described the caucus as "clearly the most small 'd' democratic" House policy-making institution. But votes within the caucus should still be rare and limited to issues such as Social Security, where a committee was clearly frustrating the desires of many members, Mikva said.

Thoughts on the Caucus

"I don't like any of these matters coming from the caucus on a direct vote."
—Speaker Thomas P. O'Neill Jr., D-Mass.

". . . almost inoperative."
—Rep. Toby Moffett, D-Conn.

"The members can determine how active the caucus is."
—Chairman Thomas S. Foley, D-Wash.

". . . fallen down miserably."
—Rep. Fortney H. (Pete) Stark, D-Calif.

Members would "have an awful time if they tried" to set party policy there.
—Rep. Richard Bolling, D-Mo.

"The only information mechanism we have now is the whip advisory."
—Rep. Norman Y. Mineta, D-Calif.

Caucus History

The queasiness many members feel when the caucus votes on legislative positions can be traced to the up and down history of caucus policy-making. Active caucus periods have been followed by long periods of dormancy, sometimes in reaction to caucus strength.

Caucuses were a vehicle for setting party legislative strategy in the earliest years of Congress. But by 1820, they had been reduced to doing little besides choosing a Speaker. The Democratic Caucus did not revive as a policy-making tool for almost a century.

In the 1800's, power was concentrated in the Speaker, who controlled such vital functions as committee assignments. That era culminated in the autocratic reign of Speaker Joseph G. Cannon, R-Ill., in the early 1900's. When Cannon was deposed and Democrats took over the House, they turned to the caucus as the means for building party unity to get legislation passed. A caucus rule bound members to vote for a bill if two-thirds of the party had endorsed it in caucus.

But the frequent use of the binding rule led Republicans to charge that "King Caucus" had become as dictatorial as Cannon had been.

A decline in party unity made it difficult to get a caucus consensus after a few years of the King Caucus era. At the same time, the seniority system for selecting committee chairmen had become a House tradition, giving chairmen a power base that was insulated from control by other House power groups.

The caucus, holding no authority to influence those chairmen, went into a long decline. Committee chairmen became entrenched, and some became unresponsive to both party and House leadership.

Caucus After 1968

In 1968, liberal and moderate members of the Democratic Study Group (DSG) became alarmed at the prospect of pushing bills that would be opposed by both the incoming Republican administration and conservative committee chairmen.

Seniority was so entrenched that it was considered out of the question to try to convince members to begin electing committee chairmen. Instead, the DSG members successfully pushed two caucus rule changes that they felt could open the way for a gradual break of the power of chairmen. The changes, adopted in early 1969, required monthly caucus meetings and gave any member the right to bring issues before the caucus for debate and action.

Over the next several years, the caucus used those rules to erode some of the power committee chairmen had accumulated. Included in the procedural changes was the crucial provision that chairmen would be elected by secret ballot in caucus, making them ultimately answerable to their party colleagues.

Despite the changes, the caucus has not rushed to tell chairmen how to run their committees. In 1969, the caucus took its first legislative position in decades by urging Ways and Means to report out legislation removing President Nixon's freeze on welfare payments to states.

The caucus did not speak out on legislation again until opponents of the Vietnam War used it as a last resort to try to get anti-war legislation out of committee. In a series of votes in the early 1970's, the caucus ordered or urged committees to act on anti-war bills that had been bottled up by those committees and by the party leadership. Those involved in the effort credit the caucus with finally moving the House against the war.

In 1975, "Phil [Burton] was interested in using his position [as caucus chairman] to advance himself along the leadership ladder," said Carr. Burton's ambitions and the zeal of the freshman class combined for a series of caucus victories.

Then came the backlash and the cries of "King Caucus," particularly from Republicans who felt that legislation was — or might be — written in a party body in which they had no part. Republicans said this would undermine the legislative process.

In answer to the criticism, Democrats abolished the binding rule — which actually was used only rarely since the early 1900's.

Privately, Democratic leaders were also passing the word that the caucus needed to confine itself to procedural questions and leave policy alone, except for occasional issues of overriding national importance. The caucus quietly went out of the policy-making business.

Rising Doubts in 1975

Some of the most searching criticism of the caucus move and its implications had come in 1975 from freshmen and liberals, the two groups to benefit most from the reinvigorated caucus. Few of them challenged the right of the caucus to debate and vote on legislative policy questions and to order committees to bring legislation to the House floor to be voted on. They were worried, however, that the caucus was still a fragile instrument which should not be abused. Their concerns followed several lines.

They feared that party unity might be seriously strained if the caucus became too involved in legislative matters. "The caucus shouldn't be overused to take positions on substantive issues," cautioned Donald M. Fraser, D-Minn, (1963-79), an early backer of an active caucus.

One congressional aide with close ties to the House Democratic leadership warned against frequent caucus votes on policy questions. "You get guys beat," he complained. "All the caucus does through votes is highlight divisive issues. It shows the division over and over again."

Several liberals warned that the situation that developed for several months in 1971, when many Democratic members refused to attend regularly scheduled meetings of the caucus, causing them to adjourn for lack of a quorum, could be repeated if attempts are made to force caucus votes on too many issues. Many of the absentees then wished to avoid discussing and voting on an end-the-war resolution sponsored by Rep. Bella S. Abzug, D-N.Y. (1971-77).

Another fear was that the caucus would no longer be usable as a safety valve in extraordinary circumstances if it was used too frequently or casually. David R. Obey, D-Wis., saw the caucus as a safeguard against procedural abuses and the place to consider policy initiatives, a role he wanted continued.

But he worried that it would cease doing so if its scope became too broad. "If you continue shotgunning things into the caucus, you run the risk of increasing the number of signatures needed for a special caucus," he warned. "That's dangerous, because it remains an important safety valve. But we could reach that point quickly if we have one or two more quickie caucuses."

In fact, one influential southern moderate who supported an activist caucus said "stricter rules" were needed for calling special caucuses. "Not only are more signatures needed, but we've got to put more responsibility on the leadership," he added.

Paul Simon, D-Ill., said that "if policy questions continue to come up at caucuses, you'll find more and more people voting to defer the issue."

There was rising doubt among some members about the value of caucus debates and votes on all but general policy questions. One midwestern liberal complained: "If the caucus votes against American troop commitments in Europe and the Far East, my reaction is, 'Big deal.' It's Mickey Mouse, and it detracts from seriously using the caucus to bring issues to the floor."

Caucus Defenders

While the 1975 Carr resolution became somewhat of a symbolic issue with caucus critics, defenders of an active caucus claimed it was a false issue. They said it was used to exaggerate how much the caucus became involved in legislative policy and to stunt the development of the caucus as the leadership body for House Democrats. Caucus action on questions involving policy was a logical extension of caucus involvement in procedural matters, they argued.

Richard P. Conlon, staff director of the Democratic Study Group and one of the key behind-the-scenes architects of the revived caucus, said the Carr resolution "shouldn't be read as a precedent. There was a lot of concern that this was the way the caucus was going to act," he explained. "But that is a misreading of the situation. Cambodia, because of the Vietnam legacy, was an extraordinary situation. There are no other suggestions that the

Caucus Role in Procedural Reforms of Early 1970s

After a 50-year hiatus, the Democrats in 1969 began to revive their House caucus as an instrument to reform the House.

The caucus had reigned supreme under the Democrats from 1911 to 1919, when it was used to enact the Wilson administration's legislative program. However, it fell into disuse with the rout of the Democratic Party in the congressional elections of 1918 and 1920.

The Republicans, who dominated the House in the 1920s, never developed a strong caucus, and the Democrats, who regained control in 1930, did not resurrect their powerful caucus.

During Rep. Sam Rayburn's, D-Texas (1913-61), 17-year tenure as House Speaker, which stretched from 1940 to 1961 (with two brief breaks), the Democrats rarely used the caucus except to elect a majority leader, a candidate for Speaker or a member of the Ways and Means Committee.

The push to revive the party caucus came in the middle and late 1960s from the Democratic Study Group (DSG), an organization of moderate and liberal Democratic members that is the largest reform bloc in the House. After the 1968 election, DSG members held several meetings in November and December to discuss ways to revitalize their party.

"After polling over 100 DSG members, James G. O'Hara, D-Mich., then chairman of the DSG, found that a proposal that received almost unanimous support was the scheduling of regular monthly meetings of the caucus," wrote Walter J. Oleszek, a former staff member of the House Select Committee on Committees.

When the 91st Congress opened in 1969, House Speaker John W. McCormack, D-Mass. (1928-71), agreed to regular monthly meetings of the caucus, and the first step had been taken in the revival. According to Oleszek, "the significance of regularizing party use of the caucus was noted by Donald Fraser, D-Minn., former leader of the DSG. 'With the monthly caucuses, we had regular opportunities to talk about House reforms. That was the turning point.'"

1970 and 1971

During 1970 and 1971, the caucus took two actions to strengthen its position. First, the caucus in early 1970 created the Committee on Study, Organization and Review, headed by Rep. Julia Butler Hansen , D-Wash. (1960-75), to study the seniority system. That was a prelude to important changes. The Hansen committee issued a report that December that recommended a modification of the seniority system. At their organizational sessions in January 1971, the Democrats established a policy that the House Democratic Committee on Committees need not consider seniority in recommending to the caucus nominees for chairmen and recognized the right of any 10 Democrats to obtain a separate vote on any committee chairman.

The caucus also adopted several changes that strengthened the autonomy of subcommittees. It passed a rule that no member could be chairman of more than one legislative subcommittee. However, that rule was evaded by at least one committee chairman, who said his subcommittees were "investigative" and thus not covered by the rule.

Second, it adopted new rules at a special "caucus on the caucus" held in July 1971 that allowed the caucus chairman to cancel any monthly caucus with sufficient notice, but not two consecutive meetings, and enabled members to continue to meet for purposes of discussion even in the absence of a quorum.

1973

In 1973, the caucus widened the seniority reforms. The Hansen committee was revived to consider various reform proposals offered by the DSG, including one that would have required a comprehensive secret ballot for each nominee for committee chairman.

The caucus eventually adopted a resolution to permit secret votes on chairmen if one-fifth of the Democrats requested them. The caucus then voted by secret ballot on each nominee for chairman. None was deposed that year, but the groundwork for the upsets of 1975 was laid.

Furthermore, the caucus in 1973 voted to create a new Steering and Policy Committee to assist the House Democratic leadership in developing party and legislative priorities, in scheduling floor debate and in coordinating with Senate Democrats. Viewed by some Democrats as the principal accomplishment of the reform caucuses, the Steering and Policy Committee was seen by some as the first step toward the transfer of the committee assignment responsibility away from the Ways and Means Committee.

Other caucus actions included adding the Speaker, majority leader and caucus chairman to the Democratic Committee on Committees and adopting a party rule guaranteeing at least one major committee assignment to all Democrats.

1974 and 1975

The House Democrats capped their procedural reform drive in the party caucuses of December 1974 and January 1975 by taking several significant steps. They removed from the Democratic members of the Ways and Means Committee the authority to make committee assignments and transferred it to the Steering and Policy Committee. They made the election of all committee chairmen automatic. They required all committees with more than 20 members to establish at least four subcommittees. They empowered the Speaker to nominate Rules Committee Democrats, subject to caucus approval, and they required that chairmen of Appropriations subcommittees be ratified by the caucus.

The caucus strengthened Democratic control of House committees by expanding the Ways and Means Committee from 25 to 37 members, adding several liberal members in the process, and giving all committees, except Ethics, a two-to-one plus one ratio.

Committee chairmen were brought under even closer control by the caucus when it deposed three senior chairmen who headed the Banking, Agriculture and Armed Services committees.

caucus be used that way." Conlon called the "sense of the caucus" resolution on Cambodian military aid "a perfectly legitimate caucus action, since it didn't bind the [Foreign Affairs] Committee."

Caucus Future

Most Democrats appeared content to keep the caucus in the background, leaving policy decisions to committee chairmen and the leadership. Some have said the caucus was not needed as much as previously because the chairmen have become more responsive, committee operations have become more democratic and O'Neill has become a powerful Speaker who usually reflects majority thinking in the party.

And those who might like to see the caucus more powerful acknowledged it would be difficult to make any fundamental changes. "Some people in leadership are nervous about any kind of dialogue that takes place that's not planned," said Moffett.

Leadership Views

O'Neill made his feelings about caucus votes clear at a press conference prior to the 1978 Social Security vote.

While acknowledging that party sentiment appeared strong enough to pass the Social Security resolution, O'Neill said, "I don't like any of these matters coming from the caucus on a direct vote." O'Neill and Majority Leader Jim Wright, D-Texas, both voted against the resolution.

The party's number three person, Majority Whip John Brademas, D-Ind., voted for the resolution but said later, "I find it easy to suppress my enthusiasm" for caucus policy votes. Leadership sources argued that even though caucus votes were not binding, they locked the party into a position and reduced its flexibility in seeking compromises to win votes.

Making the caucus more active would also involve getting a majority of the Democrats to show up for meetings, a task that several members have found impossible. Since the leadership generally opposed formal caucus action, members could not look for help there in rounding up votes. Backers of the Social Security resolution relied on DSG and an informal whip system among younger members to get a majority of the party to the floor.

The Quorum Problem

No caucus action can be taken without a quorum, a rule which has stymied action many times. Common Cause President David Cohen recalled that when his organization was backing anti-war resolutions in the caucus, it took months just to get a quorum for a vote.

Elliott H. Levitas, D-Ga., found that even with a majority of the House Democrats cosponsoring his bill on congressional vetoes, he could not get a quorum to show up for a vote at two regular caucus meetings in early 1978. Levitas' bill had been bottled up in the Judiciary and Rules committees.

While some members cited the early meeting time (9 a.m.) and leadership opposition as major factors in preventing quorums, Foley said lack of a quorum was more likely an indication that members did not want to overuse the caucus. They will show up when they consider an issue of overwhelming importance, but, "If you have too many issues thrown out in the caucus, members vote their dissatisfaction by not coming," he said.

Obscure Committee Bolsters GOP Power

The enormous square cake on the table had five candles and the great seal of the United States in blue and yellow butter cream. Tiny pennants ringed the frosted eagle, each little paper flag bearing the name of a different legislative issue: Rhodesia, labor reform, consumer protection agency, antitrust reforms, common situs. The occasion May 1, 1979, was the fifth birthday of the Steering Committee, a small band of senators who share a small staff, a conservative viewpoint and a commitment to needle the Democratic majority.

The tiny flags, Chairman James A. McClure, R-Idaho, told the assembled guests with a smile, identified "a few signs of our success." The party was organized to mark a milestone, but it also permitted a rare glimpse of the obscure group. Members have remained largely anonymous and refrained from publicizing the group's legislative activities. At the party, however, past and present members freely admitted their association with the group and lauded its accomplishments. They were celebrating something else as well.

Only a week earlier, the committee for the second time in a month had been attacked on the Senate floor by Democratic leader Robert C. Byrd, D-W.Va. To the small group of conservatives dedicated to outmaneuvering the majority, Byrd's attacks were a sign of recognition and of success.

Invisible Committee

"Here, lo and behold, is a committee, somewhere — I cannot see it, I do not know where to find it, I do not know its makeup, I do not know what the authority for it is — which calls itself 'the Senate Steering Committee,' " Byrd said April 23. "Let it be known," Byrd told Senate colleagues March 22, "that so far as I am concerned that there is no 'Senate Steering Committee.' None."

Byrd became angry when Steering Committee staff aides, identifying themselves as from "the Senate Steering Committee," polled senators by telephone on issues before the Senate. Byrd, who is chairman of the Democratic Steering Committee, a Democratic group that makes party committee assignments, accused the Steering Committee of masquerading as something it was not. Holding up the embossed calling card of Steering Committee Executive Director Margo Carlisle, he asked colleagues:

"Who pays the cost of this beautiful calling card. . .? On whose payroll is Margo Carlisle. . .? Where does the 'Senate Steering Committee' get its funds?"

Tired of Losing

The Steering Committee was founded in 1974 by Carl T. Curtis, R-Neb. (1955-79). "I got tired of being defeated on the floor," Curtis explained. "I was disappointed that one of my colleagues would have a good amendment that was defeated because no one knew anything about it. I decided what we needed was a little organization," he said.

Curtis gathered with like-minded senators on April 3, 1974. Attending were Republicans Norris Cotton, N.H.

(1947-75), Curtis, Peter H. Dominick, Colo. (1961-75), Paul J. Fannin, Ariz. (1965-77), Clifford P. Hansen, Wyo. (1967-78), Jesse Helms, N.C., Roman L. Hruska, Neb. (1953-76), McClure and Strom Thurmond, S.C.

From this, the Steering Committee was born. Members agreed to hire and share a small staff. Office space was donated by Curtis. Office equipment, supplies and local telephone service came from Curtis' own official allotment. Curtis turned over his leadership to McClure in 1975.

Financial Secrecy

According to Senate records, there is no such group as the Steering Committee. "We really are just members of the senators' staffs, so we operate the way their staffs do," explained Executive Director Carlisle. Carlisle told a reporter the group keeps no records of each senator's contributions, or of its staff's salaries. However, an examination of Senate records shows that for fiscal 1978, 12 senators contributed a total of $68,575.35 for the salaries of four staff aides — executive director, general counsel, researcher and secretary — and a consultant to help out during the Panama Canal debate.

The senator contributing the most was Wyoming's Hansen, who pitched in $11,276.88 for the 1978 fiscal year; the least contributed was $3,087, from each of four senators. The highest paid employee, Carlisle, received $23,775.82 in fiscal 1978; secretary Evelyn K. Wheless was paid the least, $9,016.94.

Although financial records for fiscal year 1979 were not available, these 14 Republican senators contributed money to the Steering Committee for shared staff and consider themselves members: William L. Armstrong, Colo., Jake Garn, Utah, Barry Goldwater, Ariz., Orrin G. Hatch, Utah, S. I. (Sam) Hayakawa, Calif., Helms, Gordon J. Humphrey, N.H., Roger W. Jepsen, Iowa, Paul Laxalt, Nev., McClure, Larry Pressler, S.D., Thurmond, Malcolm Wallop, Wyo., and John W. Warner, Va.

The sole Democrat ever to have been commonly associated with the Steering Committee was James B. Allen, D-Ala. (1969-78), who died in 1978. Charles McC. Mathias Jr., R-Md., one of the Senate's most liberal Republicans,

"I got tired of being defeated on the floor. . . . I decided what we needed was a little organization."

—Former Sen.
Carl T. Curtis
R-Neb. (1955-79).

"has cooperated with [the group] on a selective basis, but is not a member," according to an aide.

Committee's Work

The Steering Committee meets regularly over lunch each Wednesday, and also gets together on a monthly basis with a more moderate Republican group called the Wednesday Group, which has no staff or offices. Pressler, who belongs to both groups, said the luncheon meetings "are a good way to get information and to get to know your colleagues on a first-name basis."

Staff members coordinate legislative activities, plan strategy, assemble coalitions, write speeches, draft legislation, and assist their members' personal and committee staffers. Among issues on which the group has been active were the Panama Canal, strategic arms limitation talks, labor law reform, common situs picketing, cargo preference, consumer and antitrust reforms, Rhodesia, regulatory reform, campaign financing, curbs on the Senate filibuster, public broadcasting and balancing the federal budget.

Impact Debated

There has been disagreement about the committee's effectiveness. During the 95th Congress, the group had success using delaying maneuvers to exact compromises from bill sponsors anxious to get their measures onto the floor. The tactic typically involved preparing amendments to a piece of legislation and refusing to limit debate until the bill's managers accepted some of the amendments.

Because Senate leaders were reluctant to bring bills to the floor without a time limitation, the technique gave the committee leverage far in excess of the group's size. Carlisle claimed her small staff was disproportionately successful because "we're good. We work hard and we work with the staffs of other senators." Outside business and conservative groups shared the Steering Committee staff's high opinion of its operations.

"Comparing the difference in the effectiveness of conservatives before and after the Steering Committee is like comparing night and day," commented Paul Weyrich of the Committee for the Survival of a Free Congress. "Without their orchestration, we'd lose constantly."

"I think they're very competent people," stated the Chamber of Commerce's Hilton Davis.

Staff members of the regular Senate committees, however, differed with these assessments. For example, the Steering Committee claimed a major victory in the 1978 filibuster and defeat of labor law reforms. "The Senate Steering Commitee was the focal point of the opposition to the so-called labor reform bill last year," Helms remarked. Yet Robert Hunter, a Republican aide on the Labor Committee who helped organize the filibuster said in an interview: "In my estimation, it was a very limited role." Lugar, who organized the filibuster, "drew on a lot of members of the Steering Committee, but that was because the senators were against the issue anyway."

The Panama Canal debate was another issue on which the Steering Committee claimed a key role. But Robert Dockery, the Foreign Relations Committee aide who staffed committee and floor consideration of the debate, commented: "I never heard of them. I assume the group was part of that effort. I wouldn't want to characterize their effort, but the record speaks for itself — they lost." ∎

Congressional Committees

CQ

Congressional Committee System Overhauled

Beginning in the early 1970s, the congressional committee system was revolutionized by the adoption of new procedures and rules governing the selection of chairmen and members, and the way the committees operated. And in 1977, the Senate approved a major overhaul of its formal committee structure, reducing the number of its committees and revising their jurisdictions. In 1979, the House created a Select Committee on Committees to study reorganization proposals.

Reformers in Congress and interested outside groups had long sought to revise the committee system. They recognized committees as the primary legislative power centers because most legislation is born in committee. Committee members write the individual bills to be considered by the full House and Senate and make the basic decisions about what is included in them and what is not. Although changes can be made in a bill once it reaches the floor in either chamber, most of the basic, detailed work done by committees is never touched after their bills are reported.

As a result, committee members — and especially senior members — have an enormous influence on the content of legislation under their committees' jurisdictions. Over the years, that influence had evolved into centralized power, exercised by an elite handful of high-ranking senators and representatives.

In the early 1970s, reform advocates set out to dilute this power and reshape committee jurisdictions to reflect the changing legislative needs of the decade. By 1975 they had won half a victory.

They had chipped away at decades-old traditions and revised Congress' operating ground rules, not only for committees and subcommittees but for the full House and Senate and the party caucuses as well.

Committee chairmen, who had run their units arbitrarily in the past, were subdued by new procedural restrictions and forced to share power with their junior colleagues. In a further step, most committee sessions were opened to the public by new rules that all but banned secret meetings.

Conference committees were another prime target for the reformers. These committees are composed of members from the House and Senate committees which originally drafted the respective versions of a particular bill. They meet to resolve any differences left in the two versions after both houses have passed the measure. Consequently, they wield enormous power of their own, since they determine the final wording of the bill as it becomes law. Even though this final version is subject to the approval of both houses, the work of the conference committees — like that of the original legislative committee in each chamber — normally is not changed by either the full House or the full Senate. The power of these committees is so great that they are often jokingly (although not altogether inaccurately) referred to as the fourth branch of government.

Until the mid-1970s, conference committees usually were tightly controlled by their senior members and subject to a number of legislative abuses. A common trick was for one or both houses to attach immensely popular riders to routine bills in order to please the voters back home, knowing all along that these riders would be quietly dropped in conference, usually because they were unrealistically expensive. Another practice was for House or Senate conferees to frustrate the majority's will in their own chambers whenever they personally disagreed with specific provisions.

In order to prevent these and other kinds of activities, both houses approved measures in 1975 to open conference committee sessions to the public and the media.

Other pressures were affecting the House-Senate conference system as well. Junior committee members were demanding and receiving permission to participate in conference sessions — a practice unheard of prior to the reforms of the 1970s. Some members who had sponsored major floor amendments to particular bills were added to conference committees even though they were not members of the original legislative committees which had written the bills — again a first. These members claimed that they needed to be in on the conference sessions in order to defend their amendments against opposition by members from the other chamber.

This chapter examines the major changes in seniority and procedures during the period 1974-79. Other chapters in this section highlight the overall sweep of those changes, examine the evolving role of conference committees and survey the expanding powers of House subcommittees. The 1977 Senate committee reform and proposals for similar reform in the House are also examined.

1974-75 Changes

Congressional committees and subcommittees experienced numerous changes in membership, party ratios and even names when the 94th Congress convened in 1975. Factors contributing to these changes were House committee reforms adopted in 1974, the overwhelming Democratic victory in the 1974 elections and the new-found power of the House Democratic Caucus. While the most visible changes occurred in the House, many assignment switches also took place in the Senate.

The first of many changes in the House committee structure occurred a month before the 1974 elections when the House on Oct. 8, adopted the Committee Reform Amendments of 1974. Although this reorganization did not reduce the number of committees, it did consolidate some jurisdictions that had been spread among several committees. Among the provisions were:

● A requirement that committees with more than 20 members establish at least four subcommittees.

● A requirement that committees with more than 20 members establish an oversight subcommittee or require its subcommittees to conduct oversight in their jurisdictional areas.

(The two provisions originally set 15 members as the limit before subcommittees and oversight jurisdiction had to be established. The number was raised to 20 when the full House adopted rules for the 94th Congress.)

● Consolidation of most transportation matters in the Public Works Committee, renamed Public Works and Transportation. The panel, which already had jurisdiction over highways, gained urban mass transportation from Banking and Currency, renamed Banking, Currency and Housing, and civil aviation and surface transportation from Interstate and Foreign Commerce. Commerce kept railroads.

● Passing to the Interstate and Foreign Commerce Committee jurisdiction over biomedical research (from Science and Astronautics), nursing home construction (from Banking) and health care programs except those financed through payroll taxes (from Ways and Means).

● Passing to Science and Astronautics, renamed Science and Technology, jurisdiction over civil aviation research and development (from Interstate and Foreign Commerce), environmental research and development (from several committees) and all energy research and development except nuclear (from several committees).

● Giving to the Foreign Affairs Committee authority over some international trade matters (from Banking), the Food for Peace program except domestic production (from Agriculture), international commodity agreements and export controls (from Banking and Ways and Means).

● Transferring revenue sharing from Ways and Means to Government Operations.

● Transferring legal services from Education and Labor to Judiciary.

● Establishing a Select Committee on Aging.

● Establishing the Select Committee on Small Business as a standing committee with the jurisdiction of Banking's former Small Business Subcommittee.

Two further blows were delivered to the established committee system in the House, first by the 1974 election, which ushered in 75 mostly liberal Democratic freshmen and gave the Democrats a 291-144 majority. (Republicans later won a Louisiana seat, making the division 290-145.) The second blow was dealt by the House Democratic Caucus, including the 75 freshmen-elect, meeting Dec. 2-5, 1974, to organize the 94th Congress. Proposals concerning committees which the caucus adopted included:

● Stripping the Democratic members of the Ways and Means Committee of their power to make committee assignments and investing that power in the Democratic Steering and Policy Committee.

● Increasing the size of the Ways and Means Committee from 25 to 37 members.

● Establishing on all committees (except Standards of Official Conduct) a 2-to-1 Democratic majority, plus one additional Democrat.

● Requiring that all nominations of chairmen of Appropriations subcommittees be approved by caucus vote.

● Allowing the Speaker to nominate all Democratic members of the Rules Committee, subject to ratification by the caucus.

● Giving members of each committee the power to determine the number of its subcommittees.

As a result of these changes and a continuing attack on the seniority system, three committee chairmen were replaced by the caucus, another declined to seek his chairmanship again and a fifth had to engage in a hotly contested caucus election in order to retain his seat.

W. R. Poage, D-Texas, was replaced by Thomas S. Foley, D-Wash., as chairman of the Agriculture Commit-

tee; F. Edward Hebert, D-La., was deposed as chairman of the Armed Services Committee and replaced by Melvin Price, D-Ill.; and Wright Patman, D-Texas, lost the chairmanship of the Banking, Currency and Housing Committee to Henry S. Reuss, D-Wis. Wilbur D. Mills, D-Ark., whose friendship with a striptease dancer had made headlines for several months, declined for reasons of health to seek reelection as chairman of the powerful Ways and Means Committee which he had chaired since 1958. Mills was replaced by Al Ullman, D-Ore. Wayne L. Hays, D-Ohio, chairman of the House Administration Committee, was renominated by the caucus after a battle with the committee's second ranking Democrat, Frank Thompson Jr., N.J.

The chairmanships of four other standing committees changed hands due to retirements, and a fifth — Standards of Official Conduct — changed when Price was named to Armed Services.

The chairmen of two important subcommittees also lost their seats. The Banking, Currency and Housing Committee voted to replace Leonor K. Sullivan, D-Mo., as chairman of the Consumer Affairs Subcommittee and elected Frank Annunzio, D-Ill., to replace her. Sullivan was chairman of the Merchant Marine and Fisheries Committee at that time. Harley O. Staggers, D-W.Va., retained his chairmanship of the Interstate and Foreign Commerce Committee but lost the chairmanship of its Subcommittee on Commerce to John E. Moss, D-Calif.

In the Senate, the only significant change regarding committees in 1975 came about when the Senate Democratic caucus voted to elect all future committee chairmen by secret ballot.

1976-77 Changes

Meeting Dec. 6-9, 1976, the House Democratic caucus approved a number of changes in committee rules and procedures, among them:

● Committee privileges and powers were broadened; a quorum for conducting business — including markup sessions — was set at one-third of a committee's membership, and committee subpoena power was substantially broadened.

● The House Committee on Standards of Official Conduct and the Joint Committee on Atomic Energy were stripped of their legislative jurisdictions.

● House rules were changed to open all House-Senate conference committee meetings to the public except when the House specifically voted to close such a session.

● The chairmen of the Ways and Means and Appropriations committees were stripped of their power to nominate members of the Budget Committee, and that power was vested in the Steering and Policy Committee, which was given the power to nominate eight sitting members and eight new members to the panel at the start of each session.

Once the leadership was elected and new rules changes adopted, the House had one major housekeeping item left to attend to: the naming of House committee and subcommittee chairmen. Decisions were made in Democratic Caucus meetings Jan. 11, 18 and 26, 1977. On Jan. 19 and 27 the House by voice votes then adopted resolutions (H Res 117, 118 and 198) ratifying party choices for committee assignments in the 95th Congress.

Unlike 1975, when three powerful committee chairmen were toppled in a major revolt against the seniority system,

House Democrats in 1977 accepted the elevation of senior members to the top posts on most committees.

Eight committees were headed by new chairmen in 1977. Of the 22 legislative committees, 10 of the chairmen came from four states: Texas (4); Wisconsin (2); New Jersey (2) and New York (2). No other state had more than one chairman.

All the nominees for chairmen received strong endorsements from the caucus, with the largest number of reservations — 91 — expressed about Robert N. C. Nix, D-Pa., the nominee for chairman of the Post Office and Civil Service Committee.

The only close vote on a House committee chairman came Jan. 11 when the caucus selected Robert N. Giaimo, D-Conn., as chairman of the Budget Committee over Thomas L. Ashley, D-Ohio, 139-129.

More dramatic than the votes on committee chairmen was a 189-93 Jan. 26 caucus vote to oust Robert L. F. Sikes, D-Fla., as chairman of the House Military Construction Appropriations Subcommittee. In 1976 Sikes had been reprimanded by the full House for conflict of interest and for failure to disclose ownership of stocks as required by House rules. The action had grown out of an investigation of Sikes' financial holdings by Common Cause.

The margin of the 1977 vote to unseat Sikes surprised even the backers of the oust-Sikes movement, who had expected to win but by a much narrower margin. The following day the caucus elected Gunn McKay, D-Utah, to the chairmanship. The second-ranking member, Edward J. Patten, D-N.J., had removed himself from the subcommittee.

1978-79 Changes

House Democrats, meeting in December 1978 to organize for the 96th Congress, agreed to a number of committee changes. They voted to increase from two to three the number of terms members could serve on the House Budget Committee; to prohibit Democrats from serving on more than five subcommittees; and to maintain at least a two-to-one ratio of Democrats to Republicans on most House committees. Another change, which was expected to open up more choice assignments to junior members, required committees to let each member choose one subcommittee assignment before any member could pick a second one. (The Appropriations Committee was exempted from the change.)

Another proposal adopted by the caucus would lock in place existing practices for selecting subcommittee chairmen. The rule provided that all committees — except Appropriations — must continue to allow bidding for subcommittee chairmanships by seniority on the full committee. It would permit the Appropriations Committee to continue its practice of bidding for chairmanships by seniority on the subcommittee. The caucus also voted to prohibit a full committee chairman from serving as chairman of any other full, select, special, or joint committee.

There were no major upsets in the selection of committee chairmen when Congress convened in January 1979; however, three more junior Democrats scored a victory over more senior colleagues in elections for subcommittee chairmanships on the Commerce and Government Operations committees. *(See p. 64)* ∎

Senate Reorganizes Its Committees in 1977

Hoping to improve its working conditions and its legislative product, the Senate devoted the first month of the 95th Congress to reorganizing its committee system. The 1977 overhaul was the first since the Legislative Reorganization Act of 1946 (PL 79-601). The new rules went into effect fully in 1979.

Passage of the reform resolution (S Res 4) dictated major changes in the way each senator spent his time and in the way the Senate conducted its business. Only over a span of years would the full impact of the changes become evident.

The reorganization, said Adlai E. Stevenson III, D-Ill., "democratizes the Senate, rationalizes jurisdiction and cuts far back on the multiple committee assignments which pull and haul senators into time conflicts every day." Stevenson, chairman of the select committee set up to recommend reform of the system, had observed before the Senate acted that self-interest was working to encourage adoption of the reforms: "Senators are frustrated and deeply concerned about public cynicism about Congress. For their own sakes, as well as for the country, they want to make the Senate a more responsive, efficient institution."

As adopted, S Res 4 streamlined the number of Senate committees, revised their jurisdictions, set a limit on the number of subcommittees and committees a senator could belong to or chair, gave minority members an adequate share of committee staff and directed computerization of committee meeting schedules to avoid conflicts.

S Res 4 was introduced by Stevenson on Jan. 4, 1977. It was the product of the temporary Select Committee to Study the Senate Committee System, which Stevenson had chaired. The committee had published its recommendations in September 1976.

The Rules and Administration Committee began hearings on S Res 4 Jan. 5. Twenty days later, on Jan. 25, the committee unanimously ordered the measure reported with a number of major changes. After making still more revisions, the full Senate passed the measure by a vote of 89-1 on Feb. 4.

S Res 4 realigned legislative responsibility and sought to focus senatorial energies by defining committee jurisdictions to reflect current issues and by limiting the number of committee responsibilities an individual senator could take on. Under the measure, no senator could serve on more than three committees and eight subcommittees. He could chair no more than four committees and subcommittees, three after the 95th Congress.

A Revised Resolution

The original Stevenson plan called for abolition of all special, select and joint committees, except the special intelligence committee, and for the abolition of the District of Columbia Committee, the Post Office and Civil Service Committee, the Aeronautical and Space Sciences Committee and the Veterans' Affairs Committee.

The Rules Committee voted to preserve the Veterans' Committee, the Select Committee on Small Business, the Committee on Standards and Conduct (under a new name, Ethics), the Joint Economic Committee, and the Joint Committee on Taxation and to defer action on the Joint Committee on the Library and the Joint Committee on Printing.

The Rules Committee also voted to set up a new, temporary Select Committee on Indian Affairs during the 95th Congress only.

When the measure came to the floor, the full Senate voted to preserve the Special Committee on Aging, and to extend the life of the Select Committee on Nutrition and Human Needs through December 1977.

Thus, by the time the resolution passed, it called for an immediate reduction in the number of committees to 25 from 31. It also offered the prospect that by the end of the 95th Congress this number would be further reduced to 23 with the abolition of the Nutrition and Indian Committees.

The Stevenson committee plan to consolidate responsibility for transportation matters in one committee and for environmental matters in another broke down in the face of opposition from committee chairmen who resisted any reduction of their influence in these matters.

But in the area of energy, consolidation succeeded. The Interior Committee, renamed the Energy and Natural Resources Committee, retained most of its former responsibilities plus jurisdiction over naval petroleum reserves and oil shale reserves in Alaska from the Armed Services Committee, water power from the Public Works and nonmilitary development of atomic energy from the Joint Committee on Atomic Energy.

In addition, the committee gained jurisdiction over a wide range of subjects that had not been defined under the old committee system. Among these were solar energy, outer continental shelf energy reserves, energy regulation and research and coal production and distribution.

Winners and Losers

Many of the full committee chairmen gained power as their committees absorbed the jurisdictions of panels that were abolished. The Government Operations Committee, chaired by Abraham Ribicoff, D-Conn., for example, gained jurisdiction over the District of Columbia and Post Office and Civil Service matters because those two committees were blended into a new Governmental Affairs panel.

Henry M. Jackson, D-Wash., became in effect the new Senate energy czar as jurisdiction over virtually all energy legislation was concentrated in his committee, formerly the Interior Committee, now the Energy and Natural Resources Committee.

Russell B. Long, D-La., chairman of the Finance Committee, came out unscathed, despite early rumblings that liberals would attempt to strip his committee of jurisdiction over Social Security or health care legislation.

The special power of the Appropriations Committee was duly noted in a provision that exempted its members from strict limits on subcommittee service.

A number of middle level senators lost power. The Senate Committee on Nutrition and Human Needs, chaired by George McGovern, D-S.D., was to go out of business at the end of 1977, with its functions transferred to the Agriculture Committee, tightly controlled by Herman E. Talmadge, D-Ga.

Quentin N. Burdick, D-N.D., lost his bid to retain the Post Office and Civil Service Committee, which he was in line to chair. Burdick was the only senator to vote against final passage of the resolution.

A number of senators lost because of the limits on subcommittee membership and chairmanships. James O. Eastland, D-Miss., for example, who chaired three Judiciary Committee subcommittees in the 94th Congress could retain only one under the new rules. Claiborne Pell, D-R.I., who sat on 24 committees and subcommittees in the 94th Congress, was limited to 11.

Republican senators gained a proportional share of committee staff, something they had fought for years to obtain. Some Democratic senators, however, were expected to lose staff aides as a result of the changes.

But every senator also gained something under the new system. The endless scheduling conflicts, incessant demands that senators scurry from one committee meeting to another, and the nearly total dependence on staff work that were hallmarks of Senate operations for years, were expected to diminish as a result of S Res 4.

Provisions

As adopted by the Senate, S Res 4:

Committee Structure

Established 12 major Senate committees, as follows, with the following number of members each: Agriculture, Nutrition and Forestry (16); Appropriations (24); Armed Services (16); Banking, Housing and Urban Affairs (15); Commerce, Science and Transportation (18); Energy and Natural Resources (17); Environment and Public Works (15); Finance (17); Foreign Relations (15); Governmental Affairs (19); Human Resources (16); Judiciary (15).

Established minor committees with the following number of members: Rules and Administration (9); Veterans' Affairs (9); Aging (14 in the 95th Congress and nine thereafter); Intelligence (15); Small Business (14 in the 95th Congress and nine thereafter); Joint Economic Committee (10); Joint Committee on Internal Revenue Taxation (5).

Provided that the Budget Committee with 16 members would be a minor committee for the 95th Congress and a major committee thereafter, but would be a major committee during the 95th Congress for new members of the committee.

Continued the Select Committee on Nutrition and Human Needs as a minor committee with nine members through Dec. 31, 1977, but thereafter transferred its functions to the Agriculture Committee.

Established a five-member Select Committee on Indian Affairs to consider all legislation dealing with Indians during the 95th Congress.

Required the appropriate standing committees to report legislation by July 1, 1977, dealing with the future status of the Joint Committee on the Library and the Joint Committee on Printing. (The Senate Rules Committee recommended that both committees be retained.)

Changed the name of the Committee on Standards and Conduct to the Ethics Committee and specified that it would consist of six members, each of whom would serve a six-year term with the terms staggered to achieve a rotation of membership, and that the committee would not be subject to the limitations on memberships applicable to other committees.

Specified that not later than July 1, 1977, the appropriate standing committees would report legislation to terminate the authority of the Joint Committee on Atomic Energy, the Joint Committee on Congressional Operations and the Joint Committee on Defense Production. (The Joint Committee on Atomic Energy was abolished in August 1977. The Joint Committee on Defense Production was extended for two years by PL 95-37. The Senate passed a bill in July abolishing the Joint Committee on Congressional Operations; the House in March established a Select Committee on Congressional Operations to continue the Joint Committee's work on the House side.)

Committee Membership

Limited each senator to membership on two major committees and one minor committee.

Limited each senator to membership on three subcommittees of each major committee on which he served; exempted the Appropriations Committee from the limit.

Limited each senator to membership on two subcommittees of the minor committee on which he served.

Allowed a member of the Budget Committee during the 95th Congress to serve on three subcommittees of the Budget Committee.

Allowed the chairman of any full committee to serve ex officio and without a vote on any subcommittee of the committee he chaired.

Exempted the Intelligence Committee chairman and ranking minority member from the rules limiting committee membership during the 95th Congress.

Allowed a senator who served on three major committees during the 94th Congress to continue to serve on three major committees but prohibited him from serving on a minor committee.

Allowed exemption from the limits on committee service on agreement by the majority and minority leaders if exemption were necessary to maintain majority party control of committees.

Stated the sense of the Senate that in making appointments to committees and in establishing seniority, first consideration should be given to members of those committees who were serving as chairman and ranking member of committees whose functions were transferred.

Stated the sense of the Senate that no member of a committee should receive a second subcommittee assignment until all members of the committee had received a second assignment.

Allowed the temporary addition of one or two members to committees above the limits set in the resolution.

Chairmanships

Prohibited a senator from serving as chairman of more than one full committee at any one time.

Prohibited a senator from serving as chairman of more than one subcommittee on each committee.

Prohibited the chairman of a major committee from serving as chairman of more than one subcommittee on his major committees and as the chairman of more than one

How One Senator Sought to Avoid Chairmanship Limits

Rules sometimes are made to be broken — or at least avoided.

The January 1979 organizing sessions of two Senate committees illustrated how this works. Veteran Sen. Harrison A. Wiliams Jr., D-N.J., had to hustle to preserve some of the power that years of incumbency brought him. Still, he was only partially successful.

The 1977 Senate rules prohibited a senator from being chairman of more than three committees and subcommittees in total. A full committee chairman could head only two subcommittees; a senator who didn't head a full committee could chair three subcommittees. But in addition, the new rules prohibit the chairman of a major committee from serving as chairman of more than one subcommittee on all of the major committees on which he serves.

For 20-year veteran Williams, the new rules created a few problems. Williams managed to finesse one sticky situation, but he lost an attempt to squeeze his way around another.

The New Jersey Democrat began the 1979 session in a position — under the old rules — of chairing four committee or subcommittee units.

● He was chairman of the Senate Human Resources Committee, and chairman of its Labor Subcommittee.

● As the ranking Democrat on the Senate Banking Committee, he was first in line to become chairman of the important Housing Subcommittee, and continue as chairman of the Securities Subcommittee.

Both Banking and Human Resources are major committees under Senate rules.

Thus, under the new rules Williams couldn't hold all the posts and all the power that goes with them. For example, if he took the Banking's Housing Subcommittee he would have to give up the chairmanships of the Securities and Labor subcommittees.

Yet Williams is considered an expert on securities law and didn't want to lose control of that. However, he is also an ardent supporter of organized labor and was reluctant to give up control of the Labor Subcommittee. Further, that subcommittee has jurisdiction over another major law sponsored by Williams, the Employee Retirement Income Security Act of 1974.

Attempting to resolve the dilemma, Williams worked out a strategy in which he could keep as much real power as possible, although he would have to give up some of the titles. It nearly worked.

First, Williams persuaded the Human Resources Committee to disband the Labor Subcommittee and allow the full committee to handle labor legislation.

"I wanted, quite honestly, to retain the subject matter," Williams said at a Jan. 25 organizational session of the committee.

Organized labor wasn't particularly happy to see the end of the Labor Subcommittee. However the full committee was still dominated by senators who have strong alliances with organized labor.

The Human Resources Committee met in the morning. That afternoon, the Banking Committee held its organizational meeting.

Using carefully phrased language — he never pinned authorship on any individual senator — Banking Committee Chairman William Proxmire, D-Wis., said it had been suggested that the Securities Subcommittee be disbanded and its subject matter handled by the full committee. Of course, Proxmire said, Williams, with his securities expertise, would still be looked upon as the expert on securities legislation.

Williams also argued for the change.

But the committee rejected the proposal. Three of six committee Democrats voted with all six Republicans against disbanding the Securities panel.

Sen. Morgan's Role

One of the chief players in the drama was Sen. Robert Morgan, D-N.C., who also had his eye on the Housing Subcommittee.

Morgan, anxious to increase his Senate visibility in preparation for his re-election campaign in 1980, figured that blocking the effort to disband the Securities Subcommittee would force Williams to choose between the Securities and Housing subcommittees.

Morgan was not next in line for Housing if Williams chose Securities, but the North Carolina legislator had sounded out the two members who ranked above him in the seniority pecking order — Alan Cranston, D-Calif., and Adlai E. Stevenson III, D-Ill. — and neither wanted the Housing unit.

Thus, if the move to abolish the Securities Subcommittee were blocked, and Williams retained the Securities Subcommittee, Morgan would chair Housing.

But Morgan didn't quite attain his goal. Williams elected to give up Securities and take the Housing Subcommittee. Sen. Paul S. Sarbanes, D-Md., took the Securities chairmanship. Williams retained the other majority spot on the subcommittee.

Morgan wound up with what he had during the 95th session — a spot on the Housing Subcommittee and chairman of the Rural Housing Subcommittee.

subcommittee on his minor committee, effective with the 96th Congress in 1979.

Prohibited the chairman of a minor committee from chairing a subcommittee on that committee and prohibited him from chairing more than one of each of his major committees' subcommittees, effective with the 96th Congress in 1979.

Committee Business

Prohibited any committee from establishing a subcommittee without approval from the full Senate.

Allowed the majority leader with the agreement of the minority leader, to offer a privileged motion to refer a bill to two or more committees jointly or simultaneously. (Existing rules allowed such a referral only by unanimous consent.)

Required the Rules Committee to establish a central computerized scheduling service for meetings of Senate committees and subcommittees and House-Senate conference committees, and to place computer terminals in all Senate offices.

Permitted any committee or subcommittee to meet without special leave up to the conclusion of the first two

The Standing Committee System of the Senate...

The Senate committee reform effort in 1977 left the Senate with a streamlined committee structure which consisted of 15 standing committees, plus eleven special, select, joint or temporary committees.

The following list sets out the Senate standing committees, their new names, the number of members, and the subjects within their jurisdiction.

Committee on Agriculture, Nutrition and Forestry (16)

Agriculture and agricultural commodities; inspection of livestock, meat, and agricultural products; animal industry and diseases; pests and pesticides; agricultural extension services and experiment stations; forestry and forest preserves and wilderness areas, other than those created from the public domain; agricultural economics and research; home economics; plant industry, soils, and agricultural engineering; farm credit and farm security; rural development, rural electrification, and watersheds; agricultural production, marketing, and stabilization of prices; crop insurance and soil conservation; human nutrition; school nutrition programs; food stamp programs.

Committee on Appropriations (24)

Appropriation of revenue for the support of the government; rescissions of appropriations; the amount of new spending authority and new, advance spending authority as provided for in the Congressional Budget Act of 1974 (PL 93-344).

Committee on Armed Services (16)

The common defense; the Department of Defense, the Department of the Army, the Department of the Navy, and the Department of the Air Force, generally; pay, promotion, retirement, and other benefits and privileges of members of the Armed Forces, including overseas education of civilian and military dependents; military research and development; selective service system; strategic and critical materials necessary for defense; aeronautical and space activities associated with the development of weapons systems or military operations; maintenance and operation of the Panama Canal, including administration, sanitation, and government of the Canal Zone; national security aspects of atomic energy; naval petroleum reserves, except those in Alaska.

Committee on Banking, Housing and Urban Affairs (15)

Banks, banking and financial institutions; financial aid to commerce and industry; deposit insurance; public and private housing (including veterans' housing); federal monetary policy, including Federal Reserve System; money and credit, including currency and coinage; issuance and redemption of notes; control of prices of commodities, rents, and services; urban development and urban mass transit; economic stabilization and defense production; export controls; export and foreign trade promotion; nursing home construction; renegotiation of government contracts; matters relating to international economic policy as it affects United States' monetary affairs.

Committee on the Budget (16)

The committee shall be required to report matters required to be reported by it under Titles III and IV of the 1974 Budget Act, to study the effect on budget outlays of relevant existing and proposed legislation and to devise methods of coordinating tax expenditures policies and programs with direct budget outlays and to review the conduct of the Congressional Budget Office.

Committee on Commerce, Science, Transportation (18)

Interstate commerce; transportation; regulation of interstate common carriers, including railroads, buses, trucks, vessels, pipelines, and civil aviation; merchant marine and navigation; marine and ocean navigation, safety and transportation, including navigational aspects of deepwater ports; Coast Guard; inland waterways, except construction; communications; regulation of consumer products and services, including testing related to toxic substances, other than pesticides, and except for credit, financial services, and housing; the Panama Canal and interoceanic canals generally except those areas reserved for Armed Services; standards and measurement; highway safety; science, engineering, and technology research and development and policy; nonmilitary aeronautical and space sciences; transportation and commerce aspects of Outer Continental Shelf lands; marine fisheries; coastal zone management.

Committee on Energy and Natural Resources (17)

Energy policy; energy regulation and conservation; energy research and development; solar energy systems; nonmilitary development of nuclear energy; naval petroleum reserves in Alaska; oil and gas production and distribution; extraction of minerals from oceans and Outer Continental Shelf lands; energy related aspects of deepwater ports; hydroelectric power, irrigation, and reclamation; coal production, distribution, and utilization; public lands and forests, including farming and grazing thereon, and mineral extraction therefrom; national parks, recreation areas, wilderness areas, wild and scenic rivers, historical sites, military parks and battlefields, and preservation of prehistoric ruins and objects of interest on the public domain; mining, mineral lands, mining claims, and mineral conservation; mining education and research; territorial possessions of the United States, except for trusteeships.

Committee on Environment and Public Works (15)

Environmental policy; environmental research and development; ocean dumping; fisheries and wildlife; environmental aspects of Outer Continental Shelf lands; solid waste disposal and recycling; environmental effects of toxic substances, other than pesticides; water resources; flood control and improvements of rivers and harbors, including environmental aspects of deepwater ports; public works, bridges, and dams; water pollution; air pollution; noise pollution; nonmilitary environmental regulation and control of atomic energy; regional economic development; construction and maintenance of

...As Revised and Reorganized by the 95th Congress

highways; public buildings and improved grounds of the United States generally.

Committee on Finance (17)

Except as provided in the Congressional Budget Act of 1974, revenue measures generally; except as provided in the Congressional Budget Act of 1974, the bonded debt of the United States; the deposit of public moneys; customs, collection districts, and ports of entry and delivery; reciprocal trade agreements; transportation and dutiable goods; revenue measures relating to the insular possessions; tariffs and import quotas; national Social Security; health programs under the Social Security Act and health programs financed by a specific tax or trust fund; general revenue sharing; the revenue policy of the United States.

Committee on Foreign Relations (15)

Relations of the United States with foreign nations generally; treaties and executive agreements, except reciprocal trade agreements; boundaries of the United States; protection of United States citizens abroad and expatriation; intervention abroad and declarations of war; foreign economic, military, technical, and humanitarian assistance; United Nations and its affiliated organizations; international conferences and congresses; diplomatic service; international law as it relates to foreign policy; oceans and international environmental and scientific affairs as they relate to foreign policy; oceans and international environmental and scientific affairs as they relate to foreign policy; international activities of the American National Red Cross and the International Committee of the Red Cross; international aspects of nuclear energy including nuclear transfer policy; foreign loans; measures to foster commercial intercourse with foreign nations and to safeguard American business abroad; the World Bank group, the regional development banks, other organizations established primarily for economic development assistance purposes and the International Monetary Fund and other international institutions established primarily for international monetary purposes except that legislation dealing with such institutions shall also be referred to the Banking Committee on request; acquisition of land and buildings for embassies and legations in foreign countries; trusteeships of the United States.

Committee on Governmental Affairs (19)

Except as provided in the Congressional Budget Act of 1974, budget and accounting measures, other than appropriations; organization and reorganization of the executive branch of the government; intergovernmental relations; government information; municipal affairs of the District of Columbia, except appropriations; federal Civil Service; status of officers and employees of the United States, including their classification, compensation, and benefits; Postal Service; census and collection of statistics, including economic and social statistics, archives of the United States; organization and management of United States nuclear export policy; congressional organization, except that involving amending Senate rules.

Committee on Human Resources (16)

Measures relating to education, labor, health, and public welfare; labor standards and labor statistics; wages and hours of labor; child labor; mediation and arbitration of labor disputes; convict labor and the entry of goods made by convicts into interstate commerce; regulation of foreign laborers; handicapped individuals; equal employment opportunity; occupational safety and health, including the welfare of miners; private pension plans; aging; railway labor and retirement; public health; arts and humanities; Gallaudet College, Howard University, and Saint Elizabeths Hospital; biomedical research and development; student loans; agricultural colleges.

Committee on the Judiciary (15)

Judicial proceedings, civil and criminal, generally; constitutional amendments; federal courts and judges; local courts in the territories and possessions; revision and codification of the statutes of the United States; national penitentiaries; protection of trade and commerce against unlawful restraints and monopolies; holidays and celebrations; bankruptcy, mutiny, espionage, and counterfeiting; state and territorial boundary lines; civil liberties; patents, copyrights, and trademarks; patent office; immigration and naturalization; apportionment of Representatives; measures relating to claims against the United States.

Committee on Rules and Administration (9)

Meeting of the Congress and attendance of Members; federal elections generally, including the election of the President, Vice President, and members of the Congress; credentials and qualifications of members of the Senate, and contested elections, acceptance of incompatible offices; presidential succession; corrupt practices; the United States Capitol and congressional office buildings, the Library of Congress, the Smithsonian Institution (and the incorporation of similar institutions), and the Botanic Gardens; the Government Printing Office, and the printing and correction of the Congressional Record; the Senate Library and statuary, art, and pictures in the Capitol and Senate Office Buildings; purchase of books and manuscripts and erection of monuments to the memory of individuals; payment of money out of the contingent fund of the Senate or creating a charge upon the same (except that any resolution relating to substantive matter within the jurisdiction of any other standing committee of the Senate shall be first referred to such committee); parliamentary rules and floor and gallery rules; administration of the Senate office buildings and the Senate wing of the Capitol, including the assignment of office space; services to the Senate, including the Senate restaurant.

Committee on Veterans' Affairs (9)

Veterans' measures generally; pensions of all wars of the United States, general and special; life insurance issued by the Government on account of service in the Armed Forces; compensation of veterans; vocational rehabilitation and education of veterans; veterans' hospitals, medical care and treatment of veterans; soldiers' and sailors' civil relief; readjustment of servicemen to civil life; national cemeteries.

hours of a Senate meeting or up to 2 p.m. whichever was earlier, and allowed the deadline to be extended by agreement of the majority and minority leader.

Directed the Rules Committee to continue to review the committee system and to report its findings every two years.

Prohibited a committee from approving amendments on matters outside its jurisdiction.

Provided a transition period to allow for reassignment or dismissal of staff members of committees that were eliminated under the reorganization plan.

Specified that the transition would begin on the effective date of the resolution and end on July 1, 1977, or 10 days after the first resolution authorizing expenditure for a reorganized committee staff, whichever came later.

Provided that during the transition period the staff of committees abolished under the plan would work for the committee that assumed jurisdiction of the abolished committee.

Required the staff of each committee to reflect the relative size of the minority and majority membership on the committee, and on request of the minority members of a committee at least one third of the staff of the committee would be placed under the control of the minority except that staff deemed by the chairman and ranking minority member to be working for the whole committee would not be subject to the rule.

Specified that the resolution would take effect on Feb. 11, 1977.

Background

The Senate committee system—of regular standing committees which exist from Congress to Congress—began in 1816 when the Senate approved creation of more than a dozen standing committees to replace the ad hoc system of select committees which had been in use up to that time. The number of standing committees grew steadily. When the Senate in 1921 undertook reform of the system, there were 74 standing committees, which were then consolidated into 34.

The next major committee overhaul came with the Legislative Reorganization Act of 1946, which reduced the number of standing committees to 15. In the following 30 years, three new standing committees were created in the Senate: Aeronautical and Space Sciences (1958), Veterans' Affairs (1970) and the Budget Committee (1974).

While the number of standing committees changed only slightly during the 1946-1976 period, subcommittees proliferated. After the 1946 reorganization there were 44 subcommittees. By 1976 there were 140.

With this explosion of subcommittees came a steady increase in the volume of subcommittee assignments. In 1947 the average senator served on two or three subcommittees; by 1976, the average senator held 14 subcommittee assignments. The workload of the Senate as a whole increased during this period. In 1947, the Senate was in session 807 hours and took 138 roll call votes. In 1976, the Senate was in session 1,033 hours and took 688 roll call votes.

One result of these changes was an impossible scheduling situation for senators. As a report to the Select Committee on Committees described the situation: "As floor sessions have lengthened and as committee and subcommittee meetings and hearings have mushroomed, senators more frequently face the daily dilemma of reconciling two, three, or more conflicting meetings or hearings, while still

New Responsibilities

The major changes in responsibility for various programs and issues which came about within the Senate committee system as a result of S Res 4 were the result of the abolition of certain committees.

● The responsibilities of the Aeronautical and Space Sciences Committee were transferred to the Commerce, Science and Transportation Committee.

● Matters under the jurisdiction of the District of Columbia and Post Office and Civil Service Committees were transferred to the Governmental Affairs Committee.

● After Dec. 31, 1977, the functions of the Select Nutrition Committee were to be taken over by the Agriculture, Nutrition and Forestry Committee.

● The responsibilities of the Joint Atomic Energy Committee were transferred to the Armed Services, Energy and Natural Resources, and Environment and Public Works Committees.

● The jurisdictions of the Joint Committee on Congressional Operations and the Select Committee to Study the Senate Committee System were transferred to the Rules Committee.

Other changes included:

● Transfer of responsibility for school lunch legislation to the Agriculture Committee from the old Labor and Public Welfare Committee, now the Human Resources Committee.

● A shift of foreign commerce and veterans' housing programs to the Banking Committee from Commerce and Veterans' respectively.

● A shift of responsibility for the naval petroleum reserves and the oil shale reserves in Alaska and for water power to Energy and Natural Resources from Armed Services and Public Works respectively.

● Transfer of responsibility for fisheries and wildlife, except for marine fisheries, to Environment and Public Works from Commerce.

coping with ongoing floor debates and frequent roll call votes. Such conflict...is nearly constant."

Select Committee Recommendations

The recommendations of the Select Committee to Study the Senate Committee System were published in the Sept. 30, 1976, *Congressional Record*. The committee report was filed Nov. 15 (S Rept 94-1395).

The committee recommended that all special, select and joint committees be abolished—except the special intelligence committee. In addition, it recommended abolition of four standing committees—the District of Columbia Committee, the Post Office and Civil Service Committee, the Aeronautical and Space Sciences Committee and the Veterans' Affairs Committee. Remaining relatively unchanged would be seven committees: Appropriations; Armed Services; Banking, Housing and Urban Affairs; Budget; Finance; Foreign Relations and Judiciary. Undergoing change would be the Agriculture and Forestry Committee, the Commerce Committee, the Interior and Insular Affairs Committee (slated to become the Energy and Natural Resources Committee), the Public Works Committee (to become the Environment and Public Works Committee), the Government Operations Committee, the Labor and Public Welfare Committee (to become the Human Resources Committee), and the Rules Committee.

The most substantial change of jurisdiction that the committee hoped to accomplish would come in the areas of energy, environment and transportation, where overlapping and fragmented jurisdictions made the process of legislation even more complex than the subject demanded. The most salient area in which such consolidation was not proposed was Social Security and health insurance. While most social programs were to go to the new Human Resources Committee, Social Security—including Medicare and Medicaid—and national health insurance remained the business of the Finance Committee. Five members of the Finance Committee served on the Select Committee on Committees and methodically opposed efforts to narrow their committee's jurisdiction.

The Select Committee also recommended:

● Limiting senators to a maximum of eight committee and subcommittee assignments apiece. Each person could be a member of two standing committees, and of two subcommittees of each of those, plus one other committee assignment and one subcommittee assignment there. (Membership on the Budget and Select Intelligence Committees was exempted from the assignment limit.)

● Limiting to one the number of committee chairmanships a person could hold, and also to one the number of subcommittees a member could chair for each committee on which he served.

● Reporting by July 1977 of legislation to create a Congressional Revenue Office, responsible primarily to the Ways and Means and Finance Committees.

● Creation of ad hoc committees where proposed legislation falls within the jurisdiction of two or more committees of the Senate. Otherwise, joint or sequential referral of such legislation would be allowed.

● Computerized scheduling of all committee and subcommittee meetings, updated hourly with the data available through terminals in the offices of senators and the committees.

● Requiring special permission for any committee or subcommittee meeting to take place after the first two hours the Senate is in session, or any time after 2 p.m. Excepted from that rule would be Appropriations and Budget.

● Dividing the early part of the day into two "periods" for scheduling committee and subcommittee meetings. The first period would last from 8 or 9 a.m. to 11 a.m. The second period would last from 11 a.m. to 2 p.m.

● Prohibiting roll-call votes from being held before 2 p.m. unless ordered by majority vote or unanimous consent on a previous day.

● Limiting committee amendments to areas that come within the jurisdiction of the reporting committee.

● Periodic review of the committee system by majority and minority leaders.

Rules Committee Action

The ambitious Select Committee reorganization plan underwent major change in the Senate Rules Committee, which was the target for pressures from a number of special interest groups, including labor, small business, and veterans' groups, plus the jurisdictional jealousies of individual committee chairmen.

The Rules Committee voted to give new life to five committees that the Stevenson plan had slated for merger: Joint Economic; Veterans; Select Small Business; Joint Internal Revenue Taxation; and Standards and Conduct—the last renamed the Ethics Committee. In addition, the committee rejected several proposed jurisdictional shifts.

In a major victory for Republicans, the committee voted to give the GOP more staff.

Liberal senators, led by Dick Clark, D-Iowa, won modification of the Select Committee's strict limits on subcommittee and committee membership. The Stevenson proposal allowed membership on only two subcommittees of each major committee on which a senator served and one subcommittee of his minor committee. The Rules Committee modified this to allow him to serve on three subcommittees of each major committee and two of the minor committees.

The touchy problem of realigning committee jurisdictions was illustrated forcefully to the Rules Committee after it decided, Jan. 18, to support the Select Committee recommendation that jurisdiction over the coastal zone management program be transferred from the Commerce Committee to the new Committee on Environment and Public Works. The next morning when the committee met at 10 a.m. it was confronted by five angry members of the Commerce Committee demanding that the program be returned to them. Russell B. Long, D-La., the powerful Finance Committee chairman and a member of the Commerce Committee, accused Stevenson-plan backers of advocating "reshuffling just for the sake of reshuffling."

After a stormy hour, the Rules Committee by voice vote agreed to reconsider its action and then also by voice vote transferred the program back to Commerce.

They also agreed to the Commerce Committee members' demand that the jurisdiction over oceans, weather and atmosphere and the National Oceanic and Atmospheric Administration be retained by the Commerce Committee.

Committee Report

The Senate Rules Committee voted 9-0 on Jan. 25 to order S Res 4 reported. The report was filed that day (S Rept 95-2).

Despite the changes made by the committee in the original measure, Stevenson was enthusiastic about the Rules Committee version. "We went for about 150 per cent of what we wanted," he said, "It looks like we'll end up with about 75 per cent."

The unanimous endorsement of S Res 4 by the Rules Committee provided an important boost for the measure on the floor. Rules Committee members represented a broad cross section of the Senate from liberal Clark to conservative James B. Allen, D-Ala., and included two important party leaders—Majority Leader Robert C. Byrd, D-W.Va., and Republican Policy Committee Chairman John G. Tower, R-Texas.

After the vote, Byrd called the resolution "a good package." The measure also was endorsed by Minority Leader Howard H. Baker Jr., R-Tenn.

Whereas the original proposal would have reduced the number of Senate committees to 15 from 31, the measure reported by the Rules Committee retained five of the committees which would have been abolished and created a new one, a temporary Select Committee on Indian Affairs to sit during the 95th Congress only.

Senate Study Recommends Reforms. . .

A special 11-member panel appointed in 1975 concluded that the byzantine and antiquated operations of the U.S. Senate were in need of a major overhaul and an infusion of modern technology in order to bring them up to date.

The panel, headed by former Sen. Harold E. Hughes, D-Iowa (1968-74), issued its report Dec. 16, 1976, after a one-year study. The commission recommended more than 50 changes ranging from the abolition of patronage jobs to establishment of a centralized administrative body to an overhaul of the Capitol page system.

Sen. John C. Culver, D-Iowa, who originally proposed the commission, said that its report was the first study of the Senate ever made by an outside body. And Hughes added that the report was the first thorough study of the Senate ever undertaken by anybody. The Senate's administrative practices have grown "in a topsy-turvy manner," Hughes said.

The major recommendations of the commission were as follows:

Central Administration

"The administrative structure of the Senate is antiquated, fragmented and lacking in clear lines of authority and responsibility," the commission concluded.

As a remedy, it recommended that all Senate services should be administered by one central professional manager working under the guidance of an administrative council consisting of the minority and majority leaders and the chairman of the Senate Rules and Administration Committee.

The new administrative officer would have the responsibility for most administrative functions currently carried out by the sergeant at arms, the Committee on Rules and Administration, the architect of the Capitol and the president pro tempore of the Senate.

The commission also recommended that the administrator be empowered to set up a simplified and uniform system of budgeting and accounting and a "modern personnel system."

The panel's recommendation on a Senate administrator was rejected in 1978, when the Rules Committee April 26 voted instead to instruct the three officers who oversee most of these services to streamline their fragmented administrative structure.

Space

There has never been any full inventory of how the Senate utilizes its space and no overall effort to make efficient use of that space which is available, Hughes said. As a result, many operations that "could just as easily be carried out in Baltimore" are housed in the Capitol building itself.

On the other hand, many senators seeking private offices in the Capitol are unable to obtain them. Only 56 senators had Capitol offices during the 94th Congress, Hughes said.

The commission recommended that the Senate undertake an immediate inventory of its space and transfer out of the Capitol all functions that could be performed elsewhere. This included, according to Hughes, the Senate disbursing office and various repair shops and maintenance operations.

Time

In order to reduce the demands on the time of individual senators, the commission recommended that the Senate change a number of its methods of operation.

Although the report noted that the major savings in senators' time could come only from changes in the operations of each senator's office and personal schedule, it did recommend several revisions in general operations to save time. The panel recommended that:

● The Senate devote certain days of the week exclusively to floor action and certain days exclusively to committee business.

● Early in the session the Senate schedule a series of debates on national issues to provide guidance to committees as they consider legislation.

The purpose of creating the panel, the report said, was to deal with recommendations for new legislation expected to come from the American Indian Policy Review Commission.

The Rules Committee did vote to strike from the original resolution a section authorizing the establishment of more *ad hoc* committees. The report said that such a provision would "encourage the proliferation of additional temporary committees in the Senate."

Because it had voted to retain so many committees that the original resolution had proposed to abolish, the Rules Committee also found it necessary to modify the resolution's formula for committee assignments.

While the original resolution had contemplated that each senator would be limited to service on a total of eight committees and subcommittees, the measure reported by the Rules Committee permitted service on 11 panels.

Despite this increase, the report noted that the change would still represent "a far more realistic and workable format" than the existing structure under which the average

senator served on 18 committees and subcommittees and some served on as many as 30.

The Rules Committee also made a large number of changes in the jurisdictional plan recommended by the original resolution. For example, the Stevenson proposal had been to consolidate most transportation matters in the new Committee on Commerce, Science and Transportation. However, the Rules Committee voted instead essentially to retain the *status quo*, with highway construction in the Environment and Public Works Committee, urban mass transit in the Banking Committee and most other transportation issues in the Commerce Committee.

The original resolution also sought to consolidate all environmental issues within the new Environment and Public Works Committee. But the Commerce Committee insisted on retaining its jurisdiction over coastal zone management programs and ocean policy and marine fisheries and the Agriculture Committee wanted to retain control of pesticides. In both cases the Rules Committee opted in favor of retaining the existing system.

. . .Designed to Modernize the Senate

● Consider appointing someone who is not a senator to preside over routine Senate sessions.

● Make use of computers to schedule committee and other meetings.

● Encourage the use of panel formats and other time-saving devices for committee meetings.

● Organize the Senate before Congress convenes.

● Assign office space to senators at the start of a new session or assign permanent offices to each state to reduce confusion about offices early in the year.

● Provide administrative support for each senator-elect during the period between the election and the swearing-in.

Improving Legislation

A central goal of the commission recommendations, Hughes said, was to provide better legislation. Too often, he said, the Senate acts only in response to a crisis, rather than to anticipation of a need.

To provide for better foresight about coming problems, the commission recommended that the Senate:

● Assign to major committees responsibility to conduct long-range analyses of major national issues before they become crises.

● Place responsibility for monitoring Senate oversight responsibility in the Government Operations Committee.

● Establish a Senate-wide information system to collect information from individual offices and make it available to all offices and committees.

Technology

The commission recommended that the Senate use a variety of modern equipment to increase its efficiency. It recommended that the Senate:

● Use computers to provide offices with up-to-date information about legislative flow and the status of individual bills.

● Develop an integrated printing management system, which Culver said could save up to $15 million a year.

● Adopt more uniform formats for committee documents and explore the advantages of automated techniques for the preparation and dissemination of such documents.

● Experiment with closed-circuit televising of floor proceedings, running summaries of floor proceedings in each office, and the use of computers to display in each office the texts of all amendments under consideration on the floor.

Support Agencies

The commission urged the Senate to join with the House in a thorough review of all congressional support agencies—the General Accounting Office, the Office of Technology Assessment, the Congressional Budget Office and the Congressional Research Service.

Specifically the commission said that Congress should provide for better coordination between these agencies in order to avoid duplication of effort and to "increase the availability of high-quality information and analysis to Congress."

Public Relations

The public, according to the commission, often "finds it difficult if not impossible to make an objective and balanced judgment about the overall performance" of the Senate because the Senate's system of communicating with the public is "incomplete and therefore distorted."

To improve this situation, the commission recommended that the Senate:

● Experiment with audio and visual radio and television broadcasting of Senate floor proceedings.

● Hold formal briefings for the news media;

● Improve media facilities and establish a Senate briefing room;

● Assign staff to assist with Senate briefings and to develop and disseminate information materials.

The only opposition to the Rules Committee actions noted in the report came in additional views filed by Clark, Harrison A. Williams Jr., D-N.J., and Claiborne Pell, D-R.I. The three took issue with the committee's decision to recommend that the Special Committee on Aging be abolished and that its functions be taken over by the new Human Resources Committee.

"We conclude that the Senate's oversight over aging-related areas would be diminished by this transfer," the three senators noted. The views carried a special weight because Williams was slated to be chairman of the new Human Resources Committee that would have picked up the aging jurisdiction under the resolution as reported.

Floor Action

The full Senate approved the committee reforms Feb. 4 by a vote of 89-1 after deciding to retain both the Special Committee on Aging—and, for the duration of 1977, the

Select Committee on Nutrition. The Senate rejected an effort to give new life to the Post Office and Civil Service Committee. The lone vote against the resolution was cast by Quentin N. Burdick, D-N.D., who would have been that panel's chairman.

Aging

With 51 cosponsors, Frank Church, D-Idaho, was assured of victory from the beginning of the debate on his amendment to retain the Special Aging Committee as a separate Senate committee. Church was the committee's chairman.

The Rules Committee had defeated a similar amendment by a 4-5 vote and the interval between the committee action and the floor debate had provided time for an intensive lobbying effort by senior citizens' groups on behalf of the panel.

Backers of the Church amendment couched their argument strictly in terms of what would be best for elderly

Subcommittee Reform

By limiting the number of subcommittees a senator could serve on and chair, S Res 4 dictated substantial realignment of subcommittee structures. One example of this effect of the reform was provided by the changes in the Senate Judiciary Committee in 1977.

During the 94th Congress, the Judiciary Committee had as many subcommittees as it had members, many of whom had multiple subcommittee assignments within the committee. Edward M. Kennedy, D-Mass., for example, served on seven judiciary subcommittees and chaired two, John L. McClellan, D-Ark., served on 11 subcommittees and chaired two.

The reform resolution limited each senator to service on three subcommittees and to one subcommittee chairmanship. Thus, with only 11 Democratic members, the Judiciary Committee was forced to dissolve at least four of its subcommittees in order to have enough chairmen to go around.

In fact, the committee abolished five of its subcommittees, merged two, and created one new one, bringing its total number of subcommittees in 1977 to 10 with memberships of four to eight senators each. Only Majority Leader Robert C. Byrd, D-W.Va., of the Democrats on the committee did not hold a subcommittee chairmanship.

Americans. Pointing out that the Rules Committee had voted to preserve the Veterans and Small Business Committees and to establish a new committee on Indians, Church told the Senate, "I do question the denial to 23 million senior citizens the same consideration which we are extending to veterans, native Americans and small business."

Another key point was the support for Church's amendment by Williams, the chairman of the Human Resources Committee to which S Res 4 proposed transferring jurisdiction over aging.

Williams' panel already had legislative jurisdiction over most aging programs. The Special Aging Committee had no legislative powers. But the New Jersey Democrat had argued in the Rules Committee that the oversight and investigation functions of the Special Committee could not be performed by a subcommittee of Human Resources.

Church pointed out that while Human Resources had legislative jurisdiction over many aging programs, the Finance Committee had jurisdiction over Medicare and Medicaid and other committees were involved in other aspects of concern to older Americans. The special committee, Church said, offered the only forum in which the broad range of issues important to elderly Americans could be considered.

Stevenson repeated arguments he had made during the Rules Committee debate—that a vote to preserve the Aging Committee would only add to the proliferation of committee assignments that made it difficult for senators to function effectively.

But the Illinois Democrat clearly recognized that Church held all the cards. When the time for a vote approached, Feb. 1, Stevenson gave in, winning a few concessions from Church and then joining with 89 other senators in voting 90-4 to keep the committee alive.

Post Office

After losing the vote on the Aging Committee, the backers of the Stevenson plan then won a major victory when the Senate Feb. 2 tabled, 55-42, an amendment that would have retained the Post Office and Civil Service Committee as a separate panel.

Burdick, the amendment's sponsor and the acting chairman of the committee, argued that the magnitude of the problems faced by the Postal Service and by the workers in the government bureaucracy warranted attention from a full Senate Committee.

Burdick's arguments were backed up by a lobbying effort by organized labor. AFL-CIO president George Meany, in a letter to Ted Stevens, R-Alaska, the committee's ranking Republican, warned against the Stevenson proposal to merge the Post Office Committee into the new Governmental Affairs panel.

Such an action, Meany said, would "eradicate the only forum available to federal and postal employees, the people's workforce who manage the day to day operations of the federal government."

But Stevenson argued that while the committee had nine members and a fiscal 1977 budget of $564,000, "only 2.7 per cent of the bills referred to committees in the last Congress were referred to this committee. It reported 1.6 per cent of the bills reported in that Congress."

"If this committee is to be continued," Stevenson warned, "the proliferation of committees and of assignments will continue. At some point the line must be drawn."

The Senate was willing to draw the line as Stevenson urged. A provision of S Res 4, however, allowed both Burdick and Stevens to transfer to the Governmental Affairs Committee to lead a subcommittee on Post Office and Civil Service without losing their rights to serve on two other major committees as well.

Government Regulations

The Senate also adopted Feb. 1 by a vote of 74-20, an amendment sponsored by Herman E. Talmadge, D-Ga., that would require every committee to include in reports on legislation an assessment of the measure's impact on federal regulations.

Nutrition

Stevenson won narrow—and temporary—victory on Feb. 3 when the Senate tabled an amendment sponsored by George McGovern, D-S.D., that would have retained the Select Committee on Nutrition. The vote to table was 49-44.

McGovern argued that because the Nutrition Committee, which he chairs, had no subcommittees, it did not create the kinds of demands on senators' time that other committees did.

He also argued that a "certain amount of competition" between committees was healthy, and that to have all of the nutrition matters handled by a single subcommittee of the Agriculture Committee, as proposed by S Res 4, would stifle such competition.

In a last minute attempt to salvage the panel, McGovern modified his original amendment to provide that it would continue for only two years and would merge with Agriculture after the end of the 95th Congress.

McGovern argued that a two-year extension would at least enable the committee to complete an ongoing study of the effect of diet on health.

But the next day, before passing S Res 4 the Senate backtracked on its previous decision to abolish the Select Committee on Nutrition.

By voice vote it adopted an amendment sponsored by Charles H. Percy, R-Ill., to allow the committee to continue in existence until the end of 1977, but with a membership reduced to nine from 11.

Percy argued that the extension of the committee's life would allow it to complete several studies that were underway and would be aborted if the panel was abolished immediately on passage of S Res 4.

Committee Chairmanships

Junior senators won a major victory on Feb. 3, when the Senate adopted an amendment sponsored by Clark to prohibit full committee chairmen from heading more than two subcommittees. The Rules Committee had limited all senators to three subcommittee chairmanships, allowing full committee chairmen three subcommittees in addition to their full committee. The Clark amendment would take effect with the 96th Congress.

Clark's amendment was adopted by voice vote after a motion to table (kill) it offered by Stevenson was defeated by a 42-47 roll call. The chairman of every full Senate committee voted to kill the amendment, except for Talmadge, who was absent.

The debate over the amendment brought to the surface the submerged feeling among junior members that too much power in the Senate was concentrated in the hands of a few senior members. "The question before us is really simple," Clark said. "If a senator thinks that the responsibility in the Senate should be shared on a fair and equitable basis and if he thinks that freshmen members should be allowed to serve as equals in this body then it seems to me he would vote for this amendment."

Other attempts to tamper with the power of committee chairmen were turned back. On Feb. 3 the Senate tabled, 63-20, another Clark amendment that would have required each Senate committee to establish legislative subcommittees unless the full committee voted otherwise. The amendment was aimed primarily at the Finance Committee, where most major decisions were reserved for the full committee, and subcommittees had relatively little power. Long, however, promised the Senate that he would delegate more authority to subcommittees during the 95th Congress.

The Senate also rejected attempts to limit the service of committee chairmen. On Feb. 4 it tabled, 72-15, an amendment sponsored by William D. Hathaway, D-Maine, that would have limited a senator to eight years continuous service on one committee, a provision that would have guaranteed a frequent turnover in chairmen as well as members. Then the Senate tabled, 62-26, an amendment sponsored by Gaylord Nelson, D-Wis., that would have required a rotation of committee chairmanships every six years.

Final Recommendations

In its final report to the Senate on March 1, the Temporary Select Committee to Study the Senate Committee System made these major recommendations:

Staff Allowances. The Rules Committee consider the possibility of consolidating existing allowances to senators for committee staff aides into the regular clerk-hire allowance for each senator.

Committee Funding. Each Senate committee submit to the Rules Committee a single resolution to authorize total funding for inquiries and investigations for the committee in excess of statutory allowances.

Committee Staff. The Senate increase permanent committee staff by reducing investigative budgets.

Committee staff aides displaced because of the committee reorganization be given severance pay equal to four weeks salary plus one week salary for every year of Senate service over one up to a limit of 12 weeks pay, but no person shall receive severance pay simultaneously while working at another government job or while collecting unemployment insurance.

Committee Activities Summary. Each committee maintain a summary of its activities in public session and submit the summaries daily to a central office for dissemination via cathode ray tube screens or other devices to all Senate offices.

Computerized Bill Status. The Senate establish a complete computerized bill status system with information on bill status available through computers and other devices in each Senate office.

Committee Calendar. Each committee publish a tentative calendar of anticipated activities semi-annually.

Broadcasting Floor Action. The Senate establish a system of audio transmissions of floor and committee proceedings to each Senate office and the Rules Committee study the feasibility of installing closed circuit television broadcasts of floor proceedings.

Scheduling Conflicts. The Rules Committee submit to the Senate before the close of the 95th Congress recommendations to alleviate scheduling conflicts.

Meeting Rooms. The Senate establish a central computerized listing of available committee meeting rooms.

Information Office. The Senate establish a central information office to provide information about Senate activities to the press and the public.

Oversight Activities. Each committee prepare an annual report listing projected oversight activities and a separate report listing oversight activities of the preceding year.

Legislative Review. The Rules Committee direct an office of the Senate to establish a list of legislative review provisions of existing laws.

Executive Actions. The Rules Committee publish an appendix to the Standing Rules of the Senate listing exceptions to normal procedures made by laws providing for approval or disapproval of executive actions.

Conference Committee Rules. The Rules Committee work with the House to develop common rules to govern meetings of conference committees.

Information Gathering. The Congressional Research Service study alternative methods of gathering information including alternatives to hearings.

Records System. The Senate establish a uniform automated document control and microfilm records system.

Committee Information. Senate committees record and make available to the public information about all their activities, including roll call votes.

Committee Procedures. The Senate recodify its rules governing committee procedures.

Subcommittee Rules. The Senate amend its rules to require that all subcommittees be governed by their committee's rules.

Committee Continuity. The Senate revise the provision in the rules that allows committees to continue and operate until their successors have been appointed to make clear that committees may receive and report measures at the beginning of each Congress before new assignments have been made.

Investigation Procedures. The Senate specify procedures for committee investigations, including rules designed to protect the rights of witnesses.

Committee Records. The Senate establish a system for transfer of committee records to the Archives and establish rules governing noncurrent classified records.

Classified Information. The Senate establish a single committee to investigate and make recommendations concerning allegations of unauthorized disclosures of classified information. ∎

House Attempts to Reorganize Committees

The House in 1979 approved a new attempt to reorganize its committee structure and jurisdictions, but the vote indicated that revisions, if they are ever made, would not come about easily.

The House March 20 approved a resolution (H Res 118) creating a Select Committee on Committees, but by only eight votes, 208-200.

Third-term Rep. Jerry M. Patterson, D-Calif., was selected to head the new 15-member panel.

The new select committee must report by Feb. 1, 1980. Recommendations would go first to the Rules Committee.

The committee could make recommendations on committee structure, jurisdiction, rules, procedures, staffing and facilities and on media coverage of meetings.

The committee also could make recommendations concerning the optimum size of committees, the appropriate number of committee and subcommittee assignments per member and the number and jurisdiction of the House committees' subcommittees. However, these recommendations would go to the Democratic Caucus and Republican Conference rather than to the House floor.

Background

Creation of the new select committee would mark the second time in five years that the House had attempted a major reorganization of its committees, and the fourth time this decade that it has attempted substantial reforms in procedures and administration.

Critics of the new effort said that the earlier failures at committee reform made a new select committee a waste of time and money.

Nevertheless, there was considerable agreement that the committee system needed reorganization.

The basic jurisdictional framework has been little changed in almost 35 years, except for a substantial increase in the number of subcommittees in recent years. As a result, the House's committee system is not well designed to handle some issues facing Congress in the late 1970s. For example, both the House Commerce and Science committees have jurisdiction over energy issues — a division that has produced bickering between the two panels.

In addition, critics charged that the proliferation in subcommittees has resulted in overlapping jurisdictions and has brought forth a deluge of legislative proposals.

At the end of the 95th Congress, there were 22 House standing committees, 142 subcommittees and nine ad hoc and select committees. *(See chapter on subcommittees)*

Committee reorganization efforts have failed largely because members have fought fiercely to retain the jurisdictional authority of the panels on which they serve. A second important reason for past failures has been the opposition to reform from special interest groups outside Congress that have built up close ties to committee members and staffs. These interest groups were faced with the prospect of seeing old alliances in Congress dissolved overnight and new and unknown persons put in control of legislation that affected them.

Previous Reform Efforts

The existing committee structure was largely the result of the Legislative Reorganization Act of 1946, the first full-scale attempt to "modernize" the entire House committee system. That reorganization combined 48 existing committees into 19, clarified their jurisdictions and made significant changes in their powers, responsibilities and procedures.

The number of standing committees was increased to 22 when the House created the Science and Astronautics Committee in 1958, the Committee on Standards of Official Conduct in 1967 and the Budget Committee in 1974.

The Senate reorganized its committee structure extensively in 1977. *(See p. 47)*

In the House, important changes in committee operations — but not jurisdictions — have occurred since 1946. Some of the changes came from House-sanctioned reorganization efforts — most notably in 1970. Other significant changes resulted from procedural reforms imposed by House Democrats on themselves.

One of the most successful reform attempts, in 1970, produced few changes in House committee jurisdiction but did result in significant changes in committee procedures.

Bolling Committee Failure

The second House-sanctioned effort, in 1973-74, produced a far-reaching committee reorganization plan that was rejected in favor of a much weaker proposal.

This plan, of all the reorganization efforts in the 1970s, best illustrates the problem faced by reformers in taking away jurisdictional turf from powerful committees and powerful members of the House.

The 1973 effort was the work of a select committee headed by Richard Bolling, D-Mo., a close ally of then-House Majority Leader Thomas P. O'Neill Jr., D-Mass. Bolling now is Rules Committee chairman and O'Neill, the House Speaker. The Rules Committee will have to approve any changes the new select committee makes before they can be voted on by the House.

Key opponents of the Bolling committee's recommendations were:

- Rep. Phillip Burton, D-Calif., who often has pitted himself against the leadership in internal House battles and who served on a committee, Education and Labor, that Bolling's plan split in two, much to the dislike of organized labor and other liberal interest groups;
- Former Rep. Wilbur D. Mills, D-Ark. (1939-77), who was then chairman of the Ways and Means Committee which lost substantial jurisdiction under Bolling's plan;
- Former Rep. Wayne L. Hays, D-Ohio (1949-76), who was then chairman of the Administration Committee that also lost power under the plan.

The three were among the most powerful House members at the time and all were preeminent political operators in that chamber. Together, and with the aid of other members disgruntled with the Bolling plan, they managed to sidetrack the most far-reaching parts of the Bolling plan.

To accomplish this, Burton asked the Democratic Caucus to vote by secret ballot on a motion to refer the Bolling plan for redrafting to the caucus' Committee on Organization, chaired by Rep. Julia Butler Hansen, D-Wash. (1960-74). The Hansen committee was controlled by members sympathetic to views of more senior House members who didn't like the changes the Bolling plan would have made. The Hansen committee subsequently recommended a much weaker plan which was adopted by the House in October 1974.

The Hansen plan made some jurisdictional changes, but few affecting Ways and Means, Administration or Education and Labor.

In 1979, only Bolling and Burton remained of the key players in the 1974 committee reorganization fight. Burton was chairman of the Caucus Committee on Organization that Hansen chaired in 1974.

1977 Obey Commission Proposals

Following the House's failure to accomplish a major reorganization in 1974, the Commission on Administrative Review, chaired by Rep. David R. Obey, D-Wis., proposed a package of House administrative and structural changes in 1977, including creation of a new select committee on committees.

But, having swallowed its medicine on ethics reform and allowance changes that year, the House said a resounding "no" when offered a new prescription of administrative changes, committee reform and anti-discrimination efforts.

The decision came Oct. 12 on a vote rejecting a modified closed rule for consideration of a package of changes (H Res 766) drawn up by the Commission on Administrative Review. Democrats disgruntled either with portions of the package or the limited number of amendments allowed joined a unanimous Republican bloc to defeat the rule, 160-252.

Too Much Controversy

A variety of theories was offered to explain the defeat. But Democratic leaders generally agreed that they had lost by pushing a package that had enough controversial proposals to alienate a huge majority in the House.

For instance, H Res 766 called for appointment of a select committee to suggest committee reforms, an idea that potentially threatened the jurisdictions of powerful committee chairmen. Nine of the 22 House committee chairmen voted against the rule.

A recommendation for a grievance panel to hear discrimination complaints from House employees drew fire from women and minority representatives for not being strong enough, while others thought it was too strong. Advocates of a more powerful grievance panel were unhappy with the rule allowing only one amendment to that portion of the bill.

After the vote, commission chairman Obey washed his hands of the package. Although he maintained that the House still needed the changes in H Res 766, he said he would not try to revive it.

The resolution was the last official business of Obey's commission, which also produced the ethics code passed by the House in March. *(Ethics reform, p. 153)*

The final package of changes drafted by Obey's commission was aimed at streamlining House internal operations with a new administrator in charge of most housekeeping duties. It also called for an auditor to check

House Found Expensive, Wasteful

The lack of unified control over the administrative operations which support the House of Representatives costs the taxpayer in time and in money, according to a 1977 study by a management consulting firm for the House Commission on Administrative Review, chaired by David R. Obey, D-Wis.

The study, conducted by the Westinghouse National Issues Center, gave support to the commission's attack on waste and inefficiency in House operations. The commission had asked the firm to study three areas of House operations: financial management, procurement and property control.

The scattering of financial and procurement decisions throughout numerous House offices was blamed for many inefficiencies. "Decentralization, coupled with other characteristics of the system, obscures priorities of the institution and makes planning and coordination quite difficult," the report said.

In addition, management inefficiency created unnecessary demands on members' time that interfered with their legislative duties. "A consistent thread that the study team has observed is the burden which poor system performance can place on members' offices," the efficiency experts concluded.

Among the particular failings found by the Westinghouse study were:

● Failure to take advantage of discounts available on procurement and leasing arrangements. Utilization of extended leasing and prompt payment discounts could save hundreds of thousands of dollars a year on rented office equipment. For example, the report found that the House could save $18,000 a month by taking advantage of discounts offered by companies offering automatic typewriters for rent.

● A confusing and antiquated voucher system. Ten different voucher forms are currently in use, a number that the report argued could easily be reduced to one or two. The bewildering variety of voucher forms and the lack of information in members' offices about official expense policies produced a large number of "unacceptable" vouchers. The report found that almost one-quarter of vouchers submitted by members' offices during the period studied were rejected because of inadequate or incorrect information.

● Extended delays in fulfilling vouchers for official expenses. In March and April 1977 a flood of requests caused by a new official expense payment system swamped the Finance Office, causing a fifty-day delay in processing.

● Unnecessarily strict inventory requirements that kept track of almost all House office property, regardless of cost. The tight security in House buildings, which makes theft almost impossible, should obviate the need for a comprehensive inventory system on all but the most expensive items, the report said.

the books, a new $12,000 allowance for each member to purchase computer services and committee reform to free members from too many committee assignments.

Obey said opposition to the resolution represented a coalition of Republicans, who did not want Democrats to get credit for passing new reforms; members who either thought the grievance procedure was too tough or too weak; committee chairmen who "don't want their own turf invaded"; and those who resented more reforms because they were "so fed up with this institution getting shot at, sometimes for good reasons and sometimes for some pretty damn lousy reasons." He added: "What you have here is a constant drip, drip, drip of criticism."

Recommendations

The Commission on Administrative Review's major recommendations for administrative changes included:

Administrator. The Speaker should appoint a new officer, the House administrator, subject to House approval. The new officer would take over a variety of duties now handled by the clerk, the architect of the Capitol, the doorkeeper, the House Administration Committee and the House Select Committee on Congressional Operations.

The administrator would appoint a comptroller to handle financial affairs taken over from the clerk's office and the House Administration Committee. The administrator would be responsible for day to day operations such as repair and maintenance of furnishings, procurement of supplies, bill paying and operation of facilities such as the barber and beauty shops, subway, restaurants, garages and recording and photographic studios. The sergeant at arms should remain in charge of security, and the doorkeeper should continue to handle floor services.

Auditor. The chairman of the House Administration Committee should appoint an auditor, subject to approval by a majority vote of the Speaker and majority and minority leaders. He would audit all House accounts and publish an annual report. The audits would be checked annually by an outside appraiser.

Clerk. The clerk's office, which would lose the most authority to the new administrator, would be put in charge of official reporters used to record committee and floor proceedings. Reporters were currently under the Speaker's office.

The clerk would also coordinate communication between information services, such as the Congressional Research Service and the Office of Technology Assessment.

Major recommendations on work management, some of which were subsequently incorporated in House rules, included:

Select Committee on Committees. The House should create a Select Committee on Committees which would recommend changes in the committee system by July 1, 1978.

Information. Each office should be provided with computer terminals as standard equipment. Committees should require written testimony to be submitted 48 hours before a hearing and to be summarized in 10 minutes. Committees should abstract and index their hearings, as well as prepare weekly summaries of significant actions. Remarks inserted in the *Congressional Record* should be clearly distinguished from speeches actually delivered for a six-month test period, and the Rules Committee should set guidelines for identifying insertions after that. Scholars studying Congress should be given access to the House press gallery and the House library. *(Congressional Record changes, p. 120)*

Office Workload. Increases in non-statutory committee staff personnel would be limited to 3 percent over the number of staff in the previous Congress. Members should be allowed to count two part-time employees as one staffer in counting each member's allotment of 18, up to a maximum of four part-time employees. (In July 1979, the House voted to raise the existing ceiling of 18 to allow members to hire up to four additional employees.)

Personnel. The House should establish a fair employment practices panel with two majority members and one minority party member named by the Speaker. The panel would confidentially consider employee discrimination complaints and could offer suggestions but could not bring any sanctions against a member. By unanimous vote, the panel could refer a complaint against a member to the ethics committee.

The House should establish a program of maternity and sick leave for employees.

Travel. Members should file reports before and after trips explaining their purpose for travel. Financial information about each trip should be printed quarterly in the *Congressional Record*. Members should submit requests for foreign travel to the administrator for approval.

1977 Task Force Report

"Members have too many assignments, and jurisdictions are too confused for the strains and conflicts members currently endure to be substantially alleviated by piecemeal and procedural reform. Only marginal improvements can occur until a basic restructuring of the committee system takes place."

So concluded a task force of the House Commission on Administrative Review in a draft report released in late August 1977.

The report's conclusion supporting committee changes was backed by many statistics about how House members used their time. The average member, according to the report, worked 11 hours a day and had little or no time to spend studying issues.

The study said that the average House member's work day ran from 8:30 a.m. to 7:30 p.m. Of that time the member spent four hours and 25 minutes on the floor or in committee, three hours and 19 minutes in the office, two hours and two minutes in other locations in Washington, and one hour and 40 minutes in other places, including travel to and from appointments.

Meeting Demands Increase

The study found that the demands of committee and House meetings had risen dramatically in the past 20 years. In the 86th Congress, the report noted, there were 3,059 committee and subcommittee meetings. In the 94th Congress there were 6,975 meetings. During the 86th Congress the House was in session 1,037 hours. During the 94th Congress the House met for 1,789 hours.

The trend apparently was continuing. During March of 1975, for example, there were 494 committee and subcommittee meetings and the House met for 74 hours. During May of 1977, there were 730 meetings and the House met for 98 hours.

The number of committees and subcommittees had increased. In the 88th Congress there were 156 committees and subcommittees and each member served on an average of 4.3 panels. In 1977 there were 184 legislative units and each member served on 6.1. (The number of panels was slightly reduced by the end of the 95th Congress.)

The problem of the time conflicts was compounded, the study found, by the "inefficient and ineffective distribution of labor" among the committees.

"Some committees are enormously busy," the report said, while "other panels by comparison have relatively little to do." The study noted, for example, that during the first five months of 1977 the House Agriculture Committee met 61 times while the District of Columbia Committee held only five meetings and that the International Relations Committee met 49 times while the Small Business Committee had only four sessions.

Creation of Select Committee in 1979

The Republican Conference voted Jan. 15, 1979, and the Democratic Caucus Jan. 31 to ask the House Rules Committee to send to the floor a resolution establishing a new Select Committee on Committees.

Major Provisions. As reported (H Rept 96-18) by the Rules Committee Feb. 28, H Res 118 would establish a 15-member Select Committee on Committees; all members would be appointed by the Speaker. Ten would be Democrats and five, Republicans.

Under the resolution, the committee would be barred from making recommendations to the House concerning the optimum size of committees, the appropriate number of committee and subcommittee assignments per member or the number and jurisdiction of any committee's subcommittees. The select committee could make such recommendations to the Democratic Caucus or Republican Conference, however.

Opponents

The vote to approve the new study was along party lines, but a number of liberal Democrats and eight House committee chairmen joined most Republicans in opposition. Republicans voted heavily against H Res 118, 21-126. Democrats supported it 187-74.

The opposition of chairmen was expected because reorganization would encroach on committee powers. A number of chairmen who voted against the resolution

headed panels that many critics of congressional organization — including some House members — believed serve only narrow special interests and should be abolished; Veterans' Affairs and Post Office often were cited as examples.

But other chairmen opposing the resolution headed major committees with vast power that critics thought should go partly to other panels.

Committee chairmen voting against H Res 118 were Charles E. Bennett, D-Fla. (Standards); Don Fuqua, D-Fla. (Science and Technology); James M. Hanley, D-N.Y. (Post Office); Ray Roberts, D-Texas, (Veterans' Affairs); Harley O. Staggers, D-W.Va. (Commerce); Frank Thompson Jr., D-N.J. (Administration); Al Ullman, D-Ore., (Ways and Means); and Jamie L. Whitten, D-Miss., (Appropriations). The other 14 House standing committee chairmen voted for the proposal.

Ways and Means members voted heavily against the new committee; 21 other members joined Ullman in opposition while only 14 voted for it. Any significant reorganization plan probably would take from Ways and Means some of its extensive jurisdictional powers.

Rules Action Urged

In floor debate March 19, opponents said reorganization should be handled by the Rules Committee rather than a new panel. But Rules members said they were too busy. Opponents also said the select committee's two-to-one ratio of Democrats to Republicans would make the reorganization effort partisan.

Rep. Leon E. Panetta, D-Calif., a supporter of House reforms in the past who voted against H Res 118, later told a reporter some members thought the title of Committee on Committees was a mistake. "If it had been called the 'Committee to End Congressional Waste,' it would have gotten more votes." ▮

Power of House Subcommittees Enhanced

When the 94th Congress began in January 1975, the House Democratic Caucus took the unprecedented step of deposing three senior committee chairmen. To many congressional observers, that action symbolized the end of "committee government" in the House as the once powerful barons, who had dominated the lower chamber in the 1950s and 1960s, were humbled publicly by the younger, more activist Democratic members.

But the ouster of F. Edward Hebert, D-La., Wright Patman, D-Texas, and W. R. Poage, D-Texas, the three southern elders who chaired the Armed Services, Banking, Currency and Housing and Agriculture committees, overshadowed a more significant power shift in the House — the rise in importance of the subcommittee. "The significance of the 94th Congress was not the symbolic execution of a few committee chairmen," noted Rep. Barber B. Conable, R-N.Y., "but the upgrading of middle-level liberal Democrats at the subcommittee level." The subcommittee had come into its own as a new center of power.

The move to strengthen the autonomy of House subcommittees began in 1971 and culminated in decisions taken by the Democrats in the winter of 1974-75 forcing the Ways and Means Committee to establish subcommittees and authorizing subcommittee chairmen and ranking minority members to hire their own staff.

As a result, subcommittees have taken over from their parent committees much of the legislative workload. They are drafting major legislation in important areas such as energy and the environment, and their chairmen are managing bills on the House floor. On some committees, such as Interior, subcommittees are operating autonomously with large staffs of their own.

Because of these changes, some House members and congressional observers began to talk about "subcommittee government" much as they had spoken of "committee government" in the 1960s. Walter J. Oleszek, a former staff member of the House Select Committee on Committees, said a "shift from committee to subcommittee government" has apparently taken place in the House. A member of the House Rules Committee, which schedules most legislation for floor action, said that subcommittees were reporting more legislation intact, without full committee consideration. "We're now in the position where we're getting more and more legislation by subcommittee," he said. "I've seen that on Rules. We've been having more and more subcommittee chairmen coming before the committee . . . requesting a rule on a bill they're handling." Bills still must be formally reported by the full committee.

Despite general support by Democrats for strengthening subcommittees, some members began to question whether the shift had gone too far. Few talked about undoing the procedural changes that had enhanced the power of subcommittees or wanted to return to the days of the committee barons. But many members were asking the following questions:

- Had the House become too fragmented?
- Were subcommittees operating too autonomously?

- Had the House leadership exerted strong enough leadership to effectively coordinate the efforts of the committees in drafting legislation and scheduling controversial measures for floor action?

"We're going the way of the Senate," warned an influential southern member. "We've spread the action by giving subcommittees more power and making it possible for members to play more active roles on them. But there's nothing at this point to coordinate what all these bodies are doing and to place some checks on their growing independence."

Past Subcommittee Role

Until the early 1970s, subcommittees in most instances did not play a dominant role in committees or in managing bills on the floor. The major exception was the House Appropriations Committee in which the subcommittees, organized to parallel the various federal departments and agencies, have had to operate autonomously because of the heavy workload involved in considering departmental budgets.

Between 1971 and 1975, however, the old committee structure broke down. During those four years, the House Democratic Caucus set the stage for the ascendancy of the subcommittee by approving a series of innovations that guaranteed junior and middle-ranking Democrats greater power on subcommittees. The thrust of the changes was twofold: the authority of committee chairmen was curbed, and that of subcommittee leaders was strengthened. By the end of 1975, subcommittees were acting more independently and subcommittee chairmen were playing a more active role on the House floor.

The changes have had a ripple effect that was seen throughout the House — on committees, on House members themselves, on the House floor and on the leadership.

Committee Chairmen

The great losers in the House power struggle of the late 1960s and early 1970s have been the committee chairmen. By the time the 94th Congress organized, they had given up much of their control to the heads of their panel's subcommittees and to junior committee members. They still could delay bills coming before the full committee, or take a more active role in amending them, if they wanted to.

Their powers have been pared in several ways through changes in House rules and positions adopted by the Democratic Caucus.

1. No House member can be chairman of more than one legislative subcommittee. That, in effect, made it possible to break the hold of senior conservative Democrats on key subcommittees and opened up opportunities for middle-level and junior Democrats on them. Adopted at the beginning of the 92nd Congress, that rule was responsible for giving 16 Democrats elected since 1958 their first subcommittee chairmanships in 1971 on such key committees as Judiciary, Foreign Affairs and Banking, Currency and Housing.

1979 Subcommittee Battles Reflect . . .

The time-honored congressional seniority system took a beating in the House Jan. 30 and 31, 1979, as three junior Democrats bumped more senior colleagues in elections for subcommittee chairmanships on the Commerce and Government Operations committees.

The most dramatic subcommittee race ended in a victory for Henry A. Waxman, D-Calif., who was elected chairman of the House Commerce Health Subcommittee over Richardson Preyer, D-N.C. Preyer ranked three slots ahead of Waxman in seniority on the full Commerce Committee.

In another Commerce Committee upset, Bob Eckhardt, D-Texas, defeated John M. Murphy, D-N.Y., for chairman of the Oversight and Investigations Subcommittee.

Toby Moffett, D-Conn., pulled off the third coup by winning the chairmanship of the Environment, Energy and Natural Resources Subcommittee after Government Operations Committee Democrats rejected three more senior members for the job.

Traditionally, committee and subcommittee chairmanships are filled by the most senior majority party member on each panel. Only rarely has the seniority tradition been successfully challenged. In 1975, three committee chairmen were rejected in coups led by some of the same junior members who engineered the 1979 subcommittee upsets. *(See p. 44)*

However, the 1975 ousters were successful largely because the chairmen involved were considered autocratic leaders who did not give fair treatment to junior members.

This wasn't an issue in 1979 because the three defeated members were making their first try for the chairmanships.

Several members said the subcommittee upsets may have set a new anti-seniority precedent. Instead of just challenging a senior member for autocratic behavior, in the 1979 races "members were voting on whether one candidate's views are closer to theirs than the others," said Preyer.

Other Democrats agreed that ideology was a major factor in the 1979 races. Waxman, Eckhardt and Moffett were considered more liberal than the members they defeated, and a heavy concentration of liberal young Democrats on the two panels helped put them in office.

Those members have a different attitude about seniority, said Waxman, who was first elected to the House in 1974. "We don't feel bound by it," he said.

The Upsets

Waxman-Preyer. The health subcommittee race was considered the biggest upset, in part because Preyer was one of the most respected House members. Several Commerce Committee Democrats said later they voted against Preyer with some reluctance but felt Waxman would be a more aggressive chairman.

Preyer originally appeared vulnerable because of his stock holdings in two pharmaceutical companies. The subcommittee has jurisdiction over drug legislation. Preyer's financial disclosure report covering 1977 listed holdings of at least $115,000 in drug manufacturing companies.

Preyer tried to defuse the stock issue by pledging that if he were elected chairman he would not take part in subcommittee action on drug issues. However, some members still considered the holdings a conflict of interest.

Some Commerce members also were unhappy when Preyer released a statement criticizing the Jan. 11 Surgeon General's report linking smoking with several health problems. Preyer represents a tobacco-growing district.

Waxman, who began aggressively campaigning for the job in late 1978, came under attack when he gave campaign contributions to 10 Commerce Committee Democrats from a political campaign fund he established.

Such contributions, which do not violate campaign laws, are often made by top party leaders. But the practice was considered highly unusual for a junior mem-

2. Subcommittee members are now protected by a "bill of rights" adopted by the caucus in 1973. The new rules established a Democratic caucus on each committee and forced committee chairmen to start sharing authority with the panel's other Democratic members. It did that by giving the committee caucus the authority to select subcommittee chairmen, establish subcommittee jurisdictions, set party ratios on subcommittees that reflect the party ratios in the full House, provide adequate budgets for subcommittees and guarantee all members a major subcommittee assignment where vacancies make that possible.

Committee chairmen no longer could kill legislation quietly by pocketing it. Now they are required to refer bills to subcommittee jurisdictions within two weeks. Establishing fixed subcommittee jurisdictions also prevents committee chairmen from referring bills to subcommittees that they know will do their bidding.

3. All committees with more than 20 members must establish at least four subcommittees. This was directed at Ways and Means, which had operated without subcommittees during most of the 16-year chairmanship of Rep.

Wilbur D. Mills, D-Ark. It also established an important precedent in the House because it institutionalized subcommittees for the first time.

4. Another change was in subcommittee staffing. Subcommittee chairmen and ranking minority subcommittee members are now authorized to hire one staff person each to work directly for them on their subcommittees. A former representative's aide called this development "crucial." "Whether a subcommittee has its own staff is literally an index of how independent a subcommittee is," he said.

5. Committees are required to have written rules. This opened the way to checking the arbitrary power of committee chairmen and institutionalizing the subcommittees.

6. In an effort to spread participation even further, the Democratic Caucus in December, 1974, restricted senior Democrats to membership on only two of a committee's subcommittees. This was aimed mainly at the House Appropriations Committee, where senior conservative Democrats dominated important subcommittees handling defense, agriculture, and labor, health, education and welfare appropriations.

... **New Setbacks for Seniority System**

ber in a subcommittee contest. Waxman's contributions were strongly criticized by Richard Bolling, D-Mo., at a closed-door meeting of the House Democratic Steering and Policy Committee in January.

However, Waxman's contributions and Preyer's stock holdings were only side issues, agreed several committee members. When Commerce Committee Democrats caucused Jan. 30 to choose subcommittee chairmen, the choice between Waxman and Preyer was made primarily on ideology, they said.

Bidding for subcommittee chairmanships is done by seniority on the full committee. Thus, the committee Democrats first took a secret ballot "yes" or "no" vote on Preyer's bid for the health panel. Preyer lost, 12-15.

Waxman then bid for the chairmanship post and was elected 21-6.

Several members, including Preyer, credited Waxman's win to an aggressive lobbying campaign by Waxman and outside groups supporting him.

Freshman Al Swift, D-Wash., said Waxman had lunch with him in December, a month before Swift was assigned to the Commerce panel. "I just got to be very fond of him," said Swift, who committed his vote to Waxman shortly after winning the Commerce assignment. Swift said Preyer's stock holdings did not bother him because "his reputation for integrity is enormous." However, Waxman's views were "philosophically closer to mine," said Swift.

Waxman, who had the backing of consumer, environmental and labor groups, argued in his campaigning that he would be a more aggressive chairman with more liberal views on national health insurance and other major issues scheduled to come before the panel.

Preyer had the backing of House Democratic leaders, which some committee members thought worked against him. Richard L. Ottinger, D-N.Y., said: "The thing that hurt Preyer most was the leadership's very untoward efforts to intervene" in what was considered an internal committee affair.

But Preyer said he did not feel the leadership worked aggressively on his behalf. The deciding factors, he said, were "generational and philosophical. It boiled down to young liberals versus older moderates."

Eckhardt-Murphy. Murphy, chairman of the House Merchant Marine and Fisheries Committee, began campaigning for the Oversight and Investigations panel while Eckhardt was in the hospital recovering from heart surgery.

Eckhardt had already announced his plans to seek the chairmanship that former Rep. John E. Moss, D-Calif., parlayed into a national forum on a wide variety of issues.

Commerce Democrats said Murphy's bid was resented by many members because he already chaired a full committee and a Merchant Marine subcommittee and was trying to renew his chairmanship of the Select Outer Continental Shelf Committee. Murphy said if he got the Commerce chairmanship, he would give up the Merchant Marine subcommittee.

As chairman of the Merchant Marine panel, Murphy developed a reputation as a defender of special interest groups. Eckhardt was considered more likely to continue Moss' aggressive oversight of powerful industries, such as oil companies.

Moffett. Moffett began campaigning for the Government Operations post several weeks before committee Democrats caucused to elect chairmen. However, his victory caught some committee members by surprise.

The first committee Democrat to bid for the energy chairmanship at a Jan. 31 meeting was Glenn English, D-Okla., who was defeated, 10-14. Elliott H. Levitas, D-Ga., and David W. Evans, D-Ind., each were defeated, 8-16. Moffett was elected, 16-8.

Government Operations subcommittees are largely oversight panels, but Moffett was expected to use his position as chairman to aggressively pursue energy issues.

---

7. As of the beginning of the 94th Congress, chairmen of all the Appropriations subcommittees have to be approved by the House Democratic Caucus. (An attempt to extend this to Ways and Means subcommittee chairmen failed in 1977.)

8. In December 1978, the caucus approved a change requiring committees to let each member choose one subcommittee assignment before any member could pick a second one. The change was expected to open up more choice assignments to junior members.

9. Another change approved by the caucus in 1978 limited each Democrat to five subcommittee assignments on standing committees of the House.

Changes Beneficial?

The strengthening of subcommittees, and the concurrent decentralization of the House, has its pluses and minuses, said Richard Bolling, D-Mo., who helped bring about some of the changes as chairman of the Select House Committee on Committees that proposed a reorganization of the House committee structure. For the most part he considered "the pluses greater. You get greater specialization and oversight when you decentralize."

But the changes have had a much deeper impact and have transformed the character and operations of the House. They have made the legislative process much more untidy, freewheeling and unpredictable and have introduced more competing elements.

The strengthening of subcommittees has created more work for House members. Subcommittees were holding more hearings and preparing more reports. With the broadening of committee opportunities, junior members have had to cope with a heavier workload as they participate more in subcommittee deliberations and floor debate. "When you spread out power, you give people an incentive to work," said Norman J. Ornstein, a political scientist at Catholic University in Washington, D.C.

Subcommittee chairmen have gained more influence on the House floor. On routine legislation, there has been a growing tendency for them rather than the committee chairmen to give the cues to members on how to vote. On major legislation, subcommittee chairmen have been dealing almost as equals with the chairmen of other committees. The fact that subcommittee chairmen can now manage legislation on the House floor has given them new clout. Part of the subcommittee bill of rights was letting them manage legislation, Ornstein added. "That forced them to become more diligent and expert on legislation. And in the House, one of the things giving people power is expertise."

The increased independence and expertise of subcommittees have placed greater burdens on the House Democratic leadership. "In the past, the Speaker only needed to think about a bill just as it approached the House floor," said Bolling. "Now the Speaker has to know what's happening at the subcommittee level where legislation is being generated. He has to find out what members think long before a bill hits the floor."

Some House members and their staffs feel decentralization of the House committee structure has gone too far, that subcommittees are becoming too autonomous. This trend, they said, makes it much more difficult to lead the House, delays the legislative process and exacerbates the problem of overlapping committee jurisdictions, which has on occasion generated intense inter-committee squabbles.

The subcommittee reforms, as Walter Oleszek pointed out, have had contradictory effects. They came at a time when House Democrats were trying to pull themselves together by increasing the powers of the Speaker, the Democratic Steering and Policy Committee and the House Democratic Caucus to better coordinate party policy on legislation and make the Democratic members of the House a more coherent body.

"Paradoxically, just at the time when the majority party has nurtured an instrument [the caucus] to pull together a fractionalized and uncoordinated committee system, it has undermined that objective by creating numerous independent subcommittees," Oleszek said. "'Spreading the action' to subcommittees may have further diffused power at a time when many think centralization is needed."

It has encouraged jurisdictional fights not only between committees but between subcommittees and committees. Because the House did not accept most of the Bolling committee proposals for restructuring House committee jurisdictions (H Res 988) in 1974, "you now have subcommittees expending great energy protecting their own turf," Ornstein said. "You have fights between the Health Subcommittees on Interstate and Foreign Commerce and on Ways and Means, the Energy Subcommittee on Commerce and Ways and Means."

Resolving the jurisdictional problem, according to one House member, "would make leadership and subcommittee problems much easier to handle." If one committee, such as Interstate and Foreign Commerce, handled all legislation on the same subject as the Bolling committee had proposed, then that committee would be able to integrate the work of its subcommittees in that area. "You can't get a handle on a small part of the energy problem with the present jurisdictional set up," he said.

Some members, who looked at the House from an institutional standpoint, said that reform had swung too far. They saw the pendulum eventually swinging back toward stronger party and committee leadership as House Democrats realized how difficult it was to function in an overly decentralized body. The tyranny of the committee chairmen would not return, they said, but House Democrats would have to find a mean between expanding participation and stronger leadership to adopt a party legislative program. ∎

Conference Committees Opened to Public

One of the last and most traditional vestiges of secrecy in Congress disappeared in 1975 when conference committees were opened to the public and press.

Under pressure from "government in the sunshine" advocates, both the Senate and House changed their rules to require that conferences called to iron out differences in each chamber's version of a bill be open to the public.

In a major extension of the movement toward open meetings, House Democrats in December 1977 endorsed a change in the House rules that would open all House-Senate conference committee meetings to the public except when the entire House specifically voted to close such a session.

Bob Carr, D-Mich., who sponsored the amendment, said it would expose the working of the Congress to the "maximum sunlight" and prevent "powerful conference committees from bargaining and making deals in secret."

The openness requirement was the most dramatic of many new pressures on conference committees in recent years. These sessions traditionally have been the quiet preserves of senior members of Congress who exercised great power over legislation as compromises were reached behind closed doors.

This power was being eroded in the 1970s as junior members demanded more participation in conferences and as the meetings were opened to the public. Some conferences had been opened voluntarily in the past, but most were not. Participants in the open conferences generally agreed that the meetings went smoothly even when large numbers of observers were present.

Proponents of the change said the open conferences held in 1974, including one on a controversial strip mine regulation bill, disproved the claim that public scrutiny would disrupt the conference process. "The open strip mine conference in no way inhibited the need for making changes and compromises in legislation," said David Cohen of Common Cause, the so-called citizens lobby group that pushed for the change.

But some members, aides and lobbyists felt that the openness might lead some conferees to make long speeches explaining their actions and others to hold out stubbornly on issues of particular interest to constituents.

Open conferences were an issue as far back as the first session of Congress in 1789. The first conference, on import and tonnage legislation, was held in open session. Nonconferees wandered in and out of the meeting room and the Senate finally had to adjourn for the day because its members, distracted by the conference action, were paying

George Norris

little attention to regular business. The next open conference was not recorded until 1911.

In addition to complaints of secrecy and unaccountability, the conference system has been sharply criticized for the manner in which conferees are selected, their occasional reluctance to uphold the position of their chambers and the latitude they have to write final legislation.

Sen. George Norris, R-Neb. (1913-43), crusaded against conference committees during most of his political career, calling them the third house of Congress. "The members of the 'house'," he said in 1934, "are not elected by the people. The people have no voice as to who these members shall be. . . . No constituent has any definite knowledge as to how members of this conference committee vote, and there is no record to prove the attitude of any member of the conference committee." In 1934, when Norris helped redesign the Nebraska legislature, he eliminated the second house, making it the only state with a unicameral legislature and eliminating the need for conference committees.

Opening the Doors

Congress is unlikely to follow Norris' lead, but advocates of the public conference think openness is the answer to many of his criticisms. The push to open the conference committee was a logical outgrowth of the trend toward opening legislative markup sessions — where members work through the details of bills that will be presented to the full chamber for consideration. The House opened its committee bill-drafting sessions in 1973. The open meetings requirement created no major problems for House committees. The Senate applied a similar rule to its committees in late 1975.

Of the 12 open conferences held in 1974, the most important and controversial was on a bill to regulate strip mining. Conferees came from the House and Senate Interior and Insular Affairs Committees.

Explaining the decision to open the conference, Charles Conklin, special counsel on the House Interior Committee, pointed out that both committees had long held open markup sessions and that there had been several requests from the press and the public to open the conference. The motion to open the doors was made by Sen. Lee Metcalf, D-Mont. (House 1953-61; Senate 1961-78), and while there was a little discussion, Conklin said, the motion was easily approved.

The experiment apparently worked well. "I didn't let the presence of a crowd affect me at all in what I said or did," said John F. Seiberling, D-Ohio, a House conferee, "and I think that goes for the other members too."

Access to the conference "benefits both sides . . . [since] you have a better idea of what's happening on a day-to-day, hour-by-hour basis," said one mining industry source. John McCormick, a lobbyist for the Coalition Against Strip Mining, said "openness was an assurance that we weren't going to lose anything major," because members knew their positions would be reported in the press. In one case, McCormick said, his organization was

Calling a Conference

Either chamber can request a conference once both have adopted differing versions of the same legislation. Generally, the chamber that approved the legislation first will disagree to the amendments made by the second body and request that a conference be convened. Sometimes, however, the second body will ask for a conference immediately after it has approved the legislation, assuming that the other chamber will not accept its changes.

Not all legislation goes to conference. Often on minor bills, the second house will make only minimal changes in the first chamber's version. The first house will then agree to those amendments, clearing the measure for the president's signature. But virtually no legislation of any consequence or controversy escapes the conference system. Approximately one-fourth of all the bills enacted into public law in the 95th Congress, including all regular appropriations bills, were products of conference committees.

able to change a member's stand on an issue by reporting his statements in conference to constituents, who in turn protested.

Openness Mandate

The experience of conferees on the strip mining bill and in other open conferences helped ease the way for the rules change in the House at the beginning of the 94th Congress and in the Senate in November 1975.

The week Congress convened, the Democratic Caucus approved by voice vote a proposal by Dante B. Fascell, Fla., to open all conferences except when either the House or Senate conferees voted in open session to close them. Each vote could apply to only one session of the conference; separate votes would be required to close it each day. This proposal was later accepted by the full House as part of its rules.

An open conferences resolution was offered successfully in the Senate Democratic caucus by Lawton Chiles, Fla., and in the Republican caucus by William V. Roth, Del. Both were advocates of "sunshine laws," opening the legislative process to the public. However, the Senate did not approve the "sunshine" changes until November.

The Limits of Sunshine

While its advocates said the open conference would make conferees accountable to their chambers and the public, some members questioned how openly conference decisions would be made.

"Sunshine laws kid the public," said Richard Bolling, D-Mo., a chief advocate of institutional reform in the House. "They imply a total openness and there never will be." Bolling said openness was healthy but cautioned that some compromises and accommodations would have to be made in secret if the legislation was to succeed. In those cases, he added, "if we have to meet in our wives' boudoirs — if they still have such things — we will."

"I don't think very frankly that a conference can be held in open session until such time as the necessary compromises can be made," agreed Rep. Lester L. Wolff, D-N.Y., who predicted that many open conferences simply

would be window-dressing for agreements already worked out among conferees. Fascell discounted such criticisms. "There's a limit to where you can go in seeking openness," he acknowledged, "but with the open conference you will know a lot more than you know now."

The prospect of open conferences drew mixed reactions from lobbyists. A chief lobbyist for the U.S. Chamber of Commerce said he did not object to sunshine but thought it could hinder passage of effective legislation. "Compromise could be a little more difficult to come by," he said. "If you put a flock of Ralph Naders, John Gardners or Sierra Clubbers in a conference room ... it will make some conferees sweat." It was just that access, however, that Cohen of Common Cause thought would be beneficial. He said it would help public interest groups like his compete with industry and other special interest groups that were more entrenched in Congress.

A congressional liaison official in the White House said that "on the whole, the administration favors anything that will open public forums to public view" and thought that members would continue to vote their constituencies, adding that on the strip mining bill, nothing changed "even with all those environmentalists sitting around."

The official also pointed out that open conferences might cut down the number of non-germane and special interest amendments added to the legislation in the Senate. Many of those amendments are accepted on the floor with the clear understanding that they will be quietly dropped in conference. The member benefits, however, because he can tell his constituents that he had the amendment approved on the floor.

Selection and Seniority

The selection of conferees has often caused more controversy and criticism than the action they have taken.

The two chambers have different rules for selecting conferees, but in practice both follow similar procedures. Senate rules allow the chamber to elect conferees but the body has rarely done so. The common practice is for the presiding officer to appoint conferees on the recommendation of the chairman of the committee having jurisdiction over the legislation.

House rules grant the Speaker the right to appoint conferees, but he usually does so only after consultation with the appropriate committee chairman. In 1976, House Democrats adopted a rule stating that, to the extent feasible, the Speaker should appoint authors of principal amendments to conference committees.

Each chamber's delegation to a conference can range in size from three to more than 20 members; the Senate usually sends larger groups than the House. But whatever the size, a majority in each delegation must be from the majority party in the chamber. Each delegation votes as a unit on issues in dispute with the majority position in the delegation determining how the whole delegation will vote.

Few legislative committees have hard and fast rules guiding the chairman on his choice of conferees, although most chairmen consult with the ranking minority member in choosing conferees from the minority party. The lack of guidance has frequently led to complaints that a chairman has stacked the conference in favor of his own personal position rather than the will of the full chamber.

Members have also complained that reliance on the seniority system and the conservative bent of senior members combine to thwart the will of the full body.

In recent years, however, as the volume and complexity of legislation has grown, committee chairmen have begun to choose as conferees members of the subcommittee that originated the legislation. In addition to giving the delegation expertise, that practice has allowed junior members to attend conferences.

The Will of the House

Even more controversial than seniority is the question of whether the conferees, however they are appointed, are likely to uphold their chamber's position on key points in the conference. Precedent in both the House and Senate indicates that conferees are expected to support the legislative position of the chamber they represent. Obviously, conferees from one chamber must give way to conferees of the other or strike a compromise in order to reach a final agreement. But when concessions are made by conferees who did not support their chamber's decision on passage, arguments are likely to result.

A classic example in the House occurred in 1972, when a coalition of House Republicans and southern Democrats objected so strenuously to proposed conferees on a bill raising the hourly minimum wage that they blocked the bill from going to conference.

Generally regarded as more liberal than the rest of the House, the Education and Labor Committee had reported the bill in 1971. When the bill came to the floor in May 1972, after a long delay in the Rules Committee, the House on a 217-191 vote approved a more conservative substitute bill offered by John N. Erlenborn, R-Ill. Erlenborn's bill made the increase more gradual, deleted a proposed extension of coverage to additional workers, and added a controversial provision that would allow employers to hire youths under 18 at a sub-minimum wage.

Subsequently, the Senate passed a bill even more generous than the original House committee proposals.

When Education and Labor Chairman Carl D. Perkins, D-Ky., asked unanimous consent to send the bill to conference with the Senate, Erlenborn asked him for the names of members he had recommended to be conferees. Perkins said they would be 10 members from the General Labor Subcommittee which had originally considered the bill — six Democrats and four Republicans. Ten of the 11 Democratic members of the subcommittee had voted against the Erlenborn substitute.

Erlenborn objected to the unanimous consent request, thereby blocking it. He said it was unfair to send to the conference a delegation whose majority opposed the final House bill.

Certain that a second unanimous consent request would be objected to, Perkins offered a motion that the House disagree with the Senate version and request a conference to resolve the differences. Only a simple majority was needed to pass the motion. But Erlenborn again objected: "If we refuse to send the bill to conference at this time, then we may receive assurances in the future that when the bill does go to conference a majority of the managers on the part of the House will fight for the position the House had taken."

Perkins' motion was defeated, 190-198. Later the House killed the bill by voting 188-196 against a second Perkins motion to request a conference with the Senate. "All too often," Erlenborn said, summing up his opposition to the motion, "the House speaks its will by amending legislation . . . or adopting substitute bills and sending the legislation to the other body. All too often the other body

John N. Erlenborn   Carl D. Perkins

passes a bill very similar to that rejected by the House. And almost without exception the conference committee members appointed by the House accede more to the provisions of the other body than they try to protect the provisions which the House had adopted."

Instructions

In an effort to ensure that its conferees would uphold its position, the House in 1974 modified its rules on their selection. The new rules said that in making appointments to conferences, "the Speaker shall appoint no less than a majority of members who generally supported the House position as determined by the Speaker."

Either chamber may try to enforce its will by instructing its conferees on how to vote when they go to conference, but the conferees are not obligated to follow the instructions. Since the instructions are little more than guidelines, they are rarely used. In 1974 the House on three separate occasions instructed conferees on the elementary and secondary education amendments bill (HR 69 — PL 93-380) to insist on the House language limiting busing. The House conferees nevertheless agreed to a modification of the much weaker Senate version.

Many members of Congress have argued that conferees should not be bound. Wolff disagreed. "It is sometimes wise to tie the hands of the conferees" so the will of the House prevails, he said. "If a report comes to the floor of the House in violation of the instructions, the membership of the House could be required to vote to modify, annul or reaffirm the instructions previously given."

Erlenborn, on the other hand, said he thought that instructions were a wasted effort. He said that there must be considerable give and take in the conference, and that instructions could hamper that to the detriment of the legislation. But he supported the new rules guaranteeing a conference majority in favor of the bill as passed.

All or Nothing

Once conferees report the final bill, it must be approved or rejected in its entirety by both sides. Exceptions are made only for non-germane Senate amendments which may be deleted in the House, and for certain other amendments which are reported in technical disagreement because they do not conform with House rules.

Unlike the Senate, the House has strict rules forbidding consideration of amendments not germane to the bill under consideration. The Senate for years has attached non-germane amendments to House-passed bills, and they

'Sunshine' Backers See New Secrecy Trend

A House Appropriations subcommittee vote to exclude the public from a meeting on a key 1980 money bill raised concern that the House's commitment to "sunshine" could be drifting behind a cloud.

The Appropriations Labor-HEW Subcommittee voted May 16, 1979, to close a markup of the fiscal 1980 Labor-HEW appropriations bill.

"We've held open markups for the past four or five years," a subcommittee aide said. "We had every intention of holding an open markup this year, until we were inundated with people. We closed it because there were so many people in the halls and in our offices that two policemen couldn't get order. . . . We couldn't work with all those people breathing down our necks."

Trend Detected

Some members of Congress and congressional watchdogs say they fear a trend away from the open meetings commitment of the early 1970s, beginning in 1973, when the House voted to open up its committee markup sessions to the public. The Senate adopted a similar rule in 1975. In addition, both chambers voted to open conference sessions to the public.

"I definitely detect a trend toward more closed meetings in the House," commented Rep. David R. Obey, D-Wis., a champion of House openness and a member of the Labor-HEW Appropriations Subcommittee. Obey voted against closing the May 16 session.

"It seems to be a case of creeping secrecy," commented Richard P. Conlon, staff director of the Democratic Study Group.

A CQ survey of the 13 Appropriations subcommittees indicated that two subcommittees in addition to

---

"There's a great deal of confusion and bad reporting when you have [a meeting] opened and you haven't completed your press release."

—Senate Finance Committee aide

Labor-HEW had switched from open to closed markups in the past several years. They were State, Justice, Commerce, Judiciary and Agriculture.

Agriculture, according to staff aide Robert Foster, held only closed markups before 1977. The 1977 markup was partially open, he said, while the 1978 markup was entirely public.

The May 2, 1979, session was closed because the budget resolution was on the floor that same day, Foster explained. "We were concerned that we might enter into the floor discussions on the budget resolution," he said.

State, Justice, Commerce, Judiciary began closing markups two or three years ago, staff assistant John G. Osthaus said. "The members feel it facilitates their discussion of the issues and the amounts to be appropriated. When the markups were open, the members felt it was a madhouse, with people rushing in and out and

trying to command their attention. Now, the staff simply announces the results at the end of the markup."

Missing Listings

Secrecy has crept into other aspects of the Appropriations subcommittees' operations.

A number of subcommittee sessions have not been listed in advance or after the meeting in the *Congressional Record*, as House rules require. Subcommittee aides blame the omissions on administrative foul-ups.

A meeting of the Appropriations Energy and Water Development Subcommittee on May 9 to discuss fund-

---

"If the members can't stand up to the pressures in the room, they shouldn't be in the room."

—Rep. David R. Obey, D-Wis.

---

ing for controversial water projects was not listed in the *Record*. Nor was it on the official list of hearings and markups posted in the press galleries.

Staff assistant Hunter Spillan said a routine announcement of the meeting had been given to the full Appropriations Committee. As for it being closed, "our meetings generally are closed because one-third of our appropriations deal with weapons and weapons research," Spillan explained. "Every year, they forget we closed it last year."

Other Committees Affected

A spot check turned up some closed meetings other than Appropriations subcommittees.

The Senate Finance Committee, for example, in early 1979 held 11 closed sessions with public and administration witnesses to help develop trade agreement implementing legislation.

"There's a great deal of confusion and bad reporting when you have it opened and you haven't completed your press release," explained a Finance Committee aide. "I guess it's a way of keeping it pure and simple until the recommendations have been completed."

A House Ways and Means subcommittee held about 15 days of closed sessions for the same purpose. "They are sensitive hearings," a staffer said.

Obey, in an interview, blamed much of the push for secrecy on lobbyists.

"You have a number of members frustrated because things they have said or done in open markups have been garbled by trade association newsletters and lobby groups," he said. "Also, you have a feeling that the lobby groups in this country have become so single-minded and so intense that maybe it's better to operate behind closed doors. You sometimes wonder who is having more influence — the lobbyists or the members."

Obey said he sympathized with the problem, but disagreed with the closed-session solution. "If the members can't stand up to the pressures in the room, they shouldn't be in the room," he said.

are frequently retained in conference. Until 1970, such amendments could not be voted on separately in the House and many House members complained that the practice prevented them from considering the amendments at all.

In 1970 the House adopted a rule that allowed separate votes to be taken on non-germane Senate amendments. But the rule failed to achieve the desired result, partly because it did not spell out the procedure under which the separate votes could be taken, and partly because the new rule appeared to conflict with other House rules requiring an up-or-down vote on the entire conference report with no chance to amend it.

In 1972, the House again amended its rules to allow members to make points of order against a conference report after it is read but before debate begins. If any portion of the conference report is ruled non-germane, that portion is immediately subject to 40 minutes of debate and a separate vote. If no points of order are sustained or if the House accepts all non-germane amendments, the House then considers and accepts or rejects the conference report as a whole.

If any of the non-germane amendments are rejected, the House can consider a motion to accept the Senate version with an amendment — the amendment consisting of all provisions of the conference report not rejected by the House. If the House agrees to this motion, the Senate can agree to the House version, without the non-germane amendments, or request a second conference on the bill.

This rule was employed at the end of the 1974 session. The House had approved a bill calling for a White House symposium on libraries; the Senate added two non-germane amendments, one to clarify a recently enacted law on the privacy of student records and one to exempt certain organizations from compliance with federal sex discrimina-

A Quiet Place to Talk

The movement toward open conferences produced one practical problem: where to hold them. Traditionally, conferences had been held in small rooms in the Capitol itself, usually as close as possible to a point midway between the two chambers. But those rooms were not large enough for a crowd of observers and reporters.

Conferees on the 1974 strip mining bill saw a preview of the problem. "Members had to carve their way through a wall of human flesh," recalled Rep. John F. Seiberling, D-Ohio. One aide to House conferees said staff members searched every day for a room big enough to hold the throng. "If Interior Committee conferences are closed in the future," he said, "it will be solely because we can't get a place to operate in."

tion regulations. The provisions were retained in the conference and when the bill reached the House floor Dec. 19, William A. Steiger, R-Wis. (1967-78), raised a point of order against the provision dealing with sex discrimination. The point of order was sustained but the House on a 37-102 standing vote rejected the motion to delete the non-germane provision. Thus the bill was accepted as it had been reported from the conference.

While the new rule seems to be working well for the House, it has irritated a number of senators. An aide to Sen. Jacob K. Javits, R-N.Y., said there was a feeling among some senators that the Senate should reject some appropriate House amendments in an effort to force the House to relax its non-germaneness rule. ∎

Few Changes in Long's Power Preserve

Russell B. Long has influenced American domestic policy in a way that few legislators have done in this generation. In the Senate, Long controlled much of the major legislation that passed through the 95th Congress. Occasionally he was unsuccessful, as in his end-of-Congress effort to obtain a rise in the support price of sugar, but few doubted that he had become the single most influential member of Congress outside the top leaders.

The Senate Finance Committee headed by the Louisiana Democrat had a hand in shaping the 1978 tax bill that was one of the last measures to be enacted by the 95th Congress in October, and which bore little resemblance to the tax program President Carter had proposed in January of that year. In February 1978 his committee voted to move the tuition tax credit proposal to the Senate floor. In the energy field, the administration failed to pry out of the Finance Committee what was clearly the most important part of the original bill — a new policy to bring domestic oil prices up to world levels. Carter wanted to rebate the additional cost to consumers but Long wanted the oil industry to get the extra revenues. His opposition, which stalled the bill in his committee, was enough to kill the measure even though the House passed it.

It was Sen. Long, who by using his considerable powers of persuasion, pushed a compromise version of the waterway user fees legislation through both houses and on to the White House in only four days. The Finance Committee also offered a compromise proposal for countercyclical aid, considered the customs law revision, airline noise control and hospital cost control among other pieces of legislation in 1978.

The committee that has handled all this work is one that has changed remarkably little over the past decade of general congressional turmoil. While committee chairmen in both the House and Senate have grown weaker, Long has grown stronger. While subcommittees have generally taken over more and more of the legislative workload, the subcommittees on Finance do little of importance.

And this is not merely by Long's decree. For example, early in 1977, when pressure from Democrats on the Senate floor forced Long to promise a bigger role for subcommittees, it was Long's own colleagues on Finance who insisted that things be kept the way they are. The existing system, in which all important bills are considered only by the full committee, keeps all subjects under Long's personal control. But it also gives each member a role to play on every piece of major legislation considered by the committee.

The subcommittee episode illustrated one fact of life on Finance — members feel the chairman's influence enhances their own, and they fight to preserve it. Long's relationships with other senators are a complex matter, but they are the source of his control. The chairman's power over his committee surprises those who see it for the first time, prompting comparisons with ex-Rep. Wilbur D. Mills, D-Ark. (1939-77), former chairman of the House Ways and Means Committee.

"There's no doubt he runs that committee," said Sen. Spark M. Matsunaga, D-Hawaii, who joined the Senate and the Finance Committee in 1977 after 14 years in the House. "Not even Wilbur Mills was like this. Mills had factions forming against him on Ways and Means. Russell Long is close to every member on a personal basis."

Some observers who have studied the Senate for years still marvel at the personal dynamics of the Finance Committee. "The whole thing puzzles the hell out of me," said Norman J. Ornstein, a political scientist who is authoring a book on the Senate. "It amazes me because he obviously has some kind of personal charisma. Even people like Gaylord Nelson, D-Wis., and Abe Ribicoff, D-Conn., love Russell Long. You won't see any revolution coming out of the Finance Committee. He has some personal power over them."

The fact that Russell Long is powerful is not news. The adjective has appeared next to his name almost automatically during his 14 years as Finance chairman, and frequently before that. He makes fun of it. One tax lobbyist recalls Long ambling up to a group of reporters at a cocktail party and saying, "Call me anything you want to, boys, but don't call me powerful."

The other cliche about Russell Long is that he is smart. The newspaper articles that characterize him as the most powerful senator often say in addition that he is the smartest, perhaps the smartest of modern times. The late Sen. Richard B. Russell, D-Ga. (1933-71), used to say that Russell Long was the second smartest senator he had ever known. The smartest, he said, was Russell's father, Sen. Huey P. Long, D-La. (1932-35).

The kind of intelligence most often ascribed to Long is not intellectual brilliance, but sheer cleverness and cunning. His loyalists on the Finance Committee find this unfair. "Clever has a connotation of stealth," said Bob Packwood, R-Ore., who led the fight against subcommittees. "Russell is just bright. When somebody is so smart he can outwit somebody else, people get the impression he is devious. In Russell's case it's just smartness."

This article explores the "smartness" of Russell Long, the workings of his committee and the effects of that combination on legislation the Senate takes up. None of the information comes directly from Long himself; he declined to be interviewed on the subject of the Finance Committee.

"Call me anything you want to boys, but don't call me powerful."
—Sen. Russell B. Long, D-La.

Favors to Bestow

Conversations with members of the Finance Committee and with key lobbyists leave a clear picture of Russell Long's tactics and style. Most important, he has favors to bestow.

Tax bills are the basis of the Finance Committee's work. More than any other aspect of the legislative process, they attract lobbying and constituent pressure for special provisions.

The current U.S. tax system uses the Internal Revenue Code for a variety of social as well as economic goals, and any tax incentive that benefits somebody can be extended or rewritten to benefit somebody else. It is this complex network of tax incentives that makes the committee a focus for high-priced corporate lobbyists, and a target for tax revision lobbyists who feel the tax code is riddled with the giveaways the committee is persuaded to enact.

Whatever one's opinion of tax incentives is, there is no doubt that Chairman Long is a master at picking up Senate votes by promising colleagues help with incentives their constituents want. He also is in the position to threaten to take tax incentives away. This is backscratching — the single most important tool of power on the Finance Committee.

"He knows the Senate is full of guys that posture a lot but have something in their closet," said one veteran tax lobbyist. "Every one of them has some constituency, some interest that he has to deal with. Long knows their interests, he knows their weaknesses, and he exploits them."

This is especially important within the Finance Committee, whose members receive the most direct constituent pressure, but Long is able to use it on the Senate floor and in conference to make sure favorable decisions taken within the committee are sustained, or unfavorable ones reversed.

Spark Matsunaga of Hawaii arrived at the Finance Committee in 1977 to find a new Subcommittee on Tourism and Sugar created just for him. Since subcommittees have little power on Finance, it involved no substantive concession on Long's part. But Long knows it is helpful with constituents and difficult to forget at a time when the chairman wants a favor.

No Euphemisms

Long's talent for doing favors and collecting on the debts has long been familiar in the Senate. What many colleagues find remarkable is the candor with which he does it.

"I understand," said Gaylord Nelson during energy markup one day in 1975, "that in my absence we passed the tax breaks for railroads, but omitted railroad-over-water ferries — such as the one in Wisconsin."

"I'll be happy to give you that one without need of further discussion," Long replied, "but I expect you in exchange to vote for this next tax credit we're about to discuss." Only Russell Long knows for sure how seriously that remark was meant, but the "tax reform" lobbyists in the Senate take it seriously enough to cite it as an example of procedural abuses in Senate Finance that make improvement difficult. (*"Tax reform," box, p. 80*)

But not everybody on the liberal side finds Long's back-scratching so objectionable. "He's a very honest man," said one longtime aide to tax-reform-minded senators. "He's a very direct man. My feelings about him have changed over the years. I spent a great deal of my Hill career hating Long in abstraction. But he's honest. When he wants to carve out a loophole he'll tell you who he's doing it for. The goddamn liberals will tell you it's for some candy ass reason."

When Ralph Nader and other critics complained that the committee was creating new "tax expenditures" — revenues lost to the Treasury through special tax preferences — Long said he would accept their word for it. "...That label doesn't bother me," he said. "I've never been confused about it. I've always known that what we're doing was giving government money away." In his critical 1976 book, *Tax Politics,* Robert M. Brandon, former director of Nader's Tax Reform Research Group, cites this and other statements by Long.

But other observers find Long's disregard for euphemisms to be one of his most appealing traits, and one of his most effective tactics in dealing with people.

Some senators find that Long's ability to talk plain English wins him votes both in the committee and on the Senate floor. They point out that colleagues often walk into a meeting or a floor debate virtually cold, with the choice of accepting Long's explanation, which is always simple and clear, or a dissenting view, expressed in arcane economic terms. Long gets the benefit of the doubt.

Even the most vehement opponents concede this. "He always twists things around backwards and they come out reasonable," said Bill Pietz, another tax lobbyist for the Nader organization. "It's a talent that he has. It's remarkable."

In 1977, when the committee considered President Carter's proposal to phase in higher Social Security taxes, Long said it was "like cutting off a puppy's tail one inch at a time to spare him the pain. It hurts every time you cut off any of it." But Finance Committee arguments are rarely won on metaphors alone. The chairman frequently prevails because he is more tenacious than most of the people he is arguing with.

Also in 1977 Matsunaga led the effort in committee to retain an existing tax advantage for single taxpayers in the stimulus tax bill (HR 3477). Long opposed that. "I think if we had taken a vote, we would have had it," Matsunaga said. "But he wouldn't take a vote until he was certain his side would prevail." Ultimately Long found the votes, and Matsunaga's amendment lost.

But the fight was not over. Long remained concerned that a tax break for singles, a politically sophisticated pressure group, might be strong on the Senate floor. Matsunaga says Long talked President Carter into calling

Senate Finance Committee In 96th Congress

Russell B. Long, D-La., chairman

Herman E. Talmadge, D-Ga.	Robert Dole, R-Kan.
Abraham Ribicoff, D-Conn.	Bob Packwood, R-Ore.
Harry F. Byrd Jr., Ind.-Va.	William V. Roth Jr., R-Del.
Gaylord Nelson, D-Wis.	John C. Danforth, R-Mo.
Mike Gravel, D-Alaska	John H. Chafee, R-R.I.
Lloyd Bentsen, D-Texas	H. John Heinz III, R-Pa.
Spark M. Matsunaga, D-Hawaii	Malcolm Wallop, R-Wyo.
Daniel Patrick Moynihan, D-N.Y.	David Durenberger, R-Minn.
Max Baucus, D-Mont.	
David L. Boren, D-Okla.	
Bill Bradley, D-N.J.	

Matsunaga and asking him not to offer the amendment on the Senate floor. When Matsunaga said he had a commitment to the singles groups interested in the amendment, Long asked if he would offer it but not fight for it. "I've never seen anyone like him," Matsunaga said. The amendment was brought to the floor where it failed, 33-55.

Master of Compromise

When he is unable to win outright, critics say, Russell Long is a master of the "two for me, one for you" compromise. He goes into most negotiating sessions with plenty of minor points he is ready to concede in order to win on things he considers important. In conferences with the House, he often loses on a majority of the individual points in dispute. But he rarely loses a majority of the key issues. In 1975, in conference over the emergency tax cut bill, he threw enough Senate-passed amendments overboard to preserve the oil depletion allowance for independent companies, which was his ultimate goal.

Colleagues say Long is more than willing to call any victory a compromise. "Russell realizes the best way to pants a guy is when he doesn't know he's been pantsed," said Packwood. "He makes you feel you're helping to make the decision," Matsunaga explained. "Actually he's making it."

But colleagues agree that the chairman is rarely dogmatic, and will nearly always cut his losses rather than squander his influence pursuing a lost cause. "He likes to win," said Lloyd Bentsen, D-Texas, a committee member since 1973, "and he works hard at winning. He works hard to develop a consensus. But I've watched Russell time and time again start out with something, find it wasn't going to work, and drop it. He doesn't often bring it to a vote."

"He'll stand up for his position when he knows he'll have an impact," said William V. Roth Jr., R-Del., who is also on Finance. "But he won't take a stand just for taking a stand. He feels as chairman it's important to be where the majority is."

Long has frequently made it clear in public that he places no importance on moral victories. "I don't see much point," he told an interviewer in 1971, "in recommending something that the Senate won't agree to."

Long's preference for substantive rather than moral victories inclines him to look farther down the legislative road than other legislators do. When most senators offer an amendment in committee, their attention is on that amendment and its chances for adoption. Long is already thinking beyond the committee to the Senate floor and the conference with the House. Often he is not concerned as much with whether something passes as with how the action taken that day will affect the eventual legislative product.

"He has a degree of confidence that his views will ultimately prevail," said John C. Danforth, R-Mo., a committee member since 1977, "that allows him to accept temporary setbacks.... He realizes that the legislative process is complex."

One result of Long's tendency to look far down the road is a reluctance to bear a grudge. Senators say Long looks for allies wherever he can find them on a given issue, regardless of what they might have said about him or he about them on the issue before.

No senator has clashed more often with Long over the years than Edward M. Kennedy, D-Mass., who ousted him as majority whip in 1969 and consistently tries to rewrite Finance Committee tax bills on the Senate floor. Long's

The Powers of Finance

When the Senate passed a resolution in February 1977 reducing the number of committees and rearranging their jurisdictions, Finance and its immense turf were left untouched. To many observers, this was a graphic symbol of Chairman Long's power and personal influence.

"There was no way our committee was going to do anything to damage the substantive power of the Finance Committee," said one expert who helped draft the reforms. "There was no question that the implicit shadow of Russell Long was over the process. People were not willing to buck him. When Long saw something happening that would take away from his power, he would simply say, 'I don't want that'."

When the committee reform proposals reached the Senate floor, even Kennedy and other senators who routinely challenge Long on tax matters chose not to take on the Finance Committee.

As a result, the formal jurisdiction of the Finance Committee now stands as follows:

- Bonded debt of the United States.
- Customs, collection districts and ports of entry and delivery.
- Deposit of public moneys.
- General revenue sharing.
- Health programs under the Social Security Act and health programs financed by a specific tax or trust fund.
- National Social Security.
- Reciprocal trade agreements.
- Revenue measures generally.
- Tariffs and import quotas.
- Transportation of dutiable goods.

The one major challenge to Long's authority came over the question of subcommittees. And it was the Republican minority on Finance that argued most strongly against decentralizing power and in favor of keeping it under Long's full committee gavel.

"Many people who do not agree with him often lose," Packwood said then in defending Long. "They lose when they have a fair fight in committee, and they come on the floor and have a fair fight, and they lose; and they think that somehow it is because we do not have subcommittees."

aides have told lobbyists privately that the chairman likes nothing better than to defeat Kennedy in public. Yet visitors to the Senate chamber have often found Kennedy and Long engaged in amiable conversation, talking strategy or sharing a joke.

Going Along

The work of the Finance Committee is done in a small hearing room, often packed to overcrowding, with senators seated casually around a series of tables strewn with books and papers. Long avoids using the raised, horseshoe-shaped platforms common on most committees. The situation helps give Finance Committee meetings an air of informality that many observers think is as much a part of Long's strategy as his talking and bargaining. "Long's personality helps make it a bull session of colleagues," said one lobbyist.

In a situation like that, it becomes difficult for some senators to resist going along with what another "one of the boys" wants done. And the informality of the setting makes it easier for Long to maintain a casual procedure.

In many cases, proposals are not brought to a formal vote. Or senators are not all clear what the vote is about. If the consensus goes Long's way, he can point out afterward that a decision had been reached during the meeting. If it goes against him, he can say later that there was no real decision at all.

"I think I can play as well by the rule book as the other guy," Long has noted, "as long as I know what the rules are." Some watchers of the Finance Committee would add that he can play even better when there are few rules at all.

The whole procedure is frustrating to lobbyists like Pietz, Nader's tax specialist. "They sit around the table," he said. "They mumble. Half the people in the room can't hear. They banter. If a senator tries to win an argument on the merits, he's personally offending Russell."

It is nearly unanimous that Chairman Long wins most of the arguments he is involved in. But there is widespread disagreement about how fair he is in doing it. Some of the tax reform faction believes Long manipulates the committee procedures to deny them a hearing. Others on the same side of the question do not think so.

Changing Procedures

It is clear that the Finance Committee was not a very democratic operation under the late Harry F. Byrd, D-Va. (1933-65), who was chairman from 1955 until his retirement in 1965, or in the early years under Long, who succeeded him.

"When I first came there, the Finance Committee was the most closed operation on the Hill," said one former aide who arrived in the late 1960s to work with liberal Democrats on the committee. "You couldn't find out even days later what had gone on. You couldn't get committee staff to return your phone calls. . . . The lobbyists always found out. If you needed to know something, you had to call a lobbyist so you could tell your senator."

Committee markup sessions were held in secret in those days, as they were until the Senate passed "sunshine" legislation in 1973 and 1975 that forced nearly all committees to meet in public. Reporters, lobbyists for citizens' groups and aides to most senators had no first-hand knowledge of what went on. Some corporate lobbyists did manage to get inside as technical advisers.

The other thing that often remained secret was the purpose of the amendments that were being discussed. No transcripts of markup sessions were kept. Reporters were given no written explanation of key legislative provisions. "They had only two ways to describe tax amendments," the ex-aide said. " 'Technical,' or 'to end discrimination.' No matter how much money they would cost, that's what they would call them."

The Finance Committee now marks up all major bills in open session. It has made a great deal of difference in coverage of the legislation. But has it made a difference in the substance? "I don't see that open sessions changed anything at all," Packwood said. "We still do the same things and vote the same things."

Although Long has complained at times about the awkwardness of open sessions, they are no longer an important issue to most lobbyists or members of the committee. But the question of secrecy in the committee's explanation of its work does come up from time to time.

In marking up the 1976 tax bill, the Finance Committee adopted a string of narrow-purpose amendments whose beneficiaries were not identified or even known to many members of the committee. Eileen Shanahan, at that time a reporter for *The New York Times,* investigated one amendment, proposed by Robert Dole, R-Kan., and wrote that it appeared likely to provide specific financial help for the Long family's oil interests in Louisiana. Long said he had been unaware that the provision could benefit several members of his family. He subsequently sponsored an amendment drawn to keep them from benefiting.

But the surrounding controversy had a strong effect on the committee. Even Nelson, who is normally reluctant to confront Long, publicly criticized the procedure. Several weeks later, while the Senate debated the tax bill, the committee went back over all the narrow-purpose amendments and distributed statements identifying the beneficiaries of each, something it had never done before. Upon reconsideration, the committee dropped or modified a number of the amendments.

In recent years the committee has been making transcripts of the markup sessions available to the public. Some tax reform advocates believe the committee no longer has a serious procedural problem. "It's a democratic committee," said James S. Byrne, formerly of Tax Analysts and Advocates. "You can reconsider a vote on anything. You can even phone in your vote." Byrne believes Long has complied adequately with the demands of the new "sunshine" era in the Senate.

Staffing

Like Ways and Means in the House, Finance is served by two staffs. The staff of the Joint Committee on Taxation is nonpartisan and exists to provide technical information and legislative expertise to both parties on both Finance and Ways and Means. When Laurence N. Woodworth, its longtime chief of staff, left, he was replaced by another committee veteran, Bernard M. Shapiro. Although Woodworth and other top joint committee staff members have been close to Long over the years, they have had to balance loyalty to him and to the Finance Committee Democrats with the other obligations of their bipartisan role.

The Finance Committee staff has always been small. Under Byrd's chairmanship it consisted of a handful of personal aides responsible only to the chairman. Long expanded it considerably after 1966, bringing in tax specialist Thomas Vail as chief counsel and adding another tax lawyer and an economist. Vail died in 1974 and was replaced by Michael Stern. The committee staff has expanded to 29 under Stern but remains far smaller than the

"When somebody is so smart he can outwit somebody else, people get the impression he is devious. In Russell's case, it's just smartness."

—Sen. Bob Packwood, R-Ore.

70 member staff of the Joint Committee on Taxation, and more oriented to the personal concerns of the committee Democrats. There are few spots allotted specifically for the Republicans, and observers say the minority staff is not sufficient to play a significant role on most committee matters.

Each senator on the committee is also entitled to one personal aide who spends full time on Finance matters. But there are complaints that these aides, unless their senators are frequent allies of Long, often find it difficult to keep up with the proceedings. "They're almost like lobbyists," said one tax reform advocate, "dealing with Stern and the staff. They're not insiders. They don't always know what is going on."

Conservative Posture

Supporters of tax reform have charged repeatedly over the years that the Finance Committee is more conservative than the Senate as a whole. Most studies have tended to confirm this. Political scientist Thomas Reese, in a recent study, found that Democrats on Finance throughout the postwar years tended to be lower in party unity voting than other Democrats. He also noted that in years when conservatives were most influential in the Democratic leadership, they often persuaded senior conservative colleagues to join the committee in order to block anti-establishment junior members from going on and challenging tax orthodoxy.

J. W. Fulbright, D-Ark. (1945-74), is said to have joined Finance in 1961 only to stop William Proxmire, D-Wis., who had by then developed a reputation as a Senate rebel on tax and financial matters. Reese also reports that Lyndon B. Johnson went on the committee in the 1950s to block Paul H. Douglas, D-Ill. (1949-67), an articulate crusader for tax revision. Douglas finally got a slot on the committee in 1956. "I sometimes suspected," Douglas wrote years later, "that the major qualification of most aspirants for membership on the Finance Committee was a secret pledge or agreement to defend the oil depletion allowance against all attacks."

Long's own allegiance to the oil industry has been a focus for criticism of the Finance Committee over the years. He has never made a secret of it, telling reporters frequently that he would not be allowed to continue representing Louisiana in Congress if he failed to defend one of the state's most important industries. It is only when the criticism borders on accusations of corruption that he adopts a more defensive posture.

In a 1970 book, *The Politics of Finance,* political scientist John Manley quoted one liberal Democrat who finally made it to Finance after he had enough seniority that no one could block him: "I could have had the Capitol dome if I gave up my interest in getting on Finance. The lobbyists in Washington would have done anything to keep me off the Finance Committee. . . . And I've been driving them crazy ever since just to prove to them how right they were."

Reese says most senators join Finance not because they have policy goals, as Proxmire and Douglas had, but because they think they can help constituents economically and themselves politically. But he adds that the most serious problem for the tax reform side is that even those who do have liberal policy goals in general submerge them on the committee to the desire to get along with the chairman. "They see no reason to fight him on tax reform," Reese argued, "an issue they feel gains them few votes in their states. In addition, they are convinced that Long

"I think Russell Long has a great respect for the presidency. He's also a realist and he's not interested in fighting any hopeless battles. And he'll tell the President that."

—Sen. Lloyd Bentsen,
D-Texas

cannot be beat in the committee. But their fear of losing his friendship and his help on other issues keeps them from even challenging Long on the Senate floor where he can be beat."

Others point out that the liberals who do go on the committee often place its tedious tax work secondary to more glamorous pursuits on other committees, attending to Finance mainly to fulfill constituent needs. "Only the fanatics make Finance their main concern," said a former staff member. "Very few people spend any time on it at all. If Nader thinks he's going to find people willing to devote themselves single-handedly to Finance Committee business, he's crazy."

Whatever the reason, the committee in recent years has developed a relatively bipartisan consensus in favor of tax incentives for the business community and against the wholesale elimination of tax expenditures, as Nader and others continue to recommend. In many cases, this has taken in virtually the entire Republican side of the aisle, and most of the Democrats just below Long on the majority side, leaving liberals far short of the votes to challenge Long successfully within the committee.

The senator who most symbolized tax reformers' frustrations in recent years was Walter F. Mondale, D-Minn. (1964-76), now Vice President of the United States. Placed on the committee in 1973, partly at the insistence of liberal Democrats who felt they needed a stronger voice, Mondale rarely fought Long on any important tax issue. On the 1976 tax bill, he voted to keep the existing provision allowing exporters to defer payment of taxes on half their foreign trade earnings. The Nader forces called this one of the most unnecessary expenditures in the tax code. Mondale said it was important to Minnesota companies like Minneapolis Honeywell and Minnesota Mining and Manufacturing.

Also, Mondale told Finlay Lewis of *The Minneapolis Tribune,* it was just not worth his time to argue with Long. "I have to live in the real world," he said, "and I don't want to get isolated on the committee as a lone squeaking mouse." Mondale said he could accomplish more for causes he believed in — like child care and aid to the elderly — by cooperating with Long.

Varying Effectiveness

In the past several years, tax reformers have had to drop down several positions in seniority to find much sympathy with their views. Next to Long in seniority, and by common consent next to him in influence, is Herman E. Talmadge, D-Ga., who chairs the Agriculture, Nutrition and Forestry Committee but also serves on Finance.

"There's no doubt he runs that committee. Not even Wilbur Mills was like this."

—Sen. Spark M. Matsunaga
D-Hawaii

"Talmadge knows the committee and does his homework," said one tax lawyer. "He's very effective. If I were a lobbyist and I couldn't get to Long, I'd go to Talmadge. I might go to him first anyway. He's exactly what the liberals want in a senator — but he does it for the wrong side." Talmadge has rarely exercised his influence by arguing in the committee. He is usually there, but he sometimes sits through entire sessions without saying anything.

Between meetings, however, he is the most important member next to Long. "He talks a lot to the chairman," said one senator. "After the meetings you find Talmadge and Long, just the two of them, involved in serious discussions."

One of the things they talk about is their shared belief that too many people are on welfare who ought to work. Long invented the earned income tax credit, through which welfare families are given tax incentives to find jobs. Talmadge's program is the Work Incentive (WIN) program, which requires them to search for jobs and offers training to succeed in them.

Talmadge chairs the Health Subcommittee, one of the few subcommittees on Finance that is thought to have much independence from the chairman. Talmadge has used the subcommittee to develop cost control and antifraud bills for the Medicare program. Sources say that because Long and Talmadge think alike on most health matters, Long allows him considerable leeway.

Ribicoff of Connecticut, immediately below Talmadge, votes with Long on tax matters although he is far more liberal on issues outside the Finance Committee's jurisdiction. He is a close personal friend of Long, and cosponsor with him of limited national health insurance legislation covering catastrophic illnesses. A former U.S. Secretary of Health, Education and Welfare, Ribicoff has sought to use the Finance Committee to establish tuition tax credits for parents of college students. He fought — against Long — for President Nixon's family assistance welfare plan in 1970 and 1971. "If you're a liberal, you like Ribicoff on welfare and health," said one tax reformer. "But he's a disaster on taxes. He never shows up."

Harry F. Byrd Jr., Va., next in line, is more conservative than Long on most issues and comfortable philosophically with the Republican side. He caucuses with Democrats in the full Senate but has been elected twice as an independent and is only nominally a member of the majority.

One of Byrd's greatest interests on the committee is the national debt. A staunch advocate of a balanced budget, he sometimes asks Treasury Department witnesses what the extent of the debt is on a given day, and how much it has increased during the preceding 24 hours. Byrd

chairs the Subcommittee on Taxation and Debt Management Generally. The panel is one whose jurisdiction is entirely under Long's control.

Nelson of Wisconsin takes a considerable interest in Social Security matters, and chairs a subcommittee on the subject. He occasionally votes against Long on tax matters, but rarely chooses to confront him, which disappoints Naderites and other tax reform specialists. He has been extremely reluctant to speak against the committee position when bills come to the floor.

Mike Gravel of Alaska and Lloyd Bentsen of Texas both represent energy-producing states, and are frequent defenders of oil interests. While Bentsen is conservative on most economic issues and has few ideological disputes with Long, he is willing to argue with him on occasion. It was Bentsen who led the fight within Finance in 1977 for a stronger subcommittee role.

"I've disagreed with Long on many procedural matters," Bentsen said, "but I don't have a confrontation. I don't take him on in the press." Bentsen played a key role during consideration of complex pension legislation in 1974. He chairs a pension subcommittee. Gravel is less frequent in his committee attendance than Bentsen, and plays a smaller role on most issues. He spoke on the Senate floor in 1977 in favor of the subcommittee idea.

Below them in seniority are Matsunaga and Daniel Patrick Moynihan, D-N.Y., who joined the committee in 1977. Moynihan, chairman of the Subcommittee on Public Assistance, has attracted considerable attention because of his background as a welfare expert — he drafted much of the Nixon family assistance plan in 1970.

New liberal Democrats who were added to the committee in 1979 include Max Baucus of Montana and Bill Bradley of New Jersey. A third Democratic newcomer, David L. Boren of Oklahoma, vowed to protect his state's oil industry, a job with which Long is more than willing to help.

Republican Impact

Most observers feel the Republican side on Finance lost some of its impact when Wallace F. Bennett, Utah (1951-74), retired. A former president of the National Association of Manufacturers and a rigid conservative, Bennett was respected as a knowledgeable and competent legislator by the most liberal members of the committee.

The retirement of Carl T. Curtis of Nebraska and Clifford P. Hansen of Wyoming, both over 60 years of age, left Robert Dole of Kansas and Bob Packwood of Oregon as the two senior Republicans on the committee. This meant a generational change on the Republican side, with all the GOP committee members less than age 60.

But Republicans on Finance continue to face the question of whether to cooperate with Long, obtaining favors at the cost of a party identity, or to insist on alternative positions, knowing that it will freeze them out of many committee decisions. "When you're a small minority, you almost have to work with the other side," said Roth of Delaware, a quiet but respected budget specialist who ranks third among the eight GOP members of the committee.

But Danforth of Missouri, who joined the committee in 1977, leans toward the other approach. "We are in the minority," he said. "What we can accomplish by going along is relatively modest. What we need is a statement of alternatives." Pietz of the Nader organization sides with Danforth — he thinks the Republicans lost out by agreeing to help Long so often. "Russell just wraps the Republicans around his finger," he said. "He doesn't have to give them anything, and he knows that they'll always vote with him. If they began to be like Republicans on Ways and Means, they could be effective."

With the addition of four new members in 1979, the Republican contingent was somewhat more liberal than in the last Congress. Filling out the Republican roster were John H. Chafee, R.I.; H. John Heinz III, Pa.; David Durenberger, Minn.; and Malcolm Wallop, Wyo., another spokesman for an energy-producing state. This group offered little prospect of serious dissidence, with the possible exception of Heinz.

Record on Taxes

Committee members who are the least fond of tax reformers accuse them of turning too many committee votes into moral issues, making all differences of opinion appear to be questions of right and wrong. Packwood is particularly indignant about this.

"They attempt to portray members as big-bellied, key-chain-wearing reactionaries because they believe in tax expenditures rather than direct subsidies," Packwood said. "When they describe you as selfish, you tend to become insulted and vote against them on everything."

Tax reformer Pietz responded that he did not consider Packwood selfish. "Packwood is one of the most honest men in the Senate," he said. "But on the issues, he's terrible. He's a reactionary to almost a dangerous degree."

The increased visibility of tax reform lobbyists like Pietz has made them a controversial issue among the members of Finance. Some senators think they have the competence of corporate lobbyists and lack only the resources to win their case. Others disagree.

"They don't have the technique of the professional lobbyist," Matsunaga said. "The oil companies have an ex-senator, ex-congressman, somebody who knows the workings of the Senate. The public lobbyists don't have the entree — they come at you cold, and frequently without the polish of the lobbyist on the other side. Their presentation is crude, they come unprepared, most of it is based on emotion rather than fact."

Former member Floyd K. Haskell, D-Colo. (1973-79), disagreed with that. "It's a matter of numbers, of bodies," he said. "Some of the tax reform lobbyists are very competent folks. They know what they are talking about. But they lose out on sheer numbers."

Floor Challenges

Sheer numbers are also the reason the tax reformers have no better luck on the Senate floor than they do in the Finance Committee. The full Senate has developed a reputation over the years as the most generous spot in town for virtually any special interest seeking a tax advantage. With members voting for each others' narrow-purpose amendments in order to guarantee support for their own, tax bills become the gift-laden "Christmas trees" that editorial writers love to complain about.

The Finance Committee, criticized by liberals for adding too many revenue-losing tax breaks during markup, often finds itself arguing on the floor against decorating the tree even further.

Nevertheless, some critics complain that the few senators who are willing to vote against Long in the Finance Committee are rarely the ones to stand up against him on the Senate floor. "It's a crime that the brunt of tax reform isn't carried by someone on the committee," one senator said. "Kennedy deserves a great deal of credit." One tax lobbyist remarked that Ted Kennedy was "willing to take the battles to the floor. He's got terrific backup, terrific advice, and he's a learner."

One observer close to the committee said these critics fail to look at the situation from the committee's point of view. "It's a plaything for Kennedy," he said. "he can offer his amendments and walk away from it. He isn't going to be on the conference committee. He doesn't have to get along with Long all year. The same with Hollings [Ernest F. Hollings, a South Carolina Democrat]."

Whoever leads the argument against Long on the floor almost always loses. "Long controls 10-20 votes on the floor," said Pietz. "On a liberal-conservative split on tax reform, there are maybe 35 tax reform votes. But there are 10-20 swing votes, and Russell gets those. You could watch them walk into the chamber [in 1976] and get their signal from Russell Long on how to vote. And in the end they got their goodies."

Few of Long's opponents have expressed their frustrations as drastically as William Proxmire, D-Wis., did after a floor fight in 1964: "If a man murdered a crippled, enfeebled orphan at high noon on the public square in plain view of a thousand people, I am convinced after today's performance that if the senator from Louisiana represented the guilty murderer, the jury would not only find the murderer innocent, they would award the defendant a million dollars on the ground that the victim had provoked him."

Thomas Reese studied Senate votes on tax bills between 1945 and 1975, and found that Finance was reversed on the floor 18 percent of the time, compared to 12 percent for the House Ways and Means Committee. Unlike Finance, Ways and Means brought most of its tax bills to the floor under closed rules in which individuals could not offer amendments.

But Reese also found that when a majority of Finance Republicans agreed with a majority of Finance Democrats, the reversal rate was only 9 percent. He added that in most of the reversals, a majority of the Democrats on the committee were on the winning side on the floor.

Conference Record

In the years when Wilbur Mills was chairman of Ways and Means in the House, the common impression was that Mills won more often than he lost in conferences with Long and the Senate. One reason was that the House-passed bill was usually close to what Mills and the House itself

Long "has a degree of confidence that his views will ultimately prevail. That allows him to accept temporary setbacks."

—Sen. John C. Danforth, R-Mo.

actually wanted, while the Senate, which had no limits on floor amendments, had added numerous provisions Long did not ask for and chose not to fight for in conference.

So on a numerical basis, the Senate was always forced to recede from more of its amendments than the House. But even during Mills' heyday, Long often won on issues that he cared about.

Long himself said in 1971 that he won in conference most of the time. "My impression," he said, "is that we've been successful in persuading the House to take about two-thirds of the things we initiate. And I wouldn't expect to do any better than that no matter who I was conferring with."

Rep. Barber B. Conable Jr., R-N.Y., senior Republican on Ways and Means, has been attending conferences with Long for years. "It used to be that Wilbur Mills quite dominated the conference," Conable said. "My impression is that the Senate is restraining its enthusiasms a little better on the floor now and coming out better in conferences."

Since Al Ullman, D-Ore., took over as Ways and Means chairman in 1975, the most important conferences have been on tax bills in 1975 and 1976, the 1977 stimulus tax bill and energy taxes in 1978.

The general consensus in 1975 was that Long got what was most important to him, preservation of the oil depletion allowance for most independent producers. About $8 billion in amendments added on the Senate floor were dropped, however, giving the House its usual mathematical advantage in provisions won and lost.

In the 1977 conference, the major difference of opinion between Ullman and Long was over tax credits for new hiring by employers vs. increased tax credits for investment. Ullman favored the employer credit. Ullman won. "Russell has established his strength vis-a-vis Ullman," Conable said. "He doesn't need to prove it any more."

In 1975 the committee ignored a battered, House-passed energy tax bill, but eventually added most of its provisions to the omnibus tax revision bill in 1976. The provisions included credits for home insulation and installation of solar energy equipment, and investment credits for experimental technologies. They were still in the bill as passed by the Senate but were dropped in conference, significantly reducing the revenue loss in the bill. The Finance Committee then agreed to report the energy tax provisions separately, but took no further action.

Long's committee wasn't any more sympathetic toward Carter's proposals for energy taxes in 1977. After rejecting virtually all of the administration energy tax proposals, the Finance Committee wrote its own vastly different energy tax bill. Rather than trying to force conservation through penalty taxes, the committee bill tried to induce additional energy production primarily through tax incentives to industry.

Although Congress continued work on the energy bill in 1978, the tax conferees held no meetings between December 1977 and July 1978 on energy taxes, primarily because Long insisted that the gas pricing controversy be resolved before the tax issues were settled. Long had announced that the crude oil tax could not pass the Senate in 1978, stating that outraged public reaction to the stiff increases in Social Security taxes passed by Congress in 1977 made passage of the oil tax impossible in an election year. Not until late in September 1978, after the Senate had voted on gas pricing, did the conferees again turn their attention to energy taxes. By then the crude oil tax was considered officially dead. Carter's proposal for taxes on industrial use of oil and gas was also killed in conference. The final energy bill did include tax credits for home insulation and a tax on "gas guzzling" cars.

Philosophical Disputes

The questions that divide the Nader-Kennedy side from Long and most of the business community are essentially simple ones. But they are not easy to answer.

The federal government has a limited number of ways it can help people and businesses. It can vote them money directly, through the appropriations process. It can guarantee their loans. It can reduce their taxes, either by allowing deductions from income or, as Democrats have increasingly preferred in recent years, by providing a dollar-for-dollar credit on the tax payment itself.

All these kinds of financial help are federal expenditures of a sort. If they come through the tax code, they are tax expenditures — or if that word is unacceptable, tax incentives.

"I don't use the word 'tax expenditures'," said Bentsen. "I use 'tax incentives.' If you use tax expenditures you assume all income belongs to the government to begin with. The alternative to incentives is to have a government agency hand it out."

The consensus of the liberal economic community in recent years, however, has been that whatever you call them, most tax breaks are a bad policy. The argument is that they contain a built-in bias in favor of the rich, who know how to use the tax system and who pay a higher percentage of their income in tax to begin with. Critics say tax breaks are also difficult to measure in their precise impact. The conclusion is that the Internal Revenue system should be used primarily to raise money, and not to further social or economic goals.

This is the position of Edward Kennedy and Ralph Nader. It was the position Jimmy Carter generally espoused in his 1976 presidential campaign. It is not the position of a majority of the Senate Finance Committee.

In some ways, the most conservative members of the committee come closest to the tax reform position. They argue that the tax system should encourage private business, but they otherwise favor a relatively simple tax system, free of social policy experiments.

On the other side are the more moderate Republicans, such as Packwood and Danforth, who not only want the tax code to stimulate business but to serve as an instrument of social policy as well. They share some of the progressive policy goals of Kennedy but reject the argument that tax incentives are the wrong way to do it. Packwood argued successfully on the Senate floor in 1977 that expanded tax credits to private campaign contributors should be tried as an alternative to federal subsidies for congressional candidates.

Long himself is clearly in favor of using the tax code to do whatever he thinks ought to be done. "You can do a lot more than raise money with those tax laws," he told an interviewer in 1977. "You can speed up the economy or slow it down. You can encourage people to do all sorts of things that they ought to be doing for their own good as well as the good of the country."

Critics have often said Long feels that way only because the tax system is the only tool the Finance Committee has. Long himself has come close to admitting this. "When it comes to helping homeowners," he said in 1975, "if I were on the Banking Committee I'd favor a loan guarantee for them because they would be in my jurisdiction, but since I'm on the Finance Committee I favor the use of tax credits."

Comments like that have led some observers to the conclusion that Long has no ideology at all — except to win arguments and have fun doing it. "Long is satisfied to be Mr. Tax," said Byrne, "and have *The Wall Street Journal* and CBS call him up for his opinion. He doesn't have a lot of substantive policy goals."

'Mixed Populist'

Pietz thinks that even Long's friendship with the business community is essentially a tactic. "Why is Long so susceptible to business lobbying? Because he knows other people are, and the way to win is to get the business on your side."

But others see in Long's actions over the years a curious but consistent mixture of populism and deference to free enterprise, with a few remnants of the more rebellious populism of his father, Huey. "He's got that mixed populist personality," said Jack Moskowitz, former tax lobbyist for Common Cause. "He'll go to extremes to punish wayward fathers. He knows that's politically popular. But he's also the inventor of the earned income credit."

In a number of interviews in recent years, Long has made clear his commitment to the business community. "We're paying less than one half of 1 percent of our gross national product," he told one interviewer, "to these very successful people who are providing us the leadership for our democratic capitalist system. These are the people who through hard work, talent and good judgment rise to the top. The government couldn't provide this kind of leadership for this economic system if it were paying 10 times as much. It couldn't do it half as well."

Unlike other southern Democrats, Long does not base his opposition to most liberal schemes on pure fiscal conservatism. He has been more than willing over the years to spend huge sums on social programs he is convinced will work. Long's criticisms of most welfare proposals, for example, are based more on his feeling that too high a floor under income encourages laziness and undermines the work ethic.

In July 1977 the committee debated Matsunaga's proposal to make residents of Puerto Rico and other U.S. possessions eligible for Supplemental Security Income (SSI) payments to needy aged, blind and disabled persons. They have not been eligible since the program began.

Long argued against it, not because of the $150 million it would cost but because he did not want to see any more people added to the SSI rolls. "The welfare program is so attractive down there," Long said, 'that it's hard to get anybody to work. . . . The people who are paying for this in the long run are going to be compelled to revolt." Long offered to support increased federal matching money to help Puerto Rico pay its existing welfare costs — as long as it would not add new people to the rolls.

Long has been heard to say that he feels personally responsible for only three areas of tax policy. One is the earned income credit; a second is the income tax checkoff system used to finance presidential general election campaigns; the third is the tax credit for firms that have employee stock ownership plans. It is this last idea, commonly abbreviated ESOP, that strikes observers as being the closest thing in Long's philosophy to his father's platform of "share the wealth." "If Russell Long could tie the earned income credit to the ESOP program," Packwood said, "we'd all have Nirvana as far as he was concerned."

What is 'Reform'?

"Tax reform" has become a catch phrase for liberals seeking to close what they consider loopholes in the nation's tax laws. Finance Committee Chairman Long scorns the term.

"A reform by definition means a change for the better or an improvement of something that exists," Long told the Senate in 1975. "I do not know of any senator or any member of the House who ever introduced a bill who did not believe the country would be better off" if it were enacted.

Recalling that the word reform was removed from the title of the 1974 trade act at his insistence, Long said Congress should "stop playing games with the American people, and start facing these things for what they are. What is a loophole? That is something that benefits the other guy. If it benefits you, it is tax reform."

Long did not attempt to remove the word reform from the title of the 1976 Tax Reform Act. And liberals who looked upon the measure as a loophole-ridden travesty of reform were frustrated in their attempts to do so.

Long and Carter

On some issues, Russell Long appears to have given President Carter the benefit of whatever doubts exist in his mind. Less than a month after Carter was elected, Long told Carter to be liberal in his recommendations for an economic stimulus. When Carter recommended a $50 rebate for individual taxpayers, Long stuck with him despite widespread congressional criticism and Long's own comparison of such rebates to "throwing $50 bills off the top of the Washington monument." Long was still for the rebate in April 1977 until Carter announced it was no longer necessary.

To Carter's 1977 welfare initiative, Long was less than kind. After waiting over a week to say anything about the plan, Long issued a statement saying it would be foolish to take such a drastic step nationally without trying local pilot programs first. But his reaction left enough ambiguity to allow supporters of the plan to feel Long could be brought around eventually.

"The President is doing the best he can, as a man from Georgia, to come up here and try to run things," Long told his committee. "He learns something new every day." "I think Russell Long has a great respect for the presidency," said Bentsen. "He's also a realist and he's not interested in fighting any hopeless battles. And he'll tell the president that."

When Congress failed to pass President Carter's energy bill in 1977, the administration was faulted in part for poor lobbying and for consulting too little with the key committee chairmen. The various tax proposals in the bills were not thoroughly checked out with Sen. Long's Finance Committee. Since the energy package was heavily reliant on tax incentives and disincentives, the failure to sign on members of the taxwriting committee contributed largely to that committee's hostility to several crucial pieces of the program, the crude oil equalization tax and the industrial energy users' tax. When Congress finally presented Carter with a five-part energy package in 1978, the gasoline tax had been dropped and the key element — a tax on domestic

Long has "that mixed populist personality. He'll go to extremes to punish wayward fathers.... But he's also the inventor of the earned income credit."

—Jack Moskowitz, former tax lobbyist for Common Cause

crude oil to raise prices to world levels — had been defeated.

In 1979, the president's hospital cost control bill and national health plan both came under the scrutiny of Long's committee. Hospital cost control, Carter's centerpiece anti-inflation proposal, was flatly rejected by the Finance Committee in July. Long had committed himself to voting for the Carter plan but according to committee sources "he expected to be voting in the minority." The committee instead reported out a Medicare-Medicaid reimbursement bill.

Long avoided a flat endorsement of the national health insurance plan announced by Carter in June 1979. Long was noncommittal at Carter's press conference but later repeated assurances that he could support some Medicare and Medicaid improvements as well as catastrophic coverage. Long promised only that "the Finance Committee will study the president's recommendations and add some of our own and bring forth a bill."

By mid-1979, Long was off and running and had opponents of catastrophic health insurance worried; he had already moved his committee through a series of major decisions on new catastrophic health benefits, before either President Carter or Sen. Kennedy had even introduced their more extensive health insurance plans. ∎

Congressional Oversight

CQ

Legislative Oversight of Agencies, Programs

Over the years, Congress has created a vast array of agencies and programs, but often it has paid only scant attention to how the agencies are operating or the programs administered. Aware of this defect, Congress has demonstrated its concern for better oversight periodically since 1946 when it first officially recognized its responsibility for such activity in the Legislative Reorganization Act (PL 79-601). Its problem since then has been to put its intent into practice. Propelled by its struggle to regain power from the executive branch, Congress moved in 1974 to improve its conduct of oversight when it passed the Congressional Budget and Impoundment Act (PL 93-344) and the House Committee Reform Amendments (H Res 988).

But members and Capitol Hill observers were divided in their predictions as to whether Congress would carry out oversight any more vigorously than in the past. Some said that Congress finally had given itself the tools to carry out effective, comprehensive oversight and was determined to use them.

Others worried that Congress still lacked the will to undertake the task and that all the institutional tinkering would not change the final result.

An aide to Rep. John B. Anderson, R-Ill., summed up the problem: "The subjects of congressional investigations are scandals, corruption a la Watergate, or executive branch hanky-panky or law twisting. These are the things that bring headlines and turn on the TV kleig lights and the public.

"But oversight, unless it turns up a scandal or gross maladministration, is dull and politically dangerous. If effective oversight turns up an ineffective program which results in its proposed elimination, the greatest hue and cry goes up from those with a vested interest in the program, and not from taxpayers overjoyed at the prospect of reduced federal spending."

Oversight Tools

Congress exercises its oversight over federal agencies in numerous ways, the most fundamental of which is in the very establishment of new agencies and commissions and the use of the authorizing legislation to spell out the agencies' powers and limitations. And, too, members of Congress have a substantial input into the process of selecting nominees, who are then subject to Senate confirmation.

Once the agencies are established, Congress has the responsibility to see that they act in accordance with the purposes of the legislation under which they were established and that they remain politically accountable. Congress also has a responsibility to examine agency practices in light of possible abuses, costs and benefits of regulation, possible reforms and agency responsiveness to the elusive "public interest."

The appropriations process enables House and Senate Appropriations committees to scrutinize proposed agency budgets. Oversight through appropriations has been strengthened by the fact that it generally has come to involve annual, rather than periodic, review of agency budgets. In approving them, Congress specifies the purposes for which funds are to be used. Such specification in dollar terms is a direct and unambiguous method of control.

Congress also exercises control through the authorization process. A number of agencies have been given permanent authorization status. In recent years, Congress has enacted legislation requiring periodic authorization for a number of agencies, among them the Consumer Product Safety Commission and Federal Trade Commission (reauthorization every three years). Although periodic reauthorization gives Congress an opportunity to review a wide spectrum of agency operations and their *raison d'être,* most of the agencies' authorizing statutes have been couched in vague generalities, giving them considerable leeway in the performance of their functions — in some cases, running counter to congressional intent. Although Congress has amended statutes to make them more specific, more frequently amendments to the original authorizing legislation have involved giving an agency new powers.

Besides these "formal" oversight powers, Congress has a number of other tools at its disposal to oversee executive branch agencies, among them, hearings, informal contacts and directives contained in committee reports. Investigations by committees and by the General Accounting Office, Congress' investigative arm, also serve as a means to gain information and publicize the performance of agencies.

Although the number of oversight hearings has been steadily increasing, the Senate Governmental Affairs Committee concluded in a February 1977 report that

one of the most notable features of oversight by nonappropriating committees is its sporadic, unsystematic functioning. . . . This *ad hoc* approach to oversight is particularly evident in the regulatory area. Only those agencies with a periodic authorization are actually guaranteed review by a legislative committee. Between authorization periods, there may or may not be regular oversight hearings called. While the appropriations committees respond to a set agenda, other committees rarely do. The wide range of techniques available to legislative committees are seldom marshaled for an annual review. . . . Oversight tends to be done on a crisis basis only . . . in response to a newspaper article, a complaint from a constituent or special interest group, or information from a disgruntled agency employee.

The Senate committee study noted several obstacles to effective congressional oversight:

● *Committee Structure.* Because several committees usually share jurisdiction over an agency, oversight is fragmented, and coordination and cooperation among them is difficult to achieve — particularly between House and Senate committees.

● *Access to Information.* Committees sometimes have experienced difficulties and delays in obtaining requested information. Or the agency may simply not have it available.

● *Staff Resources.* According to the committee report, the total number of professional staff members on legislative committees having oversight responsibility for the regulatory agencies was fewer than 200, reflecting the great disparity in size between congressional staffs and the agencies they oversee. Perhaps more important is the problem of developing the necessary staff expertise for effective oversight, the report said.

The report noted several more intangible factors that hinder congressional oversight:

> Members of Congress have a multitude of duties and a limited time in which to fulfill them. For many members oversight is simply a low priority. Oversight is often less attractive politically than passing new legislation, with which a member can receive public identification. . . .

> Oversight suffers ... when committees are "stacked" with members who share similar backgrounds and values with the agencies they are charged with overseeing. Oversight is also inhibited by the alliance that often develops between the agencies and the committees. . . . Some committee members may have strong ties, as well, to the industry which is being regulated. These relationships may militate against vigorous oversight, especially when ineffective regulation may be in the industry's interest.

House Reforms

To a greater degree than the Senate, the House in 1975 began to take a look at itself to see how its operations, including oversight performance, could be improved.

In October 1974 it overwhelmingly adopted, 359-7, H Res 988, a committee reorganization plan offered by a Democratic Caucus panel headed by Julia Butler Hansen, D-Wash. (1960-75). H Res 988 required committees with 15 or more members to set up an oversight subcommittee or require their legislative subcommittees to carry out oversight functions. (In January 1975 the size of those committees was increased to more than 20 members.)

Legislative subcommittees carrying out oversight can do it only within their limited jurisdictions. On the other hand, most subcommittees set up specifically to conduct oversight can carry out their work within most of the full committee's jurisdiction, a much broader area.

The Hansen plan required the House Government Operations Committee to report to the House within 60 days after Congress convened on the oversight plans of all the standing committees and on any recommendations for coordinating the activities.

It also gave seven committees — Budget, Armed Services, Education and Labor, Foreign Affairs, Interior and Insular Affairs, Science and Technology, and Small Business — special oversight responsibilities that permit them to cross jurisdictional lines in any investigation.

A key man in setting the tone for oversight in the House during the 94th Congress was Jack Brooks, D-Texas, who became chairman of the Government Operations Committee in 1975.

The committee, which always has had the main oversight responsibility in the House, never was considered a major House committee. Its powers, however, were expanded under H Res 988, which gave it new oversight responsibilities as well as the legislative jurisdiction for revenue sharing. Committee staffers depicted Brooks as a scrappy, partisan chairman who would give the committee a more aggressive cast than it had under Chet Holifield, D-Calif. (1943-75), the previous chairman.

One of Brooks' first moves after taking over the committee was to reorganize the subcommittee jurisdictions. He shifted them from agency lines to functional lines. "This has ended many of the jurisdictional problems we had under the old approach and made the subcommittees more responsive to the important areas of public policy," said one aide.

Senate Oversight

The Senate and House share some of the same problems in coping with oversight chores. But the Senate has some of its own, too. Because it is smaller, the Senate's problems of time, interest and priority are more acute. And the predilections of conservative committee chairmen have often mitigated against vigorous oversight activity.

"The sheer smallness of the Senate and the large number of subcommittees spreads senators so thin that they can't give full attention to carrying out oversight," said Walter Kravitz, a former House Budget Committee staff director.

Thus, the oversight responsibility in many cases is left to the subcommittee staff members, who generally reflect the chairman's attitudes.

As in the House, oversight brings little publicity and often is neglected. "Oversight has appeal only when it brings headlines," said one Senate subcommittee staff member. "If you have an on-going review of a program that prevents graft and corruption, then there's no sex in it." A senator's activity usually is measured by how many bills he has introduced, not how much oversight he has conducted. Overlapping committee jurisdictions also work against carrying out effective oversight. Writing on the problem in 1975, former Sen. Bill Brock, R-Tenn., noted: "With so many different committees covering the same field of public policy, the chances of developing a coherent, integrated program are substantially reduced. Moreover, jurisdictional conflict works to impede the committees' oversight function — everybody's responsibility is nobody's responsibility, as the saying goes."

The problem of overlapping jurisdiction was eased in 1977, when the Senate restructured its committee system.

The 17-member Governmental Affairs Committee is the chief oversight committee in the Senate. Under Rule 25 of the Standing Rules of the Senate, it is charged with reviewing the efficiency and operations of the federal government.

Abraham Ribicoff, D-Conn., who in 1975 took over the chairmanship from retired Sam J. Ervin Jr., D-N.C. (1974-75), has concentrated oversight on energy, his main area of interest. The committee also conducted an extensive study of the federal regulatory agencies.

It also created a new oversight procedures subcommittee, chaired by Sam Nunn, D-Ga., to conduct an informal review of the oversight activities of other Senate committees. Although it was given specific jurisdiction over the General Services Administration, the Nunn subcommittee was established primarily to seek suggestions from other committees on how oversight might be improved.

The panel recognized it faced a delicate task. One committee aide said, "We don't have the mandate the House Government Operations Committee has. That means we have jurisdictional problems any time we start rummaging in somebody else's domain."

History of Oversight Legislation

Congressional concern with oversight of federal programs is a post-World War II phenomenon. It grew out of Congress' desire to check the powers of the executive branch, which had greatly expanded during the war years.

Oversight received its first formal recognition in the 1946 Legislative Reorganization Act, which reformed the committee structure of the House and Senate. Since then, four other pieces of legislation — including two passed in 1974 — have enhanced Congress' oversight authority.

The five foundation blocks of oversight legislation are:

● The Legislative Reorganization Act of 1946 (PL 79-601). Section 136 of the act assigned to each standing committee of Congress the duty of "continuous watchfulness" of the execution of laws by administrative agencies and the study of all pertinent reports the agencies submitted to Congress.

The act created three categories of oversight: 1) committees empowered to authorize appropriations were responsible for the legislative oversight of agencies and programs within their jurisdictions, 2) fiscal review was the responsibility of the Appropriations Committees and 3) investigative oversight was assigned to the Government Operations Committees, which had authority to study the operations of government activities at all levels and review whether they were being carried out economically and efficiently.

● The Intergovernmental Cooperation Act of 1968 (PL 90-577). The act required committees to review grant-in-aid programs that had no expiration dates and to report 1) whether the programs are meeting their intended purposes, 2) the extent to which the objectives could be met without further governmental assistance, 3) whether any changes in the programs are necessary and 4) whether the programs were adequate to meet the growing and changing needs they were designed to support. All programs existing before the legislation was enacted were to be reviewed by committees within four years; all programs subsequently enacted were to be reviewed within four years after they were passed.

● The Legislative Reorganization Act of 1970 (PL 91-510). The Legislative Reference Service in the Library of Congress, which became the Congressional Research Service under the act, was required to make experts available to committees to evaluate legislative proposals.

More important, the research service was required to provide each committee at the beginning of each new Congress with a list of laws under its jurisdiction that were due to expire during the Congress, along with "a list of subjects and policy areas which the committee might profitably analyze in depth."

The Congressional Research Service, however, has given its oversight agenda and list of expiring legislation only to committee chairmen, prompting Republicans to complain that the ranking minority committee members also should receive the reports.

The 1970 act authorized the General Accounting Office (GAO) to review and analyze "the results of government programs and activities, including the making of cost benefit studies," on its initiative or when ordered by either house or a committee.

All committees except Appropriations, House Administration, Senate Rules and Administration, House Rules, House Standards of Official Conduct and Senate Standards and Conduct were required to report at the end of each Congress on their oversight activities.

● The Congressional Budget and Impoundment Control Act of 1974 (PL 93-344). This act created the House and Senate Budget Committees and established the Congressional Budget Office (CBO) as the back-up agency for the committees. The act, besides giving Congress significantly greater control over federal spending and programs, also tightened oversight in several areas. For example, it authorized committees to evaluate federal programs, agencies or laws themselves, to seek outside assistance and to require the affected government agency to carry out the analysis and then report to Congress.

The GAO was ordered to develop and recommend to Congress methods for review and evaluation of government programs and to establish an Office of Program Review and Evaluation.

The Treasury Department and the Office of Management and Budget were required to provide information on federal programs and spending, not only to committees but to the GAO and CBO.

● Committee Reform Amendments of 1974. Passed as H Res 988, the amendments were the product of the House Select Committee on Committees led by Rep. Richard Bolling, D-Mo., and Rep. Dave Martin, R-Neb. (1961-75). After a stiff House fight, the Bolling-Martin recommendations were revised by a committee headed by Rep. Julia Butler Hansen, D-Wash. (1960-75), and appointed by the House Democratic caucus.

The Bolling report would have required that each standing committee except Appropriations establish an oversight subcommittee. It also would have permitted the chairman of the Government Operations Committee, or another member at the direction of the committee, to offer floor amendments to any bill so long as the amendments were related to the committees' oversight findings. Neither provision was included in the amended H Res 988.

Besides rearranging the jurisdictions of several House committees and tightening House procedures, the Hansen plan took several steps toward improving the conduct of oversight by House committees.

H Res 988 gave House legislative standing committees the option of either establishing an oversight subcommittee or requiring their legislative subcommittees to carry out oversight functions. It also gave seven committees special oversight responsibilities that permit them to cross jurisdictional lines in investigations.

The Government Operations Committee was required to submit to the House a report on the oversight plan of all the standing committees.

Although the Governmental Affairs Committee specializes in oversight, it faces several problems in carrying it out. First, it has jurisdiction over government reorganization legislation and spends at least half of its time handling legislative business.

Second, it is not a major Senate committee. That has meant that the members tended to concentrate on their major committee assignments.

Several additional tools for congressional oversight have been proposed in recent years. "Sunset" legislation considered during the 95th Congress would have set time limits on federal programs, thus requiring periodic congressional review and either reauthorization or termination of federal programs. *(Details, p. 93)*

Greater use of the controversial "legislative veto" has also been advocated. The House has attached amendments providing for legislative approval or disapproval of agency regulations to a number of bills. *(Details, p. 89)* ▮

Controversy Surrounds Legislative Veto Use

While the concept of sunset legislation has attracted a broad spectrum of supporters — particularly in the Senate — use of the legislative veto as a technique for congressional oversight has been hotly debated. This controversial mechanism has been the subject of numerous bills that have been introduced in recent years. Some versions of the veto would provide that a ruling would take effect unless one, or both, chambers passed resolutions of disapproval within a certain time period. Others would require that one or both chambers of Congress take affirmative action. And some would provide for resolutions of reconsideration of a rule already in effect.

The House in particular has attempted repeatedly to attach legislative veto provisions to bills, and the Senate has tended to strongly oppose the action. In 1978, for example, controversy over the congressional veto issue led to the defeat of legislation authorizing funding for the Federal Trade Commission for fiscal years 1978-81 (funding for the agency was contained in another bill passed subsequently). The House voted to reject the bill because it did not contain legislative veto provisions endorsed by the House when it passed its original version of the bill. A similar controversy flared up again in 1979 over the FTC authorization bill.

Advocates of the legislative veto have argued that it would help rectify existing inadequacies in the oversight process by providing Congress with a clear-cut and quick means of disapproving (or approving) a proposed regulation. Moreover, it has been contended that the threat of a legislative veto might make agencies more responsive to congressional sentiments.

Opponents of the veto, including the executive branch, have countered with arguments that the mechanism would result in additional delays in the regulatory process, that the 60-day waiting period would cause uncertainties both within the agency and for the regulated industries, and that it would represent an added burden to Congress' already heavy workload. In addition, a 1977 Senate Government Operations Committee report on regulation noted that use of the veto "may wreak havoc with regulatory programs. These programs often involve a series of interrelated rules. The veto of selected parts of such a program could distort or destroy the program."

Background

The congressional veto has attracted considerable bipartisan support in Congress, at least in part because of increasing citizen unhappiness with the peformance of government. But the idea itself is not new.

The first law containing a congressional veto clause was enacted in 1932, when Congress passed a bill allowing President Hoover to reorganize the executive branch.

Hoover signed the bill (PL 72-212), but the following year, at the urging of his attorney general, he vetoed the Urgent Deficiency Bill (HR 13975), which included a provision giving a single committee, the Joint Committee on

Taxation, the power to veto individual tax refunds of more than $20,000.

Hoover's change of position set the pattern for the on-again, off-again attitude of his successors toward legislation containing congressional veto provisions.

President Franklin D. Roosevelt, for example, signed the Lend Lease Act of 1941 (PL 77-11) which contained a congressional veto provision, but at the same time he wrote a private letter to Supreme Court Justice Robert H. Jackson explaining his constitutional objections to the veto clause.

Congress made use of the congressional veto during World War II to provide a check on the broad war-making power it had delegated to the administration. Use of the veto declined during the 1950s and 1960s but mushroomed during the 1970s.

A survey released by the Congressional Research Service in April 1976 identified 196 pieces of legislation enacted from 1932 through 1975 which carried some form of provision for congressional review of executive action. Of these, 89, or nearly half, were enacted since 1970, with 46 enacted in the previous two years alone.

The provisions had been included in bills covering a wide range of issues, with the most frequent use coming in defense, public works, interior, foreign affairs and space legislation. Examples included the 1973 War Powers Act, the Congressional Budget and Impoundment Control Act of 1974 and the Federal Election Campaign Act of 1974.

Provisions of the War Powers Act served as a model for 1976 legislation (HR 3884 — PL 94-412) that empowered Congress, through adoption of a concurrent resolution, to terminate any future national emergency proclaimed by the president.

1975-76 Action

Congressional efforts to impose new controls on the federal bureaucracy increased significantly during the 94th Congress. Use of the congressional veto device in the 94th Congress was primarily in the House; the language was inserted in at least 11 bills and prompted President Ford to veto two of the measures. The concept was resisted in the Senate.

Moreover, the House came within two votes of passing a general congressional veto bill that would have applied the concept to all regulations issued by government departments and agencies. Significantly, this proposal received a substantial majority of the votes on the passage roll call, 265-135, but was rejected nevertheless because the House was operating under a parliamentary procedure that required a two-thirds majority for approval.

Veto Added to Bills. In addition to the general veto bill, which was rejected, the House attempted to add the congressional veto to the following bills.

● **Consumer Product Safety Commission** authorization (S 644): the veto provision, added by the House in 1975,

Congressional Veto: Issues in Dispute

Critics opposed the congressional veto idea on constitutional and practical grounds.

The Office of Management and Budget (OMB), writing on behalf of the Ford administration in October 1975, said the proposal would "both undermine and conflict with the doctrine of separation of powers, wherein [agency] rules are an executive function." Others said the veto procedure would usurp duties of the courts, which review disputed regulations. The Carter administration continued to oppose the veto on these grounds.

Constitutional Objections

The OMB stressed the Justice Department's contention that the veto idea runs counter to Article I, Section 7 of the Constitution, which "clearly indicates that the veto power of the President is intended to apply to all actions of Congress which have the force of law."

The Judiciary Committee responded in its report on the House bill that the veto proposal would not violate the separation of powers principle because legislative, judicial and executive functions are not watertight categories. "The review relates to rulemaking, that aspect of administrative procedure that is obviously legislative in character...," the panel added. "Since this power has been delegated to administrators by Congress it would be anomalous if the Congress were prevented from exercising the limited oversight and option to disapprove regulations contemplated by this bill."

According to H. Lee Watson, a California lawyer who has studied the issue, "These devices may shift the balance of government power toward Congress and allow the legislative branch to dominate the executive."

Rep. Robert F. Drinan, D-Mass., a former law school dean, on Oct. 22, 1975, argued on the House floor against inclusion of a veto clause in the consumer product safety bill (HR 6844). "This amendment would probably violate the constitutional principle of separation of powers," Drinan said.

Not surprisingly, most administrations also have opposed the congressional veto, although presidents have reluctantly signed bills containing such clauses when forced by circumstances to do so.

Assistant Attorney General Antonin Scalia in October 1975 told the House Judiciary Committee's Subcommittee on Administrative Law and Governmental Relations that the veto provisions violate the separation of powers doctrine, circumvent the president's constitutional right to veto measures passed by Congress, and give one house the power to act on behalf of the entire Congress.

"The executive has repeatedly expressed the view that the use of such a device to offset executive powers is constitutionally objectionable," Scalia said.

Other Objections

On a more practical level, critics said the veto proposal would add unnecessary delay and confusion to agency operations. The Securities and Exchange Commission (SEC), for example, wrote the Judiciary Committee to warn that Congress is not equipped to evaluate the complex, technical regulations it issues, and criticized the House bill for not spelling out a "standard" to guide congressional committees in reviewing agency rules.

"If this bill is enacted into law," warned Judiciary Committee member John F. Seiberling, D-Ohio, in a dissenting opinion on HR 12048, "Congress is going to have to spend an inordinate amount of time just reviewing regulations...." Seiberling said the procedure would also increase the number of floor votes taken and force Congress to hire "hundreds of additional committee staff employees simply to review regulations...."

The Congressional Budget Office estimated the cost of additional staff members to handle the review procedure at about $150,000 a year. But a Judiciary Committee staff member said the kind of review the panel had in mind should be possible to accomplish without additional staff.

"The standing committees of the Congress have the experience and competence to perform the functions required under the bill...," the committee argued. It said resolutions on agency rules "would probably be relatively infrequent," and that the increased review activity of committees would improve congressional oversight and congressional-executive communications.

"The review of regulations contemplated by this bill does not go to the technicalities of rulemaking," the committee said. "Rather it is a means to implement basic policy and place ultimate limits upon the discretionary authority of agencies involved in the rule making process."

Critics of the proposal also pointed out its potential for manipulation. Seiberling warned that it would encourage more special interest lobbying directed at Congress and would "enable and perhaps encourage committee chairmen and key committee members to intimidate or otherwise interfere with the operations of executive departments and agencies." Agencies might feel obliged to submit proposed regulations to the appropriate committee chairman for approval in advance, he predicted.

was dropped by conferees when the bill cleared in 1976.

● Youth camp safety regulations (HR 46, S 422): approved by the House in 1975, the proposal was not passed by the Senate.

● Environmental Protection Agency fiscal 1977 authorization (HR 12704): this bill passed the House May 7, 1976, with the veto provision, but died in the Senate.

● Federal Energy Administration extension (HR 12169): the veto provision added by the House was dropped from this bill before it was cleared in August 1976.

● Water pollution control (S 2710): the veto provision of this bill, added in the House, died in the closing days of the 1976 session when conferees were unable to reach agreement.

● Outer Continental Shelf (S 521): the House-added veto provision died in conference on this bill which itself later was killed when the House in late 1976 rejected the conference report.

● Mine safety (HR 13555): the 1976 House bill contained a veto provision but the Senate did not pass the bill.

● Pesticides (HR 12944): the House-added veto provision in this 1976 bill, a simple extension of some government pesticides programs for a year, died when President Ford vetoed the measure because the provision was included.

● Toxic Substances (S 3149): conferees dropped a House-added veto provision before this bill was cleared in 1976.

● Clean Air (S 3219): the House's veto provision was kept in this bill but the entire measure died in the 1976 adjournment rush.

● Fire Prevention Funds (HR 12567): President Ford July 7, 1976, vetoed this bill because it allowed Congress by concurrent resolution to block plans to construct a professional training academy for firefighters. A substitute measure (S 2862) without the provision was then passed.

House General Veto Bill

Not satisfied with the addition of veto provisions to individual bills, House backers of the concept attempted unsuccessfully in 1976 to push through a general bill that would have made most agency rules and regulations subject to congressional rejection.

The bill (HR 12048) was drafted in the Judiciary Subcommittee on Administrative Law and Government Relations, chaired by Walter Flowers, D-Ala. In addition to Flowers, a principal sponsor of the bill was Elliott H. Levitas, D-Ga.

Veto Procedure. The congressional veto can be structured in several different ways. The most strict form bars an agency from enforcing a regulation until Congress approves the rule by majority vote. A more lenient version simply requires an agency to submit proposed regulations to Congress for review and possible action through normal legislative channels. The most frequently used version of the veto requires that, before taking effect, a proposed regulation must lie before Congress for a specified period — usually 60 or 90 days — during which time either house may, by adoption of a simple resolution, veto the regulation.

It was this third approach that was taken in the House bill, HR 12048.

A proposed rule would not go into effect if either chamber, within 60 days of continuous session, had reported or approved a concurrent resolution disapproving it. The veto would become final in another 30 days if both chambers had passed the resolution or if one chamber had passed it and the other had not acted at all. A regulation would take effect, however, if one chamber passed a disapproval resolution but the other one rejected it.

A simple resolution passed by either chamber would be enough to force an agency to reconsider a regulation.

Resolutions to veto regulations or have them reconsidered would be referred to the committee with oversight and legislative responsibility over the agency in question. The bill included procedures for discharging resolutions from committee more easily than is normally permitted in order to get them to the floor before the 60-day time limit expired. It would take one-fifth of House members, instead of the usual majority, to discharge a resolution disapproving an agency regulation.

The veto procedure was to apply to all federal agencies including independent regulatory agencies such as the Federal Trade Commission and executive units such as the Department of Transportation.

HR 12048 would have authorized $200,000 for the Administrative Conference, a federal agency that monitors administrative law, to study the veto procedure. The veto system was to begin in 1977 and expire at the end of 1982 if Congress did not extend it.

1978 Attempts

Having almost succeeded in 1976 to secure passage of the general congressional veto bill, Levitas continued his attempts in 1978, but he had no luck trying to nudge similar proposals out of two House committees in the 95th Congress. In February 1978, the House rejected a conference report on a bill (HR 3816) streamlining Federal Trade Commission procedures. A key element in the rejection was a decision by bill conferees to drop a congressional veto provision previously approved by the House.

In a second action in 1978, a House Ways and Means subcommittee refused by very narrow margins — a tie vote in one case — to add versions of the congressional veto to President Carter's hospital cost control legislation.

Some congressional observers said part of Levitas' problem was the change to a Democratic administration, which, like its Republican predecessor, said a bill allowing congressional vetoes of agency regulations would violate the constitutional doctrine of separation of powers. The Carter administration had opposed individual veto amendments added by the House to several bills in 1977 and repeatedly declared its opposition to the broad congressional veto of agency regulations proposed by Levitas.

Two bills introduced in the 95th Congress by Levitas (HR 959 and HR 116) were similar to the general veto bill that nearly won House approval in 1976. They would allow Congress to disapprove proposed rules and regulations if both houses adopted a concurrent resolution rejecting them within 90 calendar days after they were sent to Capitol Hill. Both bills would also allow congressional review of existing regulations.

Other bills introduced by Levitas would make the veto applicable only to future agency actions.

A major argument raised against Levitas' bills was the burden it would place on congressional committees to review some 10,000 regulations generated by federal agencies each year. Opponent Jack Brooks, D-Texas, said Congress already had ways to let agencies know when it feels regulations don't reflect the intent of a law drafted by Congress. As part of its oversight function, a committee can call in agency officials and "have a little chat with them," Brooks said. He described Levitas' bills as "fraudulent" because, "We can't go down and run the executive."

Levitas said he did not think a broad congressional veto would be used very often, but it should be available to block "bad" regulations. He said as the number of congressional vetoes attached piecemeal to bills increases, the need for a uniform approach in reviewing all agency regulations increases. The Georgia Democrat reintroduced his comprehensive bill in 1979.

Carter Message

In a June 21, 1978, message to Congress, Carter served clear notice on Capitol Hill that he considered the legislative veto unconstitutional and that he did not feel legally bound to comply. Estimating that 48 legislative veto provisions had been enacted in the past four years, the president denounced them as "intrusive devices" that "infringe on the executive's constitutional duty to faithfully execute the laws." He said they prolonged and undercut the regulatory process and that they "treat symptoms, not causes. The vast effort required to second-guess individual regulatory decisions could impede the crucial task of revising the underlying statutes." However, the president in his statement stopped short of saying that he would ignore congressional vetoes. He indicated he was trying to dissuade Congress from attaching such provisions to future bills. The "inclusion of such a provision in a bill will be an important factor in my decision to sign or to veto it," he said.

Members of Congress generally accepted Carter's statement as a challenge, but some agreed with the president that Congress had "overreacted" in employing the legislative veto as a safeguard against executive abuses. "The gauntlet has now been thrown down," Levitas said in a floor speech immediately after the House received Carter's message. "I suggest that we send a message back as soon as possible saying we, and the American people, want this essential control over the unelected bureaucracy."

Sen. Frank Church, D-Idaho, said that Carter appeared to be "inviting a tug-of-war with Congress." Church said the laws containing legislative veto provisions are "perfectly acceptable and ought not to be contested." He added, "I hope the curtain is not going up on another imperial presidency."

However, House Speaker Thomas P. O'Neill Jr., D-Mass., spoke as if to soften the confrontational atmosphere generated by Carter's message. He said he agreed with the president that "in some instances we have overstepped our rights."

1979: Battle Renewed

The Carter administration and Congress in March 1979 opened another round in the continuing battle over the legislative veto. At issue was a process Congress established in 1978 to review Department of Housing and Urban Development regulations. It would allow either banking committee to delay a regulation for up to three months, but it would not actually block the proposal from taking effect. As such, the process was not a strict legislative veto but rather a delaying mechanism to give Congress extra time to overturn or force revisions in regulations.

Nevertheless, the Carter administration opposed the provision as unconstitutional and asked Congress to repeal it. Moreover, the administration said it would ignore the provision regardless of what Congress did. "Our position is that no committee of Congress can bind the executive branch to do anything. . . . A committee can suggest what we should do, but that's it," said an official in the Department of Justice.

Congress established the review process for housing regulations in 1978 amid controversy over HUD efforts to assert more control over how cities and towns use community development grants.

Former Rep. Garry Brown, R-Mich., then the ranking minority member of the Housing Subcommittee, and several other members, including some Democrats, said the proposed rules were designed to circumvent legislative intent and forced the agency to back down.

Brown, joined by Levitas, won House approval by a 244-140 vote of a "one-house" legislative veto giving either chamber 90 days to reject any proposed HUD regulation. The provision was added to the fiscal 1979 housing authorization bill. The Senate rejected a similar proposal by a 29-65 vote. Conferees on the bill devised a compromise that did not give either chamber direct veto power over regulations but allowed either the House or Senate Banking Committee to approve a resolution automatically blocking a regulation from taking effect for 90 days, unless the full chamber overturns the committee action.

Regulations automatically take effect after 90 days unless Congress has taken other action to prevent this. ∎

Congress Presses for Sunset Legislation

One widely advocated mechanism to improve Congress' ability to exercise its oversight functions has been legislation mandating periodic review and reauthorization of federal agencies and programs. Under various "sunset" plans, time limits would be placed on a program's existence; if, after a certain period, there was found no justification for continuation, the program would be terminated.

In 1978, the Senate overwhelmingly passed a sunset bill that established a 10-year reauthorization cycle for most federal programs. The bill, popular with many younger members of Congress, was supported by President Carter.

Advocates of sunset legislation argued that periodic review of agency statutes would require Congress to evaluate the need for and performance of the programs, resulting in an elimination of wasteful expenditures. In addition, the threat of termination could put pressure on agencies to become more accountable to the legislative branch. However, writing in the Fall 1977 issue of *The Public Interest,* Robert D. Behm of Duke University's Institute for Policy Sciences pointed to problems in the sunset concept: An effective evaluation would not only be expensive but would also severely increase individual committee workloads. Moreover, Behm said, sunset laws — regardless of their other merits — could not be expected to change the tendency of members of Congress to bargain for support of their pet programs by agreeing to support those of their colleagues.

Background: 1978 Senate Action

The sun set on the 95th Congress before any final action was taken on sunset legislation.

A sunset bill (S 2), which required automatic termination of funds for most federal spending programs if they were not specifically reauthorized after a comprehensive review every 10 years, passed the Senate, 87-1, Oct. 11, 1978.

But despite the widespread popularity of the sunset review concept, similar bills in the House never emerged from committee.

The heart of sunset proposals, contained in S 2 and a similar House measure (HR 9533), was the requirement that Congress periodically reauthorize programs after a comprehensive review. Both bills would have ended funding of a federal program after a date set by law, unless Congress evaluated the program and took positive action to renew it.

Sunset advocates touted it as a way to get control of the federal budget and get rid of wasteful or outdated federal programs that are usually routinely renewed by Congress.

S 2 was introduced in 1977 by Edmund S. Muskie, D-Maine, with 59 cosponsors, including 30 Democrats, 28 Republicans and one independent. Supporters of sunset legislation spanned the political spectrum ranging from Barry Goldwater, R-Ariz., and Jesse Helms, R-N.C., to George McGovern, D-S.D., and Edward M. Kennedy, D-Mass.

The sunset idea, which complemented President Carter's proposals for zero-base budgeting and government reorganization, developed out of concern over Congress' ability to shape the federal budget. Three factors, according to a Senate Governmental Affairs Committee report, were particularly bothersome:

● The vast number and complexity of federal programs.
● The dramatic increase in the percentage of federal spending for so-called uncontrollable programs, which comprised more than three-quarters of all federal spending. These were programs where spending mandated by earlier congressional action could not be appreciably altered.
● The rapid growth in the cost of federal programs that were permanently authorized and thus escaped systematic and thorough congressional review.

The sunset concept drew its most significant opposition from some committee chairmen who felt it would erode their authority, give them a heavy new workload and perhaps cause inadvertent termination of some worthwhile programs.

The Road to a Vote

When the bill finally reached the floor in the closing days of the 95th Congress, the lackluster Senate debate and the overwhelming vote to pass it gave few clues to the intense parliamentary maneuvering that led up to it.

Muskie's sunset odyssey began in 1976, when he found himself trying to get a floor vote in the closing days of the 94th Congress. His sunset bill had come through three committees. But two — Rules and Finance — didn't like the bill even though they agreed to put it on the Senate calendar.

Muskie was persuaded to drop efforts for a floor vote when the Democratic leadership assured him sunset would be a "priority" bill in the 95th Congress.

In 1977, S 2 had little trouble winning approval from the Governmental Affairs Committee — although the panel did drop tax expenditures from the review process.

But Muskie could not persuade Rules Committee Chairman Howard W. Cannon, D-Nev., to set a deadline for committee action. Cannon opposed automatic termination of federal programs, which Muskie considered the heart of the bill.

When Cannon moved over to chair the Senate Commerce Committee in 1978, Muskie found a more sympathetic leader on Rules. But the new chairman, Claiborne Pell, D-R.I., still took several months to move S 2 through committee.

Once the bill left Rules in July 1978, Muskie began working on the Senate leadership to schedule it. But Majority Leader Robert C. Byrd, D-W.Va., Majority Whip Alan Cranston, D-Calif., and other influential senators wanted Muskie to make some changes. The leaders were concerned that procedures established by the committee bill would make some federal spending programs highly vulnerable to presidential vetoes or filibusters.

To calm those fears — and get his bill scheduled — Muskie devised a procedural safety valve that would allow Congress to vote for continued funding of a program one year past its sunset date if the program's reauthorization bill ran up against a veto or a filibuster.

With the safety valve in place, Byrd and Cranston signed on as cosponsors of the new S 2 introduced by Muskie Sept. 26, 1978.

But the delay caused by having to compromise with the leadership put Muskie in the same position he was in two years earlier. Competition to bring bills to the floor in the last two weeks of the session was fierce, and sunset was hardly a priority since the House had never acted on it.

Looking for a Vehicle

So Muskie presented the compromise as an amendment, hoping to attach it to a bill — such as the tax cut measure — that was certain to be enacted in 1978.

Muskie's first choice of a vehicle for sunset was the Export-Import Bank authorization bill (S 3077), which several other senators had already spotted as a potential "Christmas tree" to carry unrelated bills that would not be brought up on their own. But S 3077 was pulled off the Senate floor when it was loaded down with one too many ornaments.

Muskie and others turned next to the tax bill (HR 13511). Once the sunset amendment was introduced, John Glenn, D-Ohio, proposed an amendment to Muskie's proposal that would have added tax expenditures to the sunset process. Finance Committee Chairman Russell B. Long, D-La., began filibustering. Cloture on the tax bill prevented attaching sunset or any other non-germane amendments.

Muskie then sought a commitment from Byrd to bring up sunset on its own. Byrd said only that he would "try" to do so. But it wasn't until Glenn agreed to drop the tax expenditures amendment that Muskie could get an agreement for limited debate on the sunset bill.

That debate was notable mostly for its dullness. Several senators gave lengthy speeches filled with rhetoric about the benefits of sunset in reducing government waste and inefficiency. Muskie accepted several amendments to the bill, including one from Charles H. Percy, R-Ill., to include regulatory agencies in the sunset review process.

1978 House Bills

Several variations of sunset bills had attracted numerous cosponsors in the House in 1978. Chief sponsors of bills paralleling various versions of S 2 were James J. Blanchard, D-Mich., and Norman Y. Mineta, D-Calif.

One Blanchard-Mineta bill was HR 9533, which was identical to the versions of S 2 reported by the Senate Governmental Affairs Committee.

House Budget Committee member Butler Derrick, D-S.C., introduced a bill (HR 10421) requiring detailed congressional oversight of federal programs, with periodic assessments of whether programs are meeting their intended goals.

However, Derrick's bill did not contain automatic termination, which sunset supporters considered the key to forcing meaningful program review. Derrick's bill was considered in tandem with sunset bills by the House Rules Subcommittee on Rules and Organization of the House.

No committee action was taken on HR 9533 or on Derrick's oversight bill — which had more than 100 cosponsors — in 1978. "People are prepared to sit tight one more year," a Mineta aide said.

Outlook

Muskie made his third attempt to enact sunset legislation in 1979 by introducing a bill similar to S 2. Although Muskie left the Governmental Affairs Committee, which has jurisdiction over sunset legislation, to take a seat on the Foreign Relations Committee, his absence from the former panel was not expected to deter action on the bill. Sunset was strongly supported by both the committee chairman, Abraham Ribicoff, D-Conn., and its ranking minority member, Charles H. Percy, R-Ill., who had introduced their own version of the legislation.

The fate of sunset was much less certain in the House, although the Democratic Caucus in January 1979 adopted a resolution, offered by Blanchard, urging the House Rules Committee to report a sunset bill in 1979. The resolution specified that the bill should call for comprehensive review of most federal programs, with automatic termination of any program not specifically renewed by Congress. It also urged the Ways and Means Committee to consider applying the sunset concept to tax expenditures. (Tax expenditures had been exempted from the 1978 bill passed by the Senate.)

However, Rules Committee Chairman Richard Bolling, D-Mo., said that he wanted to study sunset and other proposals for increased oversight — such as legislative veto bills — as a group and that the study might take at least a year.

On the plus side for the House sponsors was a Common Cause survey, taken in the fall of 1978, which showed that some form of sunset legislation was favored, 325-6, by those elected to the House in November. In a December 1978 interview, House Speaker Thomas P. O'Neill Jr., D-Mass., said that sunset legislation and oversight would be among the "hallmarks" of the 96th Congress. However, O'Neill did not endorse a specific sunset bill. ∎

Senate Confirmation Procedures Weak

One of the most damaging episodes of 1977 for the Carter administration, the "Lance affair," also was unpleasant for the Senate. And early in 1978 the "Marston affair" similarly proved to be a bane for the president and the Senate.

These and other cases demonstrated that there are pitfalls for both the executive and legislative branches in the way appointments to high government office are made. As the Senate during the second session of the 95th Congress undertook its responsibility of examining and confirming a number of major Carter nominations, there was a continuing discussion of the problems in the process, and of potential remedies.

The Senate early in 1978 approved such crucial nominations as that of G. William Miller to be chairman of the Federal Reserve Board, which determines monetary policy, and that of William H. Webster to head the FBI, the nation's top law enforcement agency. Also in March it confirmed the nomination of James T. McIntyre Jr. to succeed his former boss, Bert Lance, as head of the Office of Management and Budget.

Moreover, the controversial dismissal of David W. Marston, a Philadelphia U.S. attorney who was investigating state and federal officials, doubtlessly focused extraordinary attention on the confirmation of his successor.

The Senate also passed judgment on a host of lesser presidential nominations during the year. Carter in January resubmitted to the Senate the "first group" of renominations of persons appointed in 1977 but not yet confirmed by the Senate; that list alone included 50 names. *(Statistics, box, p. 96)*

Of the 3,054 civilian nominations Carter sent to the Senate in 1978, 3,010 were confirmed. Four nominations were withdrawn and 40, mostly to relatively minor positions, failed to win confirmation.

'Rubber Stamp'

Even stalwart defenders of the Senate such as Majority Leader Robert C. Byrd, D-W.Va., have conceded that the confirmation process has not always worked as it should. Common Cause, the citizens' lobbying group, in November 1977 published a report that skewered the Senate process as a "rubber-stamp machine." And Sens. Abraham Ribicoff, D-Conn., and Charles H. Percy, R-Ill., both among those most stung by the handling of the Lance confirmation, proposed legislation to standardize and centralize Senate confirmation.

The gist of most of the dissatisfaction with the Senate's performance in confirming nominees to high office is typified by the case of Bert Lance: A brief, inadequately documented committee examination in January 1977 of his banking background failed to turn up the questionable aspects of his past career that led to his resignation under fire in September. That failure led to criticism that the Senate has been lax in examining presidential nominees.

Leading the charge for that viewpoint has been Common Cause, whose November study was based on consideration of 50 Carter nominations. It concluded that the Senate inadequately examined the background and qualifications of most nominees, failed to build an adequate public record for the confirmation decision and rushed to confirmation without any affirmative finding that the caliber of the nominees met the requirements of their offices. *(Box, p. 97)*

Sen. Byrd told reporters in September 1977 that he felt the Senate had not performed as it should in confirmations. Calling the Lance case an "indictment" of the process, Byrd said that "confirmation often have been rubber-stamped. There has been a feeling that this is a nominee the president wants, and he should have who he wants. I believe our responsibility should go deeper than that."

But these criticisms signal the complexity of the confirmation task, which presents several distinct difficulties:

● Confirmation to high office increasingly must focus on potential conflicts of interest that turn on complex evaluations of financial information about both individuals and corporations for which they work.

● Even traditional FBI inquiries into arrest records, youthful associations and other personal background data must be carefully weighed to avoid unfairly penalizing an individual for conduct that may be constitutionally protected even though not approved by many in society.

● Appointment to high office is patronage by any other name, and removing politics from patronage is no easier today than it has been since the days of Andrew Jackson.

● Besides being affected by partisan politics, the appointment process is constantly enmeshed with the conflict between the legislative and executive branches over both patronage and substantive policy.

The Constitutional Mandate

"The President . . . shall nominate, and by and with the Advice and Consent of the Senate shall appoint Ambassadors, other public Ministers and Consuls, Judges of the Supreme Court, and all other Officers of the United States, whose appointments are not herein otherwise provided for, and which shall be established by Law; but the Congress may by law vest the appointment of such inferior officers, as they think proper, in the President alone, in the courts of law, or in the heads of departments.

"The President shall have power to fill up all vacancies that may happen during the recess of the Senate, by granting commissions which shall expire at the end of their next session." *(Constitution of the United States, Article II, Section 2)*

The House has only one limited role in confirming officers of the executive branch. Under the Twenty-fifth Amendment to the Constitution, ratified in 1967, both the House and Senate must confirm, by majority vote, a new vice president to succeed to any vacancy in that office.

Conflict of Interest

As the Lance case demonstrated, an adequate examination of a presidential nominee may require evaluation of bank records, a knowledge of banking practices and the ability to sift through complex financial statements.

The case of Fed nominee Miller, who headed the giant Textron conglomerate, illustrated that evaluation of the nominee's qualifications may require an understanding of the activities of a multibillion-dollar corporation. As one congressional observer put the problem of modern nominations, "It ain't as easy as looking for the old boy's arrest record."

Ribicoff Proposal

It was primarily this problem that the Ribicoff-Percy bill addressed. A Governmental Affairs Committee aide said that the legislation was aimed at providing the Senate with the staff expertise and the time needed to discharge this complicated part of the confirmation duty. The proposal, first introduced in 1977, had not been reintroduced in the 96th Congress as of mid-1979. It called for creation of a Senate Office on Nominations, which would assume primary responsibility for conducting background inquiries into a nominee's integrity and fitness for office. The office would be headed by a director selected on a bipartisan basis and would have adequate staff to do the kind of investigative work implied by its mandate.

Moreover, the office would be empowered to demand detailed biographical and financial disclosure statements, which would be made available for public inspection. Finally, the Office on Nominations would have mandatory access to "any investigative reports prepared on the nominee by any federal agency and submitted to the President as part of his consideration of the nomination," including FBI summary reports. This central office would compile a record on each major nominee and identify any questions about his or her integrity. It would then report to the committee having jurisdiction over the nomination, which would act according to a timetable that precluded a rush to confirmation.

Critics of the proposal responded that a nominations office was not needed. They suggested there is little Senate committees cannot do now to scrutinize nominees if they take the trouble to do so. "Just because one committee got into a lot of trouble by not doing a good job doesn't mean there's a problem with all the rest of us," said one aide, referring to Governmental Affairs' role in the Lance case.

Grenville Garside, chief of staff of the Energy and Natural Resources Committee, argued that "just because of the Lance case, it would be disastrous to rush in with an office, rules and regulations." Garside said that many tools already were at the disposal of examining committees, such as the use of the General Accounting Office (GAO) to aid in complex inquiries. Above all, "we can put the burden on the executive," Garside said. "They are the advocates. If there's something we don't like, we don't have to confirm."

Those responsible for screening nominations in the White House were well aware of the ultimate weapon of Senate committees — rejection of nominees. The office of White House counsel Robert J. Lipshutz had that job for the Carter administration. Associate Counsel Michael H. Cardozo V, who handled the examination of a potential nominee's financial background and possible conflicts of interest, said he agreed that the Senate committees were in a position of strength in the confirmation process. "They

---

Confirmation: A Major Task

One of the biggest chores any president faces is simply staffing his government. Review of those presidential personnel choices is likewise one of the Senate's major duties. Despite the number of government jobs now controlled by the merit-based Civil Service system, the magnitude of the appointment and confirmation power, taken literally, remains enormous.

According to the Secretary of the Senate, the Carter administration had 124,730 appointments confirmed in 1977 and 1978. Unconfirmed nominations numbered 12,713 and 66 nominations were withdrawn during those years of the 95th Congress. That number of nominations was not exceptional. In the two years of the 93rd Congress (1973-74), for example, there were 131,254 confirmations.

Those figures are misleading, however, since the vast majority of those confirmations are of military promotions that traditionally have received no real scrutiny from the Senate. But John C. Stennis, D-Miss., chairman of the Armed Services Committee, announced in June 1977 that the committee was instituting a new confirmation practice. The committee, he said, intends to "get a better picture as to the type of men and women that are being nominated and proposed for promotion within the services," through a "system of random selection of officer nominees by the committee for confirmation hearings. . . ."

Only 7,691 civilian nominations were included in the 124,730 total, and most of those were "routine" appointments to the Coast Guard, the National Oceanographic and Atmospheric Administration and the Public Health Service. Those appointments also have not received full-dress Senate attention in the past.

Still, Senate committees and the White House Counsel's office dealt in 1977 with some 200 nominations to policy-level positions deserving careful scrutiny.

The confirmation burden is unevenly distributed among Senate committees. Judiciary (judges, U.S. attorneys and U.S. marshals), Commerce (regulatory agencies), Foreign Relations (ambassadors) and Armed Services (primarily military) are among those committees with major confirmation duties. At least 14 committees have some confirmation responsibility.

can elicit anything they want to from a nominee, or just not confirm him," Cardozo said.

Tough Procedures

Even the critical Common Cause study corroborated the contention that an aggressive Senate committee can do a thorough confirmation investigation if it wishes. That study reserved praise for a few committees, notably the Commerce Committee. In part due to its heavy responsibility for examining nominees to the numerous independent regulatory agencies, Commerce has developed tough procedures, including a comprehensive questionnaire to which all nominees before it must respond. A nominee's responses to the Commerce questionnaire may run as long as 400 pages, according to staff director Edward A. Merlis.

Several other committees also have developed extensive questionnaires that require a nominee to disclose wide-ranging information on his background, current finances and future employment plans.

As of mid-1979, however, no uniform set of questions or standards had emerged, a fact which signals the second major criticism of the Ribicoff proposal. Senate committee aides said that "turf protection" by committee chairmen was certain to stand in the way of creation of any central confirmation office. Powerful committee chairmen are considered unlikely to yield their confirmation prerogatives even partially to a staff that is not directly accountable to them. Further, a number of aides argued that standardizing the inquiry into nominees would be a mistake, since the requirements for offices vary, and what constitutes a troublesome problem in a nominee's background may also vary. They add that individual committees can best muster the staff expertise relevant to their jurisdictions.

FBI Reports

Inquiries into the personal history and integrity of nominees continued to be a crucial element in confirmations.

Common Cause Study

Procedures used by the Senate in confirmation cases were described as deficient in a November 1977 Common Cause report, "The Senate Rubber-Stamp Machine."

Common Cause examined procedures used in 50 Carter administration nominations. It was not a study of the nominees' actual qualifications.

Only two of the nominees were not confirmed:

● Donald L. Tucker was withdrawn from consideration to be a member of the Civil Aeronautics Board after opposition emerged in the Commerce Committee.

● Kent F. Hansen was rejected by the Environment and Public Works Committee as a nominee to the Nuclear Regulatory Commission.

The other 48 nominees were confirmed to Cabinet, sub-Cabinet, ambassadorial and regulatory agency posts.

Fourteen committees handled the nominations. Hearings were held on 49 of them, but only 10 of the hearings lasted longer than one day. Only 14 nominees testified under oath.

Printed hearing records were made available to senators before their confirmation votes in only six of the 50 cases. Recorded votes in committee occurred in only half the cases, and recorded Senate floor votes came on only six.

More than half the nominees were fully confirmed within four weeks of their nomination. In 18 cases, committee approval came on the day the hearing was held. In the case of Energy Secretary James R. Schlesinger, a familiar figure to the members, full Senate confirmation was obtained the same day the Senate received his anticipated nomination.

In 14 cases committees opened to the public the financial disclosure statements tendered by the nominees. In 17 cases nominees were required to make public a statement of recent political activities and campaign contributions. In 29 cases potential conflicts of interest and their intended resolution were placed in the public record.

The principal tool in this part of the examination is the FBI "full field" investigation. The resulting report has long been a mainstay in the administration's way of assuring itself that a nominee's background is adequately pristine. But there has been conflict between the White House and the Senate over Senate access to those reports, and that historic confict came into the open because of the Lance case.

Senate committees have had differing experiences with previous administrations in' gaining access to the FBI reports. With a few exceptions it appears, however, that past administrations did not allow members of confirming committees to look at the reports. At the very least, they discouraged committees from seeking access to them.

As a result, few committees regularly sought the reports. In fact, only one committee is known to have had regular access prior to the Carter administration: the Judiciary Committee. A special relationship has existed between that committee and the FBI, which the Judiciary Committee oversees. Also, the FBI in its manual of procedures has attached particular importance to the investigation of persons for life-tenure federal judgeship appointments, which are a major component of Judiciary's confirmation duties.

Carter Policy

Cardozo, of Lipshutz' office, said that Carter's administration policy was to grant access to the FBI file only to the committee chairman and the ranking minority member, and only if they requested to see it. If there was little or no derogatory information in the file, then the administration also would allow one staffer designated by the chairman to see the file.

Examination of the file was tightly guarded, however, even with committee chairmen. If a chairman asked to see a file, Cardozo, along with another counsel in Lipshutz' office personally carried the file to the senator's office. Cardozo remained with the senator while he read the file. No reproductions were allowed, although notes could be taken. Afterward, Cardozo took the file back to the White House. That practice was formalized in the wake of the Lance affair, largely because more senators expressed an interest in seeing the FBI reports after observing how the Governmental Affairs Committee was burned by not seeing them.

Ribicoff complained in 1977 that "the Senate is expected to act without having access to relevant investigative reports prepared on nominees by executive branch agencies. In the case of Mr. Lance, the [Governmental Affairs] committee was not given access to the FBI report on his nomination, nor did it have the opportunity to review reports prepared by the Comptroller of the Currency." Cardozo responded it was Carter administration policy from the beginning to make the FBI reports available under those careful precautions. Garside, for one, corroborated that. He said that even before the Lance blowup in July, the Energy Committee requested and obtained FBI reports when they were considered necessary, although it did not request the reports uniformly.

But the Carter administration has resisted granting the Senate access to the FBI reports on a routine basis. A September 1977 letter from Lipshutz to Commerce Committee Chairman Warren G. Magnuson, D-Wash., and ranking minority member James B. Pearson, R-Kan., stated that "we are extremely reluctant to allow FBI reports to be read by others; they represent a significant intrusion into any nominee's privacy. To date, the policy of this administration, like others, has been not to submit FBI reports to the Senate, except on special occasions."

Lipshutz wrote in response to an earlier request to the president from Magnuson and Pearson asking regular access to FBI reports. Lipshutz outlined in his reply the procedure described by Cardozo. "Making the FBI files available is a significant step, and can lead to invasions of privacy," Cardozo stated. "We want to be careful with it. . . . There have been problems with Senate staff. We have found that some staff members are not as discreet as they should be."

Damaging Allegations

The reason for this concern is rooted in the nature of the FBI reports themselves.

What the White House sees, and what it is now willing to show to committee chairmen, are "summary" reports that digest the results of interviews of various people who have had contact with the nominee in the past: neighbors, co-workers and friends.

The FBI does not make judgments, but passes along the statements of others. Many uncorroborated allegations about individuals may be included in the FBI reports, allegations that could be damaging to a person if leaked out, whether true or not. A number of Senate aides privately argued that the real problem with the FBI reports is that they dwell on "gossip" about a person's social and sex life, without plumbing more complex questions of the individual's honesty or corruption. A major study by the then-Government Operations Committee in January 1977 quoted a number of past White House aides of both parties criticizing the reports as an "irrelevant collection of gossip" and as "nonsense."

The FBI doesn't normally examine financial documents relevant to the individual's integrity. While the FBI report on Lance reportedly did not describe his controversial banking practices, it would have alerted the Ribicoff committee to existence of a criminal investigation of those activities in Atlanta. That investigation had been shut down at the time of Lance's nomination to the Carter Cabinet.

In addition, as the Government Operations study pointed out, the FBI inquiry has "McCarthy era" origins. The executive order mandating FBI investigations of top government appointees was signed by President Eisenhower in 1953. Under that order, one of the principal objectives is to check on a person's loyalty to the United States — and the methods used to measure loyalty are politically offensive to many observers today.

Notwithstanding those inadequacies, it seemed clear that the Lance case resulted in a heightened Senate determination to have regular access to the FBI product. Ribicoff's proposal called for mandatory access to the reports, and the current administration policy guarantees carefully proscribed access. Cardozo said he believed that the senators appreciate the administration policy. "They feel we are strengthening the process," he said. "Senators want to make the confirmation process as comprehensive as possible and looking at the FBI files is one way of doing it."

Partisan Politics

The partisan nature of the confirmation process is most evident in the realm of judgeships and U.S. attorney appointments.

President Carter as a candidate pledged to remove politics from the consideration of appointments to these judicial offices. But the case of David Marston, who was fired by Attorney General Griffin B. Bell, demonstrated the continuing political nature of those selections. Under the system of senatorial courtesy that had its beginnings under President Washington, senators from each state who are of the same party as the president are given virtually a veto power over those appointments. As a Judiciary Committee aide suggested, one reason for the practice is that these are offices held within the states themselves, not in Washington.

Thus the level of concern of a senator is apt to be somewhat higher than for an appointment, say, to a federal regulatory agency. As a corollary to the courtesy system, where the senators from a given state are not from the president's party, the president has been influenced in his choice by his party cohorts in the state's House delegation.

The Marston case stands as a clear example of the partisan approach of both parties to court-related appointments. Marston had no prosecutorial experience and was recommended for appointment as U.S. attorney by President Ford because he had been an aide to Pennsylvania Republican Sen. Richard S. Schweiker. The choice of Marston was harshly criticized at the time in many legal circles. Once in office, his anti-corruption record was good enough to turn some of his critics around. His removal by a Democratic administration responsive to the entreaties of Democratic congressmen, including one who had been touched by a Marston investigation, allowed Schweiker and other Republicans to shift the partisan label to the Democrats.

Partisan considerations historically have colored the discussion of the "merits" of an administration's nominees. President Carter has steadfastly clung to his pledge to move generally to merit consideration of nominees, but his record on overall appointments has been severely criticized by many observers. In particular, Carter has been charged with following a pattern of excessive reliance on his fellow Georgians.

In addition, some of his appointments have been criticized as political payoffs for early support in his presidential drive. A case often cited to back up that allegation was that of Donald Tucker, the Speaker of the Florida House, who was nominated by Carter to be chairman of the Civil Aeronautics Board (CAB).

The CAB post is considered vital to air-travel-dependent Florida, and Tucker was an early Carter backer in the crucial 1976 Florida primary. Yet serious allegations about financial improprieties by Tucker had surfaced even before the nomination was announced. In the end, resistance to the nomination in the Commerce Committee forced Tucker's withdrawal, at some expense to the administration's claims to high ethical standards.

Despite the Tucker example, critics of the Carter performance on nominations also have been critical of the Senate role in readily confirming most of those named. But Cardozo stated that it was erroneous to suggest that presidential friends and political associates have been protected in the confirmation process. "Our vulnerability is greater when the nominee is a friend of the President's, because it's bigger game for the press," he said. "The chase is harder. We all know that." For that reason, Cardozo said that Carter personally scribbled notes instructing them to be particularly tough in examining the finances and potential conflicts of nominees close to the president, including his fellow Georgians.

Institutional Tensions

Overlaid on the personal and political partisanship of the appointment and confirmation process is the inherent institutional struggle between the two branches of government for patronage and policy control. The point of the senatorial courtesy system is not only that members of a president's party have influence over appointments, but also that the Senate itself has wrested effective control over lower court and prosecutorial appointments from the president.

Historically, the Senate has not asserted such control over other nominations by the president, particularly those to his Cabinet. There, the sentiment expressed by Sen. Byrd that the president is entitled to "his own man" has been predominant. Only eight men nominated to become Cabinet members have been rejected by Senate votes, although some others have not been nominated due to anticipated opposition. The last Cabinet-level rejection was the 1959 Eisenhower nomination of Lewis L. Strauss to be his Secretary of Commerce.

A slightly more aggressive Senate attitude has been taken to nominations more distant from a president's official working family. Nominations to the Supreme Court and to independent regulatory agencies have been considerably more likely to meet Senate opposition or even rejection. But the Senate's power over those nominations never has approached the control of the senatorial courtesy system over lower-level court appointments.

Policy Questions

There has even been a continuing debate over whether the "advice and consent" role of the Senate was intended to allow the Senate to affect policy, or whether it was intended only as a screen to weed out unqualified or corrupt appointments. Particularly with regard to Cabinet nominees, many senators have felt that if an individual is shown to be honest and competent, then the president is entitled to name him without regard to policy beliefs.

A differing view holds that senators can and should inquire into the policy intentions and commitments of a nominee before confirming him to office. This view has been maintained by a number of Senate committees, as reflected in their insistence that each major nominee testify under oath about his beliefs and plans, and in some cases, that he submit written statements on policy.

The most prominent example of such an approach to a Carter Cabinet member was the grilling received by Attorney General Bell in his confirmation hearings before Judiciary. Suspicions about Bell's civil rights record in particular, including his personal membership in some exclusionary clubs, led to days of questioning. The result was that Bell was forced to pledge his resignation from such clubs, to commit himself to minority appointments to major Justice Department posts, and to take a number of actions once in office in the civil rights and civil liberties arena.

Common Cause and other critics of the Senate confirmation process contend that the eliciting of binding policy commitments from nominees ought to be the norm during confirmation. Some senators disagreed, however, and it appeared doubtful that the Senate would assert itself that strongly in the policy area through the confirmation process.

In any event, the lessons learned by many senators from the Lance case have resulted in a perceptible shift toward a more stringent examination of presidential nominees.

Budget Process

CQ

Committees at Center of 1979 Budget Fight

After only four years of existence, the House and Senate Budget committees found themselves at the center of the major domestic policy battle of 1979 — the battle of the budget.

The budget has long been viewed as the single most important statement of government policy, but President Carter's pledge to keep the federal deficit below $30 billion, combined with the uncertain state of the economy, gave it special significance in 1979.

As a mechanism for setting spending and tax priorities, the Budget committees were at the center of one of the tightest spending squeezes Congress had faced during the term of a Democratic president. As Congress' main instrument for setting fiscal policy, they had to walk a narrow line between mounting inflation and the strong possibility of a recession.

A few years ago, many would have doubted that the fledgling budget process could withstand the strain that 1979 was sure to produce. But in 1979, most observers believed it would survive, and many expected its strength actually would be enhanced. Still, there was considerable attention on Congress' budget-writing abilities, possibly giving rise to a new debate on how suited it was to meet its twin mandate.

Background

The Congressional Budget and Impoundment Control Act of 1974 (PL 93-344) was designed to give Congress a way of deciding on the total level of spending and taxes each year so that it could make explicit, rather than piecemeal, decisions about fiscal policy and the size of the federal government.

It was hoped that would force Congress to exert greater control over spending, establish priorities, and judge the relative effectiveness of different programs.

To achieve those purposes, the budget act established House and Senate Budget committees and the Congressional Budget Office to give them information and technical assistance; set a timetable for action on spending and tax bills; and provided for congressional approval of two budget resolutions annually — one to set overall spending and tax goals early in the budget planning process, and another to set binding figures shortly before the beginning of the fiscal year.

Different Expectations

While assessments of the process involved its mechanics to a certain extent, they also reflected the considerable differences in what various groups expected it to accomplish.

"Conservatives wanted the budget process to put a ceiling on expenditures. They saw the purpose as being to hold down expenditures," noted Congressional Budget Office Director Alice M. Rivlin, who has served in her post since the inception of the process. "Liberals, on the other hand, saw it as a way of weighing priorities. They wanted a priorities debate."

In practice, the process has not worked quite as either side hoped. Conservatives continued to complain about excessive federal spending, and liberals continued to argue that the nation's priorities need to be shifted. The expectations of conservatives and liberals about the budget process have differed in other ways. Conservatives hoped it would lead to a balanced budget. Liberals, on the other hand, hoped it would promote equity in tax policy, mainly by eliminating tax preferences. Neither expectation had been realized by 1979. Finally, lawmakers of different political stripes have argued heatedly over the fiscal policies established through the budget process. Those differences are partly political and partly technical, and they have been greatly complicated by confusion over what realistically can be accomplished by fiscal policy.

The Spending Debate

Those who expected the budget process to hold down federal spending probably took heart in the early days of the process, when it became evident that the Budget committees would interpret the non-binding "targets" in the first resolution as "ceilings." That first happened in August 1975, when the Senate Budget Committee opposed

"Conservatives wanted the budget process to put a ceiling on expenditures. Liberals, on the other hand, saw it as a way of weighing priorities."

—Congressional Budget Office Director Alice M. Rivlin

the annual military procurement bill as exceeding the defense spending target in the first budget resolution. The amount of money involved was minuscule — the procurement bill ultimately emerged from a House-Senate conference only $250 million below the Senate Armed Services Committee measure — but the budget victory set an important precedent.

Still, many conservatives were unhappy with the budget process because they considered the first resolution spending figures that were established to be too high. House Republicans in particular raised that objection. During the debate on the first resolution for fiscal year 1979, Delbert L. Latta, R-Ohio, the ranking Republican on the House Budget Committee, expressed conservative frustrations with the process: "Rather than being a threat to the big spenders, the budget process has been converted into big spenders' biggest ally. . . . The [Budget] Committee described this budget resolution as 'lean and tight,' but anyone who watched them put together this resolution knows full well that the committee acted like an adding machine without a subtract button. The Budget Committee encourages more spending by putting its blessing on many social welfare proposals so inflationary that the House, left to its own devices, would probably not approve many of them."

Democrats have been sensitive to such complaints. During the House debate on the first resolution for fiscal 1979, Paul Simon, D-Ill., claimed that the Budget Committee had pared $49 billion in budget authority and $22 billion in outlays from the sum that various legislative committees reported they expected to spend. A report by the House Budget Committee in November 1978 claimed that the committee had proposed spending levels on the average $23 billion below what legislative committees reported as their intentions during the first four years of the budget process.

Such claims are virtually impossible to evaluate. Some said that the legislative committees inflated their March 15 reports to the Budget committees in order to assure themselves enough flexibility to spend pretty much whatever they wanted. Cutting back those inflated figures reflects no real restraint, they suggested. But there is considerable disagreement on how to achieve real spending cuts, and on the role of the budget process in forcing them.

Republicans in the House argued that the budget process should be the major tool for forcing a sharp cutback in the size of the federal government. Their strategy in 1978 was to propose an alternative to the House Budget Committee that would have shaved $21 billion in budget authority and $13 billion in outlays from the first resolution totals. Democrats quickly denounced it. "Why, this is apple pie and cake with icing on it. It is just marvelous," declared Simon. "The only problem is that it is unrealistic."

House Budget Committee Chairman Robert N. Giaimo, D-Conn., criticized Republicans for proposing spending cuts on the first budget resolution that Congress would never agree to when it took up individual spending bills. "We must continue to do the best we can in the Committee on the Budget, and we do, but it will not solve this whole problem today," he argued during the debate. "The time to cut spending is when the defense bill comes up on the floor of the House. That will also be true of the other bills that will be coming up in the House."

Eliminating Waste

Many Democrats agreed that Congress needs to find a better way of eliminating waste. But that is easier said than done, they argued. "Each of us knows that there is waste and excessive spending in the federal budget," said Leon E. Panetta, D-Calif. "We know this from our own experiences with the bureaucracy and from the occasional reports in the press and elsewhere documenting fraud and waste. At the same time, finding this waste, making responsible reductions in the budget that do not jeopardize truly legitimate programs, is truly like looking for a needle in the haystack," he continued. "Even though we know there is waste, we cannot find it, so we give every program just about what it got the year before, plus a little more for inflation, plus a little more for new initiatives, plus a little more for good measure."

While the debate about how well the budget process has controlled spending continued some argued that the

process should not be judged in terms of spending totals alone.

"We tend to stand up here and argue about the size of numbers in the budget resolution but we never really focus on the improvements in the process which led to those numbers," complained Butler Derrick, D-S.C. "We are all constantly criticized by the public, particularly our constituents for runaway spending — and we find ourselves responding to those criticisms. But I believe the real complaint voiced by the public is lodged not in the totals themselves but the fact that they believe the numbers are irresponsibly derived, that spending continues to increase with no reason," he continued. "This is not true — we are making better, more careful decisions based on a better understanding of the numbers and the long-term consequences. We deserve to have that fact understood."

Derrick cited a number of ways the budget process has improved spending decisions. "Because of the timetable set down in the budget act, authorizing committees have started planning ahead in a more comprehensive and coordinated way," he said. "Appropriations bills, with a

"Rather than being a threat to the big spenders, the budget process has been converted into big spenders' biggest ally. . . ."

—Rep. Delbert L. Latta, R-Ohio

few exceptions, have been enacted before the beginning of the fiscal year. This is of great benefit to state and local governments who now find it easier to plan ahead with an indication of amount and timing of federal resources."

Derrick added that the budget process has started to focus attention on some spending programs not previously scrutinized. Programs such as housing for the elderly and the Export-Import Bank, which previously were "off-budget," have been brought into the budget so that they can be examined as part of the total federal spending picture. Others — Derrick cited the Federal Financing Bank — might come under similar scrutiny. Derrick also mentioned that the budget process has greatly increased the amount of information available to lawmakers about the cost of legislation, making it possible for them to see the long-term consequences of decisions which might have only a minor impact in the short run.

The Tax Expenditures Debate

If conservatives have been frustrated at what they consider the budget process' failure to limit spending, liberals have been even more thwarted in trying to use it to reform the tax system. Indeed, some of the biggest defeats for Senate Budget Committee Chairman Edmund S. Muskie, D-Maine, have involved tax expenditures. In 1976, and again in 1978, efforts by the Budget committees to force a re-evaluation of tax expenditures were marginal at best.

The liberals' objection to tax expenditures is based on two arguments — that tax expenditures are frequently inequitable because they go disproportionately to the wealthy, and that they are inefficient because the same goals often could be achieved at lower cost through direct spending.

Several efforts have been made to put tax expenditures under closer scrutiny, but they have run into problems because they threaten the considerable power of the tax-writing committees — especially the Senate Finance Committee. Sen. Edward M. Kennedy, D-Mass., suggested during the 95th Congress that the Senate revise its procedures to require that any tax expenditure proposal be referred jointly to the legislative committee with jurisdiction over the substantive area involved and to the Finance Committee. The suggestion got nowhere. During debate on the 1978 tax bill, Sen. John Glenn, D-Ohio, pushed an amendment that would have eliminated tax expenditures unless they were periodically reviewed and re-enacted. That idea also withered — largely because Finance Committee members vigorously objected, accusing Glenn of trying to impose an underhanded tax increase.

The Senate Budget Committee did make an effort that year to force Congress to consider the relative efficiency of providing education aid in the form of tax credits or direct grants and loans. During its markup of the first budget resolution for fiscal 1979, the committee considered the two

"We are making better, more careful decisions based on a better understanding of the numbers and the long-term consequences."

—Rep. Butler Derrick, D-S.C.

approaches simultaneously, deciding to back tax credits rather than grants and loans. The grant and loan idea was pushed by President Carter as an alternative to tuition tax credits. But as the two ideas moved through the legislative mill, there were indications that, rather than choose one or the other, Congress might enact both. That approach to budget matters — building a majority coalition by fattening legislative proposals to provide something for everyone — went directly against the purpose of the budget process. The Senate Budget Committee tried to prevent that from happening. Besides considering the two issues jointly itself, it pushed the Finance Committee to revise the credit bill to be less expensive, and it pressed to have the tax credit measure referred to the Appropriations Committee. The tuition tax credit ultimately died and the grant and loan program increase was approved — but for reasons quite unrelated to the Budget Committee's efforts.

Most observers agreed that the Budget committees have helped to increase congressional awareness about tax expenditures — House and Senate Budget committees list tax expenditures and their budget impacts in the reports on budget resolutions — but it is difficult to document any substantive shift in tax expenditure policies as a result.

In 1976 the Budget committees took some credit for tax expenditure-eliminating "reforms." But in 1978 tax reform wasn't a popular issue, and Congress undid many of those changes.

The Budget and Fiscal Policy

Conservatives' objections to the fiscal policy set by Congress through the budget process follow closely their complaints about Democratic spending policies in general. House Minority Leader John J. Rhodes, R-Ariz., summed them up during the debate on the first budget resolution for fiscal year 1979. "Nowhere in the Democrat-engineered budget process does a fiscal policy appear," he said. "Instead, they first vote *seriatim* on how much they would like to spend in all major governmental programs; they then add up this wish list and take the resulting total and call that the appropriate level of federal spending."

Liberals disagreed. They said the Budget committees have had a decisive impact on fiscal policy, urging economic stimulus programs to speed recovery from the 1974-75 recession and, more recently, shifting the focus of policy more toward fighting inflation. In 1975 the Senate Budget Committee specifically debated how much economic stimulus was necessary. In the 1976 debate on tax expenditures, the economic impact of the expenditures was a major topic.

In 1977, however, both Budget committees — and Congress with them — were quite embarrassed over fiscal policy. In March of that year, they shifted their fiscal policy gears and adopted a third budget resolution for fiscal year 1977 to accommodate fiscal stimulus programs proposed by the newly elected President Carter. But in April, Carter abruptly withdrew the centerpiece of his package — a proposed $50 tax rebate. That forced the red-faced Budget committees to revise the congressional fiscal policy again, pushing through Congress a fourth budget resolution adjusting the revenue figure for the by-then defunct rebates.

"I am troubled by this all too eager flip-flop in overall budget policy...," said a frustrated Leggett. "I believe our budget process must be capable of producing sound, independent judgments about the appropriate action which Congress should follow, regardless of which political party occupies the White House."

The budget process recovered some of its lost claim to independence from the executive branch in 1978. That year, Carter proposed a $25 billion tax cut to fuel a continued economic recovery. But from the outset the Budget committees showed more concern about inflation than Carter did. Both committees warned that it would be more effective and less inflationary for government to shift its efforts to reduce unemployment away from general fiscal policies and concentrate more on programs to eliminate structural unemployment. They also expressed concerns about the size of the deficit in Carter's January budget, and some warned that Congress was unlikely to enact a tax cut by October as the president had assumed.

Those various considerations led Muskie and Giaimo to a meeting with Carter that resulted in an announcement of a new agreement on fiscal policy shortly before final action was due on the first resolution for fiscal 1979. The agreement was to delay the effective date of the cut to January, thus reducing its fiscal year impact to $19 billion.

New Era Ahead

The shift in fiscal policy emphasis in 1978 was expected to be even more dramatic in 1979. Indeed, some

A Delicate Balance: Budget Committees'...

The framers of the budget act performed a delicate task in creating the two Budget committees. On one hand they wanted committees strong enough to influence federal spending policies. But in order to win approval of the new process, they had to convince existing committees that the new ones wouldn't be tyrannical.

The experience in the first four years of the budget process has underscored the balancing act the framers performed. In general, the Budget committees have proven to be neither omnipotent nor powerless. They have won some battles and lost others, with their success depending both on the issues they raised and the personalities they challenged.

Somewhat surprisingly, relations between the Budget and Appropriations committees have been fairly harmonious. That was partly because they have proven to be valuable allies on occasions.

The budget act requirement that legislation authorizing new spending be reported by May 15 has helped the Appropriations committees get spending bills out to the floor so that they can be enacted before the start of the fiscal year on Oct. 1.

Backdoor Spending Curbs

In addition, the Budget and Appropriations committees have sometimes worked together to control spending. They have been largely successful, for instance, in eliminating "backdoor spending" — such as contract and borrowing authority. Now, it has to go through the appropriations process. When the Senate took up legislation in 1978 to allow the United States to participate in a new lending facility (the Witteveen Facility) within the International Monetary Fund, for instance, the Senate Budget Committee supported an amendment subjecting the U.S. participation to the appropriations process.

Greater controls also have been imposed on entitlement legislation — bills that guarantee a certain level of benefits and thus leave no discretion to the Appropriations committees as to how much money to provide. Under the budget act, entitlement legislation that would generate new budget authority in excess of the amount allowed under the budget resolution now must be referred to the Appropriations committees. That provision has been invoked several times. In 1978, for instance, it was used to refer a child nutrition bill to the Appropriations Committee.

Some observers also believe that relations between the two sets of committees have been fairly smooth because the Budget committees perform a task that the Appropriations committees never did.

One high-ranking official deeply involved in the budget process theorized that Appropriations Committee work is so fragmented among various subcommittees that the full committees have never made broad decisions about the total amount of money that should be spent in a given year or how it should be divided.

Relations between the Budget committees and other legislative committees have varied. The Senate Budget Committee started on an aggressive note in 1975 by successfully challenging the Senate Armed Services Committee over that year's military procurement bill, which it charged violated the first budget resolution defense spending targets.

Muskie-Long Battles

But in 1976, and again in 1978, the Budget Committee clashed less successfully with the Senate Finance Committee.

In 1976, the issue was tax expenditures. They are exceptions to general tax law (exclusions, exemptions, deductions, credits, preferential rates or tax deferrals). Senate Budget Committee Chairman Edmund S. Muskie, D-Maine, sought to use the budget resolution to force the Finance Committee to eliminate $2 billion worth of tax expenditures. Finance Committee Chairman Russell B. Long, D-La., complained that was an infringement on his committee's prerogatives. He said that the budget resolution could set the total amount of money to be raised by taxes, but it couldn't say how it should be raised.

During Senate debate on the tax bill, the Finance Committee chairman won, but the tax bill that year emerged from conference with $1.6 billion worth of closed tax expenditures, enabling Budget Committee Chairman Muskie to claim a victory of sorts.

In 1978 the issue dividing the Senate Budget and Finance committees was the long-term cost of various provisions of the tax bill. Muskie had previously charged Long with violating the spirit, if not the letter, of the budget act by delaying the effective dates of some tax measures so that they wouldn't lower revenues so much as to violate the budget act. By making a tax provision effective late in the fiscal year covered by the budget resolution, Long was able to remain within the letter of the budget act while still enacting a larger annual tax cut than envisioned in the resolution, Muskie argued.

The 1978 battle between Muskie and Long was a logical extension of the earlier fight. Muskie claimed that the budget act prohibited Congress from enacting tax provisions that would first take effect in the fiscal year following the one to which the budget act applied. Long disagreed, and after a struggle he won a Senate vote upholding his position. That opened the floodgates, and senators rushed through them tax cuts using all of the room allowed by the budget resolution — $29 billion on a calendar year basis. The Senate action drove the cost of the tax bill to more than $55 billion annually by 1983.

"If you wipe away the protection of the next fiscal year by Senator Long's interpretation of this language, for all practical purposes, you have eliminated the discipline of the budget process from the revenue side of the budget," Muskie concluded.

Again, though, the Budget Committee chairman won back some of what he had lost. Long, after winning his turf battle with Muskie, asked the Senate to add an amendment to the tax bill urging conferees to fit the measure to the budget resolution. In conference, the cost

. . . Varied Relations With Other Panels

of the bill was brought down to $18.6 billion in the first year and $32.2 billion by 1983.

Farm Bill Fights

Relations between the Senate Budget Committee and the Agriculture, Nutrition and Forestry Committee have also been rocky. In 1977, the Budget Committee challenged that year's farm bill on the grounds that it was $700 million higher than allowed by the second budget resolution. That set in motion the budget act's "reconciliation" procedures, under which the Agriculture Committee was required to report a new bill cutting spending back to the budget resolution levels. But instead, the Agriculture Committee led a successful effort to amend the budget resolution on the floor so that it would be consistent with the previously approved farm legislation. That was the only time the reconciliation process was ever tried.

The 1977 farm bill battle helped breed ill will between the Senate Budget and Agriculture committees. It carried over to the next year. In April 1978, with farmers demonstrating in the streets and lobbying in the halls of Congress, the Agriculture Committee set up another confrontation by approving the "Emergency Agriculture Act of 1978," which was designed to raise farm prices.

Muskie denounced the measure as a "costly and dangerously inflationary bill . . . that will hit the pocketbook of every American taxpayer and consumer." But he also objected to the bill on the grounds that the Agriculture Committee had taken it to the Senate floor before action had been taken on the first resolution — a move prohibited under the budget act unless a waiver was granted by the Budget Committee.

"That provision [of the act] says that when we are dealing with the next budget year all spending decisions are to be considered together in the first resolution so that when we begin to authorize spending for the next year we do so having in mind all of the spending pressures and demands we are being asked to consider," Muskie said. "If we are going to suspend the budget act every time it is inconvenient, every time it is uncomfortable, every time it stands in the way, every time it requires us to follow a certain procedure to assure that the provisions of the act are safeguarded, then it becomes meaningless."

In spite of that plea from Muskie, the Senate agreed to bypass the budget process and approve the emergency farm bill.

Strategic Force

While some existing powers have resisted the strictures of the budget process, most have begun to use it as one of many elements in their legislative strategies. Observers report that the Budget committees are increasingly lobbied — a development that has been hastened by the fact that allegiances are more fluid, with coalitions frequently shifting from issue to issue.

Committee loyalties being much less important than they once were, lawmakers have on a number of occasions formed alliances with the Budget committees to achieve objectives they were unable to achieve in their own committees.

For instance, when Senate Banking, Housing and Urban Affairs Committee Chairman William Proxmire, D-Wis., was unable in 1978 to prevent his own committee from increasing spending ceilings for assisted housing programs, he joined forces with the Senate Budget Committee to win full Senate approval of an amendment that brought the ceilings back within the first budget resolution targets.

Changing Mood

There were indications in 1978 that the Budget committees were growing stronger.

After the Senate committee's loss to the Agriculture Committee on the emergency farm bill, the House committee helped contribute to a surprising 150-268 defeat of the measure in that chamber.

Later, the Senate committee forced the Finance Committee to rewrite its original version of tuition tax credit legislation. It also won a battle with the Finance Committee to require that the bill be sent to the Appropriations Committee because it included a "refundability" provision allowing people whose tax liabilities are less than the amount of the credit to receive cash payments.

In September the Senate Budget Committee set a new precedent by forcing a Senate vote on a specific line item as part of the budget process. The issue was President Carter's proposed labor-intensive "soft" public works. Both House and Senate had assumed passage of such a bill in the first resolution, but the Senate committee decided to oppose it later in the year on the grounds that declining unemployment and accelerating inflation made reducing the deficit a higher priority. The House conferees insisted on including room in the second budget resolution for the program, so Muskie took the issue back to the full Senate, asking for a vote instructing the Senate side not to give in. He won by a lopsided 63-21 margin.

In terms of legislative strategy, Muskie chose his issue well. The authorizing committee with jurisdiction over the soft public works bill was sharply divided on it, and Senate support was less than overwhelming.

But some observers saw Muskie's victory as indicative of the growing clout of the Budget committees. Budget Committee staff members said that power began to become evident only in 1978, when controlling spending and reducing the federal deficit emerged as increasingly popular political issues.

"There's a changed mood around here — it's really amazing," one said. "The budget process is really catching on."

Although the budget process theoretically is ideologically neutral, many observers believe its effect has been to hold spending below levels that would otherwise occur. The main reason is that, by forcing lawmakers for the first time to vote directly on the deficit, it has created a new incentive to hold down spending.

believed that 1979 could mark the beginning of a new era for the budget process. Born in the depths of recession, the process rode the wave of an economic recovery throughout its first four years. That made its task easier — both because during most of its existence the state of the economy made it fairly clear to most members of Congress that economic stimulus was the needed fiscal policy; and because the recovery produced a relatively healthy growth in federal revenues each year to finance government growth.

But a number of economists in early 1979 believed the economy had neared the peak of its recovery. Some predicted at least a mild recession. In addition, the anti-

"Each of us knows that there is waste and excessive spending in the federal budget. At the same time, finding this waste . . . is truly like looking for a needle in the haystack."

—Rep. Leon E. Panetta,
D-Calif.

spending mood in the country, the desire to hold down the deficit as an anti-inflation measure, and the expected drop-off in revenues as the economy slowed, all meant that Congress would almost surely have fewer spending options than in any year since the inception of the budget process. Besides suggesting that budget decisions would be more difficult, that situation spelled headaches on the fiscal policy front. Figuring out how to bring down the inflation rate without aggravating unemployment in 1979 would be one of the most "ticklish" policy decisions the budget process had yet faced, according to Rivlin. "It's harder to make economic policy . . . than it was a couple of years ago," she said.

How Effective?

The task was complicated by the wide divergence of opinion in Congress about what fiscal policy can accomplish. In 1978 the Budget committees had to consider three widely divergent sets of economic theory. One, the more orthodox, held that tax cuts affected the economy primarily by increasing consumer buying power — in other words, by influencing demand.

The orthodox theorists were split over whether demand could be further stimulated without increasing inflation. Some held that it could. They said there was still plenty of excess manufacturing capacity in the economy, so that increased purchasing power would merely stimulate new production without driving up prices. Others argued that further stimulus would set off higher inflation. They said the economy was actually operating near its peak capacity already, so that higher demand couldn't encourage higher production. Instead, it would drive up prices because people would have more dollars to buy the same amount of goods.

Competing with the orthodox economists, however, was a new "supply" theory which held that lower taxes would give people more incentive to save and invest, thus increasing production, creating new jobs and driving down prices by eliminating shortages.

Surveying the diversity of theories, the congressional Joint Economic Committee concluded that the persistence of inflation and the serious recession of the early 1970s had shattered a widespread belief of the 1960s that fiscal policy could be effective in maintaining stability and growth."Now . . . opinions about the stimulative potential of fiscal policy range from the skeptical to the exuberant — from the view that a tax cut will merely induce a comparable increase in private saving, with little effect on the level of activity, to the view that, if large enough a tax cut will provide the incentive for a self-reinforcing acceleration of real growth, without aggravating existing inflation," the committee reported.

The committee commissioned two private economic forecasting firms to evaluate the effect of economic stimulus programs between 1964 and 1975. Both firms concluded that the policies had been effective in moderating cyclical swings in the economy but that they couldn't completely eliminate them. One firm, Data Resources Inc., also reported that "serious miscalculations" had been made in setting fiscal policy during those years. Specifically, it reported that the government maintained an "over-expansionary" posture too long following the 1964 tax cut, and that that contributed to excess inflation during the late 1960s. The firm said that restrictive policies finally implemented in the late 1960s were kept in effect too long, and that the result was higher unemployment during the recession of the early 1970s than would otherwise have occurred.

"While most of the policies produced desirable short-term effects, a long-run perspective was lacking," Data Resources reported. ". . .[D]eveloping successful policies involves more than meeting traditional short-run criteria. It involves coordination of policies and a greater eye toward the long term. Not to recognize these requirements is naive and self-defeating, reducing stabilization policies to brush-fire tools."

Economic Goals and the Budget

In part, disagreements between liberals and conservatives about the effectiveness of the budget process in setting fiscal policy reflect political, rather than pragmatic, differences. As the focus of the fiscal policy debate shifts to the long term, those political differences should become accentuated.

The differences are substantial. That was revealed in the variety of economic goals Congress set in different bills during 1978. One, the Humphrey-Hawkins Full Employment Act, established 4 percent unemployment and 3 percent inflation by 1983 as national goals — even though most economists considered the two objectives incompatible. Another, an amendment to the Revenue Act of 1978, set national goals of reducing taxes and spending by certain amounts over the next five years — an objective that Muskie warned would be inconsistent with the Humphrey-Hawkins goals and with the budget resolution of that year too. Finally, Congress approved an amendment to the Witteveen Facility bill stating that the federal budget should be balanced by 1981 — also incompatible with some of the other objectives. And in May 1979 Congress agreed to a first budget resolution that would reduce the federal debt and set the stage for a balanced budget in 1981.

Senate, House Approaches to Budgeting

Following a familiar pattern, the Senate on April 29, 1978, approved its Budget Committee's proposed first budget resolution for fiscal year 1979 by a comfortable 64-27 margin. There were no floor amendments. But on May 10, the House approved the resolution proposed by its Budget Committee by a razor-thin four-vote margin. Prior to the final vote, the House had approved several amendments and narrowly rejected a number of others. One amendment rejected by the House by only six votes would have completely reversed the policies proposed by the Budget Committee, cutting spending by $13 billion.

The 1978 experience, typical of most of the first four years of the congressional budget process, demonstrates one of the greatest surprises for those who fashioned the new system of budget writing. While the law that created the new process was passed by both the House and Senate, the two chambers have breathed life into it in very different ways, reflecting their different rules and different political complexions.

In general, observers agreed that the House Budget Committee has been weaker, and that the budget process itself has been characterized by much greater partisanship in the House.

Different Membership

Much of the difference has been attributed to the rules by which the House and Senate established their Budget committees. The Senate's 16 members — 10 Democrats and six Republicans — are chosen from the Senate at large, and they serve indefinite terms. But the House's 25 members — 17 Democrats and eight Republicans — are selected by caucus. Also, 10 positions on the House committee are reserved for members of the Ways and Means and Appropriations committees, and two for the House leadership.

In the first four years of the budget process, members of the House were limited to serving only four years in a 10-year period, but that rule was modified by the House Democratic Caucus in December 1978 to allow members to serve six years.

Observers agreed that the membership rules in the House have weakened that chamber's committee, making it less independent of the other spending and tax committees and of the leadership. In addition, the mandatory rotation of members has made it difficult for the panel to match the Senate committee in expertise. It has also discouraged some lawmakers from joining the committee. Finally, it has impeded the Budget Committee's efforts to enforce its positions because other committees have less incentive to deal with a committee when they know its chairman and membership will soon change.

Partisanship

The greater non-partisanship of the budget process in the Senate is frequently traced to the close working relationship between its chairman, Edmund S. Muskie, D-Maine, and ranking Republican, Henry Bellmon, Okla.

In contrast, House Republicans have refused to support the Budget Committee through almost the entire history of the new process.

One reason was that Republicans were more outnumbered on the House committee. But on some other committees, House Republicans have capitalized on their unity and on divisions among Democrats to win very substantial victories. A Republican minority of 12 on the 37-member Ways and Means Committee, for instance, was able in 1978 to team up with 13 of that panel's more conservative Democrats to write a tax bill that later won full House approval despite the opposition of the leadership.

House Democrats complained that Republicans had decided to use the budget process deliberately for partisan political purposes — namely, to pin responsibility for the federal deficit on Democrats. They argue that Republicans insist on cutting spending figures contained in budget resolutions to levels that are "unrealistic" while frequently supporting individual spending bills that, in the aggregate, exceed the Republican-approved totals.

But the Republicans countered that the Democratic leadership has used the Budget Committee to promote its own partisan ends — an argument strengthened by the fact that the committee was less independent than its Senate counterpart.

Whatever the reason, the partisanship in the House has made it very difficult to pass budget resolutions there. Lack of Republican support has forced the Budget Committee to seek majority backing for its resolutions from within the ranks of the Democratic Party — a situation that has increased its dependence on the leadership and probably tilted its decisions more in favor of liberals.

One illustration of the liberal slant of the House committee came during the Democratic caucus in 1978, when representatives of organized labor lobbied heavily for the provision extending the time members could serve on the panel. Labor officials complained that the Senate committee was "too bipartisan."

Changes in the Senate

There was little indication that the partisanship of the House would diminish in 1979, but observers were closely watching the Senate, where Bellmon was reportedly coming under increasing pressure from Republicans to split more with Muskie.

In 1978, Bellmon was criticized by some Senate Republicans for failing to take the lead in pushing a Republican plan to schedule substantial annual tax cuts for several years in the future. While Bellmon did vote for the plan (the "Roth-Kemp" proposal), he was a key sponsor of an alternative pushed by many Democrats. It provided for tax cuts only on the condition that spending be reduced.

In 1979, Republicans were considering a measure that would require spending measures considered excessive to be approved by a three-quarters majority. Again, Bellmon would be under considerable pressures.

The budget process has helped spark the debate on economic goals but some believed Congress needed a better forum to establish them.

Rep. Richard Bolling, D-Mo., a prominent Rules Committee member and chairman of the Joint Economic Committee during the 95th Congress, was one of the prime sponsors of a move to include in the Humphrey-Hawkins bill a provision creating a new method for setting congressional economic policy. The provision called on Congress to adopt a resolution each year, written by the Joint Economic Committee, spelling out its long-term economic goals. Bolling said the new resolution would enable Congress to consider the complete range of economic policy in a long-term context, whereas the budget process now focuses almost completely on fiscal policy on a year-by-year basis. The proposal was supported by House Budget Committee Chairman Giaimo, who was due to leave the committee after 1978 but who was advocating a change in House rules that would extend Budget Committee members' terms.

Most members of the Budget Committee vigorously opposed the proposal, though. Some warned that it would infringe on the Budget committees, reducing them to the mechanical task of setting fiscal policy aggregates to meet the Joint Economic Committee goals. They weren't assuaged when Bolling said the JEC goals would "guide and influence — but not bind" the Budget committees. Other Budget Committee members argued that divorcing the goal-setting function from the job of writing the budget would lead to wildly unrealistic goals. Muskie said that would "destroy the credibility of economic policy."

The Long Term

The continuing discussion about the goals and effectiveness of fiscal policy has increased interest in giving Congress the ability to make better long-term decisions. Some see long-term decision making as a solution not only to fiscal policy problems, but to the budget process' shortcomings in controlling spending and setting priorities as well.

About 75 percent of the federal budget is considered "uncontrollable" on a year-by-year basis. Uncontrollable spending includes funds committed by previous Congresses for major weapons procurement or public works, unavoidable expenses such as interest on the public debt, and the costs of entitlement programs such as Social Security. The budget process has helped focus attention on the uncontrollability of the federal budget by making explicit the long-term costs of various spending proposals. The CBO provides estimates not only on the impact of proposals in the next fiscal year, but over the long run.

Some believe that Congress should take advantage of the increased information by adopting multi-year budgets. The Budget committees took a first step in that direction in 1978. The Senate committee voted not only on fiscal 1979 budget figures, but on future year figures as well. Those "out-year" figures were included in the committee's report, though not incorporated in the fiscal 1979 budget resolution.

Rivlin, a strong advocate of multi-year budgeting, said that it would also strengthen the spending priorities debate in Congress. In 1978 she warned the Budget committees that they should consider their long-run goals and plan for them now because otherwise there was a danger that relatively insignificant incremental spending decisions in the short run could swell to such proportions over the long run that little room would be left for major new initiatives such as national health insurance.

But because preparing long-term budgets involves more substantial priority decisions, it is politically more difficult. Viewing the problems of winning House approval of budget resolutions, for instance, members of that chamber's Budget Committee decided against including five-year recommendations in their fiscal 1978 reports.

Still, Rivlin believed Congress is slowly edging toward multi-year budgeting. Some developments may force it to do so. President Carter's fiscal 1980 budget, for instance, included spending figures for three years. Furthermore, the increasing discussion about long-term goals itself is pushing Congress toward more advance planning.

Finally, some budget reformers have suggested that the best way to control spending and eliminate waste was for Congress to write two-year budgets.

Some argued that the spending schedule provided by the budget act is too restrictive. While the May 15 deadline for reporting authorizing bills has helped the Appropriations committees get their bills to the floor, there were indications it has posed a tremendous burden on the authorizing committees, possibly reducing the quality of their work. "The authorizing committees are simply overworked," said one staff member involved in the study. Others suggested that the one-year spending schedule leaves little time for Congress to review how well programs are working. Panetta, for instance, has proposed a two-year budget cycle — one year for "oversight" and one for action on legislation.

Congressional Funds, Benefits

CQ

Congress Appropriates $1.12 Billion for Itself

A $1.12 billion fiscal 1979 legislative appropriations bill (HR 12935 — PL 95-391) was approved by Congress Sept. 19, 1978. The bill agreed to by House and Senate conferees carried the same price tag as the Senate version.

The annual legislative appropriations bill in recent years had been the vehicle for only one major controversy — funding congressional pay raises. Hoping to avert an election-year floor fight on that issue, House and Senate Appropriations Committees voted to deny a scheduled cost-of-living pay raise to members of Congress and other top federal officials making $47,500 a year or more. Affected would be about 16,000 executive, legislative and judicial branch employees. Federal employees making less than $47,500 would still get the raise, amounting to about 5.5 percent of their current salaries. *(1979 action, box, p. 118)*

A controversial legislative funding issue that surfaced during 1978 and could have tied up the bill instead was taken up Aug. 4 during debate of the fiscal 1978 supplemental appropriations bill (HR 13467). The controversy involved an effort by John H. Chafee, R-R.I., to stop construction of a third Senate office building. The Senate rejected Chafee's proposal and instead voted to put a $135 million ceiling on the total price of the building. However, on Aug. 25, the Senate bowed to an Aug. 17 House cut of $54.9 million for the office building. *(Box, p. 114)*

HR 12935 also became the vehicle for a surprise vote to have House employees — not commercial or public network broadcasters — control television broadcasts of House floor activities. The issue of network versus House control of the broadcasts had been simmering for several months. *(p. 147)*

Provisions

As cleared for the president, HR 12935 appropriated the following amounts for fiscal 1979:

Item	Budget Request	Final Appropriation
Senate	$185,182,000	$185,064,000
House of Representatives	306,049,900	306,016,400
Joint Items	73,773,900	73,727,100
Office of Technology Assessment	10,000,000	9,700,000
Congressional Budget Office	11,368,000	11,368,000
Architect of the Capitol	60,613,500	56,506,600
Congressional Research Service	26,379,000	25,553,000
Government Printing Office (congressional printing)	73,961,000	73,961,000
Botanic Garden	1,391,600	1,392,000
Library of Congress	167,006,500	149,093,300
Architect of the Capitol (library buildings and grounds)	2,794,700	2,776,000
Copyright Royalty Tribunal	935,000	805,000

Item	Budget Request	Final Appropriation
Government Printing Office (other than congressional printing and binding)	34,676,000	34,676,000
General Accounting Office	187,843,000	185,756,000
Cost-Accounting Standards Board	1,850,000	1,850,000
GRAND TOTAL	**$1,143,824,100**	**$1,118,244,400***

* The final bill also provided that of the total budget authority in the act for payments not required by law, 5 percent shall be withheld from obligation and expenditure. (The conference report did not spell out where the withholdings must be made.)

House Committee Action

The House Appropriations Committee May 23 voted to deny top-level government officials — including members of Congress and their highest paid aides — an automatic cost-of-living pay raise scheduled to take effect in October. The amendment was adopted during committee debate on HR 12935.

Republicans had planned to offer the amendment in full committee after a Republican pay raise deferral proposal was defeated in a Legislative Appropriations Subcommittee markup April 25.

But Democrats from the subcommittee subsequently decided to draft their own amendment in an attempt to avert a politically sensitive floor fight on the pay raise. That amendment was offered in full committee by John P. Murtha, D-Pa., who urged passage of it to "speed things up without any demagoguery on the floor."

There was little debate on Murtha's proposal. When Appropriations Committee Chairman George Mahon, D-Texas, quickly called for a vote, Edward J. Patten, D-N.J., complained that he did not know what the committee was voting on. The amendment was approved, 22-8.

The pay raise amendment required a special waiver from the Rules Committee to block parliamentary challenges on the floor. Committee sources expected the amendment to remain intact because, said one aide, "In an election year you're not going to get too many members who will vote themselves a pay raise." In 1977, Congress blocked the annual cost-of-living raise but agreed to a separate proposal raising members' salaries $12,900 a year.

As approved by the committee, HR 12935 appropriated $922,491,800 for operations of the House and related agencies during fiscal 1979. It did not contain money for operations of the Senate, which is traditionally added by the Senate Appropriations Committee as amendments to the House bill. The budget request for the Senate and its related expenses was $195,130,500.

Following a practice begun in 1977, the committee divided appropriations between two categories — congressional operations, and related agencies that do not provide "primary support" for Congress.

Controversy Surrounds Cost of New Senate Building

Spiraling cost estimates for a new Senate office building made it the subject of increasing controversy in 1978-79.

The steel skeleton for the new building, named for the late Sen. Philip A. Hart, D-Mich. (1959-76), now stands on a three-acre site near the Capitol. When approved in 1972, the building was expected to cost $47.9 million. By July 1979 the cost had risen to $174.5 million, according to an estimate prepared by a consulting firm for the Capitol Architect's office.

1978 Action

The Senate approved funds for the building in 1978 by a comfortable margin, easily defeating an attempt to block funding of the building.

Sen. John H. Chafee, R-R.I., and a handful of other senators had introduced an amendment to the legislative appropriations bill (HR 12935) to rescind about $69 million in unspent funds that were appropriated for the building in the early 1970s. In a statement announcing his amendment, Chafee chided the Senate for wanting to build itself a "palace." He said it was a taxpayer-funded project "designed solely to comfort and coddle the 100 of us."

Much of the criticism was aimed at the "luxury" items in the building. Sen. William Proxmire, D-Wis., gave the Senate in March 1978 his "Golden Fleece of the Month" award for the building, which he said "would make a Persian prince green with envy." Among the features criticized by Proxmire were the building's planned rooftop dining room for senators only, a new gymnasium (the Senate already had two gyms) and $1.5 million worth of wood paneling for senators' offices.

However, Chafee's amendment, which drew only seven cosponsors, amounted to little more than a quixotic exercise.

But the House — in a rare violation of the spirit of comity between the two chambers — rejected a $54.9 million appropriation for the building by a big vote, 133-245. The Senate had added the funds to a supplemental appropriations bill.

House opponents not only criticized the expense of the building but also attacked the main justification of the building — that the crowded Senate staff needed more room. Critics said that holding down the available room would put a lid on the rapidly growing congressional staff.

1979 Funds

To shore up support for the project, the Senate Office Building Commission July 17, 1979, cut about $35 million in costs by eliminating such items as the wood paneling in senators' offices, rooftop restaurant, gymnasium for senators and a room equipped with booths for network anchormen.

The cuts, proposed by Commission Chairman J. Bennett Johnston, D-La., were approved 7-1; the "no" vote came from Sen. Pete V. Domenici, R-N.M., who said the building should be abandoned.

The plan then went to the Senate Appropriations Committee, which the same day added back about $4.9 million for the rooftop dining room, the wood paneling and the hearing room. The vote to restore those features was 8-7.

The two actions brought the building's total estimated cost to $142.6 million. With the $85 million already approved, additional funding of about $57.5 million was needed for completion. This was $2.6 million more than the funding approved by the Senate but rejected by the House in 1978.

In floor action, the Senate first rejected the extra funds, then reversed itself and approved them.

An amendment offered by Johnston to appropriate $57.5 million for the building's completion and to set a ceiling of $142.6 million on the building's total cost was rejected on a tie vote, 47-47. That vote then was reconsidered — after two more roll calls — and the appropriation and ceiling approved 49-46.

Providing the margin of victory were Sens. Howard M. Metzenbaum, D-Ohio, who switched from "no" on the first vote to "yea" on the last, and Mike Gravel, D-Alaska, and Russell B. Long, D-La., who were absent on the first vote but voted "yea" on the last. Joseph R. Biden Jr., D-Del., voted "yea" on the first vote but was absent from the last.

Even with the legislated ceiling, however, the building was virtually certain to cost more.

Tellico Dam Controversy

The Senate then tacked the $57.5 million appropriations for the building onto the fiscal 1980 energy and water development appropriations bill (HR 4388). By August conference negotiations had been completed and the conference report (H Rept 96-388) on the bill had been approved by the House. The House trimmed about $4.9 million off the funding approved by the conferees, reducing the appropriations to $52.6 million, and setting a ceiling of $137.7 million on the building's cost. The Senate approved the conference report, with the lower funding, on Sept. 10.

Although the bill was cleared for the president, the controversial building's future still was not assured. One of the bill's provisions would continue construction of the equally controversial Tellico Dam in Tennessee. (Construction of the dam had been halted in 1978 when the Supreme Court ruled the dam's completion would violate the Endangered Species Act by jeopardizing the survival of an endangered fish, the snail darter.)

Interior Secretary Cecil Andrus and a number of environmental groups asked President Carter to veto the bill. Despite their objections, Carter signed the bill Sept. 26.

A spokesman for Sen. Johnston, floor manager of HR 4388, said it was doubtful a veto would have permanently jeopardized the appropriation for the building. He said that if the bill had been vetoed and final action on public works funds delayed, funds for the Hart structure could have been attached to another bill. Delay in approving the funds could have added some $700,000 a month to the construction costs.

Printing Clerks

Missing from the $922.5 million bill was $33,500 in salaries paid to two House printing clerks. In the past, Democrat David Ramage and Republican Thomas Lankford were paid House funds to print congressional material such as leadership notices.

In addition to their work for the House, both clerks ran private commercial printing businesses in the offices they were given to perform their public jobs. The General Accounting Office reported in 1977 that Ramage and Lankford were each doing at least $1 million a year in private business by printing press releases, bumper stickers and other political material for members of Congress.

The Legislative Appropriations Subcommittee agreed that while the clerks could continue to print material for the House, they would no longer be paid public salaries. The full committee concurred in dropping any appropriations for their salaries.

Republicans William L. Armstrong, Colo., and Lawrence C. Coughlin, Pa., offered several "reform" amendments in the full committee markup, but each was defeated. The two planned to offer the amendments again when the legislative appropriations bill reaches the floor.

The defeated amendments were:

● A Coughlin proposal to cut a total of $6.7 million from the appropriations recommended for members' district office space, constituent communications and consolidated account allowances. Defeated by voice vote.

● An Armstrong amendment to require use of office funds to pay for plants, storage trunks and calendars now provided free to all members. Defeated by voice vote.

● A Coughlin amendment providing General Accounting Office audits of House accounts. Defeated 11-23.

House of Representatives

The committee recommended $306,016,400 to pay for House operations in fiscal 1979. That was an increase of $23,344,300 from the fiscal 1978 appropriation. The committee recommendation included the following:

Members' Compensation. The bill recommended $27,699,300 to pay members' salaries and contributions for retirement, life and health insurance.

Members' Mileage. The allowance for mileage to cover one round trip to the district for each member was continued at the existing level of $210,000 for fiscal 1979. Another $3,494,000 from House contingent expenses (listed below) was recommended to cover the cost of an additional 25 round trips allowed each member.

House Leadership Offices. The committee recommended $2,147,100 for the operations of majority and minority House leaders' offices. In fiscal 1978, the officers were allotted $2,056,600.

House Employees. The clerk, sergeant at arms, doorkeeper and other House employees and officers would receive $26,407,700 for fiscal 1979 operations under the committee's recommendation.

Committee Employees. The committee recommended $24,705,000 for salaries of professional and clerical employees of the 22 House standing committees. That was the same amount appropriated in fiscal 1978.

Committee Studies. The committee recommended $2,895,000 for studies and investigations to be undertaken by its own staff. It also recommended $261,000 for Budget Committee studies.

Law Revision and Legislative Counsels. The law revision counsel office would get $435,000 under the committee recommendation, while the office of legislative counsel would get $1,879,000.

Members' Clerk Hire. The committee recommended $112,648,300 for the salaries of members' personal staff aides. The fiscal 1978 clerk hire appropriation was $107,-192,000.

The committee report noted that the current clerk hire allowance is $273,132 per member, but that some representatives used less than the full amount either by hiring fewer people than permitted or by paying less than the maximum salaries allowed. The report said that if every member used 100 percent of the allowance, the total for clerk hire would be $119,904,948.

House Contingent Expenses. The committee recommended appropriations of $106,729,000 for contingent expenses, with $59,967,000 of that allotted to pay official allowances and expenses of members. The remaining $46,-762,000 was recommended to pay for investigations by standing committees and for operations of special and select committees.

The appropriations for allowances and expenses pay for such office expenses as computer services, mail, equipment, transportation, telephone service and stationery.

Joint Items

The committee recommended appropriations of $73,-727,100 to cover the House share of expenses of committees and services shared with the Senate. That included $2,-353,000 for the Joint Economic Committee, $656,000 for the Joint Committee on Printing, and $2,375,200 for the Joint Committee on Taxation. Other recommendations:

Doctor, Police, Pages. The committee recommended $465,000 to cover costs of the House attending physician, $2,171,000 for Capitol Police operations and $205,800 for the Capitol Page School. The committee also asked the Comptroller General to evaluate education and other services at the Capitol Page School.

Official Mail Costs. The committee recommended $64,944,000 to pay the U.S. Postal Service for the cost of sending franked congressional mail. The committee said that figure was only an estimate of what the fiscal 1979 costs might be.

Capitol Guide Service. The committee recommended $544,000 for permanent and temporary Capitol guides.

OTA, CBO

The committee recommended $9,700,000 for the Office of Technology Assessment.

The committee recommended $11,172,000 for fiscal 1979 Congressional Budget Office operations — $196,000 less than CBO had requested. It also recommended that CBO cut costs by reducing the number of reports it does on its own initiative.

Capitol Architect, CRS

The committee recommended $46,014,000 for the Architect of the Capitol's maintenance of congressional grounds and buildings. That included $21,065,000 for operation of the three House office buildings and two annexes and $13,635,000 for the Capitol power plant.

The committee recommended $25,553,000 for the Congressional Research Service.

Government Printing Office

The committee recommended $73,961,000 to pay for printing and binding of documents for congressional use.

That was an increase of $2,287,000 over the fiscal 1978 level. Included in the fiscal 1979 recommendation was $5,090,400 to print the *Congressional Record,* $9,868,750 to print bills, resolutions and amendments, $4,079,700 to print committee reports, $22,425,000 to print hearings and $2,225,255 to print House and Senate committee and business calendars. However, those figures covered only the documents that would be used by Congress. Cost of printing copies of the same material for the public or other government officials was included in the GPO "related agency" recommendation listed below.

Related Agencies

The $376,348,300 recommended by the committee for related agencies was divided up as follows:

Botanic Garden. The committee recommended $1,392,000 for the Botanic Garden in fiscal 1979, an increase of $109,000 from fiscal 1978.

Library of Congress. For all Library of Congress fiscal 1979 expenses, except operation of the Congressional Research Service, the committee recommended $149,093,300 — $20,139,700 above the previous year. The committee denied most of the Library's request for $3,366,500 for its new James Madison Building. The committee said that because construction delays made it appear the building would not be ready for occupancy until late 1979 or early 1980, it recommended only $268,664 for packing and crating of research materials to move to the building.

Architect of the Capitol. To maintain Library of Congress buildings and grounds, the committee recommended an additional $2,776,000 for the Architect of the Capitol.

Government Printing Office. For expenses of printing material not used by Congress, the committee recommended $34,676,000.

The most costly printed item was copies of the *Congressional Record* sent to executive branch agencies and the public. The committee recommended $9,049,600 for those copies of the Record. The committee also recommended that the public printer increase the subscription price of the Record in order to cover more of the costs.

General Accounting Office. The committee recommended $185,756,000 for the General Accounting Office, an increase of $18,756,000 over its fiscal 1978 appropriations. The recommendation allowed for a net increase of 120 staffers, needed to cope with increased congressional demand for GAO studies, the committee said. It also would cover an increased GAO workload on Department of Defense matters. The committee said about 30 percent of GAO's work involved reports done for Congress. GAO recommendations and suggestions in fiscal 1977 had saved the federal treasury $5,637,059,000, the committee said.

House Floor Action

The House June 14 approved a 5 percent across-the-board slash in funding for Congress' own operations.

The 220-168 vote to cut the fiscal 1979 legislative appropriations bill marked the third time in two days that the House had approved what opponents called "meat ax" amendments to appropriations bills.

Across-the-board cuts had previously been approved in funding bills for the Labor, Health, Education and Welfare, State, Justice and Commerce Departments.

As passed by the House, 279-90, HR 12935 appropriated $922.5 million (before across-the-board cuts) for the House and related agencies.

Silvio O. Conte, R-Mass., who opposed a successful across-the-board cut in the Labor-HEW spending bill, offered the 5 percent slash in HR 12935.

"If we really want to be responsive to the taxpayers' revolt expressed in Proposition 13 (a property tax cut measure, in California) we have to look no further than the halls of Congress," he said. Conte suggested his proposal would "show the people that we are willing to do it right here in our own house, which is larded over with fat."

Legislative Appropriations Subcommittee Chairman George E. Shipley, D-Ill., protested that, "We truly have cut this down where we can't stand even a 1 percent cut in this bill." Shipley said Congress "deserves" the money allotted in the bill.

Clarence E. Miller, R-Ohio, sponsor of the across-the-board cut amendments to other appropriations bills, offered a substitute to the Conte amendment that would have called for a 2 percent slash in congressional spending. Miller's substitute was defeated by voice vote. The House then passed Conte's amendment.

The success of Conte's proposal signalled the House mood favored cuts.

One beneficiary of that mood was William L. Armstrong, R-Colo., whose proposal to require use of office funds to pay for plants, storage trunks, calendars and agriculture yearbooks had drawn little interest in previous attempts to pass it. This time, the House adopted Armstrong's proposal, 214-159. That margin included 16 members who switched from "nay" to "aye" after seeing that Armstrong would win.

The items covered in Armstrong's amendment, now provided to members for free, would still be subsidized by taxpayers. However, Armstrong argued that if members had to pay for them with office funds, they would be less inclined to take them, and spending would be reduced.

After Armstrong's success, Gary A. Myers, R-Pa., offered an amendment to prohibit members from using office funds to pay for flags given to constituents. Flags flown over the Capitol could currently be purchased by members from office funds.

But the House decided it had gone far enough with the calendars and plants. Shipley said it would be too expensive for him to have to use his own money to pay for the flags he gave to Girl Scouts, Cub Scouts and other groups. "What are you going to do when a disabled vet asks for a flag that has flown over the Capitol? Are we going to say we have to have him pay $5?" Myers' amendment was defeated by voice vote.

Broadcast Debate

An unexpected vote on House broadcasts was prompted by an amendment from John B. Anderson, R-Ill., an advocate of network control over House broadcasts.

Anderson, who had pushed for a House vote on the camera control issue, charged that the Democratic leadership was moving close to House purchase of color television cameras without having let the House decide who should run the system. He offered an amendment to prevent House purchase of color cameras, which was defeated, 133-249.

During discussion of Anderson's amendment, allies of House Speaker Thomas P. O'Neill Jr., D-Mass. — who favored House control of the system — announced they would bring the network versus House issue up for a vote immediately. Their amendment, offered by Adam Benjamin Jr., D-Ind., prohibited anyone but House employees from running the House broadcast system. Currently, House offices could hook up to a closed-circuit system enabling them to watch floor action. But a more sophisticated system was to be installed before the House made any television broadcasts available to commercial broadcasters.

Anderson charged that if the House adopted the Benjamin amendment, "Those who make the news are going to manage the news." He said the issue involved journalistic integrity. "You are saying that the people who are reporting electronically on the proceedings of the House must be employees of this body or they are not qualified, somehow, to operate those cameras," said Anderson.

Majority Leader Jim Wright, D-Texas, said the issue was not journalistic integrity, but "the integrity of the House." Many members feared that if the networks were allowed to bring their cameras in the chamber, they would show members in unflattering poses.

Ronald V. Dellums, D-Calif., openly attacked what he called the "white, male-dominated, chauvinist" media. He charged that journalists frequently ignore statements made by "women, minorities, progressives, thinking people."

Robert K. Dornan, R-Calif., agreed with Dellums' position that the networks should be kept out of the House. But instead of charging indifference to "progressives," conservative Dornan labeled the networks "left of center." Benjamin's amendment was adopted, 235-150.

Office Account Audits

By voice vote, the House adopted an amendment offered by Lawrence Coughlin, R-Pa., calling for General Accounting Office audits of all House accounts.

Another Coughlin amendment proposed cutting $6.7 million from members' district office space, constituent communications and consolidated account allowances. The amendment was defeated by voice vote.

GOP Offices

Allen E. Ertel, D-Pa., proposed an amendment that would force the National Republican Congressional Committee to move out of House office space by Dec. 1. The Democratic Congressional Campaign Committee, which also had used rent-free House office space, moved out of the federally owned building in November 1977.

Michael T. Blouin, D-Iowa, then offered an amendment to the Ertel proposal that would have required the GOP committee to move out of House space as soon as HR 12935 was enacted. Blouin's proposal touched off a highly partisan, sometimes acrimonious, debate.

The chairman of the GOP committee, Guy Vander Jagt, R-Mich., told the House that new office space was being built for the committee. In the meantime, the committee's attempt to pay rent on the House space it occupied had been turned down by Speaker O'Neill, he said. Vander Jagt called the Blouin proposal a "blatantly partisan proposal which would result in dumping us out in the street in the middle of a campaign at the moment our building is going up." He agreed to accept Ertel's alternative, adding that the committee planned to move into its new building before Ertel's Dec. 1 deadline anyway.

Blouin's proposal was defeated by voice vote. The House then adopted the Ertel amendment by voice vote.

An amendment offered by Robert E. Bauman, R-Md., to prohibit use of funds for legal representation of congressional employees without Congress' approval, was adopted by voice vote.

John L. Burton, D-Calif., offered an amendment to prohibit use of funds in the bill to install pay toilets in the Capitol. Although there were no pay toilets in the Capitol, "the House has been so stupid tonight that I do not know that somebody might not think that it would be improper to have free toilets, paid for at the taxpayers' expense," Burton said. The amendment was defeated by voice vote.

Senate Committee Action

The Senate Appropriations Committee reported HR 12935 (S Rept 95-1024) on July 19.

The bill appropriated $1,118,244,400 for operations of the House, Senate and related agencies. The Senate version was $195,752,600 above the bill passed by the House, but House legislative appropriations bills traditionally do not include funding for Senate operations. Most of the increase recommended by the Senate committee was for Senate operations and the Architect of the Capitol's expenses to maintain Senate offices and grounds.

The Senate bill contained $25,579,700 less than the budget request. The committee report said the reduction from the budget request actually was higher, because the bill included a recommendation that 5 percent of the total bill be cut from payments not required by law. The committee did not state how much the cut would be.

The House had approved a similar across-the-board cut, estimated to be $45 million, in its version of the bill.

Congressional Operations

The bill contained $741,896,100 to pay for congressional operations in fiscal 1979, an increase of $75,518,800 from the fiscal 1978 appropriation. Of the total, $185,064,000 was for Senate operations.

The committee agreed to the $306,016,400 the House had approved for its own operations. Its recommendations for other congressional operations, such as the Capitol Police and the Architect of the Capitol, closely paralleled the House-passed bill.

Committee recommendations for Senate and other congressional expenditures were:

Compensation and Mileage. The committee recommended $6,480,000 to pay for salaries and contributions for retirement, life and health insurance for the senators and the vice president, who serves as the president of the Senate. The recommendation also included funds for members' expenses in traveling between their home states and Congress. Members' travel allowance is 20 cents per mile.

The recommendation was $5,700 more than the 1978 appropriation for compensation and mileage, reflecting an increase in health insurance costs.

Senate Leadership Offices. The bill recommended $25,000 in expense allowances for the offices of the vice president, majority and minority leaders and party whips. The figure was the same as the 1978 appropriation.

Senate Employees. The bill recommended the following amounts for the offices of various Senate employees and officials: vice president, $767,000; president pro tempore, $116,000; majority and minority leaders, $411,-000; floor assistants to majority and minority leaders, $103,000; majority and minority whips, $239,000; secretaries of the majority and minority conferences, $132,000; chaplain, $40,000; secretary of the Senate, $4,116,000.

Congressional Action on Pay Raises

The political volatility of congressional pay increases was vividly demonstrated once again in 1979 when the issue became a key factor in a Senate-House feud. That dispute caused the government to start its new fiscal year Oct. 1 without spending authority for most agencies.

Members of Congress receive salaries that are vastly larger than those earned by all but a handful of other Americans; as 1979 began, senators and representatives were paid $57,500 a year.

Moreover, members were due for an automatic pay hike in October under the "comparability" or cost-of-living pay procedures used by the government to keep the earnings of federal workers in line with private sector employees. That increase was set at 7 percent.

But that wasn't the end of it. Added to this 7 percent was a 5.5 percent comparability increase for 1978 that Congress had voted not to take because members feared the voters wouldn't like that very much.

However, the 1978 hike was not repealed; it was just suspended until the fall of 1979. Thus if nothing were done, members would get both pay hikes, plus some interest on the 5.5 percent amount, for a total increase of 12.9 percent, or more than $7,400.

With the election just a year in the future, a move was launched to limit or even deny any increase for Congress. Also caught up in this fervor were federal judges and top-level executive branch bureaucrats who make at least $47,500; past pay freezes have covered them, also.

In June, the House rejected its own appropriations bill because the measure allowed a 5.5 percent pay hike. Then, in late September, both chambers bogged down in controversy over a continuing resolution that was being used to approve the pay hike.

The continuing resolution was needed to fund agencies for which regular appropriations bills had not yet been passed by Oct. 1 — which meant most of the government. The House, in a non-recorded vote, had accepted a 5.5 percent hike. The Senate knocked that out and said no raise.

But the House just two days before the new fiscal year was to begin insisted on the raise and adjourned for a week's recess, leaving the Senate with either accepting the increase or killing the funding resolution. The latter meant that most of the government would have no power to spend money on Oct. 1, the beginning of the new year, and that the 12.9 percent pay hike would take effect. The Senate voted to kill the resolution.

The 12.9 percent hike could later be rolled back for Congress and top-level bureaucrats, but not for judges; the Constitution says the pay of judges cannot be reduced during their term of office.

That settled the matter for judges, but everything else was left hanging in early October as the House vacationed and the Senate fumed over the House's action. Sen. Jennings Randolph, D-W.Va., said House members "left their post of duty." A colleague was even more blunt. Barry Goldwater, R-Ariz., said: "Here we are on a Saturday sitting on our duffs doing nothing because the House has taken it upon themselves to quit, to put their tail between their legs, shirk their responsi-

bility to our people, our government, and our world and wander off home."

Background

Congress completed action July 30, 1975, on a bill (HR 2559) granting members and other top government officials an automatic cost-of-living pay increase every year, beginning the following Oct. 1. President Ford signed the bill into law Aug. 9 (PL 94-82).

The measure cleared after passing the House by a one-vote margin — 214-213. It had passed the Senate the day before on a 58-29 roll-call. Final action came only five days after the proposal had first surfaced publicly as a rider to a minor postal service bill.

Two months later, Congress voted to limit to 5 percent the 1975 pay increases for members of Congress, military personnel and top-level officials and white-collar employees of the federal government. Both houses voted to uphold the 5 percent pay hike proposed by President Ford Aug. 29 rather than raise salaries by 8.66 percent, as had been proposed by the Advisory Committee on Federal Pay. The salary of members of Congress thus increased from $42,500 to $44,600.

Advocates of the raise for high-level government officials argued that an adjustment in top-level salaries was long overdue. Those affected by passage of HR 2559 had not had a pay raise since March 1969, while the Consumer Price Index had risen by 47.5 percent.

Opponents charged that the measure would allow Congress to receive regular pay raises tied to the cost of living without having to vote on the raises.

Beneficiaries of the action included 17,028 members and top officials of Congress, the executive and judicial branches, plus 600 high-ranking military officers. President Ford's salary was not affected, though Vice President Nelson A. Rockefeller's was.

The legislation did not provide any "catch-up" pay to compensate for the diminished purchasing power of these officials as a result of the six-year absence of a salary hike. Nor did it provide any increase to keep top-level government pay comparable with rising levels of compensation in private industry.

1977, 1978 Action

Congress in 1977 made up for lost time by giving itself and other top government officials a large — $12,900 — and long-postponed pay raise. But it paid a price for the boost. It repealed the procedure which had allowed raises to take effect without a congressional vote, and both chambers enacted tough new ethics codes that included tight limits on outside income. (However, the Senate in 1979 suspended those limits for four years.) It also denied itself a scheduled fall cost-of-living increase. Even so, criticism of the raise was widespread. *(See 1977 pay raise, box, p. 158)*

In 1978, members of Congress used the legislative appropriations bill for fiscal 1979 (PL 95-391) to deny the 1978 raise to themselves, their top aides, judges and all other federal officials at or over the $47,500 pay level. Some 16,000 persons were affected. Other federal workers got the raise, which was 5.5 percent.

The committee deleted $116,000 requested for the deputy president pro tempore, a post created in 1977 for Sen. Hubert H. Humphrey, D-Minn. (1949-64, 1971-78).

Committee Employees. The bill recommended $10,528,000 for salaries of professional and clerical employees of Senate standing committees. That was $1 million more than the 1978 appropriation.

Conference Committees. For the professional, administrative and clerical staffs of the Democratic and Republican conferences, the committee recommended $750,000. The $62,000 increase over fiscal 1978 appropriations for the conference staffs would provide salary increases, the committee said.

Members' Staff. The committee recommended $70,881,000 to pay salaries of senators' administrative and clerical staff.

Most of the $10 million increase over fiscal 1978 funding was due to including appropriations for legislative staffers — formerly a separate item — in the administrative and clerical allowance, according to the committee.

Sergeant at Arms and Doorkeeper. The committee recommended $19,803,000 for the Senate sergeant at arms and the Senate doorkeeper, an increase of $1,903,000 over fiscal 1978. The committee said $500,000 of the increase was necessary to keep the appropriations at fiscal 1978 levels, which had been boosted by $500,000 in leftover fiscal 1977 funds. Most of the additional increase was to pay for new positions in the Senate computer center.

Included in the sergeant at arms and doorkeeper appropriations was the funding for Capitol Police salaries. The Senate earmarked $8,112,101 to pay for 523 police positions on its payroll. The House sergeant at arms payroll included 629 positions, with a fiscal 1979 appropriation of $9,774,138.

Majority, Minority Secretaries. The committee recommended appropriations totaling $411,000 for the majority and minority secretaries.

Retirement, Insurance. To pay for retirement, life and health insurance contributions and for longevity compensation for certain Senate officers and employees, the committee recommended $7,785,000.

Legislative Counsel. The committee recommended $815,000 for the office of legislative counsel.

Senate Contingent Expenses. The committee recommended $61,662,000 for Senate contingent expenses, which included Democratic and Republican policy committee staff salaries; purchase, lease and maintenance of 20 vehicles for use of Senate officers; document folding; inquiries and investigations; postage stamps and stationery.

Joint Items

The committee recommended $2,353,000 for the Joint Economic Committee, $656,000 for the Joint Committee on Printing and $2,375,200 for the Joint Committee on Taxation. The House had approved the same amounts.

The Senate committee also concurred in these House appropriations: $465,000 for the Capitol's attending physician offices, $205,800 for the Capitol Page School, $544,000 for permanent and temporary Capitol guides, $64,944,000 to pay the U.S. Postal Service for the cost of sending franked congressional mail, and $2,171,000 for general expenses of the Capitol Police and reimbursement to the District of Columbia police department for its 34 officers detailed to the Capitol Police.

OTA, CBO

The committee recommended $9,700,000 for the Office of Technology Assessment, the same as the House-passed appropriation.

The committee restored $196,000 cut by the House from the Congressional Budget Office's (CBO) request. That put the Senate committee's recommendation for CBO operations at $11,368,000. The committee said the restored money was intended to allow CBO to regularly analyze the inflationary impact of major legislative proposals.

Capitol Architect, CRS

The committee recommended $56,506,600 for the Architect of the Capitol's maintenance of congressional office buildings and grounds. That was $10,492,600 above the House appropriation, but the increase reflected maintenance expenses for Senate office buildings and the Senate garage. The House bill did not include any funding for Senate operations.

The committee recommended $25,553,000 for the Congressional Research Service, the same as the House appropriation.

Government Printing Office

The committee concurred in the House appropriation of $73,961,000 for the Government Printing Office to print and bind documents for congressional use.

Related Agencies

The $376,348,300 recommended by the committee for related agencies was divided up as follows:

Botanic Garden. The committee recommended $1,392,000 for operation of the botanic garden and grounds. The figure was the same as the House-approved appropriation.

Library of Congress. For all Library of Congress expenses except operation of the Congressional Research Service, the committee recommended $149,093,300. The House adopted an identical appropriation.

Architect of the Capitol. The committee recommended an additional $2,776,000 for the Architect of the Capitol to pay for maintenance of the Library of Congress and its grounds. The House approved the same amount.

Copyright Royalty Tribunal. The committee recommended $805,000, the same as the House appropriation, for the Copyright Royalty Tribunal.

Government Printing Office. For printing and binding publications used by executive branch agencies and the general public, the committee recommended $34,676,000 in additional Government Printing Office appropriations.

General Accounting Office. The committee recommendation of $185,756,000 for the General Accounting Office was the same as the GAO appropriation approved by the House.

Cost-Accounting Standards Board. The committee recommended $1,850,000 for the Cost-Accounting Standards Board, which set standards for defense contractors and subcontractors.

General Provisions

The committee voted to deny to top federal officials an automatic pay raise scheduled to take effect in October. The House also voted to deny the pay raise.

Following another House move, the committee recommended a 5 percent cut in the bill's total appropriations.

Congressional Record: Past and Present

On Oct. 18, 1972, according to the *Congressional Record,* Rep. Hale Boggs D-La. (1941-43, 1947-72) addressed the House. "In the next few minutes," he is quoted as saying, "I would like to note for members the great amount of significant legislation enacted during the session." At the end of his speech, the record shows, Boggs wished every member a Merry Christmas and Happy New Year.

All of this is bizarre fiction. Hale Boggs was dead on Oct. 18, the victim of a plane crash in the Alaska mountains two days before. As was routine, he had left behind a written speech to be printed at the close of the year's session. The fact that it was printed despite his death merely reflected the truth about the *Congressional Record* — it recorded not only what was said in Congress, but what members wanted people to believe they would have said had they been present. Until 1978 there was no way to tell one from the other.

According to the law, Title 44, Section 901, the *Congressional Record* "shall be substantially a verbatim report of proceedings" of Congress. But the *Record* in years past did not distinguish between speeches delivered on the floor and those merely submitted for publication. In addition, members were allowed to radically revise the text of their remarks on the floor before publication.

Recent Changes

On March 1, 1978, at the direction of House and Senate, the Government Printing Office began using large black dots to mark the beginning and end of speeches, articles and other materials members insert in the *Record* without actually reading them on the floor.

However, despite the fact that Congress' daily journal now uses "bullets" to mark unspoken speeches, readers of the *Congressional Record* may still have trouble distinguishing spoken remarks from undelivered speeches. A loophole in the recent policy allows a member to avoid bullets without having to deliver a speech. As long as the first portion of the statement (such as the first sentence or paragraph) is read on the floor, the entire speech can be inserted in the *Record* as though it were spoken.

Another change occurred with the advent of the House TV system in 1979, when the *Congressional Record* added time cues to its pages. With the first issue for the 96th Congress, the House on Jan. 15, 1979, began printing time cues which show when a speech takes place. *(See story, p. 147)*

Verbal Inflation

Verbal inflation on Capitol Hill has joined forces with economic inflation. Congress approved fiscal 1979 appropriations for congressional printing at the Government Printing Office (GPO) totaling $73,961,000, an increase of $2,287,000 over fiscal 1978 funds. Included in the fiscal 1979 bill was $5,090,400 to print the *Congressional Record.* For printing copies of the *Record* sent to executive branch agencies and the public, the bill appropriated $9,049,600, the most costly item for expenses of printing material not used by Congress. These figures reflect the mounting printing costs and increased volume of congressional publications.

The Joint Committee on Printing, responding to repeated lengthy insertions in the *Record* as extensions of remarks, in 1972 announced changes in the procedure by which senators and representatives were permitted to insert speeches, articles and other materials in the *Record* that were not actually read from the floor of the House or Senate.

In making the changes, the committee revived a procedure, repealed in 1968, that required members planning to insert more than two pages of material first to obtain an estimate of the cost from the public printer. Even with the two-page limit on insertions, however, the size of the *Record* has crept steadily upward. Production costs per page of the *Record* have rapidly increased — from $119 in 1967 to $278 in 1975, to $386 in August 1979, to an anticipated $394 in fiscal 1980.

In 1976, a House report called for a sales price increase of the *Record* which then had an annual subscription rate of $45. Effective with the first issue of the *Congressional Record* for the 96th Congress, the yearly subscription rate was $75. This was the first increase in sales price since 1970 and "necessary to establish a more realistic price for the *Congressional Record* based on production and distribution costs" according to a notice in the *Record.*

By law, taxpayers subsidize thousands of subscriptions. In 1977 Congress cut in half the number of copies members receive for distribution to designated agencies and institutions; each senator is now entitled to 50 copies and representatives may receive 34 copies each.

The committee's only stipulation was that payments required by law could not be cut.

The committee's 5 percent cut amendment dropped House language requiring that no more than 10 percent could be cut from any one item within the bill. "The deletion of the [10 percent limit] would allow more than 10 percent to be withheld from some appropriations, activities, and projects, a necessity if the intent of the 5 percent reduction is to be accomplished," the committee report said.

Senate Floor Action

Following the lead of the House, the Senate voted Aug. 4 to cut the funds in the bill by 5 percent.

The vote was 72-0 in favor of the $55.9 million cut. The bill, which funds operations of the House, Senate and related agencies, was passed by the Senate, 67-20, Aug. 7.

Senate debate on the bill, which closely paralleled the House-passed version, was routine.

The House had approved a 5 percent across-the-board cut that would not affect spending mandated by law — such as members' salaries — but would prevent a cut of more than 10 percent in any one item. The Senate Appropriations Committee recommended a similar amendment, but without the 10 percent restriction.

To give their colleagues an election-year opportunity to vote for a spending cut in the congressional budget, the Senate committee requested a recorded floor vote on the 5 percent cut. "While we knew our colleagues would agree with the cut, we would like them to join in the record to show that we are willing to cut our own thing," said Richard S. Schweiker, R-Pa., ranking minority member of the Legislative Appropriations Subcommittee.

After approving the cut, the Senate agreed by voice vote to an amendment clarifying the committee's language, to assure that all appropriations — including those mandated by law — would be considered in computing the size of the 5 percent cut.

The funding levels approved by the Senate were the same as those recommended by the Appropriations Committee.

Conference, Final Action

Conferees quickly resolved minor differences between the House and Senate versions of the bill, and a conference report (H Rept 95-1457) was filed Aug. 9.

Traditionally, the House and Senate each have determined the appropriations needed for their own operations, and the other body has concurred. In funding other congressional operations, the House and Senate versions of HR 12935 differed only on the amount of money for Congressional Budget Office (CBO) operations. The conference committee adopted the Senate version of CBO funding, which was $196,000 more than the House bill. The conferees also agreed to the Senate ceiling of 218 CBO employees instead of the House ceiling of 208.

The conference committee agreed to the Senate language requiring a 5 percent cut in the total bill without affecting items required by law. It dropped the House stipulation that no one item could be cut more than 10 percent.

The conference report also contained some directions for applying the cut. The cut "should be applied by the various agencies, offices and other bodies encompassed by the (bill)," the report said. The clerk of the House and the secretary of the Senate were directed to determine where the cuts would be made in the House and Senate budgets.

The report also directed the librarian of Congress to avoid cuts in several programs and to avoid reducing the library's operating hours "until maximum reductions are made in non-essential library services such as excessive overhead in the librarian's immediate office and the office of the director of the Congressional Research Service."

Final Action

The House adopted the conference report Aug. 17 by a 255-123 vote. The Senate gave its approval by voice vote Sept. 19, completing action on the bill. ∎

Office, Staff Funds Bolster Members' Pay

Both the pay and perquisites of members of Congress have increased enormously since World War II. Although allowances vary from member to member, the National Republican Congressional Committee in June 1978 estimated that House offices receive an average of $575,000 annually for salary, staff, travel and office expenses.

Aside from the congressional salary, a member's single greatest perquisite is a personal staff. Staff aides multiply the member's arms, legs, eyes and ears, providing the best hope of meeting the demands on the member's time. Properly used, a personal staff can function as the member's strongest ally. Misused, a personal staff becomes little more than a reservoir of wasted talents. And abused, a personal staff can turn traitor; for like the gentleman and his valet, no member is a hero to his staff.

Among the other formal, statutory perquisites are the franking privilege, immunity from certain legal actions, free office space in federal buildings, and allowances for travel, telephone and telegraph services, stationery, office expenses and equipment, plus thousands of free publications. Other benefits members receive include free storage of files and records, inexpensive use of television and radio studios, modern recreational facilities, and discounts from Capitol Hill shops and services.

In addition, there is a vast, ill-defined collection of informal perquisites based on the deference customarily shown a VIP. Such deference appears typically in delaying the departure of a plane to accommodate the tardy arrival of a member of Congress. Other informal perquisites include free parking, assured press coverage under many circumstances, and special treatment by government agencies.

Are congressional perquisites abused? Objectively, it is difficult to tell. Probably the best answer is that members abuse their privileges about as much as such privileges would be abused by the public in general. Large-scale abuses, while rare, are uncovered periodically, touching off widely publicized scandals.

Personal Staffs of Members

For a century after the organization of Congress, no provision was made in either chamber for personal staff for a member, unless he was chairman of a committee.

The Senate was first to provide for staff aides. In 1885, a senator was authorized to employ a clerk when Congress was in session. The rate was set at $6 per day. In 1893, the House first authorized a clerk for its members and provided $100 monthly for the clerk's salary.

Over the years the number of aides and the size of their salaries have increased steadily. Staff responsibilities have expanded as well, to include clerical and bureaucratic support skills, technical and professional legislative skills and political skills. Employees usually have to perform in all three areas.

In August 1979, Sen. William Proxmire, D-Wis., awarding his "golden fleece of the month" to Congress,

stated that in the past 10 years House and Senate staffs have increased by about 70 percent, from about 10,700 to 18,400 persons. The cost of the staffs has risen by 270 percent, from $150 million to $550 million a year, he said. (Proxmire gives his award for what he regards as "the biggest, most ironic, or most ridiculous example of excessive spending for the period.")

House Staff Allowance

By 1979 the House had increased the personal staff allowance of each representative to $288,156 a year to employ up to 18 aides in the Washington and home district offices. This was an increase of about $50,000 a year from 1975. The staff increases have benefited mainly the junior representatives who do not have the additional help of committee staffs. The maximum yearly salary for one staff member was $47,500, according to the *Congressional Handbook for the U.S. House of Representatives.*

In July 1979, acting without advance notice, the House approved a rules change permitting members to add up to four additional employees to their payrolls.

The rules change did not cost the taxpayer anything because the resolution passed by the House (H Res 359) provided members no additional money for their clerk-hire allowance.

Proponents of H Res 359 said the change was needed to permit House members adequate staffing. For example, if an employee took a maternity leave, they noted, the 18-staffer ceiling prevented the member from hiring a temporary employee to fill in during her absence.

But opponents argued that the new rule was just the first step toward an eventual increase in a member's staff allowance.

The House approved the resolution, which had been reported by the House Administration Committee, by a vote of 214-120. Joining the 180 Democrats who voted for the resolution were 34 Republicans.

Under existing rules, a House member could hire a maximum of 18 "clerks" for his or her personal staff. The resolution permits members to add up to four more staffers — without counting them toward the ceiling of 18 — if their job fits into one of five specified categories:

● A part-time employee, defined as one paid $750 per month or less;

● A "shared" employee, an employee who was on the payroll of two or more members simultaneously;

● An intern in the member's Washington office, defined as an employee hired for up to 120 days and paid less than $7,800 on an annual basis;

● A person who replaces an employee on leave without pay, or

● A temporary employee, defined as a staff member hired for three months or less and assigned to a specific task or purpose.

As of 1979, House members were allowed to transfer a maximum of $15,000 from unused staff funds to their official expense allowances for use in other categories such as computer and related services. *(See chapter on Computers in Congress)*

Senate Staff Allowance

The personal staff allowance of senators depends upon the population of their states. For 1979, the annual allowance ranged from $508,221 for states with fewer than two million residents to $1,021,167 for states with more than 21 million. Senators may hire as many aides as they wish within the allowance, but only one may earn the maximum annual salary of $49,941, and eight employees may not exceed $47,500 each per year. Senate staff allowances are cumulative within a fiscal year, so that unused monthly allowances may be carried over.

In June 1975, junior senators succeeded in amending the Standing Rules of the Senate (S Res 60) to allow all senators to appoint up to three additional staff members for a total of $101,925 a year to help them with their committee assignments. The first-term senators and their allies also won the right to hire and control their own committee staff members, thus making an inroad on the seniority system.

The fiscal 1978 appropriations bill for the legislative branch (PL 95-94) recommended several changes in administrative procedures to provide greater flexibility in use of official funds. It combined the legislative assistance allowance with the administrative and clerical allowance. Each senator was authorized a set amount of $157,626 per fiscal year for legislative aides in addition to the variable clerk-hire allowance which is based on state population. There was no limit on the number of employees.

Special Allowances

The travel allowance provided in the Act of Sept. 22, 1789, fixing the compensation of members of Congress was the first of what has become a handful of special allowances that members have created for themselves through the years. Senators and representatives still receive a travel allowance. Other special allowances cover office expenses, stationery, postage, telephone and telegraph service and publications. Each legislative body largely determines its own allowances and perquisites.

The various allowances have been a persistent source of trouble for members. The stationery and other allowances have been susceptible to abuse. At the same time, some members have found that the amounts provided by the allowances failed to keep up with rising costs. One answer to the money problem was for members to apply campaign contributions to certain incidental expenses.

Until the 95th Congress, in general allowances were more specific and more restrictive for representatives than for senators. While representatives often had to limit spending within each account, senators could consolidate their allowances for stationery, postage, telephone and telegraph, travel, and state office expenses with no limitation on the amount which could be spent in any one category. Many House allowances had to be spent a month at a time, whereas Senate allowances usually were cumulative within a calendar year.

Following a sex-payroll scandal that forced Rep. Wayne L. Hays to resign as chairman of the House Administration Committee, the committee in 1976 instituted a number of reform measures dealing with (among other things) the special allowances of representatives as well as their staff allowances. *(See 1976 House changes, p. 124)*

Official Expenses Allowance

House. Provisions of the House Ethics Code passed in March 1977 provided for a single "official expenses" allowance for members' office costs both in Washington and home districts, rather than separate allowances for each category as had been in use. In addition, the amount of money each member would have available to spend on official expenses was increased by $5,000 — to $7,000 from $2,000.

In keeping with the new code, the House Administration Committee adopted new regulations providing House members with two allowances: the official expenses allowance and a staff, or clerk-hire, allowance. According to committee chairman Frank Thompson Jr., D-N.J., this consolidation would "simplify bookkeeping in members' offices and in House finance office records by making it unnecessary to make periodic transfers from one account into another" as had been previously authorized under the regulations.

The consolidated account system replaced the nine separate special allowances for travel, office equipment leasing, district office leasing, telecommunications, stationery, constituent communications, postage, computer services and other official expenses. The new House official expenses allowance was determined by using a base of $32,911, a figure which included expenses in six fixed categories, the sums for which were determined on the basis of the former separate categories. To that base which is the same for each member are added expenses for three variable allowances — travel, telephone and telegraph, and district office rental which depend upon the location of a member's district and its distance from Washington, D.C. According to an Administration Committee staff member, the totals for official expenses accounts in 1979 varied from $68,000 for a district within 500 miles of the District of Columbia to $94,000 for a California district.

At the same time the streamlined accounting system was adopted, the House Administration Committee announced a set of "guidelines" tightening restrictions on official expenses. "Official expenses" were defined as "ordinary and necessary business expenses incurred in support of the member's official and representational duties." *(See box, p. 125)*

Senate. Although both the House and Senate use similar consolidated office accounts, in the Senate allowances vary with the population of the states, in addition to factors of geographical location and distance between Washington, D.C., and the home state.

Effective Oct. 1, 1977, the senator's consolidated allowance, which had been established in 1973, was revised and renamed the official office expense account. The Senate Handbook, revised January 1979 by the Senate Committee on Rules and Administration, described this account and how it worked. *(See box, p. 126)*

A provision contained in the fiscal 1978 legislative appropriations bill (PL 95-94) signed in August 1977 was unique to the Senate. That provision permits senators to spend up to 10 percent of their official allowances on "such other official expenses as the senator determines are necessary." *(See 'Official' expenses box, p. 128)*

Other changes in administrative practices contained in PL 95-94 were designed to eliminate several widely criticized perquisites enjoyed by senators and to provide greater flexibility in the use of official funds. Among these were elimination of the free shaving mugs, hairbrushes, combs and shipping trunks that had been available to members;

1976 House Changes in Members' Benefits

The House of Representatives and its Committee on Administration adopted a number of reforms in 1976 in the aftermath of a sex-payroll scandal that forced Rep. Wayne L. Hayes, D-Ohio, to resign as chairman of the committee. Elizabeth Ray, a committee secretary, said that Hays kept her on the payroll to provide him sexual favors. Hays denied the assertion, but the widespread publicity of the assertion, and resulting adverse public and political reaction, led to Hays' resignation of the chairmanship. He resigned from Congress on Sept. 1, 1976.

Committee Actions

The House Administration Committee, meeting under its new chairman, Rep. Frank Thompson Jr., D-N.J., adopted a series of reform proposals on June 28, 1976. No House action was required. The reforms:

● Reduced the current 20-cents-a-mile allowance for automobile travel for House members to 15 cents, the amount set by the General Services Administration for federal employees.

● Required House members and chairmen of committees and subcommittees to certify monthly the salaries and duties of their staffs and to disclose any kinships between staff employees and any House member. This change would become effective 30 days after the Administration Committee approved the certification forms.

● Required quarterly reports of how House funds are spent. The reports would be indexed according to employees and employing offices, showing the titles and salaries.

● Required that disbursements be made only on the presentation of vouchers.

The following reforms, which went into effect in the 95th Congress:

● Eliminated the separate postage stamp allowance, currently $1,140 a year, and ended the so-called "cash-out" practice that permitted members to convert unused stationery and travel allowances into cash for their personal use.

● Gave the committee the power to adjust the clerk-hire allowance to reflect federal government cost-of-living raises.

● Revised the telephone and telegraph allowance to permit each member to have two WATS (wide area telephone service) lines to reduce costs for long-distance phone calls. If a member opted for the WATS lines, he would give up half of his annual telecommunications allowance.

● Revised the system of allowances used by members to run their offices by permitting members for the first time to transfer money from one fund to another.

House Actions

On July 1 the House adopted two resolutions which were also designed as reform measures. Both were attacked sharply by Republicans, but survived recommittal votes, and eventually were adopted by large majorities. One resolution (H Res 1368) established a 15-person study commission on House accounting and personnel procedures and members' benefits. The other resolution (H Res 1372) stripped the House Administration Committee in most instances of its unilateral authority to alter representatives' benefits.

H Res 1368. The resolution authorizing the study commission was adopted by a 380-30 roll-call vote after a Republican motion to recommit was rejected by a 143-269 vote that followed party lines.

The resolution created a Commission on Administrative Review, which was to be composed of eight representatives (five Democrats, three Republicans) appointed by the Speaker, and seven members of the public chosen for their backgrounds and experience, also appointed by the Speaker. The commission was to conduct a study and prepare recommendations covering the following areas: staff personnel, administration, accounting and purchasing procedures, office equipment and communications facilities, recordkeeping emoluments, and allowances. The commission's reform recommendations were submitted in September 1977, but were rejected by the House the next month. *(Obey Commission, p. 153)*

H Res 1372. The resolution dealing with the House Administration Committee was adopted by a 311-92 roll call after a Republican recommittal motion was rejected by a 165-236 vote.

The resolution would require House approval — instead of unilateral committee action — of most changes in representatives' benefits and allowances. Cases in which the committee could continue to act alone were ones in which there was a change in the price of materials, services or office space; a technological change or other improvement in equipment; or a cost-of-living increase.

changes in travel regulations *(see travel allowances, p. 125)*; and a provision that the consolidated allowance would be computed by averaging the existing allowances for the two senators from each state, increasing the amount by 10 percent and rounding the number up to the nearest $1,000. This was designed to provide for an increase in the consolidated allowance and to ensure that both senators from a state were given the same allowance.

In late summer 1979, the Senate approved a proposal to require senators to document their official expenses before being reimbursed for them by the Senate. Under existing rules, senators could request reimbursement for office expenses on their signatures alone.

The proposal (S Res 170) was reported (S Rept 96-275) by the Senate Rules Committee July 30. It was approved by voice vote of the Senate Aug. 2 without debate.

Under the new rule, senators would have to provide receipts or other documentation for expenses over $25.

The resolution offered by Mark O. Hatfield, R-Ore., originally was sponsored by all six members of the Select Ethics Committee. It grew out of that panel's investigation into charges of financial misconduct filed against Sen. Herman E. Talmadge, D-Ga. One of the charges against Talmadge was that he filed vouchers with the Senate claiming reimbursement for expenses not incurred or not legally reimbursable. *(See Ethics chapter, p. 167)*

Travel Allowance

The travel allowance of 1789 — $6 for each 20 miles — has been altered to reflect increased mobility of the nation.

House. Until 1977 representatives received a separate travel allowance which allowed them 26 free round trips each year to and from their home district plus extra staff trips. Members could choose to withdraw their travel allowance in cash, up to a maximum of $2,250 a year, and any remainder not used for travel could have gone toward members' personal expenses, if they paid income taxes on it. As part of its reform package, the House Administration Committee in 1976 ended the "cash-out" option.

Under the new consolidated official expenses allowance, a member's allowance for travel is the equivalent of 64 multiplied by the rate per mile (15 cents per mile under 500 miles), multiplied by the mileage between the District of Columbia and the furthest point in the member's district, plus 10 percent. This works out to roughly 32 round trips per year. Members are reimbursed for the actual cost of transportation and there are no limits on the number of trips.

Senate. The travel allowance for Senate offices was based on the cost of 20 round trips a year for states with fewer than 10 million people and 22 round trips for states with more than 10 million. The states' distance from Washington was figured in the computation.

PL 95-94 broadened the travel expenses that could be reimbursed to include travel anywhere within the United States (existing law had provided reimbursement only within a senator's home state) and to include per diem expenses for travel within a senator's home state, but provided that neither allowance would be permitted less than 60 days before an election in which the senator was a candidate for office, and that each senator would have to make public how he used the funds.

The Senate travel allowance sets no limit on the number of trips to be taken each year, but regulations state that office staff must make round trips.

Per Diem Travel. Members of Congress may also be reimbursed for travel on official business that is in addition to visits to their home districts or states. Representatives can receive $50 per diem for such travel within the United States. Senators and their staffs normally receive $35 per diem, but may be reimbursed at higher rates as established by the General Services Administration for high cost geographical areas.

Stationery, Postage Allowances

House. Until 1977 each representative was allowed $6,500 a year to purchase stationery and office supplies and members could convert the allowance into cash to pay for publications or gifts for constituents, or for personal expenses provided they paid income taxes on it.

And until 1977, each representative's office received a postage allowance for use on official mail that was ineligible for franking. *(See Franking privilege, p. 127)*

These allowances are now part of the official expenses allowance. An allowance for stationery of $6,500 and for special postage of $211 were among the fixed categories used in determining the consolidated account. In addition, each representative is allowed 40,000 brown "Public Document" envelopes a month without charge; the envelopes may be used anytime in a calendar year.

Senate. The stationery allowance allocations for a senator's office ranged from $3,600 to $5,000 a year, de-

House Office Expenses Defined

Under new spending limits effective in January 1978, House members could not charge sports trophies, flowers, television time or other potentially embarrassing expenditures to their office expense accounts, even if they thought these items were necessary for good relations with constituents.

The House Administration Committee in November 1977 adopted a set of "guidelines" for the accounts after news media reported spending for certain items in a report of the Clerk of the House. That report was the first to itemize members' expenditures for office expenses, as required by an administrative reform package adopted by the House in 1976.

Although termed "guidelines" by the committee, staff members insisted the new restrictions would have the force of rules. They said Committee Chairman Frank Thompson Jr., D-N.J., would not sign vouchers for expenditures barred by the guidelines.

If members labeled the proscribed expenditures as "political" and reported them as required by federal campaign statutes, they could pay for them with campaign contributions, according to a Federal Election Commission (FEC) official.

The committee action was final and did not require ratification by the House. The panel also decided to streamline expense account bookkeeping, eliminating the requirement that separate records be kept for postage, travel, office rental and other categories. This change did not affect disclosure requirements.

Under the guidelines adopted by the Administration Committee, House members could not be reimbursed from their expense accounts for the following types of expenditures:

● Employment service fees, moving allowances and other expenses relating to hiring staff.

● Purchase or rental of items "having an extended useful life," such as a tuxedo rental claimed by Richard L. Ottinger, D-N.Y., that had provoked criticism. Members could still charge office equipment relating to their duties.

● Greeting cards, flowers, trophies, donations, and dues for groups other than congressional organizations approved by the Administration Committee. Members who had claimed these expenses said that constituents expected their representatives to send flowers to funerals, award sports trophies and join lodges.

● Radio or television time or advertisements, except for notices of meetings relating to congressional business.

● Tuition or fees for education and training unless a need for a special skill, relating to House activities, could be proved.

pending on the state's population. In addition, each senator receives allotments of white envelopes and letterheads, blank sheets and brown "Public Document" envelopes, all based on the state's population.

Reimbursement is authorized for air mail and special delivery stamps for use on official mail only. Senators whose states are east of the Mississippi River were allocated an annual postage allowance of $1,390; those whose states are wholly or partially west of the Mississippi received $1,740 a year. These allowances are part of the senator's

How Expense Accounts Work

According to the "Senate Handbook," the Senatorial Official Office Expense Account is a "multipurpose lump-sum allowance" authorized each year. At the end of the year, any unused balance may not be carried over until the next year.

"Reimbursement may not exceed actual expenses," according to the handbook. Reimbursement is made by check upon presentation to the disbursing office of itemized and signed vouchers. The senator must sign beneath a statement printed on the voucher that states: "I certify that the above expenses were officially incurred."

The account may be used for official telegrams and long-distance phone calls; phone calls incurred outside of Washington; stationery and office supplies; official airmail and special delivery postage (ordinary letters may be mailed under a senator's frank); district office expenses; subscriptions to newspapers and periodicals; official travel, and "reimbursement to the senator for such other official expenses as the senator determines are necessary." The latter category of expenses is limited to 10 percent of the total official expense account.

The maximum allowable amount that can be reimbursed varies according to state population and distance from Washington. For example, in 1979 it ranged from $33,000 annually for a senator from Delaware to $143,000 annually for a senator from Hawaii. The maximum allowed Sen. Herman E. Talmadge as a senator from Georgia was $49,000 annually.

Under House rules, members are required to submit documentation of expenses incurred in order to be reimbursed. The documentation is reviewed by the Clerk's Office, but is not available for public inspection.

office expense account which may be used for a variety of authorized items.

Telephone and Telegraph Allowance

House. In computing the yearly telephone allowance for representatives in 1979, the equivalent of 15,000 times the highest long-distance telephone rate per minute from the District of Columbia to the member's district is used. In no case may the equivalent amount be less than $6,000 if WATS is not utilized or less than $3,000 if WATS is used. A member may elect to use more than this amount on calls as long as total expenses in all categories do not exceed his or her established official expenses allowance.

Senate. Prior to establishment of the consolidated account in 1973, the Senate Rules and Administration Committee fixed telephone and telegraph rates. The allowance was based on a fixed number of long-distance calls totaling not more than a fixed number of minutes for calls to and from Washington, plus a fixed dollar amount for calls outside Washington. The committee used a complicated formula to determine the telegraph allowance, based on state populations and Western Union rates from Washington. Both formulas went into the senator's total consolidated allowance, now the official office expense account.

FTS, WATS for Senate and House. Beyond these basic telephone and telegraph allowances, many members have access either to a nationwide, leased-line Federal Telecommunications System (FTS) or to wide-area telephone service (WATS) provided by telephone companies. The House Administration Committee in 1976 revised representatives' telephone and telegraph allowances to permit each member to have two WATS lines to reduce costs for long distance calls. If a representative chose to use WATS lines, half the annual telecommunications allowance would have to be given up. The change was part of the committee's reform package. Senators are allowed two free WATS lines in their Washington office. FTS is available at a charge of $31 per month.

Newsletter Allowance

House. Since 1975 each representative has been allowed $5,000 a year for production and printing of newsletters, questionnaires and similar correspondence eligible to be mailed under the frank. This figure was used in computing the base sum of $32,911 for the official expenses allowance begun in the 95th Congress. Mass mailings to constituents may be charged to that account.

Senate. Some services for printing and bulk mailing of newsletters, questionnaires, excerpts from the *Congressional Record* and other items are provided without charge by the Senate's Service Department. Senators receive a monthly printing allowance, based on state population, but they sometimes use part of the stationery allowance, tradeoffs from other accounts, or private resources to cover newsletter expenses.

Office Allowances

House. The Washington office of a representative is provided free of charge. In 1975 a lobby group, Americans for Democratic Action, figured the average size of a member's office and the average rent for office space in Washington, D.C., and estimated that the free office saves each representative about $10,480 a year. Office furnishings and decorations, housekeeping and maintenance all are free. Each member receives $5,500 a year to purchase electrical and mechanical office equipment, and $9,000 a year to lease equipment. The equipment lease is one of the fixed categories in the base allowance for the consolidated account.

In September 1977 the House approved greater funding for district office funds. The measure (H Res 687) increased the rental allowance for district office space to 2,500 square feet from the existing 1,500 square feet. With rental costs varying across the country from $4 to $13.50 per square foot, the benefit to individual House members would differ although each would have a new allowance of at least several thousand dollars. Unused funds could be transferred within a member's consolidated office account and used for other office expenses.

The home offices are provided an aggregate allowance of $27,000 for furnishings and equipment, and an inventory ceiling of $55,000 for D.C. furnishings.

Senate. The Washington office and furnishings for senators are provided free, as are housekeeping and maintenance services. Senators do not have allowances to buy or lease office equipment because it is provided by the sergeant at arms of the Senate.

A senator's home state office space is allocated according to the state's population. Within the allowed square footage there is no limit to the number of offices. Offices are provided free in federal buildings or leased from private owners at the GSA regional rate. Senators receive an aggregate furniture and equipment allowance of $22,550 for

4,800 square feet of office space, increased by $550 for each additional 200 square feet. All furnishings are provided through the General Services Administration. Each senator also is allowed to rent one mobile office for use throughout the state.

Although rent and furnishings for home state offices are not chargeable to the official office account, the expense allowance for home offices is reimbursable under that account, as are subscriptions to newspapers, periodicals and clipping services.

Publications Allowance

In addition to their special allowances for office operations, communications and travel, members of Congress receive a number of free publications. Some are used directly in the member's work — a complete set of the U.S. Code and supplements, four subscriptions to the *Federal Register,* and office copies of the *Congressional Record* and the *Congressional Directory.* Others are offered as gifts to constituents. Besides three personal copies, representatives are allotted 34 subscriptions to the *Congressional Record* and senators are allotted 50. *(See box, p. 120)* Members receive clothbound (and engraved in the case of senators) copies of the annual *Congressional Directory.* Paperbound copies are distributed to spouses and staff. Representatives may distribute 25 copies and senators 50 copies.

Members also receive allotments of special publications to send off to constituents. One of the most popular is the Yearbook of the Department of Agriculture. Each representative was allotted 400 copies in 1978, worth $2,800. Senators had an allotment of 550. Unused Yearbooks and certain other publications may be turned in to the Government Printing Office for exchange or credit toward other books and pamphlets. Among the gifts members may choose to distribute are wall calendars and pamphlets on American history, the legislative process and historic documents.

Americans for Democratic Action calculated in 1975 that each representative was allowed $10,659 worth of free publications. But it is impossible to make an accurate estimate because members also receive, and use, hundrds of bills, annual reports from federal agencies, budget documents, manuals, published hearings and committee reports. Senators are given an unabridged dictionary and stand as part of their office furnishings.

'Slush Funds' of Members

Despite all the allowances, many members in the past found their incomes insufficient to meet certain expenses associated with their duties. Thus they established special accounts of private funds. The polite name for them was "office accounts" or even "constituent service accounts," but they were often referred to simply as "slush funds."

Slush funds might be leftover campaign contributions, any donations from individuals or organizations, or part of members' personal wealth. They were used for many purposes: newsletter expenses, family or staff travel, lunches for constituents, public meetings, parking fees, opinion polls, flowers for funerals, mailings of Christmas cards, office coffee, and just about any job-related expense not covered by the allowances.

Until 1977 slush funds essentially were not regulated. Some members reported all sources and uses of slush funds; others avoided any mention of them.

However, both chambers in March 1977 took steps to rectify abuses in the use of unofficial office accounts.

Members would be prohibited from maintaining such accounts after January 1978. Moreover, effective immediately, contributions to unofficial office accounts were banned, as was the conversion of campaign funds to personal use.

Members' Honoraria

For many years members of Congress, especially senators, have supplemented their income by delivering speeches, making public appearances and broadcasts, and publishing articles for fees and royalties. Until 1975 there were no restrictions on such earnings, and it was not unusual for prominent or popular members to earn more from honoraria than from salary.

The era of no restrictions ended Jan. 1, 1975, when the campaign finance law took effect. It limited honoraria for members and other federal officials to $1,000 for any single appearance or article and a total of $15,000 a year. The 1976 campaign finance law raised the maximum on individual honorarium payments to $2,000 and a total of $25,000 a year.

In 1979 the House placed a ceiling of 15 percent of a representative's annual salary on all outside earned income — including honoraria — and a ceiling of $1,000 on each individual honorarium. Stricter limits were also to have gone into effect in the Senate, but in March 1979 the Senate voted to delay the new limitation for four years. *(Details, p. 175)*

Franking Privilege

One of the most valuable of members' perquisites is the frank, the privilege of mailing letters and packages under their signatures without being charged for postage. For fiscal 1979, Congress appropriated $65 million for its members and officials to send an estimated 357 million pieces of postage-free mail during the year.

The franking privilege is actually older than Congress itself. The first Continental Congress accorded its members mailing privileges, and one of the first acts of Congress under the Constitution was to continue the practice. Except for a brief time — the franking privilege was suspended for a few months in 1873 — the privilege remained virtually unchanged. In 1973 Congress updated franking laws for the first time since the 19th century and established machinery for self-policing of franking practices.

Franking consists of a member's autograph or its facsimile on the envelope or package where stamps normally appear. Members submit three to five copies of their signature to the House Office Supply Service or the Senate Printing Clerk, and the most legible copy is selected for reproduction. Originally, franking was allowed on mail received by members as well as on mail sent.

Title 39 of the U.S. Code, which contains the rules of the franking privilege, limits it to correspondence "in which the Member deals with the addressee as a citizen of the United States or constituent." Members of Congress are not authorized to use the frank for letters in which they are acting as a personal friend, a candidate or a member of a political party.

The U.S. Postal Service keeps records of all franked mail as it passes through the post office in Washington. Every three months it sends Congress a bill for the cost of mail sent by members. The Postal Service computes the amount by weighing a random sample of the sacks of mail it receives each day from Congress. The rate of reimburse-

Senate 'Official' Expenses: Chandeliers and TVs?

When Alan Cranston, D-Calif., set out to change the rules governing Senate office allowances in 1977, he probably made life easier for some senators, but he clearly made things tougher for the taxpayer and Senate bookkeepers.

The bookkeepers' problems could lead to a showdown in 1979 in the Rules Committee.

The controversy is over what does or doesn't constitute an "official" office expense. Nobody seems to know.

Before 1977, only certain designated office expenses could be paid for with government funds. Cranston

---

Senators have sought reimbursement for such "official expenses" as the purchase of chandeliers, office color TV sets and video tape recorders, framed prints, drapes, books for an "in-house office staff reading program," sunglasses, a press club membership for a senator's aide in the home state and a contribution to a hospital in Jerusalem.

---

argued there were numerous additional items a senator might need which also were "official" expenses.

All that was needed was a little more flexibility in the rules governing Senate allowances, he said.

In the name of flexibility, however, the taxpayer has been stuck with the bill for $2,860 worth of "modular office furniture," $600 worth of Polaroid camera equipment, $403 for 108 paperweights, and $400 in matchbooks, to name a few of the thousands of miscellaneous purchases permitted by the 1977 rules change.

Rules Change

The change allowed senators to be reimbursed for such purchases so long as they simply declared them to be for "official" purposes.

In some recent cases, however, Senate officials have refused to authorize reimbursement until the Rules Committee specifically approved it. In other cases, senators have withdrawn their reimbursement request.

Paul Laxalt, R-Nev., for example, withdrew a request for repayment of $1,788 for the purchase of two Portuguese crystal chandeliers and $500 for their air shipment to Washington after the request received some media attention.

The 1977 rules change was approved after a group of 56 senators wrote the Senate Legislative Appropriations Subcommittee requesting that the reimbursement rules be altered to permit senators to be paid back for a laundry list of items barred under the existing rules.

"We almost had a rebellion here," recalled Terrence Sauvain, a subcommittee aide. "A lot of senators were

being told by the Rules Committee they couldn't be reimbursed for a whole lot of things, such as a book on the Panama Canal or a taxi ride from the Capitol."

Rather than attempt to establish new categories of reimbursable items, or create a new type of allowance Sauvain said, "we thought we would keep the allowance at the same level but open up a part of the total for this type of thing."

The Appropriations Committee accomplished this by adding a provision to the fiscal 1978 legislative appropriations bill (PL 95-94) permitting senators to spend up to 10 percent of their total allowance on official office expenses other than those falling within the existing categories of approved expenses.

As a safeguard, the provision required senators to disclose in detail every six months how their "10 percent funds" had been spent.

Cranston was not entirely satisfied. The bill still left a determination of what constituted an "official office expense" to the Rules Committee. On the Senate floor, he won approval of a change to permit each senator, in his sole discretion, to determine what constituted a reimbursable official expense.

But the Rules Committee still was not out of the picture. The committee maintained that an 1888 law requires it to continue to monitor all reimbursement requests. As of June 1979, the committee staff had put a hold on 16 requests for repayment totaling $5,557.44, according to a report by the panel's chief counsel, Chester H. Smith.

In his report, Smith noted that senators had asked to be reimbursed for such "official expenses" as the purchase of chandeliers, office color TV sets and video tape recorder-players, framed prints, drapes, books for an "in-house office staff reading program," sunglasses, a

---

In the name of flexibility, the taxpayer has been stuck with the bill for $2,860 worth of "modular office furniture," $600 worth of Polaroid camera equipment, $403 for 108 paperweights and $400 in matchbooks.

---

press club membership for a senator's aide in the home state, and a contribution to a hospital located in Jerusalem.

"It would seem," Smith told the committee in his June report, "that senators, in all fairness, do not know the definition of 'official office expense' and neither does your staff in making approval or disapproval recommendations." Smith recommended the Senate Rules Committee spell out — for the first time — precisely what constitutes an "official expense."

His suggestion was still pending before the Rules Committee as of July 1979.

ment is based on average weight, and was an estimated 13.98 cents per piece for fiscal 1979.

Neither the Postal Service nor its predecessor, the Post Office Department, has inspected franked mail to determine whether any members were abusing the privilege by sending personal or political correspondence postage-free. Until 1968 the Post Office would issue rulings on specific abuses if private citizens made official complaints, and would ask the offending members to reimburse the Post Office. But the rulings were not binding, so some members refused to pay. On Dec. 27, 1968, the Post Office Department ruled that it no longer would attempt to collect from individual members who allegedly had abused the frank. The Postal Service has continued this policy.

No person allowed franking privileges may lend the privilege to any person, organization or committee, except House and Senate committees. Violators can be fined. Surviving spouses of members may use the frank for six months after a member's death.

Special uses of the frank occasionally lead to controversy. In the early 1960s Congress had a fight each year over whether mail addressed to "occupant" could be sent under the frank. A compromise was finally adopted which permitted representatives to send some "occupant" mail but forbade senators from doing so.

Conflicting court decisions, and a reluctance of many judges to rule on questions of congressional propriety, resulted in general confusion about proper use of the frank. The many disputes during the 1972 campaign convinced some members of Congress that new legislation was necessary. In addition, the House Post Office and Civil Service Committee in a 1973 report (H Rept 93-88) noted a marked increase in the amount of mail sent from Congress since the Post Office stopped policing use of the frank — from 178 million pieces in 1968 to an estimated 288 million pieces in 1973.

1973 Franking Law

On Dec. 17, 1973, Congress approved HR 3180 (PL 93-191), which placed specific guidelines on the types of mail members could send free under the frank, set up mechanisms to rule on individual cases, and restricted the sending of mass mailings by members during the four weeks preceding congressional elections. The bill's sponsor, Rep. Morris K. Udall, D-Ariz., succeeded in establishing definitions of the franking privilege that were acceptable to most members and that represented little change from established practices. Udall said the issue was whether Congress would define the privilege or whether "the judges are going to write the law for us."

The 1973 law provided the following:

● Authorized use of the frank "to expedite and assist the conduct of official business, activities and duties."

● Permitted use of the frank for mailings of any of the following: communications between members and the executive branch, newsletters and press releases dealing with legislative activity, public opinion polls, non-partisan information on elections or voter registration, and biographies or pictures if sent in response to a specific request.

● Prohibited use of the frank for mailings that included purely personal communications, holiday greetings, information about the family of members, or political solicitations.

● Provided that material from the *Congressional Record* could be franked only if it would qualify as frankable on its own.

● Established a House Commission on Congressional Mailing Standards to make rulings on disputes arising in House election campaigns under the law.

● Assigned to the Senate Select Committee on Standards and Conduct the responsibility to make rulings on disputes arising in Senate election campaigns under the law.

● Prohibited mailings of more than 500 pieces of identical mail for the 28-day period immediately before an election by members who were candidates for re-election except for responses to inquiries, communications to government personnel, and news releases to the media.

The reforms did not anticipate every kind of abuse. Late in 1975 Congress voted to close a loophole in the 1973 law that had allowed former Rep. Frank M. Clark, D-Pa., to send out a franked newsletter mailing to his former constituents two months after his term had expired. The new legislation permitted former members to use the frank for 90 days after leaving Congress, but only for mailings to help close down their offices.

Increased Use Leads to Reforms

Both the use and the cost of congressional franking increased enormously in the 1970s. In 1970, members of Congress and others authorized to use the frank sent 190 million pieces of mail that cost a total of $11,224,000. For fiscal 1979 the volume and cost had jumped to an estimated 357 million pieces and $64,944,000. The 1979 appropriation was $16 million more than that for 1978.

Early in 1977 when new ethics codes were passed, both chambers took steps to place tighter restrictions on the use of the frank.

House. The House imposed the following new restrictions on use of a member's frank on "postal patron" mail — mail that does not include the recipient's name:

● Required that any franked postal patron mail be sent by the most economical means practicable — third class. Effective on enactment.

● Provided that after Dec. 31, 1977, the amount of postal patron mail sent annually by a member under the frank could not exceed a number equal to six times the number of addresses in the member's district.

● Required that a postal patron mailing to be sent under the frank be submitted to the House Commission on Congressional Mailing Standards for an advisory opinion on whether the mailing met the restrictions on franked materials. Effective on enactment.

In addition the House imposed the following new restrictions on mass mailings — defined in existing law as newsletters and similar mailings of more than 500 pieces of substantially identical content — whether sent to a postal patron address or to a specific person:

● Prohibited any mass mailing under the frank unless preparation and printing costs are paid entirely from public funds. Effective on enactment. (The provision was intended to end the practice of mailing at public expense under the frank newsletters or other material printed with private funds and labeled "Not Printed at Government Expense.")

● Prohibited any member who is a candidate for statewide office from sending any franked mass mailing to residents outside his district. Effective on enactment.

● Prohibited any franked mass mailing from being sent less than 60 days before any primary or general election in which the member sending the mail was a candidate. Effective on enactment.

Senate. The Senate imposed the following new restrictions:

Retirement Benefits

Congress included in the Legislative Reorganization Act of 1946 a provision, recommended by the Joint Committee on the Organization of Congress, initiating a retirement system for senators and representatives. The Act brought members of Congress under the Civil Service Retirement Act, permitting them, at their option, to contribute 6 percent of their salaries to a retirement fund. Retirement annuities were to be calculated at 2-1/2 percent of average salary multiplied by years of service, but could not exceed 80 percent of a member's final congressional salary. A member became eligible for benefits upon retirement from Congress if the member was at least 62 years old and had served a minimum of five years (except in cases of disability).

In 1954, Congress liberalized the pension law and also adjusted retirement benefits for legislative employees. The basic rate of contribution remained 6 percent of salary, but the bill included the congressional expense allowance in the salary computation. It also provided for reduced retirement benefits at age 60 and made other minor changes in the program. In 1956 the contribution rose to 7-1/2 percent. Further changes were enacted in 1960, although the basic retirement benefits were left unchanged.

In 1969, Congress again liberalized the pension law for both members and legislative employees. Retirement benefits were increased by specifying that the annuity computation formula would use an employee's average annual earnings during the highest consecutive three-year period, rather than during a five-year period, as had been required. The method of computing annuities for congressional employees was liberalized by eliminating a 15-year limitation on number of years of service for which the annuity would be computed at 2-1/2 percent of average pay. Other benefit changes also were made. In addition, the contribution of members of Congress was increased from 7-1/2 percent to 8 percent, and the contribution of congressional employees from 6-1/2 percent to 7-1/2 percent, beginning in January 1970. The government matches participants' contributions to the plan.

With enactment in 1969 of a law making modifications in the federal pension system, government retirees became eligible to receive a bonus in their pensions every time the cost of living went up by 3 percent over the previous base period for three consecutive months. In such situations, they became eligible for an extra 1 percent "kicker" payment.

The idea behind the kicker was to make up for the delay between the time the cost of living began to rise and the time it rose high enough to trigger a raise in pensions. However, because the kicker was then included in the base for the next raise, it had a multiplier effect, which some critics charged went far beyond its intent. Responding to this criticism, Congress in September 1976 repealed the law authorizing the 1 percent "kicker" and replaced it with a system that would adjust the pensions automatically every six months without the 1 percent bonus.

Source: U.S. Congress, House. Committee on Post Office and Civil Service, *Civil Service Retirement System, Hearings before the Retirement and Employee Benefits Subcommittee,* Serial No. 94-56, 94th Cong., 1st sess., Nov. 14, 1975, pp. 88-89.

● Provided that no senator or candidate for the Senate could make use of the frank for a mass mailing less than 60 days before a primary or general election in which the senator or candidate was running.

● Provided that a senator could use only official funds of the Senate to pay for preparation of any mass mailing sent out under the frank. (The provision was intended to end the practice of mailing at public expense under the frank newsletters or other material printed with private funds and labeled "Not Printed at Government Expense.")

● Required all mass mailings by a senator under the frank to be registered with the Secretary of the Senate and the registration to include a copy of the material, the number of pieces sent and a description of the groups receiving the mailing. Required the information to be available for public inspection.

● Provided that the Senate computer facilities could not be used to store any political or campaign lists and that other mail-related uses of the computer would be subject to guidelines issued by the Rules Committee.

● Provided that the Senate radio and television studios could not be used by any candidate for election to the Senate less than 60 days before the primary or general election in which the candidate was running.

● Provided that the rules governing franking would take effect Jan. 1, 1978.

1979 Franking Bill

A bill to write into law restrictions on the use of the frank in congressional mailings was approved by a House committee in May 1979. The bill (HR 3777) would convert into statute the provisions of the 1977 House ethics code dealing with congressional use of the frank. Those provisions already were in effect in House rules.

The House Post Office Committee approved a number of additional restrictions on the frank not contained in the ethics code and therefore not currently in effect.

HR 3777 would convert into law provisions of the House ethics code requiring official approval of the content of a member's mass mailings, limiting the cost and total number of mass mailings permitted a member each year, and restricting the use of the frank in some situations that could provide a political edge to an incumbent seeking re-election.

The bill went beyond the ethics code requirements in barring the use of the frank on mail consisting solely of congratulations or condolences, and in clarifying the use of the frank by former members and a deceased member's surviving relatives.

HR 3777 as introduced by Rep. Udall banned altogether the use of the frank for mail whose sole purpose was to laud a member. During the Post Office Committee's markup, however, Rep. William Clay, D-Mo., won approval of an amendment to delete the ban.

Because, under existing law, the use of the frank is permitted on material lauding a member on the basis of his or her performance of official duties, that use would continue under HR 3777 as approved by the committee.

Additional Benefits

In addition to their pay, staff, allowances, franking privileges and other perquisites, members of Congress benefit from many other services, courtesies and special favors that go along with the job. It is impossible to compile a complete list of these other benefits or to compute their precise value. Selected additional benefits are described below. *(For a discussion of retirement benefits, see box, p. 130.)*

Life Insurance. Regardless of age or health, members receive $60,000 in term life insurance coverage under a group plan. The government matches one-third of the premium. An additional policy for $10,000 also is available, with the extra premium determined by the age of the member.

Health Insurance. Members are eligible for a generous health insurance plan. The government pays up to 40 percent of the premium.

Health Care. A staff of doctors and nurses stands by in the Capitol to give members free medical care while at work. Services include physical examinations, laboratory work, electrocardiograms, ambulance service and supplies of prescription medicine. First aid stations in every House and Senate office building offer help for members and their staffs.

Taxes. The IRS maintains a temporary office in both the Senate and House between January and April each year to help members and staff prepare their income tax returns. Because members live in two places — their home towns and Washington, D.C. — federal tax law allows them to deduct up to $3,000 a year for living expenses in Washington. In April 1979 the House Ways and Means Subcommittee on Select Revenue Measures attempted to raise the deduction to $50 a day while Congress is in session.

Because the proposal would have retained an existing provision of law designating a legislator's district home as his or her "tax home," the proposal would have permitted the legislators to deduct the cost of their housing, meals, and all other "reasonable and necessary" expenses they incurred while in Washington. Apparently feeling the heat of public scrutiny, action on the bill (HR 2550) was delayed.

Library. The Library of Congress provides members with free manpower and facilities to produce research, speechwriting and responses to constituents' questions. About 800 employees in the Library's Congressional Research Service work exclusively for members.

Books. The Library of Congress gives away to members surplus books under a donation program that may be used for official business only. Some members send the books to libraries and schools in their district or state.

Legal Counsel. The Office of Legislative Counsel, with offices on both sides of Capitol Hill, assists members in drafting bills, resolutions and amendments. Its staff provides confidential help on legislative matters only and does no personal legal work for members.

Recreation. Members of Congress have their own free health club, with a modern gymnasium in the Rayburn House Office Building and two gymnasiums in the Russell and Dirksen office buildings. Facilities include swimming pool, paddleball court and sauna.

Food. Government-subsidized food and facilities are available to members, staff and visitors. The Capitol and office buildings contain five public restaurants and cafeterias; five restaurants for members, senior staff and their guests; and eight carry-out services. In addition, members may reserve several private dining rooms or arrange banquets and parties in caucus rooms with low-cost catering from the House and Senate restaurants.

Members' Recording Studios

Nearly all the perquisites of members of Congress give incumbents certain campaign advantages over their challengers. For example, a member's staff, the franking privilege, and special allowances for travel, office expenses, stationery, newsletters, telephone and telegraph services — all at public expense — may improve the member's chances of being re-elected. In addition, incumbents have inherent newsmaking powers which their opponents lack.

One of the greatest advantages — and perhaps a decisive one as electronic campaigning grows in importance — is the availability of radio and television recording facilities. The House Recording Studio, located in the Rayburn House Office Building, and the Senate Recording Studio, located in a tunnel between the Capitol and the Russell Office Building, are available to all members.

In theory the recording studios are designed to help members communicate with their constituents. Tapes recorded at the studios can be mailed to local stations for use in regular news or public affairs programming. In fact, much of the work performed at the studios is frankly campaign material.

Studio productions are subsidized with public funds. Tapes and films are produced at cost, and the film or tape is available at congressional stationery rooms. Members are billed individually each month. They may not pay in cash. Representatives may use their stationery allowance to purchase audio and video tapes.

Both recording studios are extensive. Color films for television are processed in-house within 24 hours. Teleprompter machines are available. Telephone "beeper" reports can be sent simultaneously to several broadcast stations. Members must design their programs and write the scripts, but the studios suggest a variety of formats and provide such services as TV sets and makeup. Members are urged to make appointments for filming and taping on a regular basis.

The Senate Handbook revised January 1979 states that: "Generally, the Recording Studio may not be used during the 60 days before the date of any primary or general election, whether regular, special or runoff, in which the Senator is a candidate for public office."

It is impossible to estimate the recording studios' value to members, but they are a bargain by any measure. Opponents of incumbent representatives and senators are charged full rates by commercial recording studios; they must pay for most of their broadcast time; and they are seldom seen and heard over the airwaves except during brief campaign periods.

Source: *Congressional Handbook: U.S. House of Representatives; Congressional Handbook: United States Senate.*

Loans. In the House only, members may receive personal loans through the Sergeant-at-Arms Office. Any loan must be repaid by the end of each term. Interest rates are set by commercial banks, for whom the sergeant at arms serves as the agent. Representatives may obtain the loans for virtually any purpose. The Senate has no comparable procedure for making loans to its members.

Merchandise. Stationery stores located in the Capitol office buildings sell many gift items as well as normal office supplies, all at cost or slightly above. Members, their spouses and their staffs can buy such things as wallets, briefcases, pocket calculators, typewriters, and drinking glasses and ashtrays with the seal of either the House or the Senate. Christmas cards also are available at bargain prices.

Parking. Each representative gets a free Capitol Hill garage space for personal use, plus four additional spaces and one outside parking permit for staff use. Each senator gets two garage spaces and several outside permits for staff. By 1979 parking spaces in prime business areas in Washington were rented for as high as $89 a month.

Grooming. Six government-run barber and beauty shops in the office buildings give inexpensive haircuts to members and staff. The beauty shops are much less expensive than private salons in Washington.

Photographs. Both the House and Senate use public funds to provide official photographic services for members of Congress. These services include individual photographs taken with constituents and at official functions or ceremonial events for news and publicity use.

The Senate spends approximately $200,000 for photographers while the House photographers' payroll in 1979 was $285,000.

Democrats and Republicans in both chambers maintain separate staff and darkrooms. The Senate Democratic photographers, one of whom earns as much as $40,000 a year for taking handshaking shots of senators and constituents, are listed as "assistant clerks" and "clerk assistants" in the Secretary of the Senate's Report as of March 31, 1979. Other congressional photographers are listed as such.

House funds are used to purchase cameras, film and supplies. In the Senate, Democrats purchase photographic supplies through a revolving fund while Republicans use party campaign funds.

Office Decorations. The U.S. Botanic Garden will supply members' offices with six potted plants per year. For representatives there is a charge of $5 for additional potted plants. Additional plants for senators are free. Members may request cut flowers as well.

Members may decorate their offices also with free wall maps, scenic photographs, reproductions of paintings and charts — all of which are framed and installed at no cost to members. There are quotas on paintings and certain maps.

Other Benefits. Among the services and perquisites available to members are the following:

● Congressional license tags provided for each member permit unrestricted parking while on official business anywhere in Washington.

● American flags flown over the Capitol and certified by the Architect may be purchased at cost and presented as gifts.

● Members and staff may have packages wrapped free of charge for mailing, a service used heavily during the Christmas season. For years the man who does this for Senate offices has been called "Jack the Wrapper."

● Each year members give away thousands of wall calendars published by the Government Printing Office or the U.S. Capitol Historical Society.

● Members are allowed to accept free domestic transportation on non-commercial carriers — primarily company planes — under certain circumstances. If a member's trip is related to an appearance before a sponsoring group, transport is not considered a gift.

Congress Sets New Record for Foreign Travel

Members of Congress spent nearly $4 million in public funds traveling the world in 1978. The cost was a record, but Congress only told taxpayers about half of it.

Congressional Quarterly's annual survey of congressional foreign travel found that 293 members took a near-record 504 government-paid trips abroad at public expense last year. But in a number of instances congressmen did not fully disclose the cost of their tours and many trips went totally unreported.

In official reports published in the *Congressional Record*, members of the second session of the 95th Congress reported spending a record $2,215,922.04 on foreign travel during 1978 — almost $700,000 more than the old official record ($1,532,386.36) which Congress reported spending in 1977. *(1978 reported costs, p. 137)*

However, an examination by CQ of Defense and State Department records found that the real cost of foreign travel by congressmen during 1978 was much higher:

● Providing military jet transports for overseas congressional missions cost the Defense Department an estimated $1,464,000 more than Congress reported it paid the military for transportation, according to CQ calculations. The Defense Department absorbed the difference.

● Military escorts accompanying congressional missions reported spending $35,219 more for such things as food, beverages and camera film, than they were reimbursed by members.

Again, the excess was absorbed by the military.

When these unreported costs of congressional foreign travel are added to the expenditures disclosed, a total of $3,715,141 is reached.

Beyond that, 34 members of Congress participated in six overseas presidential missions arranged by the State Department Office of Protocol and the Office of the Vice President. The missions were to the funerals of Pope Paul VI, Pope John Paul I, Italian statesman Aldo Moro, and former Israeli Prime Minister Golda Meir, and the investitures of Pope John Paul I and Pope John Paul II.

Cost of the air flights alone for these executive branch delegations was estimated at more than $355,000. CQ did not include this figure in its determination of 1978 congressional foreign travel cost.

CQ also did not include in its overall tabulation the cost ($287.58) of two trips to Canada by members reported to the Clerk of the House as office expense, but not included in the official foreign travel reports published in the *Record*.

The executive branch data used by CQ to calculate the true cost of congressional foreign travel was not available until 1976.

Rising Costs

Overall, the reported cost of foreign travel spending rose by 44.6 percent from 1977 to 1978. Total cost, as estimated by CQ, rose 36.3 percent. According to CQ calculations, 40.3 percent of congressional foreign travel costs went unreported.

Reported House travel spending alone in 1978 exceeded 1977 foreign travel spending reported by the entire Congress by more than $300,000. Congress reported spending $1,532,386 for foreign travel in 1977. The House alone reported spending $1,851,265.70 in 1978, some $693,992.07 more than it reported spending the year before.

Members of the Senate reported spending $362,462.97 for travel abroad in 1978, an increase of more than $75,000 from the 1977 Senate figure of $287,269.03.

Money was not the only item that members of Congress used abroad. Nearly two million gallons of jet fuel

Foreign Travel

were used by aircraft of the Military Airlift Command (MAC) to shuttle many traveling legislators around.

A single MAC plane such as a VC-135 or VC-137 can use more than 2,000 gallons of jet fuel per hour in the air. CQ estimated that members of Congress flying on military planes used more than 1.7 million gallons of jet fuel on their travel abroad.

The figure does not include jet fuel used by members who traveled abroad on commercial flights.

Hidden Costs

Federal law (sections 276c-1 and 1754 (b) of Title 22, U.S. Code, as amended) requires the chairmen of congressional committees and regular delegations — such as those

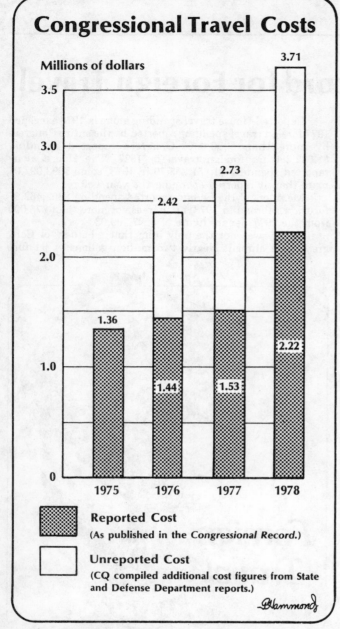

Congressional Travel Costs

Millions of dollars

3.71

3.5

3.0

2.73

2.42

2.0

1.0

1.36

2.22

1.44   1.53

0

1975   1976   1977   1978

Reported Cost
(As published in the *Congressional Record*.)

Unreported Cost
(CQ compiled additional cost figures from State and Defense Department reports.)

Hammond

to the North Atlantic Assembly (NAA) and Interparliamentary Union (IPU) — to report foreign travel expenses incurred by their members during each calendar year.

The annual reports, covering transportation, miscellaneous and per diem expenses, must be filed not later than 60 legislative days after the next session of Congress begins.

Changes in the House and Senate rules resulted in a mass of House reports being filed early February 1979, covering the period Jan. 1-Sept. 30, 1978. The final quarter of the year was covered in separate insertions in the *Record* over a two-month period. Reports of Senate committees and delegations were spread over four months — from February to May — in the *Record*.

The reports omit many congressional trips and the dollar amounts do not represent the full cost of foreign travel, for several reasons. *(Unreported trips, p. 136)*

Unreported Costs

CQ estimated the unreported cost of congressional foreign travel by using data provided by the State and Defense departments. The Defense Department provided CQ with the flight times and cost per hour of each military aircraft used to ferry congressional travelers. CQ then calculated the estimated true cost of each military-sponsored flight and subtracted those expenses for the flight actually reported in the *Record* to determine what costs went unreported.

A U.S. Air Force officer involved in providing the planes and making arrangements for congressional travel said there was no instance in which a military aircraft would have taken off if the congressional travelers had not requisitioned it in letters from the committees to the Defense Department.

When asked if congressional travelers had ever hitched rides on regularly scheduled military flights, he replied, "When they [members of Congress] lay on the requirement, they request that airlift be provided. We are providing airlifts to meet their schedules."

"The fact that they went abroad lets us (the Air Force) take advantage of that to double up and fulfill some of our training requirements for our own personnel," he added.

CQ found that in most instances members of Congress reported only part of the costs of foreign travel hosted by the Defense Department. Congressional rules allow the committees to determine reimbursement figures for Pentagon travel costs, rather than paying the actual costs of the services.

While some committees and members did reimburse DOD for the actual cost of certain trips, and reported it in the *Record*, other committees paid the department for either the equivalent first-class air fare to destinations overseas, or for whatever amount they believed covered the cost of travel. Some committees just listed the trips hosted by DOD in the *Record* with the notation "travel provided by the Department of Defense" — and provided no cost figures.

The CQ spending figure does not include any costs incurred by the Defense Department in connection with the aftermath of the murder of traveling Rep. Leo J. Ryan, D-Calif., and over 800 other Americans, at Jonestown, Guyana. The Defense Department estimates those costs to be between $3.7 million and $4.2 million.

Most Traveled Members

Rep. Stephen J. Solarz, D-N.Y., for the third consecutive year, led congressional travelers with seven trips abroad, more than any other member of Congress.

Six of Solarz' seven trips were study missions at government expense, all but one for the Foreign Affairs Committee. The seventh and part of one government-paid trip were paid for by a private foundation.

Five members finished in a tie for second place, with five trips each. They included Sen. Abraham Ribicoff, D-Conn., chairman of the Governmental Affairs Committee; three representatives, Clement J. Zablocki, D-Wis., chairman of the House Foreign Affairs Committee, Benjamin A. Gilman, R-N.Y., James R. Mann, D-S.C., and one delegate, Antonio Borja Won Pat, D-Guam.

Three senators and ten representatives had four foreign trips each in 1978. The senators were Democrats Edward M. Kennedy, D-Mass., Patrick J. Leahy, D-Vt. and S. I. (Sam) Hayakawa, R-Calif.

The ten representatives with four trips each included five New York Democrats: Joseph P. Addabbo, Charles B. Rangel, Mario Biaggi, John J. LaFalce and James H. Scheuer. They were joined by Reps. Robert K. Badham and Bob Wilson, both California Republicans, Charles W. Whalen Jr., R-Ohio, E. (Kika) de la Garza, D-Texas and G. William Whitehurst, R-Va.

Some of the above-listed trips were not at government expense.

CQ Survey

The 1978 travel study was based on a total congressional membership of 540: 292 Democrats and 147 Republicans in the House, and 63 Democrats and 38 Republicans in the Senate.

The total includes the four non-voting delegates in the House and both Sen. James B. Allen, D-Ala. (1969-78), who died in June 1978, and his wife, Maryon P. Allen, D-Ala., who succeeded to his seat. Sen. Harry F. Byrd Jr., Ind.-Va., and Resident Commissioner (Delegate) Baltasar Corrada, New Progressive-Puerto Rico, were counted as Democrats for purposes of this study.

To supplement the information available from *Congressional Record* travel reports, CQ each year sends questionnaires to all the members of Congress and non-voting House delegates, asking them to list their foreign trips taken during the preceding calendar year.

Ninety-two senators (including Maryon Allen's reply for both herself and James B. Allen) and 386 representatives responded in 1979 to the CQ survey of 1978 travel.

Eight other members died during or after the close of the second session of the 95th Congress. Aides to two, Reps. Ralph H. Metcalfe, D-Ill., and Goodloe E. Byron, D-Md., responded to the CQ survey. The other six who died are also included in the CQ survey, but are not officially listed in the "no response" figures. They are Reps. Clifford Allen, D-Tenn., Leo J. Ryan, D-Calif., William Ketchum, R-Calif., John B. Breckinridge, D-Ky., William Steiger, R-Wis., and Sen. Dewey F. Bartlett, R-Okla.

Eight senators and 48 representatives did not respond to the CQ survey. Among them were two House committee chairmen: Jack Brooks, D-Texas, and John M. Murphy, D-N.Y. CQ contacted the offices of each incumbent non-responder at least four times (twice each by mail and telephone) and attempted to contact each non-incumbent at least twice by mail. *(Non-responders box, p. 138).*

In their replies, many members voluntarily disclosed trips — such as the White House missions — that were not covered in official reports. Other members, however, maintained that all records on their foreign travel could be found in the official reports, and refused to disclose any further information.

1978 Statistics

During 1978, members of Congress took 505 government-paid trips abroad. The trips were taken by 66 senators and 227 representatives, or 54.3 percent of the 540 members of Congress surveyed.

Breaking all previous patterns, members of Congress in 1978 set two records for election-year travel: the number of members (293) taking trips in an election year, and the number of trips (505). Both records broke marks set in 1966.

The number of government-paid trips abroad also was the second-highest total since 1965, when CQ began keep-

Rep. Stephen J. Solarz   Sen. Abraham Ribicoff

ing foreign travel records, exceeded only by the 544 trips abroad taken in 1975, a non-election year.

For the first time since 1968, the number of traveling members and the number of trips both increased in an election year.

The 505 trips abroad was a 21.7 percent increase over the 1977 figure of 415 government-paid trips. The 293 members traveling was a 14.9 percent increase over the 255 traveling abroad in 1977.

Most of the increase in the number of members traveling abroad came in the House, where 227 members (145 D, 82 R) took government-paid trips in 1978, up from 197 in 1977 and 156 in 1976, the last election year. Of 101 senators surveyed, 66 (41 D, 25 R) took government-paid trips in 1978, compared to 58 in 1977, and 48 in 1976.

Only 26 senators and 170 representatives reported no foreign travel — either government or privately paid — in 1978 — down from 40 senators and 220 representatives who reported no trips the previous year.

Year	Number of members taking trips at government expense	Number of trips taken at government expense*
1978*****	293	505
1977****	255	415
1976****	204	309
1975**	308	544
1974**	185	266
1973***	218	314
1972	233	328
1971	274	447
1970	205	291
1969	217	296
1968	217	318
1967	206	306
1966	243	337
1965	232	309

    * - *Trips involving any government funds were counted as government travel in CQ totals.*

    ** - *Totals based on incomplete committee reports.*

    *** - *Totals based on unofficial CQ questionnaire response.*

    **** - *Totals based on unofficial CQ questionnaire responses, State and Defense Department records, and committee reports.*

    ***** - *Totals based on unofficial CQ questionnaire responses, State and Defense Department records, special reports from the State Department Office of Protocol and committee reports.*

In addition to the 504 government-paid trips in 1978, members of Congress took 68 trips abroad either at personal expense or the expense of private organizations.

Why Some Foreign Travel Goes Unreported

"All of the information you have requested is on file with the Clerk of the House of Representatives in the Records and Registration Office. . . ."
—Rep. Frank Annunzio, D-Ill.

Annunzio's response to Congressional Quarterly's foreign travel questionnaire illustrates loopholes in the system used by Congress to report foreign travel.

The Chicago Democrat apparently thought that all of his foreign travel in 1978 was listed in the Clerk's files, and by implication, published in the *Congressional Record.* For that reason, he refused to complete the CQ travel questionnaire.

But Annunzio was wrong. Of the three foreign trips he took overseas last year, two were not on file with the Clerk and were not published in the *Record.*

Annunzio was not alone in having trips unreported in the *Record.* Responses to CQ questionnaires and information from other sources revealed that 61 government-paid trips by senators and 66 by representatives in 1978 were not disclosed in the travel reports published by Congress. Also unreported were parts of nine other trips, five in the Senate and four in the House.

Varied Policy for Reporting

For a number of reasons, not all congressional foreign travel shows up in the *Record.* Among those reasons are:

● Reports cover only trips taken when committees have authorized travel arrangements for their members going abroad on committee business. Individual members sometimes report expenses and this becomes part of the committee report. But individual members may take solo trips and discuss committee business, but do not have to report the trip unless it is specifically authorized by a panel.

● The House and Senate follow an inconsistent policy regarding one-time delegations named by House and Senate leaders.

The new Senate policy, put into effect in 1978, was to report such one-time trips; however, not all of the trips so authorized turned up in the *Record.*

In the House, the reporting of such trips is not required, and disclosures are voluntary. One example is a House leadership-sponsored trip to Central Europe in March, that was led by Rep. Dan Rostenkowski, D-Ill.

Rostenkowski voluntarily reported the trip to CQ, although it was not listed in the *Record.*

● Federal law requires the chairmen of regular congressional delegations — such as those to the Interparliamentary Union and North Atlantic Alliance — to file their reports with the Secretary of the Senate and the House Administration Committee. The law does not require these reports to be published in the *Record.* The House voluntarily publishes the reports; the Senate publishes some of them.

Due to unusual circumstances — the death of a key staff member — the report of the second 1978 IPU delegation (Sept. 2-14) has not yet been published by either the House or Senate.

● White House-sponsored travel does not appear in the *Record* at all, although many members go overseas on White House-sponsored protocol missions.

Last year, the White House sponsored large trips to the investiture of Pope John Paul II and the funeral of former Israeli Prime Minister Golda Meir. The Meir delegation included nine members of Congress, one former member and one senator-elect among its 42 members, according to press reports. John Paul II's investiture drew 14 members of Congress, headed by House Speaker Thomas P. O'Neill Jr., D-Mass.

Also sponsored by the White House were smaller delegations to the funerals of Italian statesman Aldo Moro (two members of Congress), Pope Paul VI (two members) and Pope John Paul I (two members). The delegation to the investiture of John Paul I, which included nine members, was handled through the office of Vice President Walter F. Mondale, who headed the group; that trip, too, does not appear in the *Record.*

Reasons for No Reports

Varied reasons were given for trips failing to appear in official reports.

A Rostenkowski aide said that some members who went on the Central Europe leadership trip may have been confused by rules changes.

"Under the old system, you didn't have to file information for leadership trips. The new law [requiring such filings] may not apply to 1978 trips. That trip was run by the Speaker's staff, and it's not up to the individual members to file, as it's not a committee trip," the aide said.

Of a total of 572 trips reported for 1978, 504, or 88.1 percent, were at government expense. This figure compares with 86.3 percent in 1977, 82.2 percent in 1976, 86.9 percent in 1975, 70.2 percent in 1974 and 66.3 percent in 1973. One reason for the higher percentages since 1975 is that CQ has omitted vacation trips at personal expense since the 1975 study.

The average Democrat took 0.91 government-paid trips in 1978, slightly less than the average Republican who took 0.99 trips. The average House member took 0.88 trips at government expense, less than the average senator who took 1.17 such trips.

	Number of members who traveled at government expense	Number of government-paid trips	Number non-government-paid trips
Senate			
Democrats	41	75	6
Republicans	25	43	3
House			
Democrats	145	246	39
Republicans	82	140	20
TOTAL	293	504	68

Foreign Travel Reported by Congress

Following is the list of foreign travel expenditures for both houses of Congress in 1978 as reported in the *Congressional Record* by committees or delegation leaders. Committees not listed did not report any foreign travel in calendar 1978.

HOUSE

Committee/Group	Amount Reported
Appropriations[1]	$ 395,852.48
Armed Services	319,822.42
International Relations[2]	261,200.93
Ways and Means	102,978.27
Special Southeast Asia	89,963.21
Science and Technology	72,996.89
Government Operations	66,206.11
Merchant Marine	64,253.66
Banking	56,659.59
Judiciary	54,804.74
Agriculture	50,057.59
North Atlantic Assembly	47,203.93
Select Assassinations	46,692.29
Interparliamentary Union[3]	44,869.87
Select Narcotics	22,921.48
Public Works	22,801.43
Interstate Commerce	21,924.43
Education and Labor	20,341.68
Commission on Security and Cooperation in Europe[3]	18,395.17
Budget	13,931.01
Select Intelligence	13,282.60
Veterans' Affairs	11,265.88
Standards of Conduct	10,666.29
Interior	5,997.62
Post Office	5,668.00
Staff trips	3,285.00
Outer Continental Shelf	2,935.27
Ad Hoc Select Energy	1,814.38
House Administration	1,599.12
Select Population	874.36
House Total	**$1,851,265.70**

SENATE

Committee/Group	Amount Reported
Foreign Relations	$ 89,428.40
Delegation to Supreme Soviet	40,944.52
Appropriations	34,025.56
North Atlantic Assembly	28,635.13
16th China (PRC) Delegation	23,643.20
Energy	21,893.53
Human Resources	15,596.00
Budget	15,096.92
Finance	14,190.65
Governmental Affairs	12,459.48
Agriculture	12,436.56
Williams-Bellmon China (PRC) Trip	10,807.86
Select Intelligence	10,751.45
Robert C. Byrd Trip to Middle East	6,950.39
Environment and Public Works	6,002.15
Commerce	5,606.85
Armed Services	5,137.57
Judiciary	4,830.60
Ethics	2,670.30
Bellmon European Trip[4]	1,055.85
Staff trip	300.00
Senate Total	**$ 362,462.97**

JOINT COMMITTEE

Joint Committee on Printing	$ 2,193.37
GRAND TOTAL	**$2,215,922.04**

[1]*Includes $111,142.60 reported by the Appropriations Committee surveys and investigations staff.*
[2]*Includes $4,981.05 reported by the International Organizations Subcommittee for its investigation of alleged Korean influence buying.*

[3]*Only expenditures for House members and staff were reported by these delegates.*
[4]*Trip authorized by Senate Minority Leader Howard H. Baker Jr., R-Tenn.*

The average Democratic senator took 1.19 government-paid trips in 1978, slightly higher than the average Republican senator, who took 1.13 trips.

In the House, the average Democrat took 0.84 government-paid trips, compared to 0.95 government-paid trips for the average House Republican.

House Expenditures

Of the record $1,851,265.70 reported spent by House committees and delegations for foreign travel in 1978, over half was spent by just three committees — the three which have traditionally led the House foreign travel spending list — Appropriations, Armed Services and Foreign Affairs (formerly, International Relations).

Appropriations spent $395,852.48 for foreign travel for its members and staff in 1978, some $172,747.62 more than it reported spending in 1977. Armed Services reported spending $319,822.42 in 1978 — $102,307.80 more than the year before — and the Foreign Affairs Committee spent $261,200.93 — some $67,716.75 more than its 1977 figure.

Reported expenditures by the Appropriations Committee amounted to 21.4 percent of all House foreign travel funds reported for 1978. Appropriations also reported spending more on foreign travel than the entire U.S. Senate, not counting the unreported trips at government expense which many senators took.

Senate Expenditures

Senate reported spending on travel rose in 1978 to a figure of $362,462.97, some $75,193.94 more than the reported 1977 Senate total of $287,269.03.

However, the Senate spending level does not reflect the fact that more than half of all Senate trips did not show up on the official reports.

Though the Senate Foreign Relations Committee kept its lead in Senate foreign travel spending, both its amount and its share of Senate spending dropped substantially from 1977. In 1978, Foreign Relations reported spending $89,428.40 for travel by members and staff — 24.7 percent of all Senate spending. By contrast, Foreign Relations spent $140,594.40 on travel in 1977 — almost half (48.9 percent) of the entire Senate total. The panel has led reported foreign travel spending every year since 1969, except for 1973 when records were unavailable.

The second place finisher in reported Senate spending was not a committee at all; it was the Senate delegation to the Supreme Soviet of the Union of Soviet Socialist Republics, from Nov. 9-21, which reported spending $40,944.52.

Beginning with the 1978 records, CQ included in the respective listings of reported House and Senate travel expenditures the reports of delegations each body sent to meetings of such international organizations as the North Atlantic Assembly and the Interparliamentary Union (IPU).

Europe Favored

As in past years, Western Europe was the favorite destination of congressional travelers. Though many of the stops in Western Europe were for refueling or changing planes, most were for substantive purposes.

The Senate continued its efforts to assemble a quorum in Panama. Many Senate delegations — reported and unreported — made the trip to see the Panama Canal. Some 21 senators went to Central America and all of them went to Panama, two of them, Paul S. Sarbanes, D-Md., and Frank Church, D-Idaho, twice.

Other notable increases were registered by Africa, which had 64 congressional visits in 1978, and Russia and Eastern Europe, which had 56 visits. Those two areas had 21 and 30 visits respectively in 1977. Asia, which finished second to Western Europe in 1977 with 67 visits, again finished second — but doubled its total to 132.

Destinations visited for both government-paid and non-government-paid trips in 1978 were:

	Senate	House	Total**
Western Europe (including Turkey, Cyprus)	64	260	324
Asia	27	105	132
Japan	21	81	102
People's Republic of China	19	46	65
Southeast Asia	2	48	50
Republic of China	2	22	24
South Korea	0	16	16
South Asia	3	11	14
Africa	16	48	64
Middle East	19	42	61
Israel	11	26	37
Saudi Arabia	11	23	34
Egypt	10	22	32
Iran	6	23	29
Russia and Eastern Europe	23	33	56
Central America	23	19	42
Panama	23	8	31
South America	5	17	22
Canada	5	14	19
Cuba	0	14	14
Caribbean*	1	10	11
Mexico	5	5	10
Australia and New Zealand	0	7	7

* - U.S. territories and possessions are not included in foreign travel and are not included in CQ totals.

** - Since most members visited more than one area on each trip, the number of areas visited is greater than the number of trips reported.

The following members of Congress did not respond to Congressional Quarterly's foreign travel questionnaire. CQ contacted each incumbent member's office at least four times by mail or telephone. Non-incumbents (in *italics*) were mailed CQ questionnaires at least twice.

HOUSE

Addabbo, D-N.Y.
Ammerman, D-Pa.
Ashbrook, R-Ohio
Brooks, D-Texas
Burke, R-Fla.
Burleson, D-Texas
Burlison, D-Mo.
P. Burton, D-Calif.
Clawson, R-Calif.
Clay, D-Mo.
C. Collins, D-Ill.
Conte, R-Mass.
Cunningham, R-Wash.
Davis, D-S.C.
de la Garza, D-Texas
Delaney, D-N.Y.
Evans, D-Colo.
Flynt, D-Ga.
William Ford, D-Mich.
Fraser, D-Minn.
Gaydos, D-Pa.
Gibbons, D-Fla.
Hansen, R-Idaho
Jenrette, D-S.C.
Leach, R-Iowa
Levitas, D-Ga.
Long, D-Md.
Mann, D-S.C.
Mathis, D-Ga.
McDonald, D-Ga.
Meyner, D-N.J.
Milford, D-Texas
Miller, R-Ohio
John Murphy, D-N.Y.
Nedzi, D-Mich.
Risenhoover, D-Okla
Ruppe, R-Mich.
Schulze, R-Pa.
Shipley, D-Ill.
Sikes, D-Fla.
Sisk, D-Calif.
Skubitz, R-Kansas
Smith, D-Iowa
Teague, D-Texas
Walsh, R-N.Y.
B. Wilson, R-Calif.
J. Young, D-Texas
de Lugo, D-V.I.

SENATE

Abourezk, D-S.D.
Anderson, D-Minn
Bellmon, R-Okla.
Glenn, D-Ohio
Griffin, R-Mich.
Matsunaga, D-Hawaii
Riegle, D-Mich.
Scott, R-Va.

Travel Views

Members of Congress had differing views about the value of travel abroad. While some defended the value of travel, others derided it as a waste of money.

Rep. Jim Lloyd, D-Calif., said his failure to travel abroad in 1978 should not be misconstrued. "Do not assume that because I did not travel last year that I am against travel," he wrote. "If it falls within the needs of a member's committee requirements, I support travel."

Rep. Keith G. Sebelius, R-Kansas, said he had told his Kansas farm constituents about his Nov. 18-Dec. 3 trip to Japan and the People's Republic of China. "I have made many talks in the district since then, and I have told my Kansas constituents that I think they certainly got their money's worth."

Rep. Tim Lee Carter, R-Ky., came back impressed by the Chinese people following his trip to the People's Republic of China, Nov. 10-27. "The Chinese are a friendly, hardworking people taking care of basic needs: food, clothing, housing and health," he wrote.

Taxpayers Pay for Congressional Liquor Bills

When a congressional delegation to China took off from Andrews Air Force Base on Dec. 27, 1978, it didn't exactly travel light.

Led by Rep. Thomas L. Ashley, D-Ohio, the 20-member group boarded a VC-137 military jet transport at the suburban Washington air base that had been well-stocked for the journey. Accompanying Ashley were Reps. John J. LaFalce, D-N.Y., David W. Evans, D-Ind., Mary Rose Oakar, D-Ohio, Doug Barnard, D-Ga., Robert Garcia, D-N.Y. and Richard Kelly, R-Fla., three wives, seven staffers and three Defense Department escorts.

A U.S. Navy escort officer loaded the plane with $363.59 worth of food, enough for 22 breakfasts, 44 lunches and 22 dinners. A variety of "aircraft supplies" came to another $82.20, but the main 'supply' seemed to be alcoholic beverages.

Before departing for the Far East, the escort officer picked up $14.65 worth of beer from the U.S. Marine Corps PX at Henderson Hall. From a nearby liquor store came $537.36 worth of whiskey and wine: two cases (24 quarts) and four quart bottles (one gallon) of Johnnie Walker Black Label scotch, six quarts of Jack Daniels Black bourbon, five fifths of V.S.O.P. cognac, two fifths of Winemasters champagne, four half-quarts of Sebastiani chablis, two fifths of Smirnoff vodka, two fifths of Gilbey's gin, and one fifth of Sebastiani red wine.

There was so much to carry that the escort gave a $5 tip to the delivery man.

The beverage bill was not uncommon. Congressional Quarterly's examination of Defense Department records reveals many instances where expenses for congressional foreign delegations included bills for alcoholic beverages, food, "control room" bills, and some hotel bills — all paid for by military escorts for traveling members and staff.

In most instances, the escort officers were reimbursed by members for only part of their reported out-of-pocket expenses. Ashley's delegation, for example, reported paying escort officers $5,416.48, but the escort officers reported spending $7,708.24, leaving a net spending figure for the escorts of $2,291.76 — none of it reported in the *Congressional Record*.

Federal Law

Under federal law, traveling legislators and staffers are allowed $75 per diem when overseas. This amount is supposed to cover food, drink, hotel bills and any other necessary expenses. Per diems do not cover everything, however. Military escorts generally pay for such things as airport departure fees.

Some congressional travelers forgo the per diem and dip into private or personal funds. But other congressional travelers let the escort officer pay for meals and drinks which ordinarily should come from their per diem allowances.

Most foreign congressional missions include crowded itineraries which leave little time for the social aspects of foreign travel, and Ashley's Navy-sponsored trip was typical. In 17 days, the delegation spent 52.8 hours in the air. Members visited five cities in the People's Republic of China, and made stops in Japan, Hong Kong, Bangkok, Hawaii, Guam, and Travis Air Force Base in California.

When the Navy plane on this China trip reached Bangkok, for example, the escort officer set up a "control room" for the delegation in the Siam Continental Hotel. A Jan. 11, 1979, bill for that room discloses what such suites are used for: liquid hospitality.

That day, the escort purchased at discount prices from the U.S. Embassy commissary: four bottles of Beefeater gin, four bottles of J&B scotch, one bottle of Johnnie Walker Black Label scotch, two bottles of Smirnoff vodka, two bottles of Tanqueray gin, a case of soda water and a bottle of Gordon's gin. Four cases of Heineken beer were also shipped to the hotel.

All that, plus refreshments at the airport, added up to $74.26.

When the returning travelers arrived at Travis, they stopped for a $29.93 breakfast on Jan. 13. Since they needed some snacks and beverages for the flight home, the Navy escort picked up 40 packages of macadamia nuts, 10 packages of Fritos, 10 packages of won tons, one case apiece of Coke, Seven-Up and ginger ale, and 48 cans of Bloody Mary mix and tomato juice — all for $128.15. Thus fortified, the delegation flew back to Washington.

Ashley's China delegation was not the only overseas congressional mission in which the taxpayers paid for members' alcoholic beverages and other comforts.

Members' Comfort

Every year, for example, the Interparliamentary Union (IPU) holds at least one foreign conference for legislators. Opinions within the Congress on the value of the IPU conference tours are mixed: members who go praise them; some of those who don't call them junkets.

One fact about the IPU tours is undisputed: they are expensive. A 40-plus person IPU delegation to Lisbon, London, Geneva, Paris, Vienna and Morocco from March 22-April 2 cost an estimated $77,892.60 for flying the group's VC-137 military jet transport to Europe, plus another $4,995 for "in-theater" flights between European capitals.

The group's Army escort reported net expenses of $2,059.65 — after reimbursements by members for expenses of the 13 wives. The escort officer picked up the tab for meals, beverages, and necessities for the members.

On this trip, the IPU delegation did report in the *Record* that it repaid the escort — in fact, apparently overpaying him by $4,866.51.

Army records include six purchases of "control room supplies" during the journey for $84.97; $154.01 in four bills for refreshments (including one bill for $96.66); $646.16 handed out in tips to bellboys and porters for toting congressional baggage; one $44.50 congressional dinner and four lunches totaling $57.18; a $20.82 long-distance call, and $154.75 in other undescribed expenses.

The escorts also reported spending $152.32 to purchase electric transformers, apparently for congressional shavers.

Rep. David E. Satterfield III, D-Va., added, "All of my trips have been extremely busy and taxing. I have always learned a great deal from talking to the in-country personnel involved. I also find that while you usually go abroad for one purpose, you wind up getting information and briefings, as I did in Taiwan, on something else that later comes up on the floor."

Rep. Robert McClory, R-Ill., in a statement inserted in the *Record* on Jan. 15, 1979, noted a favorable editorial entitled "Most Junkets Serve Purpose" in the *Elgin Daily Courier News*. After praising the paper, he added, "as a delegate to many conferences of the Interparliamentary Union (IPU), I have been able to serve the interests of our nation while gaining an enlightened understanding of numerous problems and interests of other nations. . . ."

But some members took a different view of foreign travel. An aide to Rep. John J. Duncan, R-Tenn., said, "It has always been his policy not to take trips abroad at public expense."

Rep. Andy Jacobs Jr., D-Ind., who once described his only foreign trip — to fight in the Korean War — as "a waste of time," instead turned to former President John F. Kennedy for his comment on congressional travel. "The Vice President [Nixon] says if he is elected he will go to Russia," Jacobs quoted Kennedy as saying. "If I am elected, I shall go to Washington, D.C."

Jacobs' theme was echoed by an aide to Sen. William L. Armstrong, R-Colo. "He travels frequently to Washington," said press secretary Mike Kelly.

And former Sen. Maryon P. Allen, D-Ala. (1978), answering for both herself and her late husband, declared: "Neither of us ever traveled to other countries, acting officially in any manner. . . . We accepted no honoraria of any sort, no expenses, either for food, lodging or travel. In other words, the Allens weren't freeloaders!!"

The reaction of Rep. Ron Paul, R-Texas, who did not serve in the 95th Congress, was to introduce H Con Res 102 on April 10, 1979. Paul's bill would require advance disclosure of the destinations and costs of all House foreign travel, as well as a three-fourths vote of the House to authorize each trip.

"I believe the American people are sick [of] lush foreign trips for [members] and their staff," he said. "This misuse of tax funds must be ended. . . . [The trips] are as scandalous as a government grant to study Australian aborigines. Both are pure ripoffs." ∎

Computers, Direct Mail Aid Incumbents

Sen. Robert P. Griffin, R-Mich., was worried. But Derry Daly had a plan. It was 1972 and Griffin faced a tight re-election race in November. School busing was a hot issue in Michigan politics, and Daly — a direct mail expert — called for using the Senate computer, sophisticated direct mail techniques and taxpayer funds to get out the vote for Griffin. This could be done, Daly said, by obtaining a commercially available mailing list of car owners, deleting persons known to live in black areas by use of a separate computer list, and sending out computer letters outlining Griffin's opposition to busing. In addition, similar computer-produced mailings would cover Griffin's positions on pensions (directed to blue-collar areas), cutting property taxes (to higher income areas) and farm issues (to Michigan farmers).

Daly's plan is history now. On Nov. 7, Griffin rode the busing issue to a second term in the Senate by a narrow margin over his Democratic opponent. *(Details of plan, p. 143)*

Although the election is long over, the concept embodied in Daly's plan was alive, well and flourishing on Capitol Hill in 1979.

Congress has made some effort at regulating the new computer technology available to incumbents to prevent officeholders from having an unfair advantage over challengers, but success has been limited and appeared to be receding rather than advancing.

One key factor mitigating against a tougher congressional position on the issue: Dozens of members of Congress have been using techniques like those that helped Griffin. Moreover, this type of computer-aided re-election activity increasingly has been financed by taxpayers from funds that members of Congress normally use to carry out their duties as elected officials.

Legal depositions obtained by Common Cause, the self-styled "citizens'" lobby, indicated that about one-third of the members of the Senate in 1979 used official funds and sophisticated direct mail techniques to promote their re-election.

Further, rapidly changing computer technology and increasingly sophisticated techniques of direct mail communication have rendered congressional limits on Daly-type re-election efforts largely obsolete, in the opinion of direct mail experts and political campaign consultants surveyed by Congressional Quarterly. These experts said that additional technological advances and proposed rules changes were likely to make meaningless any restrictions on the political use of the free mailing privileges accorded members of Congress. Commented one computer specialist with the House: "Ultimately, the technology will get cheap enough so that everyone will have their own computer, and the crime will likely become reduced to the stature of misusing a Xerox machine."

Challenging the System

Common Cause has been the only non-congressional group that has made a major effort to combat what it considered a significant abuse of incumbent advantages through use of computers and the congressional frank. (The frank is the free mailing privilege members enjoy; it is a reproduction of the member's signature that goes where a stamp normally is placed on a letter. The cost to the Postal Service of mailing an item under the frank is covered by an appropriation from Congress.)

Originally obtained through a court deposition, the 1972 Daly plan to rescue Griffin has since become a key element in a Common Cause lawsuit filed against Congress in October 1974. (All names and other identifying details were deleted from the Daly document as a condition of its public release, but an independent investigation by CQ established that the document referred to Griffin's 1972 campaign.)

In the lawsuit, pending before the U.S. District Court for the District of Columbia in mid-1979, Common Cause charged that a congressman's free mailing privilege was unconstitutional because it promoted the re-election of incumbents and therefore denied equal protection of the law to challengers.

Acting before the courts resolved the suit, both House and Senate responded to Common Cause's evidence of abuses of the frank by adopting a series of new restrictions on the mailing privilege in their 1977 ethics codes. *(See pp. 157, 162)*

A congressional employee operates a mini-computer in a member's office. These computers are said to be excellent for targeting mail to different groups of voters. They can be located in individual offices, making supervision for compliance with Senate and House rules difficult.

However, subsequent changes in House and Senate rules and procedures have eroded the 1977 restrictions. In addition, advances in computer technology have provided incumbents with additional re-election aids far more valuable than the franking privilege alone.

Just Another Product

As advanced computer technology and techniques of building mailing lists have developed, direct mail has become a necessary ingredient of most members' recipe for re-election. This trend has occurred in part because, in many campaigns, pressure groups with single or limited legislative interests are playing an increasingly significant role. Modern direct mail techniques are a highly effective way to weave many small pockets of support into an overall winning margin.

Although a member of Congress has a special status under the Constitution, he is — to the direct mail expert — just another product.

Just as a glossy catalog of camera equipment probably would have the best results when mailed to photographers, direct mail "sells" the member by targeting the right messages to the appropriate audiences of voters. A letter strongly supporting a tuition tax credit, for example, is likely to be well received by registered voters who also are parents of children enrolled in private schools and universities.

Just as important as choosing the correct message for each particular audience is maintaining product identity. A steady stream of messages throughout the term of the member of Congress keeps the legislator's name before the electorate so that voters will recognize it when they step into the polling booth. According to the experts, the essential ingredients of any successful direct mail campaign are good mailing lists and a good computer. Persuasive letters

This file drawer in the office of a House member contains large storage discs to operate an IBM System 6 computer to target mail to voters. Each disc shown can hold up to 3,000 names and addresses, grouped by categories such as interest in particular issues, age, income, political affiliation or zip code.

and lots of money for postage and printing of an effective mail "package" are needed also.

However, members of Congress have an important advantage over commercial direct mail marketers: access to public funds to pay for the ingredients of a direct mail campaign. Letters can be drafted by staff aides or direct mail consultants paid for with official funds, mailing lists compiled or purchased at government expense, and postage and printing costs covered by the taxpayer, too.

Reforms: 'Haven't Worked'

Concern over the political use of the frank led Congress in 1973 and 1977 to adopt rules restricting the use of official funds, computers and the frank for political gain. Both houses barred use of the frank for mass mailings (defined as mailings of more than 500 pieces of identical mail) during the two-month period immediately preceding a general or primary election. Also barred were letters soliciting votes or campaign funds and such "unofficial" communications as "holiday greetings." The rules curtailed the use of members' photos and the pronoun "I" in newsletters mailed under the frank. Although the restrictions were hailed at the time, they left the door open for abuse. Simply stated, "the reforms haven't worked," said Common Cause General Counsel Kenneth Guido Jr. in mid-1979. "There's probably been an improvement since 1977," Guido said, "but the reforms didn't deal with the heart of the matter. People are still targeting mail to constituents in order to maximize its effectiveness. So long as they stop short of soliciting a vote, they can use the frank to promote their re-election."

The effectiveness of these reforms has been diminished by developments such as:
- Continued storage of political information in computers against Senate rules;
- Use of members' office funds to pay for computer and other services necessary for direct mail campaigns;
- Increased use of mailing and computer facilities outside Congress to avoid review of compliance with Senate and House rules.

Senate

In many ways, the Senate reforms went further than the House's. Senators, for example, were required to use the official Senate computer for all of their electronic correspondence management, permitting easy scrutiny of all that went into the computer as well as what came out. Rules which became effective in January 1978 barred the storage of lists of names and addresses identifying individuals as campaign workers or contributors or as members of any political party.

Once entered into the Senate computer, a list could not be removed, except in the form of a printout for "cleaning" — entering address changes, adding new names, eliminating duplicate names, and so forth. However, loopholes in the rules, as well as rules changes adopted by the Senate since the approval of the 1977 restrictions, made many of the restrictions obsolete.

Political Data Encoded

A computerized mailing list is only as effective as the information that is electronically encoded on it. Every bit of information associated with a name and address on the magnetic tape can permit a direct mail expert to more effectively choose targets for particular pieces of mail.

Targeting the Mail: Just Press a Button

The re-election plan that Derry Daly worked out in 1972 for Michigan Republican Senator Robert P. Griffin was a model of vote gathering techniques that politicians have since said they felt were essential for any candidate in a close race.

Daly was a direct mail expert with the J. Walter Thompson Co. advertising firm; in addition, he understood computers and their wonderful capacity to sort out useful groups of voters from much larger lists of citizens. His plan, essentially, called for using the Senate computer, sophisticated direct mail techniques and taxpayer funds to convince Michigan residents to vote for Griffin.

Busing Issue

A key issue in that election was school busing, which Griffin opposed. His opponent, State Attorney General Frank J. Kelley, had been wavering on the issue.

Daly proposed mass mailings to blue-collar households in three key counties which had voted Democratic in the last three congressional elections. In these counties, Daly reasoned, busing was likely to be an emotional issue.

In a memorandum entitled a "plan for making optimum use of direct mail as a medium of personal persuasion in Senator Griffin's 1972 re-election campaign," Daly told Griffin he should try to "capitalize on the unrest of this group, attempting to switch them to the Republican camp and thus gain more votes in these counties."

Griffin could accomplish this, Daly said, by blanketing these counties with a special computerized letter outlining his opposition to busing.

Dropping Blacks

Another target for the anti-busing letter, Daly said, should be "higher-income car[-owning] households in non-black tracts" in a fourth Michigan county.

As laid out in Daly's memo, Griffin was to obtain the names and addresses of such households by entering into the Senate computer the "Polk 01 list: Non-duplicating residential car households," a commercially available electronic mailing list. Then, using a second electronic list compiled from census data, all addresses on the Polk 01 list located in black census tracts were to be eliminated with a simple computer command. The computer could then electronically address the envelopes so that they would go only to the targeted households.

Other proposed mailings included 142,000 copies of Griffin's "special newsletter on pensions" to blue-collar households in 11 counties; 200,000 pieces of mail on Griffin's support for lower property taxes to "higher-income households" throughout the entire state; and letters "stressing the senator's stance on farm issues" to every farmer on the mailing list of the state department of agriculture.

To comply with Senate restrictions on the use of the free congressional mailing privilege, known as the frank, Daly specified in his memo that letters designed to get out the vote or to raise funds were to be printed, stuffed into envelopes and mailed with campaign funds.

Government Financed

Letters dealing solely with legislation or national issues, on the other hand, could be printed, stuffed and mailed at taxpayer expense, Daly said.

For the letters sent out at taxpayer expense, the sole cost to the senator's campaign committee would be the price of renting electronic mailing lists — in the form of reels of computer tape — from commercial marketing firms, the memo said. On Nov. 7, Griffin rode the busing issue to a second term in the Senate, winning a narrow victory over Democrat Kelley. Following his re-election, Griffin wrote Daly a thank-you note.

To streamline correspondence to constituents, a senator might wish to put information on the tape about a constituent's legislative interests or occupation, a bookkeeping device permitted under the rules.

Some data can be helpful for both official purposes as well as political purposes. Key demographic information such as an addressee's age, sex, race, income and home ownership, for example, could be used to predict legislative interests as well as political orientation.

Other data, however, could only be useful for political gain. An addressee's political party affiliation, past voting patterns and past political contributions fall into this category and cannot be put into the Senate computer under the 1977 reforms.

According to Senate Rules Committee Chief Counsel Chester Smith, committee staffers routinely monitor each mailing list tape at the time it is submitted to the computer center to determine its content. "When they put it into the computer, we won't let them put in the party designation or other political data," Smith said.

However, computer codes obtained through court depositions by Common Cause indicated the encoding of politically useful data was widespread. Prior to 1977, for example, one senator programmed the computer to record all individuals according to whether they had given over $1,000, over $500, over $100 or over $50 during the senator's last campaign.

After 1977, these codes were changed to "Senator **'s best supporter," "Senator **'s second best supporter," "Senator **'s third best supporter," and so forth. (The name of the senator had been deleted as a condition of the document's public release.) For other senators, pre-1977 codes indicating levels of contributions, party affiliation, and past political activity were merely converted to letter codes such as "ab" or "DD."

"We haven't run into it," commented Rules Chief Counsel Smith. "It's conceivable that they could have double codes or triple codes or something else. But this is a judgment they would have to make, and it's against the ethics code."

Paying for Mail Lists

Mailing lists are particularly important to senators because Senate rules bar the use of "postal patron" mailings — in which mail is addressed simply to "postal patron" and delivered to every address in a designated congressional district.

(A bill that would have permitted senators to make "resident" or "occupant" mailings — for which an address but no name is required to be placed on the envelope — was reported by the Governmental Affairs Committee in 1978 but died at the end of the 95th Congress.)

One way senators compile mailing lists is to collect the name and address of every person who writes to them. One advantage of this method is that senators can transfer to their campaign committees the names and addresses compiled in this manner.

To reach larger numbers, however, senators have to buy or rent computer mailing lists. Prior to 1977, senators could obtain electronic mailing lists only with their own personal funds or as gifts. However, accepting lists as gifts

---

"Ultimately, the technology will get cheap enough so that everyone will have their own computer, and the crime will likely become reduced to the stature of misusing a Xerox machine."

—House computer specialist

---

was precluded as a result of Senate adoption in 1977 of a new ethics code. The code barred unofficial office accounts — undesignated accounts that were available for whatever expenditures a member thought proper.

The Senate Select Ethics Committee subsequently ruled that the acceptance of mailing lists as gifts was the equivalent of accepting an "in-kind contribution to an unofficial office account." Senators wanting to buy lists were faced with paying for them out of their own pockets.

Cranston Change Adopted

A group of senators set out in mid-1977 to change this, and succeeded. A rules change permitted senators to buy anything they wanted — including mailing lists — with a portion of their official funds. The change permitted senators to spend up to 10 percent of their total expense allowance on whatever they deemed to be an "official expense."

The change was made in the fiscal 1978 legislative appropriations bill (PL 95-94) at the behest of the group's leader, Alan Cranston, D-Calif. The provision added the new benefit to a list of allowable expenses spelled out in a 1973 supplemental appropriations bill. The benefit was permanent and did not have to be renewed in annual funding bills.

Since July 1977, Cranston has used $1,902.90 in official funds to purchase magnetic tapes of registered voters and their addresses from the California secretary of state. Each $1.10 buys Cranston names and addresses of 1,000 households. Each of these households has at least one registered voter. According to Rich Richardson, a computer analyst in the state elections department, the tapes also contain computer codes that give each addressee's political party, sex, date of birth, date of registration, congressional district, county, precinct and preferred ballot language — English, Spanish or Chinese.

Rules Committee Chief Counsel Smith said Cranston was required to delete the party affiliation code before entering the lists into the Senate computer. The rest of the information was allowed to remain on the tapes. "Before the 1977 rules change, the senator purchased lists with money from his own pocket," explained Cranston's administrative assistant, Roy F. Greenaway. "That's why we pushed for the 10 percent discretionary fund. It was to permit us to buy mailing lists for our newsletter."

Greenaway said the lists were used solely to mail Cranston's newsletters, and for no other purpose.

County, State Lists Purchased

According to Senate records, a number of other senators have also begun using their official expense allowances to purchase county-by-county or statewide voter registration lists. Because many states permit only elected officials to purchase such lists, challengers to incumbents in those states are barred from similarly benefiting from the wealth of computerized data the lists provide.

Among those purchasing electronic voter registration lists in addition to Cranston have been Sens. William L. Armstrong, R-Colo., Harry F. Byrd Jr., Ind.-Va., John H. Chafee, R-R.I., Orrin G. Hatch, R-Utah, S.I. (Sam) Hayakawa, R-Calif., John Heinz, R-Pa., Charles McC. Mathias Jr., R-Md., Spark M. Matsunaga, D-Hawaii, Gaylord Nelson, D-Wis., and Paul S. Sarbanes, D-Md.

(The number of senators purchasing such lists probably is larger. Some senators use their district office allowances rather than their 10 percent discretionary funds to purchase the lists. Detailed records of purchases made with district office funds are not publicly disclosed, as are records of purchases made with 10 percent funds.)

Campaign consultants interviewed by Congressional Quarterly said they have advised senators to use these lists for statewide mailings intended to keep the senator's name before his constituents, to concentrate mail in precincts or counties in which the senator performed poorly in an earlier election, or to "get out the vote" in precincts or counties in which the senator performed well in an earlier election.

A spot check of these senators' offices indicated they used the lists primarily to mail newsletters. Some offices, however, said they sometimes used the list by zip code or other data to "target" mailings. For example, when Sens. Hatch and Armstrong appear at town meetings in a particular town, the senators' offices "blanket" the area with announcements of the event to promote attendance. "It's just one of those things you do to keep in touch with the folks," explained Ed Darrell, Hatch's press secretary.

Other senators have used the 10 percent fund to buy more specialized lists. For example, John C. Culver, D-Iowa, purchased in early 1978 the membership lists of the Policemen's Association and the Iowa Commission on the Status of Women; a list of subscribers to the *Iowa Conservationist* magazine, and the list of all businesses collecting sales tax in the state of Iowa. Jim Sasser, D-Tenn., purchased from the U.S. Department of Agriculture a computer tape of all Tennessee burley tobacco farmers. Mike Gravel, D-Alaska, bought a tape from the State of Alaska Department of Fish and Game listing the addresses of all licensed Alaskan hunters and fishermen. Of the three, Culver and Gravel were up for re-election in 1980.

Lists as Gifts

Though the 1977 rules changes barred a senator from accepting mailing lists as gifts, the Senate Select Ethics

Committee, in a July 1977 ruling, said senators could continue to accept lists from their principal campaign committees.

Such lists could be entered into the Senate computer so long as they were not "acquired selectively or sorted with the intent of targeting mailings to likely election supporters," the committee said in its ruling.

"The acquisition and incorporation only of lists selected on the basis of high incidence of partisan behavior, for example, is not acceptable," the ruling stated.

A number of senators have capitalized on this ruling by using campaign funds to purchase lists and then transfer them to the official Senate computer for addressing franked mail, according to Smith of the Rules Committee. However, Smith said the committee staff has blocked other senators from entering into the Senate computer politically oriented lists such as those obtained from political consultants, political organizations and state and national political party committees.

Apparently dissatisfied with the Ethics Committee's ruling, four of the panel's six members in 1978 and again in 1979 reported a resolution (S Res 25, S Rept 96-1) to permit a senator to transfer to the Senate computer mailing lists acquired from national and state political party commit-

---

"The senators are using [the IMB letter-writing computer] now for casework . . . but they'd be ideal for targeting mail by legislative interest or for sending out a senator's newsletter."

—IBM account manager Leo Tims

---

tees. Those voting to report the resolution were Harrison "Jack" Schmitt, R-N.M., Mathias, Robert Morgan, D-N.C., and John Tower, R-Texas. Voting against reporting the resolution were Adlai E. Stevenson, D-Ill., and Abraham Ribicoff, D-Conn.

Because a list from a state Democratic committee, for example, would presumably contain only the names and addresses of Democrats, the effect of the resolution — if approved — would be to permit for the first time such highly partisan lists to be entered into the Senate computer.

Computers in a Closet

Senate officials have been among the first to admit there is plenty of gray in the rules governing the frank and the use of computers. "This is going to be nebulous, because the rule doesn't have any criteria to decide anything with," one Rules Committee aide said when asked to interpret a rule.

Whatever authority the rules do have, these officials say, the centralized Senate computer is the key to their enforcement because it allows Rules Committee staffers to scrutinize everything going into and coming out of it.

A group of senators led by California's Cranston, however, is pushing to decentralize the system by permitting each senator to have his own computer unit. Computer experts say the change could spell an end to the rules' effectiveness.

Existing Senate rules bar the purchase or lease of individual office computers or computerized automatic typewriters for correspondence management, unless authorized by the Rules Committee.

Cranston, however, used his 10 percent discretionary funds to lease an IBM System 6 automatic letter-writing and addressing unit representing the latest in correspondence technology. The IBM System is not authorized by Rules. When he had exhausted the 10 percent fund, Cranston — joined by Russell B. Long, D-La. — asked the Rules Committee to change the rules to permit such equipment to be leased with funds from a senator's regular office allowance.

The two argued that the existing Senate equipment was obsolete. Long called for the General Accounting Office to investigate the competing systems' relative effectiveness and economy. Though it didn't change the rules, "We bailed you out," Rules Chairman Claiborne Pell, D-R.I., told Cranston at the time.

Rather than approve use of the mini-computers for all senators, Rules authorized an in-service "test" by permitting Sens. Cranston, John A. Durkin, D-N.H., Paul Laxalt, R-Nev., Long and George McGovern, D-S.D., to operate the machines, at Senate expense, for a year. All five senators involved in the "test" were up for re-election in 1980.

According to IBM account manager Leo Tims, the IBM System 6 is particularly well suited for direct mail use, especially if equipped with a separate "memory" unit, to store names and addresses for repeated use. Though Cranston's unit did not have a separate memory, other IBM units involved in the test had this capacity. "The senators are using them now for casework, follow-up mailings and responding to constituent mail," Tims told a reporter, "but they'd be ideal for targeting mail by legislative interest or for sending out a senator's newsletter."

For a System 6 not equipped with a separate memory, names and addresses can be electronically stored on plastic discs. The number of discs that can be produced and maintained is unlimited. Each disc can store about 3,000 names and associated data — useful for categorizing groups of correspondence by legislative interest, zip code, occupation, or whatever, Tims said.

If a larger memory capacity were needed, Tims said, a congressional office could store additional names in leased computer memory space in a remote location. The remote computer, linked to the senator's office via a telephone tie-line, could then command the System 6 to automatically write pre-programmed letters and address them.

House

House rules and procedures governing mailings are less strict than the Senate's and virtually unenforceable.

While the Senate computer is centralized, for example, House members are permitted to lease their own office computer facilities for correspondence management. This ensures the members complete confidentiality in their computer use and electronic codings.

About 300 members in 1979 used funds from their office allowances to lease some form of computer capacity to help them with their correspondence needs, according to Patricia Dowling, a House Information Systems staff aide. Members were first permitted to contract for computer services in 1975. The 1975 rules change allowing this specified that members could use up to $1,000 a month from unused staff-hire funds to lease computer and related services.

Of the 300, about 90 have IBM System 6 self-contained computer units or their equivalent. The remaining approximately 210 members lease some form of computer time-sharing capacity from a private computer firm. In time-sharing, the computer firm provides computer services and storage capacity, on a shared basis, in its own computer, located away from the Capitol. A member's office typically is equipped with a keyboard which can communicate with the computer through an ordinary telephone tie-line.

No Coding Restrictions

House rules contain no restrictions on the source of electronic lists or the information that can be encoded on them when purchased or compiled with official funds.

"It's not unusual for them to buy voter registration lists, motor vehicle lists or agency lists, such as a list from the Federal Aviation Administration of all licensed aviators, or from the Federal Communications Commission of all licensed ham radio operators in their state," commented Franklin Reeder, House Information Systems deputy director.

House members also would be free to buy mailing lists from their state and national political committees or from campaign consultants, Reeder acknowledged, so long as they were used for "official" mailings. "If the mail had an information dissemination function, then there would be no prohibition on these kinds of mailings," Reeder said.

Making it easier for members to put a political slant on their mailings was a June 1974 ruling by the House Commission on Congressional Mailing Standards. The ruling upheld the right of a congressman to ask a recipient's political affiliation in a constituent questionnaire mailed under the member's frank. The commission said knowing a constituent's party affiliation was relevant to a member's official duties.

A returned constituent questionnaire — signed, filled out with a return address, and marked with the correspondent's political preference — commonly provides new members with the basis for their first electronic mailing list. A spot check by Congressional Quarterly confirmed that a number of House offices encode constituents' political affiliation — as well as past campaign giving — on the electronic lists they compile in this manner.

Typical List Size

A typical list maintained by a House member contains about 20,000 to 30,000 names, according to figures furnished the House Information Systems office by representatives of several area computer firms serving congressional clients. Armed with such extensive electronic lists and the leased computer services, House members have at their

The flat storage disc shown can feed into a mini-computer up to 150 pages of letter texts or up to 1,000 names and addresses along with related bits of information. The reel of magnetic tape can store about 60,000 names and addresses and related data.

disposal all they need to run a first-rate direct mail operation. About 60 members have gone even one step further. They also lease "off-line" mailing services.

"The majority of the time, the computer processing firm merely prints the letters and mailing labels and then sends them to the member's office, where the letters are signed, sealed, and the labels attached," Dowling said.

However, off-line mailing permits mass mailings to be printed, addressed and sent out from the computer firm's offices rather than from the member's office.

Mail sent from a member's office goes through the House folding room, where House employees are supposed to monitor compliance with House rules governing the use of the frank. Mail sent out from the computer firm's offices does not.

No matter where the mail is sent from, or what it contains, commented Dowling, "the member is responsible for abiding by the rules." In short, as one congressional campaign consultant put it, "you can use your incumbency to get re-elected right up to the last minute, perfectly legally."

"Putting aside the moral aspects of the question," the consultant said, "it would be effortless to do that." ∎

House Launches TV Broadcasting System

Gavel-to-gavel television coverage of the House had its long-awaited public debut March 19, 1979. The House proceedings were televised through the House's own $1.2 million system, operated by House employees. The House began experimental closed-circuit, black-and-white telecasts of its proceedings in March 1977, but installed high-quality color cameras for public viewing in early 1979.

The television system began operating Feb. 19 but broadcasts were sent only to Capitol Hill offices. On March 19, telecasts were made available to broadcast and cable systems. Some public television stations and cable systems carried all House proceedings live, but the networks carried only small portions during evening news programs.

On April 3, cable television systems in more than 370 communities in all 50 states began carrying broadcast proceedings of the House. The television signal was made available to the cable systems by the Cable Satellite Public Affairs Network (C-SPAN) using an RCA communications satellite to beam the program nationwide. By September, according to C-SPAN President Brian Lamb, 500 stations would be linked up, representing a potential viewing audience of 15 million.

But static over a related issue — whether members should be able to buy House-produced tapes of their floor speeches — could cloud the picture a little. Some members have said the tapes would be just another perquisite for incumbents, and the policy of allowing members to buy them with office funds could be challenged.

However, the beginning of House-controlled broadcasts officially resolved another major broadcast controversy — whether to allow television networks to bring their cameras into the chamber. The House is hiring its own professional broadcasters to operate House-purchased color cameras that will record all floor proceedings. Networks, individual stations with Washington correspondents and cable television systems would be able to pick up the live, unedited broadcasts from a "feed" provided by the House. They also would be able to make their own tapes from the House feed for use in later broadcasts. But the outside broadcasters would have no control over what is shown on camera. The networks — still unhappy about the decision to lock them out of the chamber — showed little enthusiasm about using many of the House broadcasts.

Although the network issue was laid to rest, new controversies were expected to crop up once the House began broadcasting floor debates for the first time in history.

Rep. John B. Anderson, R-Ill., who argued unsuccessfully for a network-controlled House broadcast system, has attacked the tapes policy agreed to by Democratic leaders. In a Feb. 7, 1979, letter to House Speaker Thomas P. O'Neill Jr., D-Mass., Anderson charged that the policy allowed the House-controlled system to become "one more incumbent protection device at taxpayers' expense." In addition, he said it would "distort and prolong our proceedings by encouraging more and longer speeches for home consumption." Anderson's complaint was aimed at a Democratic decision permitting members to use their official expense accounts to buy tapes of the broadcasts for distribution to local television stations. Some junior House Democrats expressed the same concern to House Speaker Thomas P. O'Neill Jr., D-Mass., at a private meeting Feb. 1.

Rep. Charlie Rose, D-N.C., acknowledged that "We could end up encouraging little on-the-floor press conferences if we made those [tapes] available like hot cakes." But, said Rose, one of three Democrats named by the Speaker to recommend House broadcast policy, the charge that incumbents would abuse the availability of the tapes was unfounded. "We are going to make recordings and sell them to anyone who asks for them, on a first-come, first-serve basis," said Rose. No one — House members, television stations or the general public — would be able to get a tape of a debate the same day it occurs, Rose said, thus reducing the newsworthiness of any tapes a member might send to a local station.

"Hot issues just don't tend to last that long," he said.

Long Debate

The idea of televising House floor proceedings first surfaced more than 34 years ago, but it began to be discussed in earnest only in the early 1970s.

In 1944, Rep. Claude Pepper, D-Fla., introduced the first resolution calling for television coverage of floor proceedings. The idea of House radio broadcasts had already been kicking around for a couple of decades. In 1947, the House let television cameras record its opening session. But after making its film debut, House leaders quickly pulled the plug on broadcasting anything other than special events, such as the president's annual State of the Union message.

While House rules did not spell out prohibitions against network access to the floor, they did give the Speaker authority over the House chamber. And House Speakers had traditionally barred radio microphones and television cameras from being used in the chamber.

Although House leadership was instrumental in postponing the issue for years, technological problems were also a big factor. Only in recent years has it been feasible to photograph the House floor for prolonged coverage without use of very bright, hot lights.

The issue began to make a little headway when the House worked on its 1970 Legislative Reorganization Act (PL 91-510). Rep. B. F. Sisk, D-Calif., one of the architects of that plan, wanted it to include provisions for broadcasting floor action. But he only succeeded in opening up House committee hearings to broadcast coverage, something Senate committees had traditionally allowed. *(See box, p. 149)*

In 1974, the Joint Committee on Congressional Operations, headed by Rep. Jack Brooks, D-Texas, and Sen. Lee Metcalf, D-Mont., filed a report based on a lengthy study of broadcasting House and Senate proceedings. The committee recommended broadcast tests in both chambers, and

Brooks and Metcalf each introduced resolutions to implement the plan.

Activity picked up in 1975, when the House Rules Committee formed an Ad Hoc Subcommittee on Broadcasting to study Brooks' proposal. Brooks wanted to give the broadcasting responsibility to the House Commission on Information and Facilities, which he chaired. But Sisk, chairman of the Rules subcommittee, and other subcommittee members such as Anderson and Pepper advocated a network pool.

They introduced an alternative resolution calling for a House-network contract allowing commercial and public broadcasters to bring in their own equipment and personnel to film the House. In exchange for filming proceedings gavel-to-gavel for House use, the network pool would get a fee from the House and would be able to sell its live coverage at reasonable fees to other television and radio outlets.

O'Neill, majority leader at the time, opposed the Sisk-Anderson resolution and reportedly warned the Rules Committee, "If you think the public's rating of the Congress is low now, just wait until we get TV." House leaders persuaded Rules to send the resolution back to the Sisk subcommittee in early 1976. But as soon as the 95th Congress convened, the network pool advocates introduced a resolution (H Res 75) worked out in 1976. The new version left the camera-control decision to the Speaker but also stated the sense of the House that a network pool should do the job. It drew 65 cosponsors.

O'Neill pulled the rug out from under that plan March 2 by announcing a 90-day test of House-operated television coverage and putting Brooks' committee in charge of it. Using cameras designed for security surveillance, the test provided closed circuit broadcasts to the Rayburn Office Building. When Brooks' Select Committee on Congressional Operations sent O'Neill an evaluation of the test in September, there were no surprises. Brooks heartily endorsed a House-run system. O'Neill then pressed for Rules Committee approval of a Brooks-sponsored resolution (H Res 821) that would give the Speaker the authority to decide who would run the broadcasting system. The committee crossed O'Neill only slightly, by approving a substitute (H Res 866) that told the Speaker to make the decision after Rules sent him recommendations by Feb. 15, 1978. The House approved it, 342-44.

But the broadcasts, originally expected to begin in early 1978, were postponed when the House Rules Committee gave O'Neill a report criticizing Brooks' system. Rules members who viewed test film from Brooks' system said the picture was unflattering, especially to black members of the House. The overhead lighting in the chamber produced a "raccoon effect" of deep shadows around members' eyes. O'Neill then appointd a three-member panel, consisting of Rose, Brooks and Rep. Gillis W. Long, D-La., to come up with some improvements. The panel studied broadcasting systems in other legislatures, including Canada's House of Commons, where professional broadcasters were hired to set up and operate a system that was ultimately controlled by the legislators.

Rose's panel eventually spent about $44,000 to hire several consultants — including professional broadcasters — for advice on how to set up a system. Another $1.2 million of House funds was used to buy six color cameras, monitors, sound equipment, and tape recording machines.

Actual cost of setting up the system was higher, said Joan Teague, an aide to Rose, because labor to install wiring and equipment was provided by House employees. However, Teague said she did not have an estimate of the total cost to set up the system. The equipment — including remote controls for the six cameras — was set up in a basement room of the Capitol. Following the lead of the Canadians, Rose's panel decided to hire professional broadcasters to operate the House system. The clerk of the House, who would be responsible for day-to-day operation of the system, advertised in more than two dozen cities for broadcasters with at least five years experience to fill the 12 positions. The employees were to be on the clerk's payroll, drawing annual salaries totaling $278,000, according to Bill Hartnett, assistant to the clerk.

Tapes Issue

The tapes issue first arose when the House agreed in 1978 to begin radio broadcasts of floor proceedings. O'Neill's office told members they could tape floor speeches broadcast into their offices and send the tapes to radio stations in their districts, as long as they were not put to commercial or political use. The ban on commercial and political use was contained in the resolution (H Res 866) passed by the House in 1977, giving the Speaker authority over radio and television broadcasts. The same language, which permits use of the broadcast material in commercially-sponsored programs only if they are "bona fide news" or "public affairs documentary" shows, was adopted as part of the House rules on the first day of the 96th Congress.

Anderson first blasted the practice at a Jan. 9, 1979, press conference. He denounced the policy on radio broadcasts and said it would be even worse to apply it to television broadcasts. Only the media should be able to get tapes of House broadcasts, he said.

Also concerned were members active in the caucus of Democrats first elected to the 95th Congress. "The whole point [of the broadcasts] was to get television into the House, show the people how this body operates," said Leon E. Panetta, D-Calif., one of the sophomore members who met with O'Neill. "I don't want to see it turned into what might be viewed as a perk," Panetta said. Despite O'Neill's assurances that there were safeguards to prevent abuse of the tape system, Panetta said he still believed members should not be able to buy tapes. "I share John Anderson's concern. I think the danger is there," he said.

But Rose said the claims that members would make long speeches and buy lots of tapes to generate publicity back home were exaggerated. "I think members should be able to tape what happens on the floor and use it. The problem comes when members use that right and privilege to grandstand in such a way that the legislative process is disrupted," said Rose.

But, he added, "that simply is not going to happen." Members and anyone else who wants to order a tape will have to wait until the day after a debate to get the time cue in the *Congressional Record*. Time cues, which the House began printing in anticipation of the television broadcasts, show when a speech took place. They are numbers next to an open box (for example, □1525) that appear throughout the House proceedings in the Record.

On top of the one-day delay, members — and others — may have to wait a few more days to get their tapes, Rose said. Tapes would be made only when the House is not in session, and in the order they are requested, he said.

In addition, said Rose, the price should discourage members from ordering lots of tapes. A 30-minute tape —

the shortest the House would sell — cost $104; 60-minute tapes ran $176. The cost can be charged to members' office accounts, "if the tapes are to be used in direct support of [members'] official representative duties," according to the House clerk's office. House rules barred the use of the tapes for political or commercial purposes.

But Anderson and Panetta indicted they would watch to see how members took advantage of the taping system before proposing any policy changes.

After two months on the market, however, sales of the tapes were less than a roaring success. Only seven House members ordered tapes between Feb. 19 and the end of April 1979, according to House records. No other orders had been placed during that time.

Pros and Cons of House System

Among the most frequently voiced viewer complaints of the House broadcast system has been that there was a blackout while a vote was being taken, with the screen showing only a placard with the running vote tally — not the individual members' votes. Another complaint has been that the cameras do not show an overall view of the House floor. Finally, many viewers have said they would like some explanation of the often complex and unfamiliar parliamentary procedures and phrases used in Congress.

O'Neill in late summer 1979 asked the House Government Operations Committee to study the possibility of turning off television coverage as soon as the regular legislative business has been finished on the grounds that it led to lengthy floor proceedings and speeches given for a member's hometown consumption at the general taxpayers' expense. O'Neill said members "notify everyone at home" when they were going to make a speech that was frequently not connected with the regular legislative business. "And when they give it, there's no one out there in the audience," he said. "They're just speaking for home consumption. And that wasn't the object of the television system. The object was to make a record of Congress."

On the other hand, many members have said that the fact that they and their staffs could watch floor proceedings on television while in their offices saved time, contributed to better-informed voting and more independence. And some of them have said that the system should be opened up to allow the cameras to pan the chamber and televise the actual voting process.

In September, O'Neill said he was dropping his request after the proposal met with bipartisan criticism.

Senate Hesitation

A few years ago, the Senate appeared more inclined to allow broadcast coverage than the House. Among those who endorsed the idea at 1974 hearings before the Joint Committee on Congressional Operations was Majority Leader Robert C. Byrd, D-W.Va. However, Byrd leaned toward a system giving Senate employees control over the cameras "to avoid the possibility of media-provoked theatrics."

But Senate aides said two events considerably dampened enthusiasm for television on their side of the Capitol. The first event was the swearing-in ceremony for Vice

Cameras in Committee

Most House and Senate committees allow television and radio to cover hearings that are open to the public.

The Senate has a long tradition allowing broadcast coverage of committee hearings. Senate rules leave to individual committees the decision whether or not to admit radio and television. That decision usually is made by committee chairmen or, if there is an objection by a member, by a majority of the committee. In practice, most committees encourage coverage and require only advance notification from the news crew in order to provide suitable accommodations. "There's usually no problem," explained a Senate Commerce Committee aide, "because senators like to be on TV."

The House has traditionally been less hospitable to broadcasters than the Senate. After permitting a historic first telecast of floor proceedings in 1947, the leadership of the House closed the chamber to television and prescribed the same policy for House committees. It was not until passage of the 1970 Legislative Reorganization Act (PL 91-510) that broadcast coverage of committee hearings was legally sanctioned by the House.

While the Senate leaves broadcast decisions to its committees, the House has adopted a stringent set of standards for use by committees that do admit cameras. Among them are requirements that broadcast coverage not "distort the objects and purposes of the hearings . . . cast discredit or dishonor on the House, the committee, or any member into disrepute." When those provisions were adopted by the Interior and Insular Affairs Committee in 1975, some questions were raised in the written press about setting limitations on "journalistic integrity." But broadcasters have said that the rules have not interfered with their coverage of committees.

President Nelson Rockefeller in December 1974. The ceremony marked the first time television cameras have been allowed in the Senate chamber. And those who remember the occasion also remember how hot it was under hastily-assembled lights.

The other event came in 1975, when the Senate faced the bitter, divisive issue of settling the outcome of the 1974 New Hampshire Senate election. Republicans offered a resolution calling for broadcast coverage of the debate. Although the resolution was not enacted, it started some members thinking about the potential embarrassment of having such a bitter partisan dispute aired to all the voters back home.

Following the House's 1979 TV debut, Senate Minority Leader Howard H. Baker Jr., R-Tenn., urged the Senate Republican Conference to support the televising of Senate procedures. However, Majority Leader Byrd said March 17 he favored studying how television worked out in the House more before bringing it into the Senate.

In the meantime, the major networks were negotiating with the Senate over televising the debate on the U.S.-Soviet Strategic Arms Limitation Treaty (SALT II), expected to begin in the fall of 1979. ∎

Congressional Ethics

CQ

Congress Approves Tough Ethics Codes

"Congressmen see the responsibility for disciplining colleagues guilty of improper behavior as having three dimensions—each congressman personally, the House [or Senate] as an institution, and constituents are all capable of curbing a legislator's actions, although not with equal effectiveness," wrote authors Beard and Horn in their 1975 study of congressional ethics.[1] "Often the least effective and most difficult way to discipline congressional behavior is to have individual members attempt it.... A more viable approach is for the House [or Senate] to assume responsibility for defending itself against behavior that weakens it as an institution.... [T]he third approach—having the district take responsibility for the behavior of its chosen representative...could be the most effective, even if it has not always been in the past. As one member said, 'It's up to the district; if they want to send a bum here, what can we do?'

"...[T]he lack of ethical standards in Congress...[is] rooted in the nation's political institutions," the authors continued. "How, then, can the reforms be achieved that low public confidence in government seems to call for? Ironically, the very climate that has accelerated the erosion of public trust may bring forth the answer. The atmosphere surrounding a heavily publicized scandal is conducive to the reordering of old standards; indeed, it appears to be vital for such change to take place."

These observations appeared to be borne out in early 1977. Prompted by the scandals of 1976 and critical public reaction to the tendency of Congress to do nothing about them, both chambers began work on drawing up new ethics codes. With House Speaker Thomas P. O'Neill Jr. (D Mass.) riding close herd on his Democratic colleagues, the House March 2 overwhelmingly adopted a resolution (H Res 287) imposing strict new regulations on the financial activities of its members. The Senate followed suit one month later, adopting a similar ethics code. In 1978, the rules governing Congress were codified and extended to cover top executive and judicial branch employees.

Obey Commission

In the House, the job of drafting the new code had been given to a bipartisan, 15-member study commission (the Commission on Administrative Review), chaired by David R. Obey (D Wis.). Similarly, the Senate Jan. 18 passed a resolution creating a special 15-member committee, chaired by Gaylord Nelson (D Wis.) to formulate a comprehensive code of ethics for that chamber by early March.

The House panel was created July 1, 1976, in the wake of the chamber's sex-payroll scandals involving Wayne Hays. The commission had been recommended by the House Democratic Caucus to follow up on the housekeeping and administrative reforms adopted by the House Administration Committee in late June. The panel included five Democratic and three Republican House members and seven from the public.

The commission had a tough job ahead: improving ethical standards on Capitol Hill is a complex matter, involving changes in the nature and use of perquisites, new rules on financial disclosure and acceptance of gifts and favors, limits on campaign contributions, tighter lobby disclosure regulations and a general willingness on the part of Congress to undertake a thorough self-appraisal of its conduct and character as an institution. Although the Obey commission addressed itself to only some of these issues, it soon became apparent that members of the House differed on the nature of the proposed reforms.

At hearings held on Jan. 14 and 15, 1977, the commission heard conflicting recommendations about financial regulations and enforcement of standards of conduct for members.

House Speaker O'Neill said he felt the new membership of the House Committee on Standards of Official Conduct (ethics committee) would give that panel the prestige it needed to handle all questions of ethics.

"These appointments will mean that the ethics committee will have the [public] confidence [it] will need to handle all of these things," O'Neill said.

But Rep. Bill Frenzel (Minn.), the ranking Republican member of the commission, appeared to disagree. Supported by Peter G. Peterson, chairman of the federal salary commission, Frenzel argued in favor of some kind of outside body to audit House members' accounts and review the handling of public money by both the members and committees.

The Obey commission also heard conflicting opinions about what kinds of standards should be set for members of Congress. Peterson argued in favor of abolishing honoraria, private office accounts and other mechanisms by which special interest groups could exert financial influence on members. "I have heard special interest groups speak very arrogantly about the effect of a few thousand dollars on legislation," he said.

Chesterfield Smith, the former president of the American Bar Association, urged the panel to ban all outside earned income by members, saying that serving in Congress should be a full-time job.

But a panel of members of Congress disagreed. John B. Anderson (R Ill.), the chairman of the House Republican Conference and a leading advocate of House reform, took sharp issue with the suggestion to limit outside earned income. "If you are serious about limiting outside income to between 10 and 15 per cent of a member's salary, I'll soon leave this place," he said. "I don't want to try to educate five college age children with that."

Morris K. Udall (D Ariz.) objected to the proposal to limit honoraria. "You're saying that if I have all kinds of inherited wealth in stocks and bonds it's okay. But if I get out on weekends and hustle and get some money from speaking engagements it's not okay," Udall said. The Arizona

---

1. Edmund Beard and Stephen Horn, *Congressional Ethics: the View from the House*, Brookings Institution, Washington, D.C.

Democrat said that he favored full disclosure as the best way of preventing abuses.

Commission Recommendations

On Feb. 7, the full commission endorsed a series of proposals on financial accountability recommended by a seven-member task force for the panel. The task force recommendations had been made on Jan. 31—three days before the commission released a poll of the public and a survey of House members to determine their attitudes towards various proposals to revise the rules governing financial accountability and other standards of conduct.

Several of the proposals endorsed by the commission were likely to arouse considerable controversy when brought before the full House. Among them was the proposal to ban private office accounts. Private office accounts were maintained by an estimated 140 House members, purportedly to help defray expenses not fully covered by official allowances. However, the accounts were not subject to any regulations. Members were not required to reveal the sources or amounts of contributions to the accounts or even to admit maintaining them. In addition, the funds in the accounts could be used for virtually any purpose.

Obey said that the commission staff estimated that the average office account in the House was maintained at a level of $5,000 and that the largest accounts ran up to $25,000. Office accounts became an issue in late 1976 when then-House Majority Whip John J. McFall (D Calif.) admitted having received a $4,000 secret contribution to his office account from South Korean businessman Tongsun Park, the target of a Justice Department probe into allegations of influence peddling on Capitol Hill.

The task force proposal to ban the office accounts was coupled with a recommendation that the official expense allowances for members be increased by $5,000.

Another proposal likely to arouse opposition in the House limited each member's outside earned income to 15 per cent of his salary. With the Feb. 20 pay raise that increased members' salaries to $57,500, the limit on outside earned income would be $8,625 per member per year for a total of $66,125.

Earned income would include fees for speeches or articles and other so-called honoraria, as well as income from law practices or other business activities. It would not, however, cover unearned income such as interest and dividends from stocks or bonds.

The existing ceilings on honoraria were $2,000 for a single speech, article or appearance and an aggregate of $25,000 in any single year. There was no limit on other forms of outside earned income.

The commission staff estimated that during 1975, 62 per cent of all members had income from honoraria or investments. It noted that 56 members had reported aggregate amounts of honoraria for that year ranging from $100 to the then legal limit of $15,000 (which was later raised to $25,-000) and that the average income from honoraria exceeded $5,000. The staff report also estimated that 50-75 members received over $5,000 annually for personal services rendered in private business.

Another proposal adopted by the commission that stirred debate would reduce to $750 from $2,000 the limit on individual honoraria payments to members. (The task force had recommended a $500 limit.)

The commission also proposed that the House:

Gifts to Members. Prohibit gifts of more than $100 in value per year to members of Congress from persons or groups with an interest in legislation, but exclude gifts of personal hospitality.

Mass Mailings. Require that mass mailings sent by representatives go third class, a change that the commission staff estimated would save $9.5-million a year in postage.

Use of the Frank. Require that postal patron district-wide mailings by members be submitted to the Franking Commission for an advisory opinion before mailing to avoid abuses of the frank.

Lame Duck Travel. Prohibit travel by lame duck members (i.e. those who have not been re-elected to the succeeding Congress in November or when Congress adjourns *sine die,* whichever comes first) and prohibit members from claiming per diem reimbursement for travel expenses covered by other sources, such as private organizations or other governmental agencies.

Financial Disclosure. Substantially widen financial disclosure regulations for members to cover all income, including honoraria, of over $100 from any one source; gifts of $250 or more from one source and all other gifts aggregating $100 or more from one source except gifts from a relative, gifts of less than $25 in value and gifts of "personal hospitality"; reimbursements of $250 or more from any individual source; holdings of property valued at $1,000 or more; debts of more than $2,500; securities transactions of more than $1,000.

Campaign Contributions. Ban the use of campaign funds to pay off personal debts. (House Democratic Majority Leader Jim Wright of Texas had disclosed on Jan. 26 that he had converted $98,501 of his 1976 campaign contributions to personal funds to pay off debts, a transaction which, although highly unusual, was legal under existing rules.)

House Committee Approval

The House commission recommendations were split into three sections and sent to three different committees. The House Administration Committee was given jurisdiction over the section dealing with unofficial office accounts, the Committee on Standards of Official Conduct was given the section covering gifts to members, and the rest of the measure was sent to the Rules Committee.

The code cleared its first hurdle with ease as the Standards Committee voted 8-0 on Feb. 16 to report its section of the resolution (H Rept 95-21, Part 1). The only change it made was to delete a section that exempted gifts of personal hospitality and gifts of under $35 in value from the ban on gifts to members from lobbyists.

More Money for Expenses

The fireworks began in the House Administration Committee. A central target of Republican opposition to the commission recommendations was the provision to increase official expense allowances by $5,000. Bill Frenzel (R Minn.), a member of both the commission and the Administration Committee, charged that the increase was an attempt to "buy" votes for the commission package by increasing the level of spending for all members to the level of the "hogs."

In the first go around the Republicans Feb. 17 prevailed as the committee, on a vote of 12-11 struck from the resolution the $5,000 increase. When word of the committee action reached the House leadership, however, O'Neill swung into action. A second committee meeting was hastily called that afternoon and the Democrats were able to round up enough proxies from absent members to reverse the committee's previous decision. The panel voted 13-12 to reconsider the resolution, then voted to restore the $5,000 provision, and then to reapprove the resolution.

Republicans were incensed, charging in minority views attached to the committee report (H Rept 95-21, Part 2) that the procedure was a "railroad" and accusing the House Democratic leadership of "arm twisting."

Outside Income Limit

But the biggest hurdle was yet to come. The most widely opposed provision of H Res 287 was that which restricted outside earned income to 15 per cent of a member's official salary. A crucial core of opposition came from the Democratic membership of the Rules Committee.

At committee hearings on Feb. 22, Morgan F. Murphy (D Ill.) charged that by excluding unearned income from the limit the resolution would discriminate in favor of the wealthy. "The American people are not going to be fooled by this," Murphy said. "They will perceive it as protection for the millionaires and very wealthy people around here."

Claude Pepper (D Fla.) called the limit "a gross violation of the Constitution"; Shirley Chisholm (D N.Y.) charged: "People who sit on boards of directors have their interest protected." The Rules Committee had two chores before it: to make substantive changes in the resolution and to decide the rules under which the full House would consider the measure.

After a bit of last-minute maneuvering, including a reportedly heated breakfast meeting between O'Neill and Rules Committee members the morning of the Feb. 24 committee vote, a deal was struck. Murphy and other opponents of the income limit agreed not to press their case in the committee in return for a promise that the full House would be allowed to vote up or down on the issue.

The only matter left unresolved was the leadership's desire to have a fall-back position in the form of a floor amendment that would increase the income limit to $15,000 from 15 per cent of salary ($8,625 at the current salary level of $57,500).

Opponents of any limit charged that the $15,000 amendment was merely designed to give backers of the measure room to maneuver on the floor in case the House rejected the 15 per cent limit. But a motion in the Rules Committee that would have denied the House a chance to vote on the $15,000 amendment, and forced a vote up or down only on the 15 per cent limit, failed on a tie vote.

Thomas P. O'Neill Jr.   **David R. Obey**

Principal forces behind House ethics code

Thereafter all the Democrats fell into line. The committee rejected a motion by John B. Anderson (R Ill.) to allow the full House to vote to amend the $5,000 increase in office accounts. The vote was 2-14 with only Anderson and Delbert H. Latta (R Ohio) voting "aye."

On a straight party line vote of 11-5 the panel then voted down a motion by James H. (Jimmy) Quillen (R Tenn.) that would have provided for a fully open rule on the resolution.

The only major substantive change the Rules Committee made in H Res 287 was to strike a section that would have established a new committee to write the statutory ethics code. Committee member Richard Bolling (D Mo.) explained that this issue would be better dealt with by a separate resolution after the code itself had been adopted.

Money for Speeches, Articles

The panel also voted to increase to $1,000 from $750 the amount of money a member could accept for making a speech or appearance or for writing an article. The move came in response to a similar change in the ethics code that the Senate committee had made the day before at the request of Jacob K. Javits (R N.Y.). Javits, in arguing for the increase, said that there was no reason the Senate should have the same limit on speaking fees as the House, and said that the increase was justified in order to "try to preserve a measure of personal dignity for ourselves."

When Bolling presented the amendment in the Rules Committee the next day to make the same change in the House code, he said that the report on the measure would justify the amendment with a single word, printed in boldfaced type: "Dignity."

House Floor Action

Having been cleared by the three standing committees, the Obey commission proposals went before the whole House on March 2, where they were adopted very nearly intact by a vote of 402-22.

On a key procedural vote leading to the adoption of a modified closed rule providing for floor consideration of H Res 287, only 15 of the 279 Democrats voting deserted the leadership. The vote, on moving the previous question and thereby ending debate on the rule, was 267-153: R 3-138; D 264-15.

Had the leadership lost on this vote, the rule would have been rewritten to open the ethics package to many individual floor amendments that probably would have changed the code's character dramatically. But once the issue was settled on the procedural vote, the rule as backed by the leadership was adopted by voice vote.

Democrats also held together in defeating the Republican-backed amendment to strike from the bill a section banning unofficial office accounts and increasing members' official allowances by $5,000. The vote was 187-235.

After O'Neill told the House that a section of the resolution imposing a limit on outside earned income was needed to restore the "collective integrity of the House," the House crushed an amendment to strike that section. The vote was 79-344. On final passage only a handful of disgruntled Republicans and Southern Democrats were willing to risk being labeled anti-ethics and to vote against the resolution.

Outside Income Limit

By far the most controversial section of H Res 287 was that which limited the amount of outside income a member could earn to 15 per cent of his official salary ($8,625 at the current salary of $57,500).

Backers of the provision argued that it was needed to ensure that members devoted full time to their House duties and to avoid the appearance of conflict of interest with other jobs.

Opponents charged that the limit—which did not apply to unearned income such as dividends from stocks or bonds—discriminated in favor of wealthy members, that it would force many members to leave Congress in order to support their families, and that it would create a class of professional politicians.

Otis G. Pike (D N.Y.) made an impassioned speech to a crowded House chamber in which he said that the restrictions on outside income would "create a Congress of two kinds of people. Some will have large unearned income and the rest will need their political jobs in order to feed and clothe and educate their families. Whether this will be a more ethical Congress only time will tell, but I think not."

But O'Neill, in an equally strong statement, told the House that "to allow us the privilege of continuing to earn outside income, no matter how stringent a provision of financial disclosure, creates in the public mind a suspicion of conflict, a suspicion of impropriety."

Calling the limit on the outside earned income, "the heart and soul of the entire package," O'Neill told his colleagues that "the issue before us is not unofficial office accounts, honorariums, outside income, earned or un-earned. The issue is credibility, restoring public confidence in this Congress." "I appreciate deeply that there are those members who will be greatly affected by this provision," O'Neill said. "It is a sacrifice we all must make."

Office Accounts

The closest vote of the evening, 187-235, came on an amendment sponsored by Frenzel to strike from the bill a section banning unofficial office accounts and increasing the official expense allowances for each member to $7,000 from $2,000.

Frenzel argued that because of the closed rule, the only way he could move to kill the $5,000 increase in the official allowances was to kill the entire section on unofficial office accounts. He said that if his amendment carried he would later offer a separate resolution to kill the unofficial office accounts without the increase in official allowances.

Frenzel said that the $5,000 boost was included in the resolution "as some kind of payoff" to those members who had maintained private office accounts.

"When we get down to it, the whole point of the $5,000 was to buy out those people with slush funds. We seem to be told that the people who have engaged in what we now term to be unethical or no longer tolerable behavior have to have this $5,000 or they will not vote for the whole ethics package," Frenzel said.

But Obey, who had engaged in similar debates with Frenzel during the commission deliberations on the ethics package, said that "what we are trying to do is to meet official expenses in an official, honest, aboveboard, open fashion," and that the only way to do that was to increase the official allowances to pay for expenses that members had been meeting out of their private office accounts.

The debate heated up, with Obey referring to Frenzel's arguments as "baloney" and then retracting his statement from the record, and William M. Ketcham (R Calif.) calling the Obey proposal "the most ridiculous thing I have ever heard of."

Other Amendments

In other action on amendments proposed by commit-tees that had reported the resolution, the House:

● Rejected by a standing vote of 14-43 an amendment to strike the exemptions from reporting requirements granted in the resolution for gifts of less than $35 in value and gifts of personal hospitality;

● Rejected by voice vote an amendment to increase to $1,000 from $750 the limit on individual fees a member could receive for a speech, appearance or article;

● Adopted by voice vote an amendment to include grandsons and granddaughters in the meaning of the term "relative" as used in the resolution's sections dealing with disclosure of gifts and financial activities;

● Adopted by voice vote an amendment to strike from the resolution a title establishing a Select Committee on Ethics.

The rule also allowed an amendment to increase the ceiling on outside earned income to $15,000 from the 15 percent of official salary, or $8,625. However, after the landslide vote against the amendment to strike the limit altogether, no member brought up the $15,000 amendment.

House Code Provisions

As passed by the House March 2, H Res 287:

Title I—Financial Disclosure

Required House members, officers, principal assistants and professional committee staff employees to file a finan-cial disclosure statement with the Clerk of the House by April 30 of each year beginning in 1978 to cover the preceding year's financial activities. (The 1978 statement would cover only Oct 1-Dec. 31, 1977 activities.)

Information Covered. Specified that the disclosure statements had to include the following information:

Income. The source and amount of all income received during the year from a single source aggregating $100 or more.

Gifts. The source and value of all gifts from a single source aggregating $100 or more per year. Exempted from the disclosure requirements were gifts from relatives, gifts of personal hospitality, gifts with a fair market value of $35 or less, and gifts of lodging, food or transportation aggregating less than $250 for the year.

(The Obey Commission, which drafted the basic ethics proposals, said in an explanation of H Res 287 that it understood "personal hospitality" to mean hospitality ex-tended for a non-business purpose by an individual, not a corporation or organization, on property or facilities owned by that individual or his or her family.)

Reimbursements. The source and identity of any reim-bursements received from a single source for expenditures aggregating $250 or more.

Financial Holdings. The identity and category of value of any property held at the close of the calendar year in a trade or business or for investment with a market value of at least $1,000. Specified that the categories within which the holdings had to be designated were less than $5,000; $5,000 to $15,000, $15,000 to $50,000, $50,000 to $100,000 and above $100,000.

Liabilities. The identity and category of value of each liability owed that exceeded $2,500 at the end of the calen-dar year. Specified that the categories of value were the same as applied to financial holdings *(see above).*

Exempted from the disclosure requirements mortgages for members' personal residential homes in the Washington, D.C., area or home district, or for the principal residence of any other person covered by the rule.

Securities, Commodity Transactions. The identity, date and category of value of any transaction in securities or commodities futures that exceeded $1,000 in value. Specified that the categories of value were the same as applied to financial holdings *(see above).*

Real Estate. The identity, date and category of value of any purchase or sale of real property exceeding $1,000 in value in the previous calendar year except for personal residences.

Specified that the categories of value were the same as applied to financial holdings *(see above).*

Spouses. Directed that with respect to the spouse of the person reporting, the report include information about all the financial dealings which were under the constructive control of the person reporting.

Exemption. Exempted from the reporting requirements members who announced before April 30, 1978, that they would not seek re-election to the 96th Congress.

Public Inspection of Reports. Directed that all financial disclosure reports be printed and made public by the Clerk of the House and that copies of each report be kept on file by the Committee on Standards of Official Conduct for public inspection and that a copy of each report filed by a member be sent to the secretary of state in the member's home state.

Title II—Gifts, Testimonial Funds

Prohibited any member, officer or employee of the House from accepting any gifts aggregating $100 or more in value in any one calendar year from any lobbyist or lobbying organization, or from foreign nationals or their agents.

Amended House rule 43 to prohibit members from converting to personal use proceeds from testimonial dinners and other fund-raising events.

Title III—Office Accounts

Prohibited any member from maintaining an unofficial office account after Jan. 3, 1978.

Prohibited new contributions to any unofficial office account, effective on adoption of the resolution.

Increased by $5,000—to $7,000 from $2,000—the amount of money each member would have available to spend on official expenses, effective Jan. 3, 1978.

Amended House rule 43 to prohibit members from converting campaign funds to personal use.

Provided a single "official expenses" allowance for members' office costs both in Washington and the home district, rather than separate allowances for each category as currently provided.

Title IV—Franked Mail

Postal Patron Mail. Imposed the following new restrictions on use of a member's frank on "postal patron" mail—mail that does not include the recipient's name:

Required that any franked postal patron mail be sent by the most economical means practical, currently third class. Effective on enactment.

Provided that after Dec. 31, 1977, the amount of postal patron mail sent annually by a member under the frank could not exceed a number equal to six times the number of addresses in the member's district.

Required that a postal patron mailing to be sent under the frank be submitted to the House Commission on Congressional Mailing Standards for an advisory opinion on whether the mailing met the restrictions on franked materials. Effective on enactment.

Mass Mailings. Imposed the following new restrictions on mass mailings—defined in existing law as newsletters and similar mailings of more than 500 pieces of substantially identical content—whether sent to a postal patron address or to a specific person:

Prohibited any mass mailing under the frank unless preparation and printing costs are paid entirely from public funds. Effective on enactment. (The provision was intended to end the practice of mailing at public expense under the frank newsletters or other material printed with private funds and labeled "Not Printed at Government Expense.")

Prohibited any member who is a candidate for statewide office from sending any franked mass mailing to residents outside his district. Effective on enactment.

Prohibited any franked mass mailing from being sent less than 60 days before any primary or general election in which the member sending the mail was a candidate. Effective on enactment.

Title V—Foreign Travel

Prohibited a member or employee traveling abroad from claiming per diem reimbursement for expenses which were met by other sources. Effective on enactment.

Prohibited a member or employee from receiving reimbursement for transportation in connection with travel abroad unless the member or employee had actually paid for the transportation. Effective on enactment.

Prohibited travel abroad at government expense for any member after the date of the general election in which the member was not elected to the succeeding Congress or, in the case of a member who was not a candidate in the general election, the date of the general election or the date of adjournment *sine die* of the Congress, whichever came first. Effective on enactment.

Title VI—Outside Earned Income

Prohibited any member from earning income at a job outside Congress in excess of 15 per cent of his official salary effective Dec. 31, 1978. The limit did not apply to unearned income—such as dividends from stocks or bonds—or to income from a family controlled business or trade in which the personal services of the member did not generate a significant amount of income.

Effective Dec. 31, 1978, prohibited any member from accepting any honorarium of more than $750. Defined "honorarium" to mean a payment of money or anything of value for an appearance, speech or article by a member.

Senate Action on Ethics Code

While the Obey commission was at work on the House side, the Senate Special Committee on Official Conduct began the task of writing an ethics code for that chamber on Jan. 26. The committee had been directed to report back to the Senate with a recommended code of ethics by March 1.

1977 Pay Raise Tied to Ethics Code

In a supplement to his Jan. 17, 1977, budget message, outgoing President Ford requested a salary increase averaging about 28 per cent for the top echelons of the executive, legislative and judicial branches. An integral part of the proposed increases, endorsed by President Carter, was a rigid new code of ethics applying to all three branches.

The pay raises took effect Feb. 20. According to a 1967 statute *(see below),* proposed salary increases would take effect automatically 30 days after a President submitted his recommendation unless either house vetoed the measure. Neither chamber did so.

The increases were a trimmed-down version of the recommendations made Dec. 6, 1976, by the Commission on Executive, Legislative and Judicial Salaries. The nine members of the commission were appointees of the President, Congress and the Chief Justice of the United States. By statute—the Federal Salary Act of 1967 (PL 90-206)—the commission was required to review top-level federal salaries every four years. The chairman of the commission was Peter G. Peterson, board chairman of the New York City investment banking firm of Lehman Brothers Inc., and Secretary of Commerce in 1972 and 1973.

The last pay raise voted by Congress—the only one top federal officials had had since 1969—came in 1975, when Congress approved a 5 per cent cost-of-living increase for itself and the other branches.

Ford's recommendations raised the salary of the Vice President, Speaker of the House and Chief Justice to $75,000 from $65,000; for Senate president pro tem and majority and minority leaders of both houses, to $65,000 from $52,000; and for other members of Congress to $57,500 from $44,600. The increase for members of Congress amounted to 29 per cent.

In its December 1976 report proposing the salary hikes, the Peterson commission called for a new Code of Public Conduct as "the indispensable prelude to a popular acceptance of a general [pay] increase in executive, legislative and judicial salaries.

"Such a reform must be sufficiently tangible to persuade a substantial majority of Americans that the post-Watergate era has truly begun," the commission wrote. "Such a majority is by no means persuaded now."

The code had seven elements:

- Persons covered by the code would be required to file periodic financial reports showing all income, by source and amount, reimbursements for travel and other expenses, gifts, debts and personal holdings. Such information would be made public unless there were some unusual reason for maintaining confidentiality.
- Salaries would be set high enough so that individuals would be prohibited from receiving honoraria, legal fees, gifts, or the proceeds from testimonial dinners for personal use.
- Conflicts of interest would be minimized or eliminated through tight new provisions.
- "Appropriate and accountable expense allowances" would be established, with more consistency throughout government.
- Consistent and explicit rules would be made to restrict arrangements whereby executives, judges or legislators leave public service to take private jobs, especially in institutions and industries which they had been regulating.
- Regulations governing public conduct would be broadly applicable across all three branches of the federal government.
- A mechanism would be established to fully enforce, audit and report all provisions of the new code.

Senate Majority Leader Robert C. Byrd (D W.Va.), a cosponsor of the resolution creating the panel, said that the strict timetable was needed to make it clear that the code was tied to the Feb. 20 pay raise. *(See above)*

The resolution also provided that the recommendations of the special committee would be made the pending business of the Senate as soon as they were reported and that debate on them would be limited to 50 hours.

But as the committee held its first organizational meeting Jan. 26 it became clear that the deadline would be difficult to meet. "The questions are a lot tougher than I thought they were," said committee Chairman Gaylord Nelson (D Wis.)

To expedite the committee's work, Nelson said that he would make extensive use of the record compiled by the special House Commission on Administrative Review during its deliberations.

He appointed a four-member subcommittee to draft a list of issues that the committee would have to confront. The first set of hearings were held Feb. 1.

But all this activity did not allay the concerns of committee-member John Glenn (D Ohio) who called the attempt to rush through a code of ethics in order to tie it to the pay raise "ridiculous."

"It is important that we take the time to do this job right," Glenn said. "I don't see how we can develop new information and hold the hearings we need by March 1."

While the House committee action on the ethics code had been marked by a series of partisan confrontations, the Senate exercise was conducted in a less intense, often jovial atmosphere. Nelson was able through wit and compromise to defuse many of the sharp controversies.

Provisions Criticized

Nevertheless, opposition remained, particularly to provisions limiting outside earned income and speaking fees and requiring full financial disclosure.

Daniel K. Inouye (D Hawaii), summed up the opposition in a single stinging speech on Feb. 23. "Why are we singled out of all the millions of people in the United States?" he asked the committee. "Are we that bad?" He added that he found it "insulting and demeaning in many ways" to be forced to report gifts and other details of his financial operations. He echoed Javits' contention that the limit on speaking fees would be a blow to senators' "personal dignity."

But Dick Clark (D Iowa) countered that there was "a clear conflict of interest in accepting honoraria from groups with an interest in legislation...."

The issue came to a head in the form of an amendment sponsored by John H. Chafee (R R.I.) to increase the limit on an outside earned income to $15,000. The amendment lost on a vote of 6-9.

Voting for the Chafee amendment were: Inouye, Javits, Robert P. Griffin (R Mich.), Robert W. Packwood (R Ore.), Paul Laxalt (R Nev.) and Chafee.

Voting against the amendment were Abraham A. Ribicoff (D Conn.), Thomas F. Eagleton (D Mo.), Sam Nunn (D Ga.), Clark, John Glenn (D Ohio), John Melcher (D Mont.), Strom Thurmond (R S.C.), Robert T. Stafford (R Vt.) and Nelson.

Restrictions Tightened

From there on it was all downhill for the reformers. The committee did accept Javits' amendment to increase the limit on honoraria, and another Javits proposal to exempt advances for books from the outside-income limits.

But the major committee actions were all in the direction of tightening the restrictions. The panel adopted Thurmond's amendment that would prohibit a senator from practicing any profession for compensation.

The original committee draft had contained a provision to ban law practice. But Thurmond argued that "if a man is a member of the United States Senate what business has he practicing any profession for compensation."

The committee also adopted a sweeping amendment sponsored by Clark to prohibit discrimination against employees on the basis of race, sex, religion or handicap and to prohibit senators from requiring aides to perform personal services. Griffin said that the enforcement of these provisions would "turn the Ethics Committee into an Equal Employment Opportunity Commission" and predicted that large numbers of employees might make use of the grievance procedure.

"The equal opportunity employment law applies to everybody else in the United States," Clark responded. "Why shouldn't it apply to us?" His amendment was adopted by voice vote.

Another change voted by the committee would require that all statewide postal patron mailings to senators' constituents go by third class mail.

This provision was adopted by voice vote over the objections of Melcher who said that "to have third class mail is demeaning. If it is worth your writing, it is worth going first class."

In the end, despite the opposition of individual senators to particular points of the resolution, the measure passed by a unanimous vote of 15-0 Feb. 24. Nelson said that it was "the most comprehensive disclosure law in the United States," and said that it would not have been possible to pass such a sweeping code "even three or four years ago."

Common Cause, the citizens' lobby group that had worked in favor of many of the changes embodied in the Senate code, also was pleased with the outcome.

Ann McBride, the Common Cause lobbyist who followed the Senate markup, praised Nelson for an "outstanding job," and said that the code the committee produced "is tough and meaningful and really goes to the heart of the problem."

She predicted, however, that several sections of the code, especially the limit on outside earned income, would face stiff opposition on the Senate floor.

Nelson agreed with this assessment, but said that Majority Leader Byrd was fully committed to passing a tough code and predicted that "we'll prevail on all of the major points of the resolution."

Major Senate Provisions

Although the House-passed and Senate Committee versions of the code differed in detail, the broad outlines of most of the major provisions were nearly identical.

The Senate version of the code also extended many of its provisions to employees making more than $25,000 a year. In addition, it included a number of provisions not included in the House measure. Some of these the House panel planned to consider later.

Among the provisions included in the Senate resolution alone were those to:

● Prohibit members who leave the Senate from engaging in lobbying activities in the Senate for a period of one year after they retire and to impose the same restrictions on employees of the Senate with respect to the member or committee for whom they worked;

● Provide that no senator could discriminate in employment or promotion practices because of race, religion, sex or physical handicap;

● Prohibit employees from being required to perform personal services for senators;

● Prohibit employees from engaging in substantial amounts of campaign activities during office hours;

● Provide for enforcement of the code by the Senate Ethics Committee and provide that the committee must justify in public all its decisions with respect to allegations brought to it;

● Permit any two members of the committee who disagreed with a committee decision not to investigate an allegation to bring the issue directly to the floor of the Senate.

Senate Floor Action

The proposed code of ethics for the Senate reached the floor on March 17 and immediately encountered sniper fire from nearly all sides.

Even before it reached the floor, the resolution underwent a major overhaul. Objections to a number of its provisions came from members of the Senate Ethics Committee which would be charged with enforcement of the new code.

Adlai E. Stevenson III (D Ill.), the Ethics Committee chairman, said that many of the resolution's provisions would be unenforceable in the form in which they emerged from committee.

He objected, for example, to the lack of flexibility allowed the Ethics Committee in dealing with complaints about senators' conduct, and to provisions requiring the committee to deal with complaints of discrimination against employees.

To meet these objections the subcommittee that had originally drafted the resolution went back to work and came out with another version, introduced on the floor in the form of a substitute amendment by Nelson.

Nelson said that the new version of the resolution solved many of the problems raised by Ethics Committee members without altering the basic scope of the code.

But the changes did not defuse other objections to the resolution. Some senators charged that the proposed code did not go far enough, while others maintained that it went too far.

The whole issue presented a major challenge to the leadership of newly elected Majority Leader Robert C. Byrd (D W.Va.), and Minority Leader Howard H. Baker Jr. (R Tenn.). Both had supported the $12,900 pay hike senators received in February and tied their support to a pledge that the Senate would pass a tough code of ethics.

As debate opened on the resolution, it became apparent that opposition to several features of the proposed new code was stronger in the Senate than it had been in the House. Most senators, for example, were able to command larger speaking fees than House members, and consequently the code's proposed limits on outside earned income was more painful to senators than to representatives.

In addition, the Senate rules allowing unlimited numbers of amendments to be proposed presented a more difficult parliamentary challenge to the Senate leadership than it had to the House. In the House debate the leaders were able to limit the number of amendments offered to two, and to win passage of their resolution after a single day's debate.

But the back of the opposition was broken on March 22, when the Senate defeated two amendments sponsored by Edmund S. Muskie (D Maine) to modify the provisions dealing with outside earned income.

Final Passage

After two weeks of debate and action on 64 amendments the Senate April 1 adopted a new code of ethics to govern the conduct of all senators and top level Senate employees.

The 86-9 vote in favor of passage of S Res 110 by no means reflected the depth of feeling in the Senate against the new code. Nor did the action guarantee that the Senate will be any more willing in the future to investigate allegations of misconduct by its own members than it has been in the past.

Gaylord Nelson (D Wis.), the floor manager of the resolution, said after the vote that the many of those senators who voted for the measure did so out of fear of the political hazards of a negative vote.

The implementation and enforcement of the new code would be in the hands of the Senate Ethics Committee, two of whose six members—Harrison Schmitt (R N.M.) and Lowell P. Weicker Jr. (R Conn.)—voted against passage of the resolution. A third committee member, John G. Tower (R Texas) missed the final vote, but expressed strong opposition to the measure during floor debate.

Penalties for violations of the code were not changed from the traditional penalties available to the Senate in disciplining its own members—reprimand, censure, expulsion or loss of seniority.

Nevertheless, Senate adoption of the code represented a major departure from the previous, loosely worded and general code of conduct.

Chief among the provisions of the new code was a requirement that all senators and Senate employees making $25,000 or more a year disclose virtually all of their finances—income, assets, holdings, liabilities and transactions—and the sources of all income of their spouses and dependents.

Nelson said that the widespread Senate acceptance of full financial disclosure was a "milestone" because past efforts to force senators to make public their financial operations had been hotly contested.

"The Senate's vote today confirms that a quiet revolution has taken place," Nelson said. "The principle that citizens have the right to full information has been fully established."

Opposition to the code focused on several specific provisions and on a general feeling that the overall result of the code would be to create a Senate full of professional politicians.

Edmund S. Muskie (D Maine) who was recorded against passage although he did not vote, had led a fruitless fight to kill the provision limiting outside earned income, charging that it discriminated in favor of wealthy senators with large amounts of unearned income such as dividends from stocks or bonds.

Weicker argued that full disclosure alone would be sufficient to guard against conflicts of interest and that the limits on outside earned income were unconstitutional.

And Republican Senate Minority Leader Howard H. Baker Jr. (R Tenn.) expressed concern that adoption of the code would spell an end to the concept of the "citizen legislator" which, he said, had been the original intent of the framers of the Constitution.

But Majority Leader Robert C. Byrd (D W.Va.) whose lobbying tactics were crucial in persuading reluctant senators to support the code and vote against crippling amendments, argued on the floor that "the necessity of the times," and the "climate created by the errant actions of a minority of public officials," demanded that the Senate adopt the code to restore public confidence in the Congress.

Broader than House Code

The financial aspects of the code adopted by the Senate were quite similar to the financial code of conduct adopted by the House on March 2.

But the Senate code also included enforcement provisions, a section guaranteeing that senators would not discriminate against employees because of race, sex, national origin or age, and other provisions not covered by the House action.

The House Commission on Administrative Review was drafting additional recommendations to deal with these matters. The panel expected to have its suggestions before the House sometime during the summer of 1977.

Once that action was completed, Congress then drafted a comprehensive code of ethics based on the codes adopted by the House and Senate and enacted the measure into statutory law so that it covered all federal employees.

Baker Sunset Amendment

The last challenge to the code was rejected one hour before passage when the Senate voted 63-31 to table an amendment sponsored by Baker that would have terminated the code on March 1, 1981.

The tabling motion was made by Byrd.

Baker argued that the time limit would offer a chance to see how well the code worked and force the Senate to reexamine the measure.

But opponents of the amendment said that improvements could be made at any time through the normal legislative process and charged that the so-called sunset amendment was merely a disguised attempt to kill the code.

"If the Senate passed this amendment," said Dick Clark (D Iowa), "we will be saying to the people of this country, 'Yes, we're concerned about ethics and we're passing a tough code of conduct. But in a few years, when the heat dies down, our code will quietly self-destruct.' "

Senate Code Provisions

As passed by the Senate April 1, S Res 110 contained the following major provisions:

Financial Disclosure

Required each member, officer or employee of the Senate making more than $25,000 a year and employed for more than 90 days in a year, each Senate employee designated to handle campaign funds, and each candidate for the Senate to file a financial disclosure statement with the Secretary of the Senate every year by May 15 covering previous year's activities.

Provided that the financial disclosure provisions would take effect Oct. 1, 1977, and that the first report, filed on May 15, 1978, would cover activities from Oct. 1, 1977, through the end of 1977.

Directed the Secretary of the Senate to compile a list of all those covered by the requirement every year.

Gifts

Prohibited any member, officer or employee from knowingly accepting or permitting his spouse or dependents to accept any gift of over $100 in aggregate value during a year from any individual or group having a direct interest in legislation before Congress or from any foreign national acting on behalf of a foreign organization, business or government.

Defined those having a direct interest in legislation as lobbyists, organizations that maintain political action funds, or officers or employees of such organizations.

Exempted from the prohibition gifts from relatives, gifts with a value of less than $35 and gifts of personal hospitality of an individual.

Directed that if a member, officer or employee unknowingly received a prohibited gift that he must, on learning of the gift, return it or reimburse the donor for its value.

Outside Earned Income

Limited to 15 per cent of his official salary the amount of outside earned income a member, officer or employee of the Senate employed for 90 days and making over $35,000 a year could receive.

Limited to $1,000 the amount of money a senator could receive as an honorarium for making a speech or appearance or writing an article.

Limited honoraria for employees making $35,000 a year to $300 per speech, appearance or article and $1,500 aggregate in any one year.

Provided that a member, officer or employee of the Senate could receive honoraria up to $25,000 a year if the proceeds are donated to charity and if no tax benefits accrue to the donor.

Defined outside earned income as income received as a result of personal services rendered if such services are material income producing factors.

Excluded from the definition of outside earned income royalties from books, income from family enterprises if the services provided by the senator or Senate employee are managerial or supervisory in nature and are necessary to protect family interests and do not require "significant amounts of time" when the Senate is in session; gains derived from dealings in property or investment, interests, rents, dividends, alimony and separate maintenance payments, annuities, income from discharge of in-

debtedness, distributive shares of partnership income if the services of the individual covered were not material income producing factors, income from an interest in an estate or trust, proceeds from the sale of creative or artistic works, and any "buy out" arrangement from professional partnerships or businesses related to the fair market value of his interest. Provided that all restrictions on outside earned income would take effect Sept. 30, 1979.

Conflict of Interest

Prohibited any member, officer or employee of the Senate from receiving compensation where such compensation would occur by virtue of influence improperly exerted from his position as member, officer or employee.

Prohibited any member, officer or employee from engaging in any outside business or profession for compensation that is inconsistent with conscientious performance of official duties.

Prohibited any officer or employee from working outside the Senate for compensation without notifying his superior in writing first.

Prohibited any member, officer or employee from aiding in the progress of legislation the purpose of which was to further his own financial interests.

Provided that a member could decline to vote on a matter when he believed that voting would be a conflict of interest.

Prohibited former members from lobbying in the Senate for one year after leaving office.

Prohibited an employee on a senator's staff from lobbying that senator or staff for one year after leaving Senate employment and prohibited committee staff from lobbying any member or staff of the committee for which he worked for one year after leaving the committee service.

Provided that conflict of interest rules would take effect April 1, 1978.

Office Accounts

Provided that no member could maintain an unofficial office account into which funds are received to pay for the expenses of a member's office.

Provided that for existing unofficial office accounts no contributions could be accepted after passage of the resolution and that no expenditures could be made after Dec. 31, 1977.

Provided that expenses incurred by a member could be paid for only by personal funds of the member, official funds appropriated for that purpose, funds derived from a political committee and funds received as reasonable reimbursements for expenses incurred by a member in connection with personal services provided by the member to the organization making the reimbursement.

Prohibited members from converting political contributions to personal use.

Foreign Travel

Prohibited a senator during the last year of his term from receiving funds for foreign travel after the date of the general election in which his successor was elected or, in the case of a member who was not a candidate in the general election, either the date of the general election or of the adjournment *sine die* of the second regular session of that Congress, whichever came first.

Prohibited a senator, officer or employee from claiming funds for reimbursement for foreign travel when the reim-

Senate Postpones Outside Income Limit . . .

For the second time in the 95th Congress, the House in late 1978 voted on one of the most ticklish internal issues it had faced in recent years: limiting the outside income of members.

As in 1977, House members in 1978 voted overwhelmingly in favor of the income ceiling. In 1977, the vote was 79-344; in 1978 it was 97-290.

The votes reflected in part the reluctance of many members to support a proposal that the public might interpret as strictly self-interest — particularly when representatives already were earning $57,500 a year.

Both the Senate and House limited the outside earned income of members, starting in 1979, to the equivalent of 15 percent of congressional salaries. At the existing level, that would be $8,625. The limits were part of the ethics codes of both chambers. The House votes came on efforts to remove the limits from the code.

Effectiveness Questioned

The one-sided House votes did not end debate over the effectiveness of the limit, however. Several House members with substantial outside earned income argued that they would get around the limit by incorporating their businesses and taking the income in dividends rather than salaries.

But the drafters of the ethics code, and staff members of the House Select Ethics Committee, argued that members will not be able to avoid the limit.

Ethics Committee member Rep. Lee H. Hamilton (D Ind.), who helped draft the ethics code, said the limit "will be difficult to get around" because the rule is "clear-cut." But Hamilton refused to rule out the possibility that some members will be able to avoid the limit.

Disputes over whether income is earned or unearned will be settled "on a factual basis" by the Committee on Standards of Official Conduct, Hamilton said.

Ethics Code Definition

The ethics code defines outside earned income as "wages, salaries, professional fees, honorariums and other amounts (other than copyright royalties) received or to be received as compensation for personal services actually rendered."

In other words, income that is earned as a result of performing a service is subject to the limit.

But there is a major exception: "In the case of a member engaged in a trade or business in which the member or his family holds a controlling interest and in which both personal services and capital are income-producing factors, any amount received by such members [is exempt from the limit] so long as the personal services actually rendered by the member in the trade or business do not generate a significant amount of income."

That section was inserted to protect members from having to give up family farms and other small businesses. Opponents have questioned the phrase "significant amount of income," saying it is vague and subject to varying interpretations.

Two Views of Issue

At least three members said they planned to use that exemption in order to get around the income limit:

● Rep. Claude Pepper (D Fla.), an attorney who reported $26,285 in legal fees during the fourth quarter of 1977, said he would incorporate his law firm and start drawing dividends.

● Rep. Gene Snyder (R Ky.), said he planned to incorporate his real estate and law firms. He reported earning $58,431 from his real estate business and $4,362 in legal fees in 1977.

● Rep. Bud Shuster (R Pa.), said his income was already protected under his tire store-real estate business of BTI Investments Inc. He reported fourth quarter 1977 income of $42,406 from that firm.

"As a general rule, a person who owns a business can take his income in dividends," Shuster said. "This limit doesn't apply to anybody like me who owns a small, family-type business." Shuster said he was a minority stockholder, but held no position in his business. "I don't spend much time at all" on the business, he said.

bursement had been made by another organization and from receiving reimbursement from the government for the same expense more than once.

Permitted senators or Senate employees to take trips paid for by foreign private educational and charitable organizations if approved by the Ethics Committee.

Franked Mail

Provided that no senator or candidate for the Senate could make use of the frank for a mass mailing less than 60 days before a primary or general election in which the senator or candidate was running.

Provided that a senator could use only official funds of the Senate to pay for preparation of any mass mailing sent out under the frank. (The provision was intended to end the practice of mailing at public expense under the frank newsletters or other material printed with private funds and labeled "Not Printed at Government Expense.")

Required all mass mailings by a senator under the frank to be registered with the secretary of the Senate and the registration to include a copy of the material, the number of pieces sent and a description of the groups receiving the mailing. Required the information to be available for public inspection.

Provided that the Senate computer facilities could not be used to store any political or campaign lists and that other mail-related uses of the computer would be subject to guidelines issued by the Rules Committee.

Provided that the Senate radio and television studios could not be used by any candidate for election to the Senate less than 60 days before the primary or general election in which the candidate was running.

Provided that the rules governing franking would take effect Aug. 1, 1977.

Political Fund Activity

Effective 30 days after passage, provided that no officer or employee of the Senate may handle campaign contributions in any way except for two staff aides in Washington and one in the senator's home state who are designated by the senator to perform such functions and

...House Questions Its Effectiveness

But Rep. Hamilton and other supporters of the ethics code argued that members would not be able to get around the income limit just by changing the name of a company or by calling their income dividends rather than salaries.

"The source of income, I don't think, is the pertinent point," Hamilton said. "The question is whether personal services were rendered" to the company by the member.

The only income that is exempt from the limit, Hamilton and others said, is "return on equity" such as profits, dividends, rent or royalties.

They contended the income is earned if the member renders any services on behalf of the firm, such as meeting with law clients or showing property to a prospective purchaser of real estate.

Hamilton conceded that "it is possible for a member to have return on equity" from a law firm, and thus escape the limit. "But this applies to a very few members, because most members who are lawyers . . . it is clear that they are giving services" to the law firm.

If the character of a member's income is in doubt, Hamilton said, "we're going to have to get the facts. There will have to be a factual determination made by the ethics committee."

Obey Commission Opinion

The Commission on Administrative Review (the Obey Commission) which drafted the ethics code, foresaw the possibility that some members would try to evade the income limit. In addition to nearly total financial disclosure by members, the panel called for limits on outside income.

In its report (H Rept 95-73) to the House in February 1977, the commission warned that "care should be taken to prevent members from circumventing [the limit] by incorporating themselves into a family business and then withdrawing what in reality are fees for personal services in the form of dividends or profits."

But the commission did not specifically recommend what should be done to prevent such a practice.

1979: Delaying the Income Limit

In a surprise move, the Senate early in 1979 voted to delay for four years the strict limitation on outside income it had approved in 1977. Based on past financial disclosure figures, probably more than half the Senate would have suffered income losses under the limitation. Before the Senate acted, that ceiling was $8,625.

The action came on short notice in the Senate and without a recorded vote. Only about six senators were on the floor when the delay resolution (S Res 93) was approved March 8 by voice vote.

Financial disclosure figures for 1977 showed that 42 senators still in office in 1979 earned more than $8,625 in honoraria that year. In total, 81 senators reported $1,087,638 in honoraria in 1977. Minority Whip Ted Stevens (R Alaska) and Sen. Daniel Patrick Moynihan (D N.Y.), the two principal sponsors of S Res 93, earned $11,108 and $23,900, respectively in honoraria in 1977.

As a result of public outcry ensuing from the March 8 voice vote, the Senate March 28 placed itself on record in favor of the income limit delay. By a recorded vote of 44-54, the Senate rejected an attempt by Sen. Gary Hart (D Colo.) to reimpose the income limitation that was to have started Jan. 1, 1979. Hart later said he was satisfied with the result because it forced senators to take a position. "The primary issue was that no one knew where we stood on this," Hart told reporters following the vote.

Though the 44-54 vote merely reaffirmed the Senate's earlier action, it appeared to satisfy senators stung by the widespread criticism of the March 8 vote.

With the Senate rule delayed for four years, senators in 1979 were limited solely by a ceiling on honoraria in the 1976 Federal Election Campaign Act (PL 94-283). That law limited to $25,000 annually the amount of money a senator could earn in honoraria; it also limited each honorarium to a maximum of $2,000. By contrast, House members were bound by the same 15 per cent cap on outside earned income and a limit of $1,000 on each honorarium. (The $750 ceiling approved in its 1977 ethics code was raised to $1,000 in January 1979.)

---

who are paid over $10,000 a year and who file a financial disclosure statement with the secretary of the Senate.

Provided that no member, officer or employee could utilize the services of an individual who was not an employee of the Senate or of the United States government for more than 90 days a year unless such individual agreed in writing to comply with the Senate Code of Official Conduct.

Prohibited senators or former senators from converting political contributions to private use.

Employment Practices

Provided that effective Jan. 3, 1979, no member, officer or employee could refuse to hire an individual, discharge an individual or discriminate with respect to promotion, pay or terms of employment on the basis of race, color, religion, sex, national origin, age, or state of physical handicap.

Ethics Committee

Charged the Select Committee on Ethics with enforcement of the Senate Code of Official Conduct.

Effective Date

Except as otherwise noted, provided that all sections of the resolution would take effect on adoption.

1978 Ethics Bill

Detailed financial disclosure by top federal officials and new restrictions on post-government activity by former federal officials were mandated by the government ethics bill (S 555 — PL 95-521) signed into law by President Carter, Oct. 26.

Carter said the bill "responds to problems that developed in the highest levels of government in the 1970s."

The final bill codified the public financial disclosure requirements passed as new ethics codes in the House and Senate in 1977. It also required public disclosure by top executive and judicial branch employees. The bill provided administrative procedures to assure compliance with the disclosure requirements, but civil penalties could be imposed for knowing and willful violations.

Obey Commission Survey of House, Public Opinion

A survey released Feb. 3, 1977, by the House Commission on Administrative Review, chaired by Rep. David R. Obey (D Wis.), indicated that both the House and the general public would endorse many of the changes in standards of conduct recommended by the commission.

The results of the survey of both public opinion and House members provided what Obey termed a "unique" insight into the opinions of average Americans and their elected representatives about the duties of a congressman and the ethical standards to which he should adhere. On many specific issues related to ethical conduct the two polls found that the majority of Americans and the majority in the House held remarkably similar opinions.

However, on several points relating to the job of a congressman—both what it should be and what it really is—there were some glaring differences. The public opinion poll also revealed that there remains a deep dissatisfaction with Congress as an institution and a widespread skepticism about the ability of Congress to reform itself.

The public opinion poll, conducted by Louis Harris and Associates Inc., was based on a survey of 1,510 Americans representing a cross section of the population 18 years and older. It cost the commission $53,000.

The members' survey was based on confidential in-person interviews of 153 of the 372 members who sat in the 94th Congress and were re-elected to the 95th Congress. The sampling was conducted by Victor J. Fisher, director of survey research for the commission, who said that it reflected a statistically representative cross section of the House.

More Information on Congress

The public survey also revealed a strong desire by many Americans for more detailed information about Congress and its activities. By a margin of 88-7 per cent the survey respondents said that they would like Congress to make more information about itself available, and large majorities favored televising House and committee meetings as a way of doing this.

District or National Interests

When asked whether they felt that a congressman should be primarily concerned with looking out for his district or looking after the interests of the nation as a whole, the public by a margin of 57-38 said that the top priority should be the interests of the district.

House members, on the other hand, by a 45-24 per cent margin said they viewed their primary responsibility to be looking after the interests of the nation.

Paying Official Expenses, Office Accounts

Both the public and the members indicated a desire to have all official expenses paid for out of public funds. The Harris poll, for example, revealed that by a 76-19 margin the public believed that congressmen should have all of their travel within their districts paid for and by a 78-15 margin that all official travel between Washington and the home district should be paid for out of public funds.

Existing rules provide for 26 free round trips a year for a member between Washington and his home district and a $2,000 allowance for district expenses, including travel in the district.

The members' survey revealed that 53 per cent of those surveyed felt a need to increase official allowances, with the travel allowance most often cited as being inadequate.

The members were not, however, unanimous in their opinion of what to do about private office accounts. Although only 10 per cent said that there was no need to change the existing arrangement, the rest split on what to do; 46 per cent said that the accounts should be permitted with some restrictions, and 30 per cent said they should be abolished.

Outside Earnings, Disclosure

Both the House members and the public reflected a strong viewpoint that service in Congress should be a full-time job. Some 54 per cent of the public and 64 per cent of the members said that members of Congress should give up their private careers entirely when elected to office.

A heavy majority of both the House (69 per cent) and the public (63 per cent) indicated that they would like to see full financial disclosure by both House members and candidates for the House.

Conflicts of Interest

On the issue of potential conflicts of interest, the House members appeared to be more skeptical and to favor more stringent restrictions than the public.

For example, 94 per cent of the members said that they would be "bothered" by a situation in which a member received a share of the profits from a law firm that did business with the government, even if the member did not actively work for the firm. Only 59 per cent of the public said that such a situation would disturb them.

Similarly, 67 per cent of the public and 85 per cent of the members said they would be bothered by a situation in which a member received a large fee for speaking to a group that had an interest in legislation.

Negative View of Congress

Despite the similarity of opinions by members and the public on ethical issues and an overwhelming approval by the public of initiatives to tighten the congressional code of conduct, most Americans remained skeptical of Congress and its ability to reform itself.

Those surveyed continued to give Congress a negative rating by a margin of 64-22, a slight improvement over 1974 but still a long way from the 64-25 per cent favorable rating of 1965.

This negative view of the Congress as an institution, Harris found, had still not affected the public view of their individual representatives. By a margin of 40-22 per cent the public rated its representatives as positive.

Restrictions were tightened on the "revolving door" that allows government employees to move freely to private jobs lobbying their former agencies. As cleared by Congress, penalties for violation of the post-government restrictions ranged from administrative actions to criminal fines or jail sentences.

In addition, the bill established an Office of Government Ethics to monitor financial disclosure and conflicts of interest in the executive branch.

The bill also set up a mechanism for appointment of a temporary special prosecutor to investigate criminal wrongdoing by the president, vice president and other top executive branch officials.

The final version also permitted the Senate to set up an Office of Senate Legal Counsel to represent members, officers, committees or the Senate as a whole in litigation.

Two-Year Gestation

Both chambers passed their ethics codes, covering members of Congress, at the beginning of the 95th Congress. But action on bills to require disclosure by other federal officials lagged.

The requirements of the ethics codes were enforceable only through congressional procedures such as disciplinary actions against a member. Stiffer penalties through the legal system, such as civil or criminal charges, weren't possible without more legislation.

The final bill passed by Congress covered the executive and judicial branches and provided civil fines but no criminal penalties.

The Senate passed its version of S 555 in mid-1977. However, companion legislation languished in the House until late in the year when it was reported by several different committees, all of which had some jurisdictional responsibility.

In 1978, the jurisdictional problem had to be resolved in order to make the bill manageable on the floor. This was accomplished eventually when the four committees involved agreed to back one compromise bill on the floor. However, the bill had languished for several months before the compromise was struck.

Penalties, Income Limit Issues

One key issue that contributed to delay was a provision in early versions of the bill imposing criminal penalties on persons who violated the disclosure requirements. Opponents said that a criminal charge, even if later disproved, could ruin a politician's career. Criminal penalties were dropped from the compromise.

A second issue involved a provision in the ethics codes limiting outside earned income of members to 15 per cent of their salaries — $8,625 at the salary level in effect in 1978. That limit, which was to go into effect in 1979, had drawn criticism from a small but vocal group in Congress.

House opponents of the limit mounted a campaign to get a vote on repealing it when the House took up the financial disclosure legislation. The fear that they might win contributed to the Democratic leadership's reluctance to bring the bill to the floor.

However, the ceiling opponents lost, and lost big. The House in September rejected by a 97-290 vote a proposal to repeal the earned income limit. Members who backed the repeal claimed that they were hurt by the vote's proximity to the November elections. Some said members had told them privately they did not like the income limit but could not vote against it just before the elections.

After the income issue was settled, the House went on to pass its version of the disclosure legislation (HR 1) with little controversy. That occurred Sept. 27 by a 368-30 vote.

Conferees reached agreement surprisingly quickly. The conference report on the bill (S 555 — H Rept 95-1756) was adopted by the Senate Oct. 7 by voice vote and by the House Oct. 12 by a 370-23 roll call. Before that final vote, the House defeated a motion by Charles E. Wiggins (R Calif.) to reject the section setting up a mechanism for appointment of a temporary special prosecutor. The vote on Wiggins' proposal was 49-344.

Provisions

As signed into law, Title I of S 555 contained the following provisions concerning legislative branch disclosure:

● Required all members, their principal assistants, congressional officers and employees paid at the GS-16 salary level or higher, and any candidate for congressional office to file annual public financial disclosure reports.

● Required all reports, except those from congressional candidates, to be filed by May 15 each year with the clerk of the House or the secretary of the Senate.

● Required candidates for congressional office in 1978 to file reports by Nov. 1, 1978, but exempted 1978 candidates from any penalties for failure to comply with the disclosure requirements.

● Required candidates in future elections to file reports within 30 days of becoming a candidate or by May 15, whichever was later.

● Required new officers and employees who are principal assistants or are paid at the GS-16 salary level or above to file reports, beginning Jan. 1, 1979, within 30 days after assuming their positions if they had not previously held legislative branch positions covered by the bill.

● Required all members, officers and employees covered by the legislative branch disclosure requirements to report the source, type and amount of earned income from any source (other than their U.S. government salaries) and the source, date and amount of honoraria received during the preceding calendar year and aggregating $100 or more in value.

● Required members, officers and employees to report the source and type of unearned income received from dividends, interest, rent and capital gains received during the preceding calendar year and aggregating $100 or more in value.

● Required candidates and new officers or employees to file the same information about income for the year of filing and the preceding calendar year.

● Required reporting of each item of unearned income in one of the following categories: Not more than $1,000, greater than $1,000 but not more than $2,500, greater than $2,500 but not more than $5,000, greater than $5,000 but not more than $15,000, greater than $15,000 but not more than $50,000, greater than $50,000 but not more than $100,000, or greater than $100,000.

● Required all persons covered except candidates and new officers and employees to disclose the source and a brief description of any gifts of transportation, lodging, food or entertainment aggregating $250 or more in value received from any source other than a relative during the preceding calendar year.

● Exempted gifts of food, lodging or entertainment received as personal hospitality from the reporting requirements.

● Required all persons covered except candidates and new officers and employees to disclose the source, a brief description and estimated value of all gifts (other than transportation, lodging, food or entertainment) aggregating $100 or more in value received from a source other than a relative during the preceding calendar year.

● Exempted gifts with a fair market value of $35 or less.

● Required all persons covered except candidates and new officers and employees to disclose the source and a brief description of reimbursements from a single source aggregating $250 or more in the preceding calendar year.

● Required all persons covered to disclose the identity and category of value of any interest in property held in a trade or business, or for investment or production of income, with a fair market value over $1,000 at the close of the preceding calendar year.

● Excluded from disclosure personal liabilities owed by relatives to the reporting individual or any deposit of $5,000 or less in a personal savings account.

● Required all persons covered to disclose the identity and category of value of the total liabilities owed to any creditor (other than a relative) exceeding $10,000 at any time during the preceding calendar year. This did not include a mortgage on the individual's personal residence or loans for cars, household furniture or appliances.

● Exempted reporting outstanding liabilities on revolving charge accounts unless the liability was more than $10,000 at the close of the preceding calendar year.

● Required all persons covered except candidates and new officers and employees to include a brief description, the date and category of value of real property (other than personal residence) or stocks, bonds or other securities purchased, sold or exchanged in the preceding calendar year if the amount involved exceeded $1,000.

● Exempted from reporting requirements any transaction solely between the reporting individual and his or her spouse or dependent children.

● Required all persons covered to report any positions held during the current calendar year with businesses, non-profit organizations, labor groups or other institutions, except for religious, social, fraternal or political groups.

● Required all persons covered except candidates and new officers and employees to report terms of agreement about any future employment planned by the reporting individual.

● Provided that in reporting property holdings, liabilities and purchase, sale or exchange of real property or securities, individuals should list each item in one of the following categories: Not more than $5,000, greater than $5,000 but not more than $15,000, greater than $15,000 but not more than $50,000, greater than $50,000 but not more than $100,000, greater than $100,000 but not more than $250,000, or greater than $250,000.

● Permitted reporting of real property values as the price on the date purchased or the assessed value for tax purposes, as long as the method used for determining the assessed value was described in the report.

● Required reporting individuals to list the following information about a spouse's finances: source of any earned income over $1,000; source and type of unearned income received from dividends, interest, rent and capital gains received during the preceding calendar year and aggregating $100 or more in value; source and brief description or estimated value of any gift or reimbursement which is not received totally independent of the spouse's relationship to the reporting individual; and certain assets, liabilities and transactions of the spouse (unless the reporting individual certified that he or she had no control over them and would not receive any economic benefit from those interests).

● Required reporting individuals to list unearned income of dependent children, and to list their assets, liabilities and transactions unless the individual certified that he or she had no control over them and did not receive any economic benefit from them.

● Exempted from reporting requirements a spouse permanently separated from the reporting individual.

● Required that an individual with holdings in a qualified blind trust report the category of the amount of income received by the individual, the individual's spouse or dependent children, but did not require reporting of the holdings or source of income.

● Defined the requirements of a qualified blind trust, and gave House and Senate ethics committees authority to determine whether a blind trust qualified under the law.

● Authorized the attorney general to bring civil charges against a reporting individual or the trustee of his or her qualified blind trust for negligent or knowing and willful disclosure or receipt of information specifically required to be kept confidential about a qualified blind trust.

● Required the clerk of the House and secretary of the Senate to make reports available to the public within 15 days after they are filed.

● Provided that reports be available to the public for five years, after which they were to be destroyed.

● Barred use of the reports for any unlawful purposes, commercial use (other than in news reporting), solicitation of money or determination of an individual's credit rating.

● Provided civil penalties of up to $5,000 for persons who make illegal use of the reported information.

● Provided that designated committees in the House and Senate should review all reports to see if they were properly and completely filed.

● Required the committees to notify any reporting individual who did not file an accurate report and give the individual an opportunity to correct it.

● Provided that an individual who complied with recommendations of the committees shall not be subject to any sanctions provided in the bill.

● Provided for civil penalties of up to $5,000 against any persons who knowingly and willfully filed a false report or failed to file a report.

● Required the General Accounting Office (GAO) to monitor compliance with the legislative branch disclosure requirements. ▮

Major Congressional Ethics Cases, 1976-79

Congress' image with the public suffered during the years 1976-79 as a number of present and former members were officially accused of criminal or unethical behavior. Indeed, Congress, which in 1974 had forced President Nixon from office for misdeeds, by 1976 had found itself the target of widespread charges of unethical and illegal conduct.

For the first time in seven years, the House moved against one of its own members when it voted on July 29, 1976, to reprimand Robert L. F. Sikes, D-Fla., for financial misconduct. The threat of a House committee probe into charges that he had kept a mistress on the public payroll forced Wayne L. Hays, D-Ohio, to resign his seat and prompted the House to set up a special committee to study reforms in the congressional payroll system.

But Congress seemed reluctant to investigate or take any other action concerning the possible misdeeds of many of its members in 1976.

While the Hays scandal drew the most publicity, the most pervasive scandal of the year involved campaign contributions. It began in December 1975, when a special committee of the Gulf Oil Corporation reported to the Securities and Exchange Commission (SEC) that Gulf over the previous decade had contributed more than $5-million in illegal corporate funds to the campaign efforts of dozens of members.

Those named in the SEC report included some of the most influential members of the legislative branch, among them Senate Minority Leader Hugh Scott, R-Pa.

James R. Jones, D-Okla., pleaded guilty to a misdemeanor in connection with failure to report a Gulf contribution, and John Heinz, R-Pa., publicly admitted having received illegal contributions from the oil company.

One Senate aide, Henry Giugni, administrative assistant to Daniel K. Inouye, D-Hawaii, admitted that he lied to a federal grand jury when he denied having passed on $5,000 in Gulf money to his boss.

Yet Congress took no action against these three or any other members implicated in the case.

Inouye declined to dismiss Giugni and the Senate Select Committee on Standards and Conduct voted overwhelmingly not to investigate Scott, even though the minority leader reportedly admitted to the panel that he had received $45,000 in Gulf money.

John J. McCloy, who headed the committee which investigated the Gulf affair for the SEC, concluded that "nobody seems able to make the Senate [E]thics [C]ommittee do its job."

In February 1976, 18 members of Congress, including both chairmen of the House and Senate ethics committees, Rep. John J. Flynt Jr., D-Ga., and Sen. Howard W. Cannon, D-Nev., admitted having received unreported free hunting trips from various defense contractors, an apparent violation of House and Senate rules. No formal congressional action was taken.

An Ethics Committee investigation of charges reported in *The Wall Street Journal* on March 23 that 10 House members had filed false claims for travel expense reimbursement never got beyond the preliminary stages.

With its image stained by scandals and an automatic pay raise, Congress began its 1977 session with a strong effort toward internal reform. Both chambers passed sweeping ethics codes early in the year and enacted the rules into law and extended them to other branches of government late in 1978.

But in some repects, the 95th Congress was as noteworthy for the laws its members violated as for those they passed. At adjournment time, more than a dozen current or former senators and representatives had been officially accused of criminal or unethical behavior.

Rep. Charles C. Diggs Jr., D-Mich., and former Rep. Richard T. Hanna, D-Calif. (1963-74) were convicted of felonies in 1978. On July 31, 1979, Diggs was censured by the House. Rep. Daniel J. Flood, D-Pa., was indicted on 13 criminal charges in the fall of 1978, and former Rep. Joshua Eilberg, D-Pa. (1967-78) pleaded guilty in February 1979 to charges that he illegally accepted compensation for helping a Philadelphia hospital obtain a federal grant.

House Speaker Thomas P. O'Neill Jr., D-Mass., and John Brademas, D-Ind., the Democratic whip, among others, were cleared by the House ethics committee of charges stemming from a Korean influence-peddling investigation, but Reps. John J. McFall, D-Calif., Edward R. Roybal, D-Calif., and Charles H. Wilson, D-Calif., were officially reprimanded by the House as a result of the investigation. But the commitee had recommended censure of Roybal; the House cut that to a reprimand. Moreover, the debate on the reprimands left observers wondering if the House really took the issue very seriously.

In the Senate, the Select Committee on Ethics early in 1979 concluded an investigation of former Sen. Edward W. Brooke, D-Mass., by reporting that it should not pursue the matter further. However, on Sept. 16, the panel unanimously voted to denounce Sen. Herman E. Talmadge, D-Ga. on grounds of financial improprieties.

Following are highlights of some of the major congressional ethics cases arising during the years 1976-79.

Rep. Robert L. F. Sikes

The House July 29, 1976, voted to reprimand Rep. Robert L. F. Sikes, D-Fla., when it accepted, by a vote of 381-3, the House Ethics Committee finding that Sikes was guilty of financial misconduct. It was the first time the House had punished one of its members since the Powell case in 1969 and was the result of the first known investigation of a House member by the Ethics Committee.

Sikes, chairman of the House Military Construction Appropriations Subcommittee, had been charged with conflicts of interest and failure to disclose certain financial holdings. *(See below.)* The complaint against Sikes had been filed by Common Cause, the self-styled citizens' lobby, and transmitted to the Ethics Committee by 44 House members. The formal backing for a complaint against a House member by other members was unprecedented in the history of the committee.

The Ethics Committee April 28 initiated an inquiry into the conflict-of-interest allegations. On May 12, by a 9-0 vote, the panel authorized a "factual investigation" into the charges. Chairman Flynt told reporters that "so far as I know" it was the first investigation of a House member by the panel. By elevating the probe from the status of an inquiry to an investigation, the panel gave itself the authority to subpoena financial records and question witnesses under oath.

The committee July 21 voted 10-2 to approve a report (H Rept 94-1364) on Sikes' dealings which recommended the House adopt H Res 1421 reprimanding Sikes.

The report cited three instances where it said Sikes' actions "have violated standards of conduct applicable to all members of Congress." They were:

● Failure to report ownership of stock in Fairchild Industries Inc., in annual disclosure statements from 1968 through 1973, and in the First Navy Bank at the Pensacola Naval Air Station, Pensacola, Fla., in his 1973 disclosure statement, as required by House Rule 44. (Sikes first disclosed stock ownership in both companies in his 1974 financial disclosure statement.) Although Sikes' failure to report these holdings did not appear to be "an effort to conceal" them from Congress or the public, the report declared: "The committee believes that the failure to report . . . is deserving of a reprimand."

● Sikes' investment in stock of the First Navy Bank which he was active in establishing violated Section 5 of the Code of Ethics for Government Service and was cause for a reprimand. "If an opinion had been requested of this committee in advance about the propriety of the investment, it would have been disapproved," according to the report.

● The sponsorship of legislation in 1961 that removed restrictions on Florida land parcels without disclosing that Sikes had an interest in the same land. The committee did not recommend any punishment for this action because, it said, it took place so long ago and "at least to some extent" the circumstances "appear to have been known to Representative Sikes' constituency which has continually re-elected him to Congress." The committee also noted that Sikes had sold some of the land after the bill he had sponsored passed the House, but before it passed the Senate. Although recommending no punishment, the committee said Sikes' involvement with the legislation "created an obvious and significant conflict of interest."

In the first two instances, the committee specified that adoption of the report would constitute a reprimand.

On another charge, the committee concluded that Sikes did not violate House rules when he voted for a fiscal year 1975 defense appropriations bill (HR 16243 — PL 93-437) that contained a $73-million appropriation for an aircraft contract with Fairchild Industries. The committee determined that Sikes' ownership of 1,000 shares out of the more than 4.5 million shares outstanding in Fairchild was not "sufficient to disqualify him from voting on the bill."

Rep. Wayne L. Hays

Less than a month after undertaking the Sikes investigation, the Ethics Committee began a probe of a sex-and-public-payroll scandal involving Wayne L. Hays, D-Ohio, the powerful chairman of the House Administration Committee and the Democratic National Congressional Committee. In a story which broke in *The Washington Post* May 23, 1976, Elizabeth Ray accused Hays of giving her a $14,000-a-year job on the House Administration Committee in exchange for sexual favors.

Hays at first denied the Ray charge but then admitted to the House May 25 that he had a "personal relationship" with Ray. However, he denied that he had hired her to be his mistress.

On May 25, Hays asked the Ethics Committee to investigate the matter. The same day 28 House members, in a letter to ethics Chairman Flynt, asked the committee to take up the Hays case. On June 2, the committee voted 11-0 to begin an immediate investigation into the charges.

The Justice Department and FBI had entered the case soon after Ray made her charges, and by May 26, a federal grand jury in Washington, D.C., began hearing testimony relating to her allegations.

Pressure built up quickly in the House to oust Hays from his leadership positions. He relinquished June 3 his chairmanship of the Democratic Congressional Campaign Committee. Hays won renomination to his House seat in a close Democratic primary in Ohio's 18th District June 8. Then, bowing to pressure from the House Democratic leadership, Hays resigned the chairmanship of the House Administration Committee June 18 and Aug. 13 announced he would not run for re-election to Congress in 1976. On Sept. 1 Hays resigned from Congress. The ethics panel then voted, 12-0, to end its investigation of Hays.

1977-78 Korea Lobby Probe

A year and a half after they began their investigations, ethics committees in the House and Senate wound up their probes into alleged South Korean influence-peddling on Capitol Hill without recommending any severe disciplinary action against colleagues linked to the scandal.

The investigation by the House Committee on Standards of Official Conduct drew to a close Friday, Oct. 13, 1978, in a bang of hyperbole, a whimper of approbrium and a mass of uncertainties about the future of the House ethics process.

The investigation, which began some 18 months earlier with reports that as many as 115 members of Congress had taken illegal gifts from South Korean agents, ended with the House voting its mildest form of punishment, a "reprimand," for three California Democrats: John J. McFall, Edward R. Roybal and Charles H. Wilson.

Similarly, the Senate Ethics Committee, concluding its 17-month Korean investigation, issued a report Oct. 16 that recommended no disciplinary action against any incumbent or former senator.

A third committee investigating U.S.-Korean relations concluded that the South Korean government sought to bribe U.S. officials, buy influence among journalists and professors, extort money from American companies and rig military procurement contracts to win support for what the panel called the "authoritarian" government of President Park Chung Hee. In its final report, released Nov. 1, the House International Relations Subcommittee on International Organizations said that the South Korean government's illegal activities went beyond its legal and extra-legal lobbying efforts. The 450-page report, which outlined the history of U.S.-Korean relations, indicated that the South Koreans frequently pursued policies antithetical to U.S. interests. The most notable of these incidents involved

South Korean efforts to develop nuclear weapons, a project the subcommittee said was abandoned by 1975.

Completing its "Koreagate" investigation Oct. 13, the House Committee on Standards of Official Conduct issued reports (H Repts 95-1741, 1742, 1743) charging McFall, Roybal and Wilson with official misconduct involving cash contributions from Korean rice dealer Tongsun Park and statements made to the House Standards Committee concerning these payments.

In the closing arguments on the House floor, heard by fewer than a third of the members, questions about the ability and willingness of the House to discipline its members were raised anew. The Standards Committee was criticized both for being too harsh in its findings and, in the end, for its inability to make the toughest of its charges stick.

Presented with reports on the committee's findings only hours before being asked to vote on them, few members evidenced any reluctance to uphold the committee's suggested reprimands of McFall and Wilson (H Res 1415 and H Res 1414). But confronted with the choice of voting to uphold the panel's recommended "censure" of Roybal (H Res 1416), who was of Hispanic descent, and suggestions that such a vote would be perceived as racist, a majority of the House backed off from the tougher recommendation.

The House rejected the resolution to censure Roybal 219-170 and then adopted a reprimand on a voice vote. Wilson's reprimand was voted 329-41 and McFall's was approved on a voice vote.

In another development related to Korean lobbying practices, former Rep. Otto E. Passman, D-La. (1947-77) was acquitted April 1, 1979, of all charges against him by a Monroe, La., federal district court jury. The trial had begun March 5.

Passman had been indicted in the spring of 1978 on charges that he conspired to obtain $213,000 in bribes from South Korean businessman Tongsun Park, conspired to defraud the United States in connection with rice sales to South Korea, failing to report $143,000 on his income tax returns and evading $77,000 in income taxes on the alleged bribes. The trial had begun March 5.

Sen. Edward W. Brooke

The Senate Select Committee on Ethics in March 1979 ended its 10-month preliminary investigation of former Sen. Edward W. Brooke, R-Mass., by concluding there was "credible evidence" of wrongdoing on Brooke's part but that the violations were not sufficiently serious to continue the investigation or to warrant punishment.

The investigation, which the committee called an "initial review," had explored since early June 1978 charges that Brooke made false statements under oath, failed to list required information on his Senate financial disclosure statement, took improper deductions on his 1975 income tax return and used his official position to improperly obtain benefits for members of his family.

The probe was begun after *The Boston Globe* reported discrepancies between the senator's financial disclosure report and sworn testimony he gave in an earlier divorce proceeding.

The fact that the probe was not concluded before election day in 1978 was credited with contributing to Brooke's defeat by Rep. Paul E. Tsongas, D-Mass.

In a report (S Rept 96-40) filed with the Senate March 21, the Ethics Committee concluded that it should not

pursue the Brooke matter any further because Brook no longer was a member of the Senate and because the committee "does not believe the violations mentioned in its report are sufficiently serious to justify" censure, expulsion or loss of seniority.

It added, however, that "there is credible evidence which provides cause to conclude that violations within the jurisdiction of the committee have occurred."

Brooke issued a statement sharply critical of the investigation. Except for a single "misstatement" which he said he had acknowledged and apologized for, the probe had found nothing "more serious than poor recordkeeping," Brooke said.

The "misstatement" Brooke referred to concerned the amount of a loan from A. Raymond Tye, a Massachusetts liquor distributor. In the divorce proceeding, Brooke said under oath that he owed Tye $49,000; in his Senate disclosure form he said he owed Tye $2,000.

In its report, the Ethics Committee said Brooke's financial disclosure form concerning the Tye loan was "substantially correct." However, the report went on, "the giving of false testimony under oath by a United States senator is improper conduct which reflects unfavorably on the United States Senate."

The committee cited a number of other instances where Brooke had failed to report to the Senate financial holdings and liabilities that Senate rules required him to report. In other instances, the committee said it did not have sufficient information to determine whether Brooke's disclosure form was correct or not.

In several matters, Brooke was cleared by the Ethics Committee. The committee said it had no evidence indicating that Brooke knew his mother-in-law was improperly receiving Medicaid benefits or that he had knowingly voted in the Senate to liberalize the eligibility to his mother-in-law's advantage. It also found no evidence that Brooke had used his position as senator to obtain a reduction in medical fees for his mother-in-law or that he had improperly claimed his daughter Remi Brooke as an exemption on his income taxes for 1975.

Rep. Daniel J. Flood

Rep. Daniel J. Flood, D-Pa., a senior member of Congress, was indicted on 13 criminal charges in the fall of 1978.

The 13 charges against Flood — which he termed "absurd" — alleged that he and his former top aide Stephen B. Elko conspired during a six-year period to collect bribes from several businessmen. The money allegedly was paid in exchange for Flood's help in getting the businessmen grants, contracts or other aid from federal agencies.

Federal bribery statutes forbid public officials from accepting anything of value in exchange for official acts.

Several of the men who allegedly bribed Flood have cooperated with Justice Department prosecutors working on the case, and some have been given immunity for their testimony.

One of those involved — a Brooklyn rabbi — in May 1978 pleaded guilty to charges in New York that he paid Flood more than $5,000 in bribes.

Flood was not indicted at the time of Rabbi Lieb Pinter's trial. But an indictment handed down by a Washington, D.C., grand jury in October alleged that Flood accepted about $6,500 from Pinter in exchange for Flood's help in getting government grants for groups headed by the rabbi.

Flood pleaded innocent to all of the charges against him, which included 10 counts of bribery and conspiracy alleged in the Washington indictment and three counts of perjury in an earlier indictment handed down in September by a Los Angeles grand jury. The Los Angeles and Washington indictments were combined so that Flood faced only one trial, in Washington.

Each conspiracy and perjury charge against Flood carried a maximum penalty of $10,000 and five years in prison. Top penalties for each bribery charge were $20,000 and 15 years in prison.

Delay Request

In December, Flood filed a motion asking for a delay in his trial. His attorneys argued that the Supreme Court's decision to review the constitutionality of a bribery indictment against a former House member could have an important effect on the case against Flood.

The Supreme Court case involved former Rep. Henry Helstoski, D-N.J. (1965-1976), who was indicted in 1976 on charges that he took bribes in exchange for introducing private bills allowing individual aliens to immigrate into or remain in the United States. Helstoski challenged the indictment, arguing that the speech or debate clause of the Constitution made him immune from prosecution for legislative activities.

The clause states that "for any Speech or Debate in either House, [members of Congress] shall not be questioned in any other Place."

Helstoski's argument was rejected by a lower court, but the Supreme Court agreed to review that decision in 1979.

Defense attorneys asked District Court Judge Oliver Gasch to delay Flood's trial until after the Supreme Court decides whether Helstoski's indictment is constitutional. They argued that a decision favorable to Helstoski could affect a claim of speech or debate immunity by Flood.

Government prosecutors responded that the Helstoski decision would not affect Flood's case because they had not presented evidence involving legislative acts to the grand juries investigating Flood.

On Jan. 4, Judge Gasch rejected the request for a delay, saying "[I]t would be unwise to continue this case indefinitely."

[The Supreme Court ruled June 18, 1979, that present and former members of Congress accused of corruption in office are protected by the Constitution from the introduction of trial evidence relating to their past legislative acts. In a separate decision, however, the court declined to block Helstoski's prosecution altogether; it did so by rejecting an appeal from Helstoski himself to quash the indictment pending against him.]

The Trial

Flood's trial began Jan. 15, 1979, the day the 96th Congress convened. Flood left the Washington courthouse during a long lunch break and traveled the few blocks to Capitol Hill to be sworn in for his 16th congressional term.

Two bribery charges against Flood were dropped before the trial, leaving three charges of perjury, one of conspiracy and seven of bribery.

On Feb. 3, U.S. District Court Judge Gasch declared a mistrial after the jury said it was hopelessly deadlocked. A retrial had been set to begin June 4 but was indefinitely postponed because of Flood's hospitalization May 30.

Rep. Joshua Eilberg

Former Rep. Joshua Eilberg, D-Pa. (1967-78), pleaded guilty Feb. 24, 1979, to charges that he illegally accepted money for helping a Philadelphia hospital get a $14.5 million federal grant.

Eilberg's plea — which came as a surprise shortly after his trial began in Philadelphia — permanently barred him from holding federal office.

Under a deal worked out between Eilberg's attorney and federal prosecutors, the former congressman changed his plea to guilty and was sentenced to five years' probation and fined $10,000.

As part of his probation, Eilberg must perform six hours of unpaid community service every week. In addition, he cannot hold state or local office during the probation period.

Eilberg was originally indicted on one conflict of interest charge in October 1978, just two weeks before the congressional elections in which he was seeking his seventh House term.

The charges against Eilberg alleged that he received compensation from Hahnemann Medical College and Hospital in Philadelphia for help that he and fellow Pennsylvania Democrat Daniel J. Flood gave the hospital in getting the grant.

Rep. Charles C. Diggs Jr.

Rep. Charles C. Diggs Jr., D-Mich., was censured by the House July 31 for misuse of his clerk-hire funds.

The vote to censure Diggs was 414-0, with four members, including Diggs, voting present. The other three were Reps. Robert Garcia, D-N.Y., Augustus F. Hawkins, D-Calif., and Parren J. Mitchell, D-Md.

The House voted to censure Diggs (H Res 378) after rejecting a Republican-led move to force a vote on a separate resolution to expel him. The resolution (H Res 391) to expel Diggs was tabled — and thus killed — July 30 by a 205-197 vote. Twelve Republicans joined 193 Democrats in voting to table; 134 Republicans and 63 Democrats voted against tabling.

The close margin on the tabling vote wasn't a clear reflection of House sentiment on expulsion because, under the Constitution, a two-thirds majority is required to expel.

The disciplinary proceeding against Diggs marked only the second time in this century — and the first time in more than 50 years — that a House member was censured by his colleagues. The last person censured by the House was Thomas L. Blanton, D-Texas (1917-37), who was disciplined for having objectionable language printed in the *Congressional Record.* That was in 1921. *(Box, p. 172)*

Including Diggs, only 18 members and one delegate have been censured in the history of the House. Of the 17 members and one delegate censured by the House prior to Diggs, 10 were re-elected.

Background

Diggs had been sentenced Nov. 20, 1978, to a maximum of three years in prison for illegally diverting more than $60,000 of his congressional employees' salaries to his personal use. Diggs won re-election to a 13th term in the House Nov. 7, 1978.

Diggs was indicted March 23 on 35 charges of mail fraud (the mails allegedly were used in the salary kickback scheme) and making false statements to the government.

Diggs Censure Resolution

Resolved,

(1) that Representative Charles C. Diggs, Junior, be censured;

(2) that Representative Charles C. Diggs, Junior, forthwith present himself in the well of the House for the pronouncement of censure;

(3) that Representative Charles C. Diggs, Junior, be censured with the public reading of this resolution by the Speaker;

(4) that Representative Charles C. Diggs, Junior, is ordered to execute and deliver to the House an interest-bearing demand promissory note for $40,031.66, made payable to the Treasury of the United States;

(5) that Representative Charles C. Diggs, Junior, is ordered, for the remainder of the Ninety-sixth Congress, to require his employees to certify to the Committee on Standards of Official Conduct that the funds he or she receives from clerk-hire funds are received in full compliance with current House rules; and

(6) that the House of Representatives adopt the report of the Committee on Standards of Official Conduct dated July 19, 1979, In The Matter of Representative Charles C. Diggs, Junior.

Specifically, Diggs was accused of taking kickbacks from three of his congressional employees and putting three other persons on his congressional payroll who did no work for Congress. The three congressional staffers allegedly were given raises by Diggs with the stipulation that they use the extra money to help pay the congressman's debts.

The three persons who allegedly drew federal pay for no work were employees of Diggs' funeral home business in Detroit.

December Caucus Action

In December, the House Democratic Caucus voted to change its rules so that the full caucus would have to vote on whether Diggs or any other member convicted of a felony could retain a subcommittee chairmanship. Previously, only chairmen of Appropriations subcommittees were subject to a caucus vote. Diggs chaired a Foreign Affairs subcommittee.

But the caucus appeared satisfied with that mild rebuke, and it rejected what would have amounted to a more stringent punishment for Diggs. The rejected proposal would have automatically forced a member convicted of a crime with a two-year prison sentence to step down from a committee or subcommittee chairmanship.

Not considered at the December meetings was a proposal recommending that a member convicted of a felony carrying a two-year prison sentence should not vote in committee or in the House, even if the member were re-elected after the conviction.

That proposal, drafted by Rep. Peter H. Kostmayer, D-Pa., was not offered in December because "the climate did not seem favorable," said Kostmayer aide Ed Mitchell.

Early in 1979, Diggs dropped plans to seek re-election to the chairmanships of the House District of Columbia Committee and the Foreign Affairs Subcommittee on Africa.

Standards Committee Action

The House Committee on Standards of Official Conduct began a preliminary investigation of Diggs on Feb. 7, 1979. On April 4, the committee unanimously adopted a motion saying that it had "reason to believe" Diggs had committed 18 different violations of House rules.

The Standards Committee alleged Diggs violated House rules by placing two employees on his payroll without duties in order to have their salaries help pay some of his personal bills; inflating the salaries of three other employees to cover Diggs' personal and congressional expenses; and putting one employee on his congressional payroll though her duties were to work for Diggs' private business, the House of Diggs Funeral Home in Detroit, Mich.

Diggs, in a printed statement, criticized the panel for proceeding with the case while the federal conviction still was being appealed. The committee earlier had rejected a request that its investigation be delayed until after Diggs' appeals were exhausted.

Diggs and his attorneys had 21 days to respond to the charges. After the Standards Committee staff had 30 days to respond to Diggs' defense, the committee would have to vote on whether to proceed with hearings on the charges.

However, in a June 27 letter to the committee, Diggs admitted he violated House rules and agreed to be censured by his colleagues in return for ending the committee investigation.

In the letter, Diggs admitted he padded his office payroll and accepted kickbacks from five present and former employees, and agreed to repay the House $40,031.66 plus interest.

The Standards Committee June 29 voted 12-0 to accept Diggs' admission, end its investigation, and approve a resolution (H Res 378) recommending to the House that he be censured.

In recommending censure rather than expulsion, the committee explained in its July 19 report (H Rept 96-351) on the Diggs investigation that it had "considered his admission of guilt of serious offenses against the House rules, his apology to the House therefor, his agreement to make restitution of substantial amounts by which he was unjustly enriched, and the nature of the offenses charged."

Floor Action

The 414-0 vote on the censure resolution July 31 came after limited debate.

H Res 378 required that Diggs present himself in the well of the House and hear a public reading of the censure resolution by the House Speaker; that Diggs be required to give the House a note promising that he repay the $40,031.66 with interest, and that Diggs' employees be required to certify to the House for the remainder of the 96th Congress that the funds they receive from Diggs' clerk-hire allowance are received in full compliance with House rules. *(Text, above)*

Following the vote to approve the resolution, House Speaker O'Neill asked Diggs to stand and approach the rostrum. With a full House chamber looking on, O'Neill then read Diggs the censure resolution.

After he had finished reading, O'Neill rapped his gavel once and announced: "The matter is closed."

With that, Diggs turned and began walking out of the chamber.

Outside the House chamber, Diggs told reporters he expected to serve out the remainder of his term and would seek re-election in 1980.

During debate on the censure resolution, Standards Committee members argued that expulsion was too severe

Censure Proceedings in the House

Congress	Session	Year	Member	Grounds	Disposition
5th	2nd	1798	Matthew Lyon (Anti-Fed Vt.)	Assault on representative	Not censured
5th	2nd	1798	Roger Griswold (Fed Conn.)	Assault on representative	Not censured
22nd	1st	1832	William Stanbergy (D Ohio)	Insult to Speaker	*Censured*
24th	1st	1836	Sherrod Williams (Whig Ky.)	Insult to Speaker	Not censured
25th	2nd	1838	Henry A. Wise (Tyler Dem. Va.)	Service as second in duel	Not censured
25th	3rd	1839	Alexander Duncan (Whig Ohio)	Offensive publication	Not censured
27th	2nd	1842	John Q. Adams (Whig Mass.)	Treasonable petition	Not censured
27th	2nd	1842	Joshua R. Giddings (Whig Ohio)	Offensive paper	*Censured*
34th	2nd	1856	Henry A. Edmundson (D Va.)	Complicity in assault on senator	Not censured
34th	2nd	1856	Laurence M. Keitt (D S.C.)		*Censured*
36th	1st	1860	George S. Houston (D Ala.)	Insult to representative	Not censured
38th	1st	1864	Alexander Long (D Ohio)	Treasonable utterance	*Censured*
38th	1st	1864	Benjamin G. Harris (D Md.)	Treasonable utterance	*Censured*
39th	1st	1866	John W. Chanler (D N.Y.)	Insult to House	*Censured*
39th	1st	1866	Lovell H. Rousseau (R Ky.)	Assault on representative	*Censured*
40th	1st	1867	John W. Hunter (Ind N.Y.)	Insult to representative	*Censured*
40th	2nd	1868	Fernando Wood (D N.Y.)	Offensive utterance	*Censured*
40th	3rd	1868	E. D. Holbrook [1]	Offensive utterance	*Censured*
41st	2nd	1870	Benjamin F. Whittemore (R S.C.)	Corruption	*Censured*
41st	2nd	1870	Roderick R. Butler (R Tenn.)	Corruption	*Censured*
41st	2nd	1870	John T. Deweese (D N.C.)	Corruption	*Censured*
42nd	3rd	1873	Oakes Ames (R Mass.)	Corruption	*Censured*
42nd	3rd	1873	James Brooks (D N.Y.)	Corruption	*Censured*
43rd	2nd	1875	John Y. Brown (D Ky.)	Insult to representative	*Censured* [2]
44th	1st	1876	James G. Blaine (R Maine)	Corruption	Not censured
47th	1st	1882	William D. Kelley (R Pa.)	Offensive utterance	Not censured
47th	1st	1882	John D. White (R Ky.)	Offensive utterance	Not censured
47th	2nd	1883	John Van Voorhis (R N.Y.)	Offensive utterance	Not censured
51st	1st	1890	William D. Bynum (D Ind.)	Offensive utterance	*Censured*
67th	1st	1921	Thomas L. Blanton (D Texas)	Abuse of leave to print	*Censured*
96th	1st	1979	Charles C. Diggs, Jr. (D Mich.)	Misuse of clerk-hire funds	*Censured*

1. *Holbrook was a territorial delegate, not a representative.*
2. *The House later rescinded part of the censure resolution against Brown.*

Sources: Hinds and Cannon, *Precedents of the House of Representatives of the United States,* 11 vols. (1935-41); Joint Committee on Congressional Operations, *House of Representatives Exclusion, Censure and Expulsion Cases from 1789 to 1973,* committee print, 93rd Cong, 1st sess., 1973.

a penalty for Diggs' crimes. They pointed out that only three members have ever been expelled in the history of the House. In those cases, all of which took place in 1861 at the beginning of the Civil War, the expelled members were accused of treason, they noted.

The three expelled members were Reps. Henry C. Burnett, D-Ky. (1855-61), John B. Clark, D-Mo. (1857-61), and John W. Reid, D-Mo. (1861).

Standards Committee Chairman Charles E. Bennett, D-Fla., argued that members could reconsider Diggs' expulsion after the federal courts completed consideration of Diggs' appeal.

Richard B. Cheney, R-Wyo., stated that "most men in Mr. Diggs' position would have resigned." Even though Diggs chose not to resign, however, the House should not assume the burden of expelling him, he argued. To do so, he maintained, would deprive Diggs' constituents of their right to choose their elected representatives.

F. James Sensenbrenner Jr., R-Wis., said the House's adoption of the censure resolution would end a precedent holding that the House could not punish a member convicted of a crime prior to the member's re-election.

Rep. Louis Stokes, D-Ohio, commended the House for the "high quality of debate" on the resolution to censure Diggs, and the Standards Committee for the "conscientious job" it did in investigating Diggs.

Sen. Herman E. Talmadge

Sen. Herman E. Talmadge, D-Ga., one of the Senate's senior members, faced a number of charges in 1978 growing out of personal and political finances.

By the end of the year, Talmadge's finances were under investigation by a federal grand jury and by the Senate Select Ethics Committee. In December, the committee set in motion a trial-like process to determine what, if any, action should be taken on alleged wrongdoing by Talmadge. The committee said there was "substantial credible evidence" of possible improprieties by Talmadge.

Among the issues being investigated were charges that a former aide to Talmadge falsely obtained Senate funds and passed them on to the senator and his family.

Former Talmadge administrative assistant Daniel Minchew told *The Washington Star* in August that he had withdrawn Senate expense money, totaling almost $13,000, in Talmadge's name during 1973 and 1974. Minchew said he acted on Talmadge's instructions. He said the money went to the senator and his family.

The Star reported that a knowledgeable source who had reviewed Talmadge's financial records said the vouchers filed by Minchew were false. Talmadge said he never received any of the $13,000 and denied that Minchew acted on his orders. The grand jury and the Ethics Committee, both of which were looking into the matter, subpoenaed records from the Riggs National Bank in Washington, D.C., where Minchew deposited the money.

Senate Ethics Committee Action

It was not until late in the year that the Senate Ethics Committee decided to move to formal proceedings in the case. By a 4-1 vote Dec. 18, the committee decided to proceed into formal adjudicatory hearings.

The last ethics trial of a senator was in 1967 when then-Sen. Thomas Dodd, D-Conn., was censured after the Senate Select Committee on Standards and Conduct said he had used money raised at political affairs to pay personal bills.

In accordance with Senate and committee rules, Ethics Chairman Adlai E. Stevenson III, D-Ill., and Vice-Chairman Harrison Schmitt, R-N.M., sent the Georgia Democrat a letter specifying the charges that would be taken up at the hearing and a summary of supporting evidence.

The letter, later made public, indicated that the five charges to be considered by the committee were:

● Talmadge converted campaign contributions to personal use.

● Talmadge submitted false expense vouchers to the Senate for reimbursement of expenses that were never incurred.

● False reports of campaign receipts and expenditures were filed with the Senate secretary.

● Taxes on gifts of stock to Talmadge's ex-wife Betty were not reported.

● Gifts and property owned were not reported, as required, to the Senate.

One allegation, however, was not included in the committee's charges. Stevenson said that the panel could not find enough evidence to pursue charges that Talmadge had "committed any impropriety or violated any Senate rules" during various real estate transactions in Georgia.

Talmadge Opens Own Defense

In a dramatic and unexpected gesture, Talmadge on April 30, 1979, opened his own defense before the Senate Select Ethics Committee with a strong denunciation of his principal accuser.

Calling the bulk of the charges against him "trivial" and "petty," he appealed to his six colleagues on the ethics panel to use their common sense to conclude that the remainder of the charges — the "serious" ones — were untrue or the result of negligence.

Speaking forcefully, his voice sometimes strained with emotion, Talmadge acknowledged many of the basic facts concerning some of the charges against him. However, he disputed the significance that the committee's attorneys had given them in framing the charges.

Talmadge said he did not pay taxes on certain gifts of stock made to his wife because he owed no money on the gifts. He said his accountant had advised him that no taxes were due. "At most, it is an argument between account-

ants," he said. "I ask the committee to dismiss this allegation now and save us all much time and needless bother." Even if the Ethics Committee's attorneys are right, Talmadge said, "if I owed $1,070 in tax, this is still a minor matter."

He said a failure to file a campaign financial disclosure report for 1973 occurred because his staff had decided under Georgia law that he was not technically a candidate during that year. Errors in his 1974 report, which initially listed no campaign receipts or expenditures for the year, were due to "confusion" by staff, he said.

Though he was reimbursed "around $12,000" by his campaign committee in January 1975 for his 1974 expenses — a total not reported to the Federal Election Commission until 1978 — Talmadge told the ethics panel that "there is not the slightest basis for concluding that those errors were due to anything but inadvertence and confusion."

Talmadge, charged with failing to report the receipt of gifts, told Ethics Committee members he received "only a few" during the period 1970-76 — "around $1,000" — as well as a number of free plane rides. Evidence to be presented during the hearing concerning these gifts, he said, as well as a claim to ownership of stock in a company called Terminal Facilities Inc. — the subject of a court dispute with his former wife Betty — "will establish that there was no intent to conceal anything in this matter," he said.

Talmadge said the fact that he repaid the Senate more than $37,000 in 1978 for expenses that were claimed in prior years, but were not reimbursable under Senate rules, should put that charge to rest. He laid the improper claims to his staff.

Talmadge reserved his harshest words for former aide Daniel Minchew, who had accused the senator of ordering him to set up a secret bank account to convert Senate reimbursements and campaign contributions into cash for the personal use of the senator and family members. Talmadge called Minchew "a proven liar, cheat and embezzler." Talmadge said that when he first decided to order the independent audit of his finances — which ultimately led to his discovery of the secret account — Minchew had tried to talk him out of it.

"No reasonable person could believe that I would have ordered that independent audit if I had known about the Minchew account and the theft," Talmadge said. "Even my enemies don't claim that I'm stupid!" He implied the committee's attorneys had attempted to prejudice the case against him through "leaks" to the press.

Minchew Reliability Questioned

The second week of proceedings in the Talmadge case focused on the reliability of the senator's chief accuser, former aide Minchew. The committee heard additional testimony from a Talmadge aide who attempted to place blame on Minchew alone for diverting illegally claimed Senate expense funds to a secret Washington bank account. The committee also heard conflicting reports on Minchew's truthfulness from three lie detector examiners.

In testimony before the committee May 21-23, Minchew acknowledged that he had earlier participated in attempts to cover up Talmadge's involvement with the bogus bank account. But he said that his role was to provide the senator with "insulation" and "deniability" in case the scheme ever was uncovered.

"Let's keep this between us," he quoted Talmadge as telling him in June 1978 when investigators first began looking into allegations of financial misconduct being made against Talmadge in the press. He said he and Talmadge agreed at the time that a full investigation of the senator's finances would be dangerous, and that a "sanitizing" of the senator's records would be necessary in order to hide the secret account's existence.

He later learned, however, that a month after their talk Talmadge had gone to the Justice Department and labeled him an embezzler.

Ex-Wife Testimony

In a June 12 appearance before the committee, the senator's former wife, Betty, testified that the senator had for years kept a roll of cash — most of it in hundred dollar bills — in his overcoat pocket in a closet of their Washington residence. On at least one occasion, she said, the wad of bills in the overcoat may have totaled as much as $45,000. Both she and the senator drew regularly from the overcoat pocket "for years" to pay for their expenses, she testified. "It was a way of life for me" to live off money from the overcoat pocket, she said. "I did it often."

Talmadge Testimony

Reversing his earlier stand, Talmadge agreed to present a defense to the charges pending against him. His action followed a unanimous "request" from the Senate Select Ethics Committee that he testify under oath on the allegations the committee was investigating. After the committee's action, Talmadge said he would appear and present other evidence in his defense.

Talmadge June 19 said he would present no defense after the Ethics Committee refused to dismiss all the charges against him, as he had sought. Talmadge's lawyers argued the committee did not present enough evidence to show that Talmadge had done anything wrong.

However, the committee's attorney, Carl Eardley, argued that "there is more than enough evidence to require [Talmadge] to proceed with his proof" on four of the five charges made against him. Eardley indicated he would not object to dropping a fifth charge.

In a June 26 letter to the Ethics Committee, Talmadge said that he originally had decided not to present a formal defense in order to "avoid painful, private matters relating to my personal and family life." The committee's request that he testify, he said, had "made it impossible to do this."

He said the committee's decision not to dismiss the charges against him "in my view was wrong. I believe that in any court in the land the case would have been dismissed."

During two days of sworn testimony before the committee in July, Talmadge steadfastly maintained his innocence of all the charges against him and urged the panel to quickly conclude its investigation so he could "get on with my business." Talmadge's appearance concluded the committee hearings into the five charges of financial wrongdoing. The committee would then begin considering disciplinary action against the senator. Four of the committee's six members would have to approve any disciplinary recommendations.

In his appearance, Talmadge said all the charges against him were the result of staff errors or were caused by staff members acting without his knowledge.

In the face of stiff questioning from several committee members, he acknowledged that, as a senator, he took responsibility for his staff's mistakes. However, he added, "I assume no responsibility whatever for any crime committed by any subordinate."

At one point, Ethics Chairman Stevenson noted Talmadge had expressed no regret "for this whole sordid episode" and asked him point-blank if he felt any. "I am human," Talmadge responded. "I have made errors, and I am confident I will make errors in the future. But I have never used my office for profit and I never will."

"Let he who is without sin cast the first stone," Talmadge continued, quoting from the Bible. "I'm sure none of us has led exemplary lives. Please complete this as soon as you can so I can get on with my business."

Asked by reporters after the hearings whether he felt any contrition, Talmadge said: "I paid the Senate back $37,000. If that's not contrition, I don't know what is."

This was the money he repaid the Senate in 1978 for official Senate expenses that had never been incurred and for expenses that were not reimbursable under Senate rules.

During close questioning by committee lawyers on every detail of his office and personal finances, Talmadge insisted over and over that he had permitted his staff to handle his money and never questioned their work.

Even after evidence came to his attention of over-reimbursements, a secret bank account and diversions of campaign funds, Talmadge acknowledged, he made no effort to determine who was responsible for the erroneous acts and how they had come about.

"We assume personal responsibility for everything we do as a senator," Talmadge told his colleagues on the panel, "but you know and I know . . . that we must delegate certain of our responsibilities."

Talmadge also denied that he had possessed a substantial roll of hundred dollar bills during his marriage to Betty Talmadge, as his former wife had testified four weeks earlier.

His cash supply "at no time approached the huge amounts indicated by Mrs. Talmadge," Talmadge said. "At no time did I maintain a cash hoard in the pocket of an overcoat or anywhere else. In fact, I wore the overcoat apparently referred to by Mrs. Talmadge from time to time in 1973 and 1974, and still do."

Ethics Committee Action

Ending 15 months of investigation, the Ethics Committee Sept. 15, 1979, unanimously voted to denounce Talmadge, characterizing his conduct as "reprehensible." In using the recommendation of denouncement, the panel's resolution fell short of censure, the strongest action that could have been recommended. The last senator to be censured was the late Thomas J. Dodd, D-Conn. (1959-71), in 1967.

During its deliberations, the committee had rejected proposals to "condemn" or to "reprimand" the Georgia Democrat. Talmadge said that the committee's recommendation was a "personal victory." "There is no finding of intentional wrongdoing. There is no recommendation of censure," he said.

Following the panel's submission of its final report, the full Senate would have to act on the committee resolution to denounce Talmadge. ∎

Outside Earnings Swell Wealth of Congress

Senators think of themselves as members of the "upper chamber" of Congress. Their personal financial disclosures show that most senators are upper income as well.

The Senate clearly is a club of the wealthy. Possibly a third of the 100 senators in 1978 could claim net worths of $1 million or more. Moreover, two-thirds of the senators counted on outside incomes of $20,000 or more to supplement their $57,500 congressional salaries.

The House, too, had its share of wealthy members. Probably 30 or more House members in 1978 were millionaires, and nearly 100 had outside incomes of more than $20,000. But the House is the lower chamber of Congress when it comes to personal finances, because the proportion of wealthy members is much lower in the House than in the Senate.

In 1979, for the first time ever under the 1978 Ethics in Government Act, all members of Congress were required to publicly disclose their sources and general amounts of income for the previous year — 1978.

In 1978, members of both houses of Congress disclosed all their financial holdings for the first time. Previously, only House members had been required to disclose some of their financial interests.

The new disclosures revealed, in detail never before available, that most members of Congress are financially much better off than most Americans. Their $57,500 congressional salaries alone put them far above the economic state of most workers. But the difference goes beyond this: Most members of Congress would be financially secure with other income and financial interests even without their government salaries.

Financial Interests

With few exceptions, members of Congress were successful lawyers or businessmen before coming to Washington. Most members kept and expanded their lucrative

---

With few exceptions, members of Congress were successful lawyers or businessmen before coming to Washington. Most members kept and expanded their lucrative financial investments after election.

---

financial investments after election to Congress. Many of the wealthiest members of Congress, however, inherited their fortunes.

The personal financial interests of members of Congress spanned the world of business. But far and away the most prevalent were investments in real estate, banks and agriculture, and stocks in major businesses. Most popular among members were blue chip stocks such as IBM, General Electric, General Motors and American Telephone and Telegraph. Only three members reported stock holdings in the financially troubled Chrysler Corp.

All but a handful of members owned at least a few stocks or bonds, in addition to bank savings accounts and personal residences. The heaviest financial burden for many members was maintaining two residences: one in the home state or district, and one in the Washington, D.C., area. Some members rented their residences back home and stayed in hotels or with relatives when visiting constituents. In 1977, some members said that heavy expense helped justify the congressional pay raise from $44,600 to $57,500.

Outside Jobs

A dwindling number of members continued to receive sizable salaries for part-time jobs back home. But a new earned income limit in the House forced most of those members to abandon their jobs, or at least to seek new ways to receive the same income. Several members apparently have tried to avoid the income limit by changing their income from "salaries" to "dividends" or some other unearned income. *(Income limit, ethics story.)*

Although more than half of all members of Congress were lawyers by training, most have given up their private practices. *(See p. 185)*

Senate rules virtually prohibit legal practices by senators. Only 23 House members who served in Congress during 1978 actively practiced law. The new earned income limit in the House would force most of them to quit, or substantially curtail, their legal work.

At least three dozen members of Congress were partners in real estate investment firms, and 26 House members served as directors of banks or savings and loan associations.

Although few members devoted significant amounts of time to their outside jobs, some received large salaries.

Jack Brooks, D-Texas, for example, received more than $56,000 in salary as director of two banks in which he was a major stockholder. House Minority Leader John J. Rhodes, R-Ariz., was paid $32,573 as vice president of an insurance company.

Cecil (Cec) Heftel, D-Hawaii, reported earned income of $879,967 and unearned income of over $189,900 from various business investments.

Unearned Income

All but 75 House members and five senators supplemented their congressional incomes with "unearned" income such as dividends on stocks or rent from investment real estate in 1978.

Senators, on the average, received about $53,000 in unearned income during 1978. The average was boosted by the enormous unearned incomes of the Senate's wealthiest members. Ketchup and pickle heir John Heinz, R-Pa., reported unearned income of $437,101 to over $836,000. John C. Danforth, R-Mo., of the Ralston Purina Co. family, had unearned income of $230,801 to over $385,000.

House members, by and large, received much smaller unearned incomes, but 29 did have unearned incomes of at

Sen. John Heinz

Sen. John C. Danforth

Rep. Richardson Preyer

Rep. James T. Broyhill

Substantial Unearned Income

least $50,000. As in the Senate, members who inherited their wealth had the largest unearned incomes. For example, furniture heir James T. Broyhill, R-N.C., received over $133,000 from family investments and drug company heir Richardson Preyer, D-N.C., received over $123,000 from various holdings.

Honoraria

Seventy-five senators and 249 House members accepted "honoraria" payments for speeches to outside groups, usually lobbies interested in legislation. Nineteen well-known members and senior committee members received the $25,000 maximum in honoraria permitted by federal law. Unlike campaign contributions, honoraria payments are personal income for members of Congress. *(Honoraria background, p. 181)*

As in previous years, big lobbies such as the American Bankers Association, the Grocery Manufacturers of America and the Food Marketing Institute provided the bulk of honoraria. The bankers paid more than any other group, $28,000 to 16 members of Congress. Their interest probably was spurred by congressional consideration and passage in 1978 of a major banking regulation bill.

Conflicts of Interest

By the very nature of their positions, members of Congress face frequent conflicts of interest between their personal lives and their responsibilities in Congress. They are as affected by taxes and most other legislation as all Americans.

But there are other, potentially more serious conflicts, that involve members' particular personal finances and their roles as public servants. A member with substantial holdings in oil company stocks, for example, may have to reconcile his own financial interests with a wider but divergent public interest, especially if he serves on a committee that writes energy legislation.

Congress has taken few steps to curtail conflicts, on the assumption that it is up to each member, and his constituents, to judge what is proper. Many members of Congress have said that the disclosure of possible conflicts is a sufficient deterrent.

Many members have avoided direct conflicts of interest with their congressional committee assignments by declining to invest in businesses that might be affected by legislation before those committees.

But in a limited survey, Congressional Quarterly counted 54 senators and 105 House members who faced possible conflicts between their own holdings and committee assignments.

In most cases, the potential conflicts involved members with limited holdings that were infrequently affected by legislation. But some of the most prominent members of Congress dealt almost daily with legislation that could have a direct impact on their financial interests.

In the Senate, for example, Agriculture Committee Chairman Herman E. Talmadge, D-Ga., owned a 1,388-acre farm worth $1 million-$2 million. Other members of the committee with farm holdings were Richard G. Lugar, R-Ind., and John Melcher, D-Mont.

Talmadge was facing charges before the Senate Ethics Committee of improper financial dealings. But as of fall 1979, no conflict of interest charge had been raised.

Senate Finance Committee Chairman Russell B. Long, D-La., whose committee writes key energy tax legislation, owned $1.2 million in oil and gas property. His oil earnings in 1978 topped $100,000. Other members of his committee with oil holdings were: Lloyd M. Bentsen, D-Texas; Harry F. Byrd Jr., Ind-Va.; William V. Roth Jr., R-Del., Danforth and Heinz.

Danforth was an example of a wealthy member whose widespread financial interests were affected by virtually every bill before Congress. His personal and family trust portfolios included stocks in defense contractors, oil companies, communications firms, banks and several other businesses that are directly concerned with federal laws and regulations. Danforth sat on two committees — Finance and Commerce, Science and Transportation — that write much of the legislation that affects business.

Some committees were heavily weighted with members who had personal interests in legislation before those committees.

In the House, for example, 18 of the 43 members of the Agriculture Committee owned farms or other farm interests, including: Berkley Bedell, D-Iowa; David R. Bowen, D-Miss.; Glenn English, D-Okla.; Floyd Fithian, D-Ind.; Charles E. Grassley, R-Iowa; Tom Hagedorn, R-Minn.; Kent Hance, D-Texas; Jerry Huckaby, D-La.; James P. Johnson, R-Colo.; Ed Jones, D-Tenn.; Richard Kelly, R-Fla.; Ron Marlenee, R-Mont.; Charlie Rose, D-N.C.; Ike Skelton, D-Mo.; Steven D. Symms, R-Idaho; Charles W. Stenholm, D-Texas; James Weaver, D-Ore.; and Charlie Whitley, D-N.C.

One possible way of eliminating at least the appearance of a conflict of interest is to establish a blind trust, completely controlled by independent trustees. But few members have taken that step.

Senate Trims Future Disclosure Rules

With uncharacteristic speed and little forewarning, the Senate in August 1979 significantly trimmed back its financial disclosure requirements for senators and their top aides.

The change in the rules (S Res 220) was approved by the Senate Aug. 3 by a vote of 50-29.

Besides requiring less stringent disclosures, the rules change eliminated audits of senators' disclosure statements by the General Accounting Office (GAO) and sharply reduced — from 1,600 to 300 — the number of Senate aides that were required to file annual disclosure forms.

The change — proposed originally by Sen. Robert Morgan, D-N.C. — eliminated the disclosure requirements in Senate rule 42 and substituted for them the requirements of the 1978 Ethics in Government Act (PL 95-521). The disclosures required by the 1978 act are in almost every respect less detailed than the disclosures that had been required by Senate rule 42.

A parallel change was made by the House on the first day of the 96th Congress, with little public notice.

The net result of the changes would be to make it more difficult — beginning in 1980 — for the public to determine their elected representatives' financial status and interests, including the value of their biggest assets, the detailed holdings of their spouses and dependents; the existence and value of their personal residences; their real estate dealings, and many details of their personal liabilities.

The change was the second made in the Senate ethics code since its adoption in April 1977. In March 1979 the Senate put off for four years a limitation on the amount of outside income a senator could earn. *(Ethics codes, p. 153)*

Audits Stopped Immediately

Senators and their aides were required for the first time in May 1979 to file disclosure forms that met the requirements of both the Senate rule and the 1978 Ethics Act. The forms filed at that time covered senators' 1978 financial activities.

Because of the rules change, senators would be able to file the less detailed reports beginning in May 1980. The reports due at that time would cover senators' 1979 financial activities.

The Senate did not wait until 1980 to stop the GAO from auditing senators' disclosure forms, however.

Under Senate rule 42, the audits were to have been conducted on a random basis, so that every senator was audited at least once each six-year term, and 5 percent of all staff forms were audited each year.

Under the new rule, senators would be subjected to an audit only if the ethics panel ordered one "for cause."

Only one disclosure form covering 1977 financial activities was brought to the attention of the Ethics Committee because of a GAO audit, according to an Ethics Committee aide.

The old rule also required senators to furnish the GAO with copies of their income tax returns to help with the audits. Following the rules change, senators will no longer be required to furnish the GAO with copies of their tax returns.

The GAO spent about $400,000 in 1978 advising senators on how to fill out their disclosure forms, receiving and storing Senate tax returns and conducting Senate audits, according to a GAO official.

Other Differences

Other differences between the requirements of Senate rule 42 and the 1978 Ethics in Government Act which the Senate substituted for the rule centered on what was required to be disclosed and by whom, and how much information was required to be given. For example:

Spouses, Dependents Holdings. Under the Senate rule, the holdings of spouses and dependents as well as senators were to be disclosed according to categories of value up to "over $5 million." Under the government ethics law, however, the highest category of value was "in excess of $250,000."

Personal Residence. Under the rule, all real estate worth over $1,000 had to be disclosed. Under the law, the existence and value of personal residences did not have to be disclosed.

Real Estate Transactions. Under the rule, all real estate transactions exceeding $1,000 in value had to be disclosed. Under the law, real estate deals were not required to be reported.

Liabilities. Under the rule, every liability over $2,500 had to be disclosed. Under the law, only liabilities of over $10,000 had to be reported; further, a senator or aide did not have to disclose the existence or details of a mortgage for a personal residence or of a personal loan for a car, household furniture or appliances.

Only three senators had blind trusts: Edward M. Kennedy, D-Mass.; Abraham Ribicoff, D-Conn.; Howard M. Metzenbaum, D-Ohio. In the House, Margaret M. Heckler, R-Mass. and Steven J. Solarz, D-N.Y., said they had part of their holdings in blind trusts. The wife of Robert Dole, R-Kan., also had a blind trust.

Millionaires

Because the disclosure system is so vague, especially in the House, it is impossible to determine exactly how many millionaires serve in Congress. But it is possible to make a general determination of which members probably have net worths of $1 million or more.

The two wealthiest senators in 1978 were Heinz and Danforth. According to rough calculations based on their disclosures, Heinz could be worth at least $16 million and possibly more than $23 million. Danforth's net worth could be between $5 million and $17 million.

One senator, Louisiana's Long, revealed a net worth of $2.8 million.

Other senators who qualified as millionaires were: William L. Armstrong, R-Colo.; Bentsen of Texas; Rudy Boschwitz, R-Minn.; Byrd of Virginia.; Dennis DeConcini, D-Ariz.; John Glenn, D-Ohio; Barry Goldwater, R-Ariz.; S. I. (Sam) Hayakawa, R-Calif.; Nancy Landon Kassebaum, R-Kan.; Kennedy of Massachusetts; Howard

Top Honoraria Providers

Following is a list of the 15 organizations that gave the most in honoraria to members of Congress in 1978. The figures in parentheses indicate the number of senators and representatives who received honoraria from each group.

American Bankers Association (16)	$28,000
Grocery Manufacturers of America (18)	$20,750
Brookings Institution (57)	$16,900
Food Marketing Institute (13)	$16,000
General Electric Co. (11)	$15,494
U. S. Chamber of Commerce (26)	$14,935
Pfizer Inc. (18)	$14,285
Outdoor Advertising Association (12)	$14,200
AFL-CIO (9)	$12,500
United Jewish Appeal (8)	$12,000
Brown & Williamson Tobacco Co. (8)	$10,500
Mortgage Bankers Association (6)	$10,500
Washington Discussion Group (11)	$10,500
Distilled Spirits Council (10)	$10,285
American Mining Congress (12)	$10,000

M. Metzenbaum, D-Ohio; Claiborne Pell, D-R.I.; Charles H. Percy, R-Ill.; Richard Stone, D-Fla.; Talmadge of Georgia; Malcolm Wallop, R-Wyo.; John W. Warner, R-Va.; and Lowell P. Weicker Jr., R-Conn.

Other senators who might qualify as millionaires included: Howard H. Baker Jr., R-Tenn.; Henry L. Bellmon, R-Okla.; Bill Bradley, D-N.J.; Howard W. Cannon, D-Nev.; Lawton Chiles, D-Fla.; Thomas F. Eagleton, D-Mo.; Mark O. Hatfield, R-Ore.; Charles McC. Mathias, R-Md.; Sam Nunn, D-Ga.; Ribicoff of Connecticut; and Adlai E. Stevenson, D-Ill.

Two financially secure, but non-millionaire, senators listed their exact net worths: Daniel Patrick Moynihan, D-N.Y. ($350,000) and Ernest F. Hollings, D-S.C. ($437,163).

The richest House member probably was Fred Richmond, D-N.Y., who was the majority stockholder in Walco National Corp., a manufacturer of small machinery and electrical equipment. Richmond owned approximately 748,000 shares of stock, worth more than $16 million.

Other probable House millionaires were: Glenn M. Anderson, D-Calif.; Jonathan B. Bingham, D-N.Y.; Richard Bolling, D-Mo.; Brooks of Texas; Broyhill of North Carolina; Tim Lee Carter, R-Ky.; James C. Cleveland, R-N.H.; James M. Collins, R-Texas; Robert W. Daniel Jr., R-Va.; Millicent Fenwick, R-N.J.; Bill Green, R-N.Y.; Heftel of Hawaii; Robert J. Lagomarsino, R-Calif.; Jim Leach, R-Iowa; Stewart B. McKinney, R-Conn.; Richard L. Ottinger, D-N.Y.; Preyer of North Carolina; James H. (Jimmy) Quillen, R-Tenn.; William H. Royer, R-Calif.; Harold Runnels, D-N.M.; Harold S. Sawyer, R-Mich.; James H. Scheuer, D-N.Y.; and Fortney H. (Pete) Stark, D-Calif.

Other House members who could be millionaires included: Bedell of Iowa; William E. Dannemeyer, R-Calif.; Robert H. Mollohan, D-W.Va.; Bill Nelson, R-Fla.; Ray Roberts, D-Texas; Gene Snyder, R-Ky.; James Weaver, D-Ore.

The Non-Wealthy

In contrast to the millionaires, a handful of members of Congress reported little or no outside income and virtually nothing in the way of financial assets.

Sen. Spark M. Matsunaga, D-Hawaii, for example, said he had no outside business earnings, aside from $7,000 in honoraria. His sole financial interest was his house in Washington, D.C., purchased in 1965 for $56,000.

Les Aspin, D-Wis., said he had no outside business earnings and no financial interests. He did accept $3,050 in honoraria payments.

Generally, the least wealthy members were young House members in their first or second terms. An example was David E. Bonior, D-Mich., a Vietnam veteran in his second term, who reported no outside income and no holdings.

Spouses

Congressional rules require members to disclose the financial interests of their spouses, unless they do not benefit from or maintain control over their spouses' holdings. Members also were required to reveal the sources, but not the amounts, of their spouses' incomes.

Although most members did disclose information about their spouses, a few refused to do so. Senators, but not House members, were asked to indicate if they withheld information about their spouses.

One senator who refused to disclose the financial assets of his spouse was John Tower, R-Texas. He said, "I have no knowledge whatever" of the estate of his reportedly wealthy wife Lilla Cummings Tower, whom he married in 1977.

Virginia's senator, Warner, said he had no control over the property of his wife, actress Elizabeth Taylor. Warner was a millionaire by virtue of a divorce settlement with his previous wife, heiress Catherine Mellon.

Other senators who did not report the holdings of their spouses were Wendell H. Ford, D-Ky. and Jacob K. Javits, R-N.Y.

The wives of at least five members were congressional staff aides. Four worked directly for their husbands.

Elsie J. Hawkins, the wife of Rep. Augustus F. Hawkins, D-Calif., worked for her husband in two paying jobs. As a clerk on his personal staff, she earned approximately $3,624 in 1978, according to clerk of the House records. She earned approximately $22,200 as a clerk for the House Administration Committee's printing subcommittee, which Hawkins chaired.

Martha A. Ford, the wife of Rep. William D. Ford, D-Mich., was an assistant clerk for the House Administration Committee. She earned $12,000 in that post in 1978, according to House records. Ford was not a member of the committee.

Vyonne Rousselot was executive secretary on the staff of her husband, Rep. John H. Rousselot, R-Calif. According to Clerk of the House records, she was paid at the rate of $22,600 in 1978.

Jeanette S. Williams was a senior staff member on the Senate Labor and Human Resources Committeee, chaired by her husband, Harrison A. Williams Jr., D-N.J. She earned $33,500 in 1978, according to Senate records.

Patricia B. Young was executive secretary on the staff of her husband, Sen. Milton R. Young, R-N.D. Young reported her 1978 earnings as $24,677.

Ford and Rousselot did not mention their wives on their financial disclosure forms.

The federal anti-nepotism law, adopted in 1967, prohibits federal officials, including members of Congress, from appointing, promoting or recommending for appointment or promotion, a relative to serve in the same agency or department. However, the law does not prohibit a member

Top Honoraria Collectors in Senate and House

Senate

The 1976 Federal Election Campaign Act limited to $25,000 annually the amount a senator could earn in honoraria for speeches and articles. But it said a senator could earn over $25,000 if he used some of his earnings to defray out-of-pocket expenses or donated a portion to charity. In 1978, the top 25 earners of honoraria in the Senate were:

Richard G. Lugar, R-Ind.	$38,500*
Jake Garn, R-Utah	$27,814*
Howard H. Baker Jr., R-Tenn.	$27,750*
Daniel Patrick Moynihan, D-N.Y.	$27,388*
Robert Dole, R-Kan.	$27,000*
Jacob K. Javits, R-N.Y.	$26,085**
Robert C. Byrd, D-W.Va.	$25,000
Ernest F. Hollings, D-S.C.	$25,000
Henry M. Jackson, D-Wash.	$25,000*
Edmund S. Muskie, D-Maine	$25,000*
William Proxmire, D-Wis.	$25,000
Harrison A. Williams Jr., D-N.J.	$25,000
George McGovern, D-S.D.	$24,995
Frank Church, D-Idaho	$24,975
Alan Cranston, D-Calif.	$24,926
John C. Culver, D-Iowa	$24,924
Orrin G. Hatch, R-Utah	$24,875
Herman E. Talmadge, D-Ga.	$24,750
Richard S. Schweiker, R-Pa.	$24,749
Donald W. Riegle Jr., D-Mich.	$24,632
J. Bennett Johnston, D-La.	$24,350
Barry Goldwater, R-Ariz.	$24,250
Joseph R. Biden Jr., D-Del.	$24,009
Bob Packwood, R-Ore.	$24,000
Abraham Ribicoff, D-Conn.	$23,760**

Senator donated all or a portion of his honoraria to charity.
**Senator used a portion of his honoraria to defray out-of-pocket expenses.*

House

The 1976 Federal Election Campaign Act limited to $25,000 annually the amount a representative could earn by giving speeches or writing articles. In 1978, the top 25 House earners of honoraria were:

Thomas L. Ashley, D-Ohio	$25,000
James C. Corman, D-Calif.	$25,000
Ken Holland, D-S.C.	$25,000
John M. Murphy, D-N.Y.	$25,000
Dan Rostenkowski, D-Ill.	$25,000
Al Ullman, D-Ore.	$25,000
Guy Vander Jagt, R-Mich.	$25,000
Jack F. Kemp, R-N.Y.	$24,950
Henry S. Reuss, D-Wis.	$24,950
Jim Wright, D-Texas	$24,750
Philip M. Crane, R-Ill.	$24,450
John J. Rhodes, R-Ariz.	$24,220
Thomas P. O'Neill Jr., D-Mass.	$23,500
John D. Dingell, D-Mich.	$19,190
Shirley Chisholm, D-N.Y.	$18,983
Morris K. Udall, D-Ariz.	$18,022
Barry M. Goldwater Jr., R-Calif.	$16,800
Frank Thompson Jr., D-N.J.	$16,800
William D. Ford, D-Mich.	$16,450
Bob Eckhardt, D-Texas	$16,300
John Conyers Jr., D-Mich.	$15,566
Thomas S. Foley, D-Wash.	$15,000
John J. LaFalce, D-N.Y.	$14,900
Henry J. Hyde, R-Ill.	$14,828
Jim Santini, D-Nev.	$14,750

from marrying a staffer and keeping his spouse on his payroll.

Compliance

Although most members generally complied with the letter and spirit of the disclosure rules, a few members in each house filed disclosure forms that were seriously incomplete, inaccurate or misleading.

Ethics committees in both houses attempted to correct the most serious errors, but committee aides admitted they did not have the time or staff to strictly enforce the rules. The Senate voted in March to discontinue GAO spot audits of forms filed by senators and their top aides.

Some members voluntarily revealed much more than the rules required. Rep. Morris K. Udall, D-Ariz., revealed his entire 1978 federal income tax form. Rep. Paul Simon, D-Ill., continued his longstanding practice of disclosing in detail his finances and those of all his aides.

Honoraria Payments

Members of Congress were paid almost $2.3 million in 1978 by businesses, trade associations, educational and ideological groups, publications and other organizations eager to hear the members' insider views on issues facing the federal government.

Of the total honoraria payments, $1,086,451 went to 75 senators and about $1,180,000 to 249 representatives, according to financial disclosure forms filed by all 100 senators, all 435 voting representatives, the resident commissioner representing Puerto Rico, and the three non-voting House delegates.

Twenty-five senators and 190 House members reported receiving no honoraria for speaking engagements or writing fees in 1978.

The total paid senators in 1978 was just slightly less than the record for honoraria payments set in 1977. In that year, 81 senators earned $1,087,638 in honoraria, while 19 reported receiving none.

Senators have been required to disclose their earnings from honoraria since 1969.

The slight decrease in 1978 probably was due to 20 senators leaving office at the end of that year. Those senators were not required to file details of their 1978 finances with the Senate. But the 20 freshmen who took their seats at the beginning of 1979 were. As candidates

What Members of Congress Must Disclose

Representatives

• For members: The source and exact amount of earned income (including honoraria and date received) aggregating $100 or more during the 1978 calendar year. For spouses and dependents: The source of income of $1,000 or more; the exact amount wasn't required.

• The source and category of value of unearned income in excess of $100 for member, spouse and dependents. Included were interest, dividends, royalties, capital gains, trusts and other financial arrangements. The value categories for unearned income were: $101-$1,000; $1,001-$2,500; $2,501-$5,000; $5,001-$15,000; $15,001-$50,000; $50,001-$100,000; and over $100,000.

• The source and a brief description of gifts of transportation, food, lodging or entertainment aggregating $250 or more in value in calendar year 1978 for the member, spouse or dependent. Exempted were gifts from relatives, gifts of personal hospitality, and any gift received by spouse or dependents totally unrelated to their relationship to the reporting individual.

• The source and a brief description of gifts other than transportation, food, lodging or entertainment aggregating $100 or more from any source during 1978. Any individual gift valued at less than $35 did not have to be reported.

• The source and a brief description of reimbursements received from any source aggregating $250 or more in value during calendar year 1978 for a member, spouse or dependent. Excluded were reimbursements received by spouse or dependents totally unrelated to their relationship to the reporting individual.

• Real and personal property held, including trusts, with a fair market value exceeding $1,000 on Dec. 31. Property had to be identified by the category of value.

• Total liabilities owed to any creditor which exceeded $10,000 at any time during 1978. Liabilities must be identified by the appropriate category of value.

• The purchase, sale or exchange of real property, stocks, bonds, commodities futures or securities which exceeded $1,000 during 1978. Property must be identified by the category of value.

• The value categories for property, liabilities and transactions were: $1,001-$5,000; $5,001-$15,000; $15,001-$50,000; $50,001-$100,000; $100,001-$250,000; and over $250,000.

• Positions as an officer, director, trustee, partner, employee, consultant, etc. of any institution.

• Agreements and arrangements for future employment or continuation of benefits by a former employer.

Senators

(1978 requirements; 1979 change p. 177)

• The source, amount, services rendered and date of each honorarium received during the calendar year 1978 and which, if any, were donated to charity.

• The exact amount and each source of earned income exceeding $100 during 1978 for self, spouse and dependents. Earned income includes wages, salaries and other fees for services.

• The source and a brief description of each reimbursement aggregating $250 or more during calendar year 1978. It was not necessary to report the exact amount of the reimbursement. Included were reimbursements to the senator's spouse where the reimbursement was not totally independent of the spouse's relationship to the senator.

• The source and category of value of each item of unearned income in excess of $100 for the senator, spouse and dependents. Included in this section were interest, dividends and royalties, capital gains, rental income, distributive shares of partnership income, and distributions from estates and trusts. The value categories for unearned income were: not more than $1,000; $1,001-$2,500; $2,501-$5,000; $5,001-$15,000; $15,001-$50,000; $50,001-$100,000; and over $100,000.

• The source, value and a brief description of all gifts, worth $100 or more, received by the senator, spouse or dependents from any one source during 1978. Individual gifts valued at less than $35 didn't have to be reported.

• The source, value and a brief description of all gifts of transportation, lodging, food or entertainment received by the senator, spouse and dependents during the calendar year aggregating $250 or more.

• Interest in real property held directly or indirectly at any time during the calendar year that had a fair market value in excess of $1,000. For each property, a brief description and location and the value category had to be provided.

• Personal property held directly or indirectly for the production of income and having a fair market value in excess of $1,000 at any time during the calendar year.

The categories for real and personal property values were: not more than $5,000; $5,001-$15,000; $15,001-$50,000; $50,001-$100,000; $100,001-$250,000; $250,001-$500,000; $500,0001-$1 million; $1 million-$2 million; $2 million-$5 million; and over $5 million.

• Liabilities owed directly or indirectly by the senator, spouse or dependents which exceeded $2,500 at any time during the year, except obligations to relatives.

• Transactions in securities or commodities futures.

• The purchase, sale or exchange of real property by the senator, spouse or dependents where the value of the property exceeded $1,000. Also the date of the transaction and the property's category of value.

• Patent rights held by the senator, spouse or dependents at any time during the 1978 calendar year.

• Agreements for future employment or continuation of payments or benefits to the senator only.

Spouses and Dependents

Members of both houses had to report property holdings for spouses and dependents except for those holdings:

a) which the member certified represented the spouse's or dependent's sole financial reponsibility and which the member had no knowledge of;

b) which were not in any way, past or present, derived from the income, assets or activities of the member; or

c) from which the member neither derived, nor expected to derive, any economic benefit.

during 1978, these individuals couldn't command the high speaking fees normally given incumbent senators.

Because 1978 was the first full year for which House members were required to disclose their honoraria payments, no figures for earlier years are available for comparison purposes.

Time-Honored Practice

The payment of honoraria is a time-honored way to entice representatives and senators to provide various groups with an "insider view" of Washington through speeches, personal appearances or published articles. In addition to the honoraria, members of Congress often receive expenses-paid trips to the sites where the speeches are given, as well as lodging and meals.

Most of the honoraria payments are in return for speeches to conventions held by trade associations and other business groups. Others are for briefings or addresses to educational groups, ideological organizations, religious and ethnic groups and think tanks.

Some are for intimate meetings over dinner or lunch with a corporation's board of directors, or a small group of businessmen, lawyers and lobbyists such as the Washington Discussion Group. These small groups say a meal and a chat with a prominent senator or representative is worth the $1,000 or $2,000 payment because of the opportunity it provides for an off-the-record discussion of Washington goings-on.

Honoraria are perfectly legal, but most of the groups that provide such payments also are interested in legislation before Congress. The most harsh critics of honoraria payments say the system is little more than legalized influence buying. Less harsh critics contend that the groups making the payments are more interested in gaining the friendship of elected officials, and easy access to them in the future, than in hearing the comments of the senators and representatives.

Organizations that give honoraria — and members of Congress who accept them — deny any impropriety.

Many freely admit, however, that inviting a member of Congress to address a company's board of directors or a trade association's annual meeting — and paying him for his appearance — can have important benefits. It can give top management a better understanding of the Washington scene, provide an occasion to get to know an important member, or ensure better access to the member in the future. It also can be used to let the member know that he has a supporter on the "outside."

Groups Target Payments

An examination of the honoraria paid members of Congress in 1978 indicates that interest groups often concentrated their payments on members in a position to help them with their concerns. This is the pattern that has been present in other years, also. For example, the Outdoor Advertising Association gave a total of $7,000 in honoraria to five members of the Senate Environment and Public Works Committee which in 1978 rewrote the Highway Beautification Act of 1965, weakening key provisions regulating outdoor advertising.

While the House Ways and Means Health Subcommittee considered hospital cost containment legislation, its chairman, Rep. Dan Rostenkowski, D-Ill., received $14,000 in honoraria from health groups.

The American Bankers Association funneled five honoraria totaling $10,500 to five Democratic members of the House Banking Committee in 1978, while five state banking associations provided one senator alone — Jake Garn, R-Utah, ranking Republican on the Senate Banking Committee — with $8,000 in honoraria for five different speeches.

The Banking committees worked on a number of major revisions in federal legislation regulating banking practices during 1978.

Banking Industry Honoraria

Banking groups gave heavily in 1978. The American Bankers Association gave more honoraria to members of Congress than any other group during that year, paying out a total of $28,000 to 16 different senators and representatives. At the same time, various state banking associations paid out $20,100 to 17 different senators and representatives in the same period.

"We hold over 300 meetings a year," commented Edward F. Smith, a spokesman for the American Bankers Association, explaining why his group gives honoraria to members of Congress. "You can't get away with always using only [the trade association's] staff. You need a big name. And you can't ask them to take time off and not give them something."

Smith said the association seeks out members of the congressional banking and tax committees to address its meetings because those members are most familiar with the industry's legislative concerns. He added that the association was proud of its record on honoraria payments.

"We're not opposed to it [paying honoraria]," he said. "We're not like some trade associations who try to hide under a bushel. I'm glad we're on top. I'm only sorry we don't have more money to spend on this."

Informing Management

Two companies that only began in 1978 to pay members of Congress for speaking engagements told Congressional Quarterly they did so to keep their firms' managers informed of important Washington activities.

One firm, Rexnord Inc., a Milwaukee, Wis., manufacturing company, paid out $1,585 in 1978 to four members of Congress for addressing Washington seminars. The sessions were set up to educate management on "how the process works," according to company spokesman John Bartels. A fifth member of Congress was paid $1,000 plus travel expenses to address the firm's annual meeting.

Bartels said the company had been holding Washington seminars for at least five years, but before 1978 had

Sen. Spark M. Matsunaga   **Rep. Les Aspin**

The Unwealthy in Congress

brought company officials to the Capitol to meet with members. In 1978, the company decided to invite the members it wanted to meet to dinner. The dinners were intended "to get to know them better," Bartels said. They were paid honoraria because to leave the Capitol in order to attend was "overtime," he said.

The Dana Corp., a Toledo, Ohio, automotive parts manufacturing firm, also paid out honoraria to members of Congress for the first time in 1978. The firm paid $6,500 to eight members for the year. The members were paid to address a Washington seminar for Dana's middle management, according to the firm's Washington vice president, Howard Haugerud.

"Many people believe government workers are not the swiftest in the world," Haugerud explained. "It's important for our employees to see that, in the upper echelons, at least, this is not the case."

Honoraria Limitations

The 1976 Federal Election Campaign Act (PL 94-283) limited to $25,000 annually the amount of money a senator or representative could earn in honoraria in a year. The law also limited each individual honorarium payment to a maximum of $2,000.

A stricter limitation on the amount of money a senator may earn in outside income was to have gone into effect in 1979, but the Senate voted in March to delay enforcement of that rule for four years.

A similar House rule was unaffected by the Senate action. The House rule placed a ceiling of 15 percent of a representative's annual salary on all outside earned income — including honoraria — and a ceiling of $1,000 on each individual honorarium, beginning Jan. 1, 1979.

The House approved the 15 percent cap and a ceiling of $750 on each honorarium as part of its ethics code, adopted in 1977. However, the $750 limit was raised to $1,000 in January 1979 after the House Democratic Caucus recommended the increase at the end of the 95th Congress.

At the existing annual salary of $57,500, the limitation meant that, as of 1979, a representative could earn no more than $8,625 a year in outside income, including honoraria. In 1978, 45 representatives and 48 senators earned more than $8,625 in honoraria alone.

1978 Honoraria Champion

Sen. Richard G. Lugar, R-Ind., was the honoraria champion in both House and Senate in 1978, earning $38,500. He donated $13,500 of his honoraria earnings to charity in order to comply with the $25,000 limitation.

"We're aware that he was No. 1, but he's still here for every vote," commented Lugar spokesman Lou Gerig. He said Lugar ranked third in attendance in the Senate in 1978, and gave no outside speeches on Senate time.

The 1976 law permits members to deduct any funds donated to charity or used to pay for out-of-pocket expenses from their total honoraria earnings in order to comply with the $25,000 limitation.

In 1978, six senators — Lugar, Jake Garn, R-Utah, Howard H. Baker Jr., R-Tenn., Daniel Patrick Moynihan, D-N.Y., Robert Dole, R-Kan., and Jacob K. Javits, R-N.Y. — earned more than $25,000 in honoraria and either donated some of the money to charity or used some of it for expenses related to speech-giving in order to comply with the $25,000 ceiling.

Javits stated in his financial disclosure report that, in order to comply with the $25,000 ceiling, he had deducted

some money from his total speechmaking earnings to pay members of his staff who "in non-working hours helped me with the speeches and writings that earned the honoraria."

This deduction is not permitted by the 1976 law. Spokesmen for both the Senate Select Ethics Committee and the Federal Election Commission refused to discuss the matter.

Javits' executive assistant, Gregory G. Jones, told a reporter the senator's accountants felt the deduction was proper. He added: "If we are advised that it is improper by either the Ethics Committee or the Federal Election Commission, then we will do anything that is necessary to clean it up."

In all, 13 senators and six representatives donated all or a portion of their honorarium income to charity in 1978.

Members donating all their honoraria to charity were Sens. Henry M. Jackson, D-Wash. ($25,000), Howard M. Metzenbaum, D-Ohio ($500), Claiborne Pell, D-R.I. ($3,200), Strom Thurmond, R-S.C. ($5,550), and Reps. Carlos J. Moorhead, R-Calif. ($1,000), and Mary Rose Oakar, D-Ohio ($3,146).

No Limit on Number

Though members were limited by the 1976 election law to $2,000 for any one speaking engagement, some members managed to earn more than $2,000 from one source by making repeat appearances.

Javits, for example, was paid a total of $8,000 for four speeches to Touche Ross & Co., an accounting firm. Lugar was paid $4,000 for two speeches to the U. S. League of Savings Associations. Rep. Guy Vander Jagt, R-Mich., was paid $3,000 by Dow Chemical Co. for three speeches, while Rep. James J. Howard, D-N.J., was paid $3,000 for three speeches to the American Public Transit Association.

Overall, senators drew larger speaking fees than House members, probably because of greater national fame.

Although the total paid all senators in honoraria was slightly less in 1978 than in 1977, the average amount earned by those senators accepting honoraria increased to about $14,600 in 1978 from about $13,400 in 1977. For House members, the average amount earned by those accepting honoraria was $4,700 in 1978.

Spouse or Aide Often Invited

A side benefit often provided members delivering speeches is an invitation to take along one's spouse or staff aide at no personal expense.

Sen. Paul Laxalt, R-Nev., for example, took his wife with him on trips to Albuquerque, Des Moines, Las Vegas, Los Angeles (twice), Phoenix and Reno (four times) in 1978, according to his financial disclosure form. In each case, her travel expenses were paid for by the groups he addressed. The Laxalts' home was in Reno.

Howard W. Cannon, D-Nev., reported accepting payment for his wife's travel expenses on four different speechmaking trips to Las Vegas in 1978. The Cannons' home was in Las Vegas.

S. I. (Sam) Hayakawa, R-Calif., reported taking along aides on speechmaking trips to Providence, Miami, Tuscaloosa, Los Angeles (twice), San Francisco (twice), Albuquerque, Columbus, Kansas City, Tucson, Jacksonville, Fresno and Palm Springs in 1978. Most of the trips were to make campaign speeches for other Republican office-seekers.

Speechmaking trips can lead a member and his spouse far from home, often to glamorous vacation spots. James A.

Disclosure That Doesn't Disclose

The extensive disclosure requirements imposed on Congress in recent years have given voters more information than ever before about the financial dealings and personal wealth of elected representatives.

But, ironically, the methods of disclosure can distort the true picture of a member's wealth; moreover, the structure of the disclosure forms, in certain cases, presents an open invitation for members to obfuscate or to conceal information.

These problems make an exact calculation of a member's net worth impossible unless the individual voluntarily supplies additional information.

Several members have been doing this for years, most notably Rep. Paul Simon, D-Ill., who released his 24th annual public financial disclosure statement in 1979. It has been his practice since first taking public office in 1955 as a member of the Illinois state House.

Rep. Philip M. Crane, R-Ill., a presidential hopeful, filed a statement over 100 pages in length. Sen. Claiborne Pell, D-R.I., released 67 pages of financial information, the most lengthy disclosure statement in the Senate.

Categories of Value

The financial disclosure rules require a member to reveal the "category of value" owned by him or his spouse and dependents. Each category represents a "range" of wealth and not an actual amount. Examples are: "between $15,001-$50,000" and "between $100,001-$250,000." *(Box, p. 180)*

The misleading nature of the categories can be shown in the disclosure of Sen. Russell B. Long, D-La., who listed all his income and holdings, and voluntarily showed a net worth of $2,817,731. Using the categories, however, Long's net worth could be anywhere between $2,127,000 and $4,760,000.

Walter (Dee) Huddleston, D-Ky., gave the exact amount of his unearned income as $14,901. Using the categories, his income could be $12,301 to $38,000.

For most members, the most serious distortion was in the $15,001-$50,000 category.

If a member had three holdings of about $16,000 each, the actual total would be $48,000. But under the category system, those three would total $45,000-$150,000.

Another distortion inherent in the category system was the largest category value. In the House it was over $250,000; in the Senate it was over $5 million.

Rep. Fred Richmond, D-N.Y., reported his holdings in Walco National Corp. as "over $250,000," which is all that is required by law for House members. Richmond held 750,000 shares of stock in Walco National in 1977, and sold 2,000 shares in June 1978, leaving him with 748,000 shares. At current stock market value in 1979, his financial interest in Walco National should be about $16.5 million — or $16.25 million more than he was required to disclose.

Problems With the Forms

The structure of the disclosure forms also permitted errors.

The House forms for 1978 were short on space for anything but the most minuscule of holdings for an individual member. The instructions were short on detail and briefly printed on the reverse side of each member's disclosure cover sheet. House Ethics Committee staffers were deluged with questions on procedures for filling out the forms.

On the other hand, the Senate Ethics Committee published a 43-page manual for senators and employees, and received far fewer procedural questions.

The different forms allowed the accuracy of information to vary, especially the value of financial interests.

The Ethics in Government Act requires members to disclose "the current value" of their real property holdings unless the current value "is not ascertainable without an appraisal."

If the latter case is true, members could use different calculation methods to determine the value, providing the method used is explained.

Because of limited space on the House forms and the brevity of instructions, information about real property holdings was more likely to be reported at fair market value than through other methods.

The Senate forms provided a separate column for senators to list the method used to value their property. This appeared to invite senators not to report the current value.

Hence, Sen. Long reported an interest in "133 acres of timberland, Winn Parish, La." at a value of "not more than $5,000, purchase price in 1935."

The county assessor's office in Winn Parish, La., told a reporter that timberland there was valued between $500 and $750 per acre. This suggests that the 1979 value of Long's timberland might be between $66,500 and $100,000. If the timber on the land is top quality southern pine, the value could be as high as $1,500 per acre, which means Long's holding could be worth as much as $200,000.

Long also reported 800 acres of timberland in Livingston, La., at a 1935 purchase price of $36,246. Based on the U.S. Forest Service assessment that virtually no timberland in the United States today is worth less than $300 per acre, 800 acres would be worth at least $240,000 and could be worth over $1 million.

Although this avenue of disclosing as little as possible was open to all members, few took advantage of it. Only six senators listed most of their real estate holdings at acquisition cost.

Filling out the Forms

Some members simply filled out the forms incorrectly or incompletely.

Several, such as Rep. Harold Runnels, D-N.M., reported income from dividends but listed no stockholdings. Rep. Charles Wilson, D-Texas, reported rental income without listing an interest in real property.

The winner of the "most illegible handwriting award" in 1979 went to freshman Rep. Ron Paul, R-Texas, who filled out his form himself in longhand. Paul is a doctor.

McClure, R-Idaho, for example, was able to take his wife along with him on a speechmaking trip to Honolulu at the expense of the National Association of Realtors. Bob Packwood, R-Ore., had his wife's way paid to Tel Aviv by the American Jewish Committee in return for a speech by the senator.

Outside Income

Members of Congress each year are paid $57,500 from the U.S. Treasury — and all but a handful have outside sources of income to help them meet expenses.

In lists compiled by Congressional Quarterly showing the outside incomes members reported for 1978, only two senators and 16 House members reported no income from outside businesses, speechmaking or investments. Another 19 House members reported outside incomes of less than $1,000.

The lists included freshmen members who were not serving in Congress in 1978.

Generally, the lists showed:

● House members were more likely than senators to have earned income from outside jobs;

● Senators, many of whom are nationally known, take home substantially more money in honoraria from speechmaking than House members; and

● Virtually all members of Congress have at least a few thousand dollars in unearned income from stocks, savings or other investments.

With a little imagination, a few House members have found that they needn't make any financial sacrifice in order to comply with a new limit on their outside earnings that went into effect in January 1979.

Many others, however, took substantial pay cuts in order to comply with the limit.

But an examination of financial disclosure reports for 1978 shows that even with the cuts in outside pay, a number of representatives in 1979 could be capitalizing on loopholes in the new House rule in order to comply with the letter but not the spirit of the new limitations. The rule was intended to limit members' outside business activities and potential conflicts of interest.

"I'm sure before it's all over we're going to be seeing some very imaginative situations," commented a staff aide to the House Committee on Standards of Official Conduct.

The Standards Committee is charged with enforcing the House rule.

A better idea of whether members were complying with the rule would not be possible until May 1980, when members file their disclosure reports covering 1979 financial activities. Even then, the Standards Committee will be hampered in its enforcement efforts because members are not required to provide the committee with copies of their tax returns. Moreover, members do not routinely provide the Standards Committee with copies of their returns voluntarily. In many cases, only an examination of a tax return could show whether a member was complying with the rule or not.

A Standards Committee aide said that panel had provided advice on how to comply with the rule to House members who requested it. But he declined to identify members who had sought advice, the details of the members' requests, or the advice actually given.

Origins of Rule

At the heart of the new House rule was a ceiling on outside earned income. The limit went into effect on Jan. 1, 1979, and thus did not affect the earnings reported in financial disclosure statements for 1978. The ceiling was approved as part of the House's new code of ethics in 1977. *(1977 ethics code, p. 153)*

The ceiling was placed at 15 percent of a representative's annual salary. At the existing annual salary of $57,500, this meant that, as of 1979, a representative could earn no more than $8,625 a year in outside income, including honoraria.

In 1978, 167 representatives reported earning more than $8,625 in outside earned income. Of those, 45 representatives reported earning more than $8,625 in honoraria alone.

A similar ceiling for senators also was to have gone into effect in 1979. However, the Senate voted in March to delay enforcement of that limitation for four years.

This meant that, in contrast to House members, senators could earn as much as they wanted in outside income other than honoraria. The 1976 Federal Election Campaign Act (PL 94-283) limits honoraria earnings of members of Congress to no more than $25,000 annually.

Full-Time Attention to Congress

When it was adopted by the House in March 1977, the ceiling on outside earned income was the new ethics code's most controversial provision.

To its supporters, the income limit had two purposes:

● To ensure that members devote their full-time attention to their congressional duties rather than to any outside business activities.

● To minimize the potential for conflicts between a member's financial interests and legislative activities.

Acceptance of the limit also was seen as a trade-off for an increase in congressional pay, which in early 1977 went from $44,600 to $57,500.

Those opposing the ceiling noted that it would not affect unearned income such as dividends, interest, rent and capital gains.

In debate, these members argued that curbing earned income while leaving unearned income alone favored wealthy members and harmed those who depended more on

---

The new House limit on outside earned income has forced big pay cuts for some members. But with a little imagination, others are finding that they needn't make any financial sacrifice.

---

such activities as speechmaking and the practice of law for their income.

"People who sit on boards of directors have their interests protected," commented Rep. Shirley Chisholm, D-N.Y., at the time.

Converting Earned Income

When the income limit rule was drafted, its supporters called it "clear-cut." But the official interpretation of the rule, published by the House Select Committee on Ethics in October 1978, left some room for members to make adjustments in their finances that apparently would enable them to continue to make substantial sums of outside income and to remain active in their outside businesses.

The Select Ethics Committee disbanded at the end of the 95th Congress, leaving further interpretation of the rule to the Standards Committee.

One way to evade the income limitation could be the ability to convert what a member formerly considered "earned income" into a return on investment.

The Select Ethics Committee's interpretation stipulated that "income may not be recharacterized in order to circumvent the rule." Income should be considered "earned," the interpretation said, if it represented "compensation for personal services actually rendered."

If, however, the income were "essentially a return on equity, then it would generally not be considered to be earned income." The interpretation added that if a member were not active in a business, yet had invested in that business, the member also could engage "in the general oversight and management or protection of his investment" without recording his earnings from that business as "earned income."

A handful of members seemed to have seized on the qualifications in the interpretation in order to "recharacterize" their income and avoid the limitation on it.

In addition, a number of House members controlled or owned their own companies. In order to comply with the earned income limit, they said they would reduce their salaries while maintaining the same level of activity with the firm.

Such total control gives a member increased authority in hiring employees, determining the company's dividend payments, and setting the salaries paid other company employees. This gives a member more opportunity to take income in the form of dividends instead of salaries, or to hire a spouse or dependent.

Outside Jobs

Although the House and Senate have widely differing regulations governing outside employment of their members, the proportion of members in each house actually holding positions outside Congress was remarkably similar.

Income disclosure reports for 1978 showed that 33 percent of the House's members held positions outside of Congress; 37 percent of the Senate's members held outside positions. In numbers this amounted to 143 representatives and 37 senators who were engaged in employment activities in addition to their duties as public officials. These figures covered all outside employment reported by members except for law practices. *(See below)*

Some of these positions were actually paying jobs; others were non-paying relationships such as company directorships.

The average member engaging in outside employment held only one position. Sen. Herman E. Talmadge, D-Ga., held eight outside positions, the most among senators.

In the House, Rep. Jim Courter, R-N.J., held 12 positions, the largest number among House members.

Although no one activity dominated, the most prevalent appeared to be in real estate and agricultural ventures. In the House, bank directorships were numerous.

Differences between House and Senate outside employment activities may stem partly from demands inherent in the jobs of senators and representatives. But a more important reason probably is the different employment restrictions in the two houses.

Members of the House are bound by relatively few limitations on their outside private employment. Although there is no statutory provision or House rule to specifically prohibit a member from engaging in outside activity which could cause a possible conflict of interest, ethical standards serve to restrict members in certain aspects of outside employment.

House rules limit the amount of income a member can earn outside his official salary to 15 percent of the salary ($8,625 at the current annual salary level of $57,500).

In addition, there are these restrictions on outside employment for members of the House:
- The official position of a representative may not be used as a means for making personal gains;
- A member of the House may not receive compensation for services rendered before federal agencies or departments;
- Direct or indirect contracting with the federal government is prohibited;
- There is a prohibition against "self-dealings" with private foundations without incurring specific tax penalties;
- A House member may not receive emoluments or compensation of any kind from a foreign government.

Outside of these basic guidelines, members of the House have been generally free to decide whether or not they might be involved in conflicts of interest.

Senate More Restricted

Senate rules, on the other hand, specifically prohibit senators from engaging in outside employment for compensation if the work creates a conflict with their official duties.

A 1977 Senate Ethics Committee report on the Senate's ethics code said the rules "should be read to prohibit any outside activities which could represent a conflict of interest or the appearance of a conflict of interest." These rules apply to all employees of the Senate. The Senate ethics code also bans members of the Senate from practicing professions for more than 90 days in a calendar year. Professional services included under this rule are "engineering, real estate, insurance, legal, medical, architectural, consulting and other services."

Members of the Senate also are restricted in serving as officers or members of the board of any publicly held or publicly regulated corporation, financial institution or business entity.

Decline in Legal Work

In contrast to the overall figures for outside employment, the toughened ethics standards have all but eliminated the once widespread practice among members of accepting thousands of dollars for part-time legal work.

Financial disclosure reports show that only 23 House members who served in Congress during 1978 received fees from actively practicing law. And many of those members have withdrawn from their law practices because of the new House ethics code. Under that code, no member of the House can accept more than $8,625 per year in outside earned income, starting in 1979. The Senate postponed the effective date of a similar rule until 1983. Senate rules, however, effectively prevent senators from practicing law.

Twenty-one House freshmen and five freshman senators reported collecting legal fees in 1978, before entering Congress. All five senators and at least four of those House members have since withdrawn from their law practices.

The House earned income limit would force some members to take substantial cuts in legal fees. Freshman

Frank J. Guarini, D-N.J., for example, reported $624,129 in legal fees for 1978. He said he would continue to practice law, but would accept only the $8,625 allowed by the rule.

Five members of the House continued in 1978 to allow their names to be used by their law firms, even though they no longer actively practiced with the firm. The American Bar Association Code of Professional Conduct expressly forbids such "false front" law firms.

The code states that a lawyer who becomes a judge or public official "shall not permit his name to remain in the name of a law firm or to be used in professional notices of the firm during any significant period in which he is not actively and regularly practicing law as a member of the firm." An ABA opinion modifying the rule said a public official may allow the partnership to retain his name if he intends to remain in public office "only temporarily."

Although the ABA code does not say so, the intent of the rule is to prevent law firms from using the name of a prominent public official to attract clients.

House members who did not actively practice law in 1978, but who permitted their names to be used by law firms were: Charles A. Vanik, D-Ohio; James C. Cleveland, R-N.H.; Robert C. McEwen, R-N.Y.; John W. Jenrette Jr., D-S.C.; and Claude Pepper, D-Fla. ▮

Selected Bibliography on Congress

Books

Asbell, Bernard, *The Senate Nobody Knows,* New York, Doubleday, 1978.

Bailey, Stephen K., *Congress in the Seventies,* New York, St. Martin's Press, 1970.

Barber, Sotirios A., *The Constitution and the Delegation of Congressional Power,* Chicago, University of Chicago Press, 1975.

Bardach, Eugene, *The Implementation Game: What Happens After a Bill Becomes a Law,* Cambridge, Mass., MIT Press, 1977.

Beard, Edmund and Horn, Stephen, *Congressional Ethics: The View from the House,* Washington, D.C., Brookings Institution, 1975.

Bolling, Richard, *House Out of Order,* New York, Dutton, 1965.

Bolling, Richard, *Power in the House: A History of the Leadership of the House of Representatives,* New York, Putnam, 1974.

Bolton, John R., *The Legislative Veto: Unseparating the Powers,* Washington, D.C., American Enterprise Institute for Public Policy Research, 1977.

Can Congress Control Spending? Proceedings of the Town Hall Meeting on Domestic Affairs, Washington, D.C., American Enterprise Institute for Public Policy Research, 1973.

Chelf, Carl P., *Congress in the American System,* Chicago, Nelson-Hall, 1977.

Christopher, Maurine, *Black Americans in Congress,* New York, Crowell, 1976.

Clausen, Aage, *How Congressmen Decide: A Policy Focus,* New York, St. Martin's Press, 1973.

Congressional Quarterly's Guide to Congress, Second Edition, Washington, D.C., Congressional Quarterly Press, 1976.

Congressional Voting Records: 95th Congress, 2nd Session, Washington, D.C., Democratic Congressional Campaign Committee, 1979.

Cotton, Norris, *In the Senate: Amidst Conflict and Turmoil,* New York, Dodd, Mead, 1978.

Davidson, Roger H. and Oleszek, Walter J., *Congress Against Itself,* Bloomington, Indiana University Press, 1977.

de Grazia, Alfred, ed., *Congress: The First Branch of Government,* Garden City, New York, Doubleday, 1967.

Dodd, Lawrence C. and Oppenheimer, Bruce I., eds., *Congress Reconsidered,* New York, Praeger, 1977.

Douglas, Paul H., *Ethics in Government,* Westport, Conn., Greenwood Press, 1972.

Drew, Elizabeth, *Senator,* New York, Simon & Schuster, 1979.

Fenno, Richard F., *Home Style: House Members in Their Districts,* Boston, Little, Brown, 1978.

Fenno, Richard F., *The Power of the Purse: Appropriations Politics in Congress,* Boston, Little, Brown, 1973.

Fiorina, Morris P., *Congress — Keystone of the Washington Establishment,* New Haven, Yale University Press, 1977.

Fox, Harrison W. and Hammond, Susan W., *Congressional Staffs: The Invisible Force in American Lawmaking,* New York, Free Press, 1977.

Galloway, George B., *History of the House of Representatives,* 2nd rev. ed. New York, Crowell, 1976.

Goodwin, George, *The Little Legislatures: Committees of Congress,* Amherst, University of Massachusetts Press, 1970.

Groennings, Sven, ed., *To Be a Congressman: The Promise and the Power,* Washington, D.C., Acropolis Books, 1973.

Hamilton, James, *The Power to Probe: A Study of Congressional Investigations,* New York, Random House, 1976.

Havemann, Joel, *Congress and the Budget,* Bloomington, Indiana University Press, 1978.

Hinckley, Barbara, *Stability and Change in Congress,* New York, Harper & Row, 1978.

Hinckley, Barbara, *The Seniority System in Congress,* Bloomington, Indiana University Press, 1971.

House Republican Task Force on Congressional Reform and Minority Staffing, *We Propose: A Modern Congress,* New York, McGraw-Hill, 1966.

Jones, Charles O., *The Minority Party in Congress,* Boston, Little, Brown, 1970.

Kingdon, John, *Congressmen's Voting Decisions,* New York, Harper & Row, 1973.

Manley, John F., *The Politics of Finance: The House Committee on Ways and Means,* Boston, Little, Brown, 1970.

Matsunaga, Spark M. and Chen, Ping, *Rulemakers of the House,* Urbana, University of Illinois Press, 1976.

Morrow, William L., *Congressional Committees,* New York, Scribner, 1969.

Murphy, Thomas, *Politics of Congressional Committees,* Politics of Government Series, Woodbury, New York, Barron's Educational Series, Inc., 1978.

Nader, Ralph, *Ruling Congress: How the House and Senate Rules Govern the Legislative Process,* New York, Penguin Books, 1977.

Nader, Ralph, et al., *The Money Committees: A Study of the House and Senate Banking and Currency Committees,* Ralph Nader Congress Project Series, New York, Viking Press, 1975.

Ogul, Morris S., *Congress Oversees the Bureaucracy: Studies in Legislative Supervision,* Pittsburgh, University of Pittsburgh Press, 1976.

Oleszek, Walter J., *Congressional Procedures and the Policy Process,* Washington, D.C., Congressional Quarterly Press, 1978.

Ornstein, Norman J. and Lambert, Richard D., eds., *Changing Congress: The Committee System,* Philadelphia, American Academy of Political and Social Science, 1974.

Ornstein, Norman J., ed., *Congress in Change: Evolution and Reform,* New York, Praeger, 1975.

Peabody, Robert L., *Leadership in Congress: Stability, Succession and Change,* Boston, Little, Brown, 1976.

Peabody, Robert L. and Polsby, Nelson W., eds. *New Perspectives on the House of Representatives,* 3rd ed., Skokie, Ill., Rand McNally, 1977.

Pressman, Jeffrey L., *House vs. Senate: Conflict in the Appropriations Process,* New Haven, Yale University Press, 1966.

Price, David Eugene, *Policymaking in Congressional Committees,* Tucson, University of Arizona Press, 1979.

Rieselbach, Leroy N., *Congressional Politics,* New York, McGraw-Hill, 1973.

Rieselbach, Leroy N., *Congressional Reform in the Seventies,* New York, McGraw-Hill, 1977.

Ripley, Randall B., *Congress,* New York, W. W. Norton, 1975.

Ripley, Randall B., *Majority Party Leadership in Congress,* Boston, Little, Brown, 1969.

Ripley, Randall B., *Power in the Senate,* New York, St. Martin's Press, 1969.

Ripley, Randall B. and Franklin, Grace A., *Congress, the Bureaucracy and Public Policy,* Homewood, Ill., Dorsey Press, 1976.

Schick, Allen, "The Battle of the Budget," in *Congress Against the President,* edited by Harvey C. Mansfield Sr., pp. 51-70, New York, Praeger, 1975.

Schneider, Jerrold E., *Ideological Coalitions In Congress,* Westport, Conn., Greenwood Press, 1979.

Schwartz, John E. and Shaw, L. Earl, *The United States Congress in Comparative Perspective,* New York, Holt, Rinehart & Winston, 1976.

Shepsle, Kenneth A., *The Giant Jigsaw Puzzle: Democratic Committee Assignments in the Modern House,* Chicago, University of Chicago Press, 1978.

Truman, David, ed., *The Congress and America's Future,* Englewood Cliffs, New Jersey, Prentice-Hall, 1973.

Volger, David J., *Politics of Congress,* 2nd ed., Boston, Allyn & Bacon, 1977.

Welch, Susan and Peters, John G., eds., *Legislative Reform and Public Policy,* New York, 1977.

Articles

Abrams, Elliott, "The Senate Since Yesterday," *American Spectator,* February 1978, pp. 12-14.

Ace, G. "Who Was Minding the Store? Senate Subcommittees," *Saturday Review World,* November 20, 1973, p. 8.

Asher, Herbert B., "Committees and the Norm of Specialization," *Annals of the American Academy of Political and Social Science,* January 1974, pp. 63-74.

Aspin, Les, "Billion Dollar Loopholes: Conference Committees," *Progressive,* January 1974, pp. 35-36.

Backstrom, Charles H., "Congress and the Public: How Representative is the One of the Other?" *American Politics Quarterly,* October 1977, pp. 411-435.

"The Balance of Congress," *Economist* (London), October 29, 1977, pp. 36-37.

Behn, Robert, "The False Dawn of the Sunset Law," *The Public Interest,* Fall 1977, pp. 103-118.

Bolling, Richard, "Committees in the House," *Annals of the American Academy of Political and Social Science,* January 1974, pp. 1-14.

Brenner, Philip, "Committee Conflict in the Congressional Arena," *Annals of the American Academy of Political and Social Science,* January 1974, pp. 87-101.

Brenner, Philip, "Congressional Reform: Analyzing the Analysts," *Harvard Journal on Legislation,* April 1977, pp. 651-681.

Brock, William E., "Committees in the Senate," *Annals of the American Academy of Political and Social Science,* January 1974, pp. 15-26.

Burks, Stephen W. and Cole, Richard L., "Invisible Power on Capitol Hill," *Wharton Magazine,* Spring 1977, pp. 23-29.

Cohen, D., "Congressional Reform," *Current,* April 1975, pp. 38-44.

Cohen, Richard W., "Junior Members Seek Approval for Wider Use of the Legislative Veto," *National Journal,* August 6, 1977, pp. 1228-1232.

"Congressional Featherbedding: Senate Staffs and the Committee System," *New Republic,* March 1, 1975, pp. 3-4.

"Congressional Record," *New Republic,* December 7, 1975, pp. 7-8.

Cooper, Joseph, "Strengthening the Congress: An Organizational Analysis," *Harvard Journal on Legislation,* April 1975, pp. 307-368.

Davidson, Roger H., "Representation and Congressional Committees," *Annals of the American Academy of Political and Social Science,* January 1974, pp. 48-62.

Finley, James J., "The 1974 Congressional Initiative in Budget Making," *Public Administration Review,* May/June 1975, pp. 270-278.

Fisher, Louis, "Congress, the Executive and the Budget," *Annals of the American Academy of Political and Social Science,* January 1974, pp. 102-113.

Fisher, Louis, "Congressional Budget Reform: the First Two Years," *Harvard Journal on Legislation,* April 1977, pp. 413-457.

Garay, Ronald, "Implementing Televised Coverage of Sessions of the U.S. Congress," *Journalism Quarterly,* Autumn 1978, pp. 527-539.

Gardner, John W., "Restructuring the House of Representatives," *Annals of the American Academy of Political and Social Science,* January 1974, pp. 169-176.

"Guide to the Congressional Budget Process: Interview with Alice M. Rivlin," *Challenge,* July/August 1975, pp. 26-31.

Havemann, Joel, "Budging the Budget Committees," *National Journal,* December 3, 1977, p. 1891.

"Honorarium Industry: Speaking and Writing Fees," *Nation,* October 19, 1974, p. 356.

"House Probes Its Committees," *Business Week,* January 19, 1974, pp. 20-21.

Kravitz, Walter, "Evolution of the Senate's Committee System," *Annals of the American Academy of Political and Social Science,* January 1974, pp. 27-38.

Ladd, Everett Carll, "The Democrats Have Their Own Two-Party System," *Fortune,* October 1977, pp. 212-218.

Malbin, Michael J., "Congressional Committee Staffs: Who's In Charge Here?" *Public Interest,* Spring 1977, pp. 16-40.

Malbin, Michael J., "The Obey Commission Report—The House Braces for More Reform," *National Journal,* September 3, 1977, pp. 1368-1371.

Mineta, Norman Y., "Update From Capitol Hill: Power and Seniority in the House of Representatives," *Public Affairs Report,* December 1976, pp. 1-6.

Nathanson, I., "Congressional Power Shift: The Caucus vs. the Barons," *Nation,* January 11, 1975, pp. 6-9.

Nelson, Garrison, "Partisan Patterns of House Leadership Change, 1789-1977," *American Political Science Review,* Summer 1977, pp. 918-939.

Oleszek, Walter J., "House Senate Relationships: Comity

and Conflict," *Annals of the American Academy of Political and Social Science,* January 1974, pp. 75-86.

Ornstein, Norman J., Towards Restructuring the Congressional Committee System," *Annals of the American Academy of Political and Social Science,* January 1974, pp. 133-146.

Peabody, Robert L., "Committees from the Leadership Perspective: Party Leadership in the House," *Annals of the American Academy of Political and Social Science,* January 1974, pp. 133-146.

Polk, J. R., "On the Take: The Secret Fringe Benefits Enjoyed by Congress," *New Republic,* September 13, 1975, pp. 10-18.

Polsby, Nelson W., "Carter and Congress: The No Deal Coalition," *American Spectator,* November 1978, pp. 16-19.

Rapoport, Daniel, "No Revolution in the House," *Progressive,* August 1975, pp. 6-7.

Renfro, William L., "The Future and Congressional Reform," *American Bar Association,* April 1978, pp. 561-563.

Rohde, David W., "Committee Reform in the House of Representatives and the Subcommittee Bill of Rights," *Annals of the American Academy of Political and Social Science,* January 1974, pp. 39-47.

Rosenthal, Paul C. and Grossman, Robert S., "Congressional Access to Confidential Information Collected by Federal Agencies," *Harvard Journal on Legislation,* December 1977, pp. 74-118.

Schick, Allen, "Budget Reform Legislation: Reorganizing Congressional Centers of Fiscal Power," *Harvard Journal on Legislation,* February 1974, pp. 303-350.

Stratton, Samuel S., "New Ethics Code: What You Can and Can't Do in Dealing with Congress," *Association Management,* July 1977, pp. 32-34.

Thurber, James A., "Congressional Budget Reform and New Demands for Policy Analysis," *Policy Analysis,* Spring 1976, pp. 197-214.

Van Der Slik, Jack R. and Stenger, Thomas C., "Citizen Witnesses Before Congressional Committees," *Political Science Quarterly,* Fall 1977, pp. 465-485.

Warren, Sara E., "The New Look of the Congressional Caucuses," *National Journal,* April 29, 1978, pp. 677-679.

Documents

Committee Structure and Procedures of the House of Representatives, Washington, D.C., Library of Congress, Congressional Research Service, December 13, 1973.

Deschler, Lewis, *Deschler's Precedents of the United States House of Representatives.* H. Doc. 94-661, Washington, D.C., Government Printing Office, 1977.

Deschler, Lewis, *Deschler's Procedure in the United States House of Representatives,* 2nd ed., Washington, D.C., Government Printing Office, 1977.

Jones, Charles O., *Congressional Committees and the Two Party System: Working Papers on House Committee Organization and Operation,* Presented to House Select Committee on Committees, Washington, D.C., Government Printing Office, 1973.

Oleszek, Walter, *Congressional Oversight Methods and Reform Proposals: Working Papers on House Committee Organization and Operation,* Presented to House Select Committee on Committees, Washington, D.C., Government Printing Office, 1973.

Peabody, Robert L., *House Leadership, Party Caucuses and the Committee Structure: Working Papers on House Committee Organization and Operation,* Presented to House Select Committee on Committees, Washington, D.C., Government Printing Office, 1973.

Ripley, Randall B., *Party Leaders and Standing Committees in the House of Representatives: Working Papers on House Committee Organization and Operation,* Presented to House Select Committee on Committees, Washington, D.C., Government Printing Office, 1973.

U.S. Congress, House, *Constitution, Jefferson's Manual and Rules of the House of Representatives of the United States,* Washington, D.C., Government Printing Office, 1977.

U.S. Congress, House, *Report of the Clerk of the House,* Washington, D.C., Government Printing Office, 1979.

U.S. Congress, House Budget Committee, *Congressional Budget and Impoundment Control Act of 1974: A General Explanation,* Washington, D.C. Government Printing Office, 1974.

U.S. Congress, House Commission on Information and Facilities, *Automated Information Resources for the U.S. House of Representatives,* Washington, D.C., Government Printing Office, 1976.

U.S. Congress, House Commission on Information and Facilities, *Congressional Budget Office: A Study of its Organizational Effectiveness,* H. Doc. 95-20, Washington, D.C., Government Printing Office, 1977.

U.S. Congress, House Committee on Government Operations, *Oversight Plans of the Committees of the U.S. House of Representatives,* Washington, D.C., Government Printing Office, 1975.

U.S. Congress, House Committee on Government Operations, Subcommittee on Legislation and National Security, *Sunset Legislation: Hearings, Oct. 17, 1977,* Washington, D.C., Government Printing Office, 1977.

U.S. Congress, House Committee on House Administration, *Information on Computer Terminal Equipment for Member and Committee Offices,* Washington, D.C., Government Printing Office, 1977.

U.S. Congress, House Committee on House Administration, *Providing for the Reform of the Administrative Organization and Legislative Management Services of the House of Representatives,* H. Rpt. 95-651, Washington, D.C., Government Printing Office, 1977.

U.S. Congress, House Committee on Rules, *Amending the Rules of the House of Representatives,* H. Rpt. 95-21, Washington, D.C., Government Printing Office, 1977.

U.S. Congress, House Committee on Rules, *Establishing A Select Committee on Ethics,* Washington, D.C., Government Printing Office, 1977.

U.S. Congress, House Committee on Rules, *Providing for Radio and Television Coverage of House Proceedings,* Washington, D.C., Government Printing Office, 1977.

U.S. Congress, House Committee on Standards of Official Conduct, *Code of Official Conduct,* Washington, D.C., Government Printing Office, 1977.

U.S. Congress, House Select Committee on Committees, *Committee Organization in the House, 3 vols.,* Washington, D.C. Government Printing Office, 1975.

U.S. Congress, House Select Committee on Committees, *Committee Organization in the House: Index to Hearings and Panel Discussions, 3 vols.,* Washington, D.C., Government Printing Office, 1974.

U.S. Congress, House Select Committee on Committees, *Committee Reform Amendments of 1974, Report, March 21, 1974,* Washington, D.C., Government Printing Office, 1974.

U.S. Congress, House Select Committee on Congressional Operations, *Televising the House,* H. Doc. 95-231. Washington, D.C., Government Printing Office, 1977.

U.S. Congress, House Select Committee on Ethics, *Legislative Branch Financial Disclosure: Hearings, June 2 and 7, 1977, on H.R. 7401,* Washington, D.C., Government Printing Office, 1977.

U.S. Congress, Joint Committee on Congressional Operations, *Broadcasting House and Senate Proceedings, Interim Report, October 10, 1974,* Washington, D.C., Government Printing Office, 1974.

U.S. Congress, Joint Committee on Printing, *Current Procedures and Production Processes of the Congressional Record,* Washington, D.C., Government Printing Office, 1978.

U.S. Congress, Senate, *Report of the Secretary of the Senate,* Washington, D.C., Government Printing Office, 1977.

U.S. Congress, Senate, *Toward a Modern Senate: Final Report of the Commission on the Operation of the Senate,* Washington, D.C., Government Printing Office, 1976.

U.S. Congress, Senate Committee on Governmental Affairs, Subcommittee on Intergovernmental Relations, *Public Attitude Toward Congressional Review of Programs: Hearings, April 26, 1978,* Washington, D.C., Government Printing Office, 1978.

U.S. Congress, Senate Committee on Government Operations, *Congressional Budget and Impoundment Act of 1974: Legislative History,* Washington, D.C., Government Printing Office, 1974.

U.S. Congress, Senate Committee on Public Works, Subcommittee on Buildings and Grounds, *400 North Capitol Street: Hearings, April 9, 1976,* Washington, D.C., Government Printing Office, 1976.

U.S. Congress, Senate Committee on Rules and Administration, *Senate Cloture Rule: Limitation of Debate in the Congress of the United States, and Legislative History of Paragraphs 2 and 3 of Rule XXII of the U.S. Senate,* Washington, D.C., Government Printing Office, 1977.

U.S. Congress, Senate Committee on Rules and Administration, Subcommittee on Computer Services, *Information Support for the U.S. Senate: A Survey of the Computerized CRS Resources and Services,* Washington, D.C., Government Printing Office, 1977.

U.S. Congress, Senate Special Committee on Official Conduct, *Senate Code of Conduct: Hearings, February 1, 2, 1977,* Washington, D.C., Government Printing Office, 1977.

INDEX